# Integrating ISA Server 2006 with Microsoft Exchange 2007

**Fergus Strachan**

| KEY | SERIAL NUMBER |
|-----|---------------|
| 001 | HJIRTCV764 |
| 002 | PO9873D5FG |
| 003 | 829KM8NJH2 |
| 004 | BAL923457U |
| 005 | CVPLQ6WQ23 |
| 006 | VBP965T5T5 |
| 007 | HJJJ863WD3E |
| 008 | 2987GVTWMK |
| 009 | 629MP5SDJT |
| 010 | IMWQ295T6T |

PUBLISHED BY
Syngress Publishing, Inc.
Elsevier, Inc.
30 Corporate Drive
Burlington, MA 01803

Integrating ISA Server 2006 with Microsoft Exchange 2007

Printed and bound in the United Kingdom

Transferred to Digital Print 2011

ISBN 13: 978-1-59749-275-1

Page Layout and Art: SPi Publishing Services
Technical Editor: Henrik Walther
Copy Editor: Beth Roberts

For information on rights, translations, and bulk sales, contact Matt Pedersen, Commercial Sales Director and Rights, at Syngress Publishing; email m.pedersen@elsevier.com.

# Lead Author

**Fergus Strachan** has not been working with Exchange Server since version 4.0, because he's not that old. He has, however, been designing and implementing Exchange Server-based solutions for over 10 years, primarily in London for academia, central government, banks, and private businesses. He is co-author of the Exchange Server 2003 Resource Kit, and has published numerous papers and magazine articles. Despite this, he thought it would be great to jump back in as the lead author on this book. Fergus is available for consultancy work, parties and bar mitzvahs.

# Technical Editor

**Henrik Walther** (Exchange MVP, MCSE Messaging/Security) is a senior consultant working for Interprise Consulting A/S (a Microsoft Gold Partner) based in Copenhagen, Denmark. Henrik has more than 14 years of experience in the IT business, where he primarily works with Microsoft Exchange, ISA Server, MOM, IIS, clustering, Active Directory, and virtual server technologies. In addition to his job as a senior consultant, Henrik runs the Danish Web site Exchange-faq.dk. He is also the primary content creator, forums moderator, and newsletter editor at the leading Microsoft Exchange site, MSExchange.org. Henrik is the author of *CYA: Securing Exchange Server 2003 & Outlook Web Access* and *How to Cheat at Configuring Exchange Server 2007* (Syngress Publishing), and he has been a reviewer on several other messaging books (including another Exchange 2007 book).

# Contributing Authors

**John Karnay** is a freelance writer, editor and book author living in Queens, NY. John specializes in Windows server and desktop deployments utilizing Microsoft and Apple products and technology. John has been working with Microsoft products since Windows 95 and NT 4.0 and consults for many clients in New York City and Long Island helping them plan their migrations from current platforms to XP/Vista and Windows Server 2003/2008. When not working and writing, John enjoys recording and writing music as well as spending quality time with his wife Gloria and daughter Aurora. You can contact/visit John at: www.johnkarnay.com.

**Jesse Varsalone** (A+, Linux+, Net+, iNet+, Security+, Server+, CTT+, CIW Professional, CWNA, CWSP, MCT, MCSA, MSCE 2000/2003, MCSA/MCSE Security, MCDBA, MCSD, CNA, CCNA, MCDST, Oracle 8i/9i DBA, Certified Ethical Hacker) is a computer forensic senior professional at CSC. For four years, he served as the director of the MCSE and Network Security Program at the Computer Career Institute at Johns Hopkins University. For the 2006 academic year, he served as an assistant professor of computer information systems at Villa Julie College in Baltimore, MD. He taught courses in networking, Active Directory, Exchange, Cisco, and forensics.

Jesse holds a bachelor's degree from George Mason University and a master's degree from the University of South Florida. Jesse was a contributing author for *The Official CHFI Study Guide (Exam 312-49)* and *Penetration Tester's Open Source Toolkit, Second Edition*. He runs several Web sites, including mcsecoach.com, which is dedicated to helping people obtain their MCSE certifications. He currently lives in Columbia, MD, with his wife, Kim, and son, Mason.

# Contents

# Foreword

xvi Foreword

I can't remember the last time I read a book foreword, except to get ideas as to what to write just now. If you're reading this, then thanks for buying the book.

I've tried to make it a bit different than typical Exchange books that have a very regimented, formal writing style, because I think technical writers should try to present information in a digestible manner, rather than just showing off how much they know. Good job, really, otherwise I'm sure nobody would publish me.

There is a lot of material covered here so you should find some interesting information in it to help you implement Exchange server in a published environment.

After my last book – the Exchange Server 2003 Resource Kit – I swore never to write again, but the lovely folks at Syngress piqued my interest. For all the ups and downs, the hard work and the frustration, it is very rewarding to have something printed with your name on it...and even more so if people write nice things about it.

There are a number of people who have been instrumental to this piece of work, so in true Gwyneth Paltrow style:

My very good friend Kay Unkroth, a former enterprise support guy for Microsoft and probably the most intelligent person I know, who got me involved in the Exchange training kit and introduced me to this whole area of work all those years ago; Henrik Walther, the technical editor, was been very encouraging throughout and made sure I'm not writing a load of nonsense; Tiffany Gasbarrini, my editor at Syngress, has kept me sane over the last few months with her wonderfully dry European sense of humour, and the poor girl did brilliantly keeping things on an even keel; Julian Datta at Microsoft UK for helping me with hard to get information from those in the know, and Ian Parramore and Clint Huffman for general tips.

Thanks to my family for supporting this venture, and for lending me money for much-needed whisky. Pleas also go out to Celtic Football Club not to sue me for referencing them and their staff. "'Mon the hoops."

Finally, thanks to my kitten, Norman Bates, for keeping me company. Okay, he constantly woke me at 6am, broke a monitor and keyboard and tried to get in on the writing process, too, but his little internal motor kept me smiling.

With any luck, this book will give you a smile once in a while too. After all, life's too short to read boring Exchange books all the time!

—*Fergus Strachan*
Perth, Scotland

# Chapter 1

# Introducing Exchange Server 2007 SP1

## Solutions in this chapter:

- ■ What's New?

- ■ Upgrading to Service Pack 1

# Introduction

It's something of an unwritten rule with Microsoft software that you don't deploy software such as Microsoft Exchange Server or Windows Server until the first service pack comes out. This may be a little unfair on occasion, as certainly the 2003 RTM version of Exchange was a good product.

With Exchange Server 2007, however, you can't help get the impression that it was "RTM'd" way before they actually finished writing it. In fact, this is a view supported by numerous articles on the Microsoft Exchange Team Web site (www.msexchangeteam.com). A number of aspects of the product are re-written from scratch (OWA for one), and it's such a departure from the last version that it was bound to happen. For the first six months Exchange 2007 was out, we were itching to bring it out at customer sites, both to enhance the feature-set of their Exchange environments and to gain more exposure to the product ourselves. However, there always seemed to be one or more major deal-breakers. A number of our conversations with customers looking to "transition" or migrate to Exchange 2007 went something like this:

"We want to migrate to this cool new version of Exchange."

"Okay, great. Do you need to access public folders via OWA?"

"Yes."

"Oh. Do you want to retrain your GUI-mollycoddled admins to use PowerShell?"

"No."

"Oh. How about we wait until December then?"

It's a shame that this had such an impact on the take-up of Exchange 2007, but such is the nature of software development. The good news is, with Service Pack 1, Exchange 2007 is a much more rounded individual. It's the difference between a 15-year-old who talks back and goes in a huff, and an 18-year-old who talks back but at least in a more coherent and reasoned manner.

A number of features were lost in the RTM version of Exchange 2007, and the majority of these have been addressed in SP1. Beyond the features that come under the "should have been there from the beginning" category, there are a number of major improvements in SP1—ESE (and therefore I/O) efficiency improvements, TransportConfig object cloning, and of course Standby Continuous Replication and other high-availability improvements.

This chapter details the important changes in SP1 that have an impact on the decision to go to Exchange 2007 and the design and deployment of your Exchange environments.

# What's New?

## Features They Couldn't Finish in Time

Let's start with some nice new features and improvements that we got used to in 2003 but somehow lost in 2007 RTM.

# Public Folders through OWA

This is the great deal-breaker for many companies. Despite being a good idea, public folders never really managed to do what they promised, and Microsoft is trying to get rid of them in the next couple of versions of Exchange. However, this is no excuse for taking it out of OWA in RTM! Whether they ran out of time to implement it, or they meant to take it out but bowed to public pressure, it's back into OWA and that's a welcome step.

You'll notice public folders are published via the /owa virtual directory rather than the old /public directory, so you don't need to modify your Exchange publishing rules in ISA Server. The redirection to the public folder store is cleverly written into the /owa directory rather than using a separate one.

# S/MIME

Another feature present in previous versions but not in 2007 RTM was the ability to sign and encrypt messages in OWA. Not a major deal for most companies, but a deal-breaker for others, S/MIME is back into OWA. It also includes an update to the cryptology API and "Suite B," an NSA-compliant suite of cryptology algorithms that über-techy security people might get excited about.

# Monthly Calendar View

This speaks for itself. What would we do without our monthly calendar view?!

# OWA Customization

Exchange 2007 RTM allowed the standard customization of OWA themes, allowing you to brand your own OWA to match your company's look. This is limited to modifying or replacing graphics files and cascading style sheets to modify the appearance, but the bones or OWA are still the same.

With SP1, the Front End Team within the Exchange Product group are giving us another two themes—Xbox and Zune—in a typically modest Microsoft way, so if you're so inclined you can make OWA look a little bit like your games console.

However, there are more interesting changes with SP1 in the form of proper customization of OWA. If you look in the ClientAccess\Owa\forms folder, you'll notice a new folder called "Customization." In this folder are a couple of template files you can use to build your own customizations. Possible customizations are:

> **Custom OWA forms** Just as in Outlook, you can customize forms and publish them to Outlook clients or public folders. OWA allows you to produce custom Web forms that are then stored in the ClientAccess\Owa\forms\Customization folder in the Exchange installation folder. Custom forms can be linked to content classes so they open automatically depending on the action taken. These forms must

be registered in a Forms Registry (registry.xml) file, which is picked up automatically by Exchange 2007 SP1 (as long as it's within the \forms folder).

**Application integration via navigation pane links** The navigation pane is the one normally at the bottom-left that has the links to the OWA functions—Mail, Calendar, Contacts, etc. Additional links can be added in the UIExtensions.xml file to point to external URLs or other applications. Settings consist of a large icon, small icon, text, and external URL.

**New drop-down menu customization** It is now possible to customize the "New" launch button in OWA to add custom links to external applications or custom forms. Using the UIExtensions.xml file in the Customizations folder, you can register these within the New drop-down. These extensions consist of an icon, text, and the relevant custom class. The custom form you create for that custom class will open automatically when you select this menu link.

**Icon mappings** Also within the UIExtensions.xml file, you can map your own small icon to custom content classes. With this, you can use an icon of your choice for the custom content you use in OWA, rather than the standard envelope, calendar, contact, etc. icons.

# Right-Click Move/Copy

You can now move/copy items in OWA using the right-click menu. Previously, although you could drag and drop items from folder to folder, there was no option to move or copy by right-clicking.

Figure 1.1 shows the difference in RTM and SP1.

**Figure 1.1** SP1 Provides More Right-Click Options on Objects

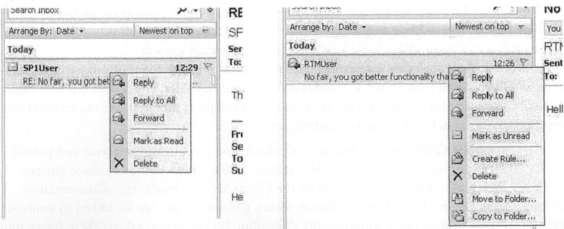

# Server-Side Rules

Rules are now accessible through the Rules section of the OWA settings page. Server-side rules can be modified via OWA; client-only rules are present as well (in gray) and can be deleted but not modified (Figure 1.2).

**Figure 1.2** The Client-Side Rules Are Grayed Out

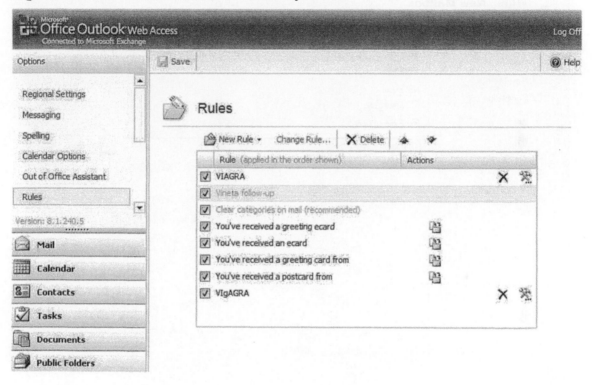

# Bulk Mailbox Creation

It's not inconceivable that an administrator might want to mail-enable more than one mailbox at a time, yet trying to do this in EMC in Exchange 2007 RTM will frustrate you to no end. Using the console to create a mailbox, you are able to select a single mailbox as in Figure 1.3.

**Figure 1.3** Only One Name Fits in the Box

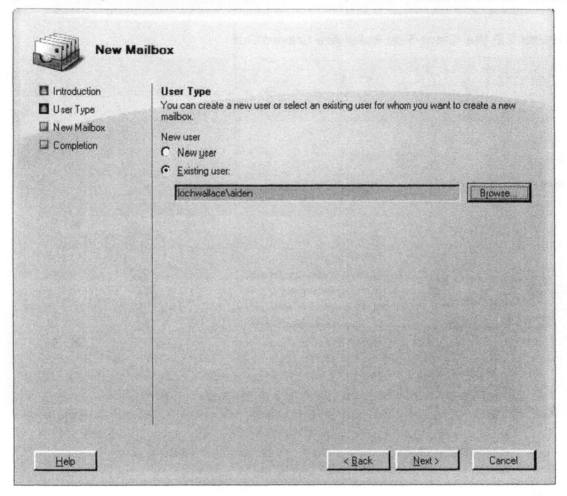

Again, it is possible through the shell, but this requires code that is not simple to write, and most Exchange admins are not great at command-line tasks. For example, to create mailboxes for all users within the "New Users" OU, you can use a command such as:

```
get-user -organizationalUnit "new users" | where-
object{$_.RecipientType -eq "User"} | Enable-Mailbox -Database
"EXCH07TEST\First Storage Group\Mailbox Database" | get-mailbox |
select name,windowsemailaddress,database
```

The output will be something like Figure 1.4.

**Figure 1.4** Mailbox-Enabling Multiple User Accounts in the Shell

However, SP1 enables you to do this, and create users and mailboxes at the same time, using the console. In SP1, you can select a list as shown in Figure 1.5.

**Figure 1.5** Creating Mailboxes for Multiple Users

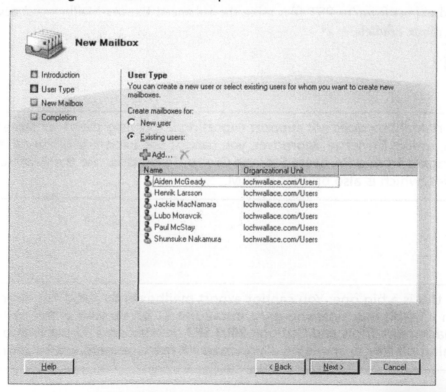

**TIP**

The terms *mailbox-enable* and *mailbox-disable* are not used in Exchange 2007. If you want to remove a mailbox while leaving the user account intact, you have to select the mailbox in the console and "Disable" it. The shell command is *Disable-Mailbox -Identity [MailboxID]*.

## Import/Export PST Files

RTM didn't include a utility to export and import mailbox data using Personal Folder (PST) files. There is an Export-Mailbox shell command, but it merely exports/imports in the same process and only between mailboxes in the same organization. We guess the main use for this command in RTM was to merge mailboxes, as otherwise it is almost identical to the Move-Mailbox command.

With Exchange 2007, the Exchange Product group decided to bring the ExMerge functionality within the same codebase as Exchange, as opposed to the separate utility it has always been. (ExMerge was actually produced by Microsoft Support way back in the days of Exchange 5.5 and taken on by the Product Team because it was such a useful tool.) With SP1, we still don't have the full functionality of ExMerge, but at least we can now import and export from/to PST files using the enhanced Export-Mailbox and new Import–Mailbox cmdlets.

**NOTE**

Export-Mailbox does not support exporting/importing client- or server-side rules, unlike ExMerge. Moreover, you cannot use Export-Mailbox to recover mailboxes from a Recovery Storage Group. To do this, use the Restore-Mailbox cmdlet, which is also present in RTM.

**NOTE**

And this is a big one: You cannot export mailboxes to a PST file directly from a 64-bit machine; you must install the 32-bit version of the Exchange Management Tools and Outlook 2003 SP2 or later on a 32-bit Windows installation (for example on a Windows XP management workstation).

To export and then import a mailbox using these cmdlets, you would use commands such as:

```
Export-Mailbox -Identity Fergus -PSTFolderPath "c:\MyMailbox.pst"
Import-Mailbox -Identity Fergus -PSTFolderPath "c:\MyMailbox.pst"
```

Easy! You can also specify filters based on date/time, subject and recipient keywords, etc. For more information, type **Get-Help Export-Mailbox –Full** in the EMS.

# Public Folder Management

**Public Folder Permissions** Configuring PF permissions through Outlook has not changed and is usually the best way to set individual user/group permissions. We say that because despite the new Public Folder admin GUI, the only way to change permissions through the Exchange admin tools is using the command line. Great if you want to script a lot of things, but poor if you want to add a single permission for users.

To add public folder permissions for clients using the EMS, use the Add-PublicFolder-ClientPermissions cmdlet, or the AddUsersToFPRecursive.ps1 management script.

**Public Folder Administrator Permissions** A new administrator role in SP1 called "Public Folder Administrator" gives the user rights to control specifically public folders. This gives slightly more granular delegation of administrative rights within the organization.

**Mail-enabled public folders included when reviewing address lists, e-mail address policies, and group memberships** When previewing the recipients who are members of an address list, e-mail address policy, dynamic distribution group, and distribution group, you can now see the mail-enabled public folders that are included in the membership criteria.

**Public Folder Management Console** This is covered under *Toolbox* in the next section.

# POP3/IMAP4 Management

POP3 and IMAP4 configuration options are now a part of the console. The new configuration pages are similar to those in Exchange Server 2003 and allow you to modify security settings, ports, and other standard POP3/IMAP4 settings without getting dirty and frustrated in the management shell.

# More GUI Options

A few additional tabs here and there in the EMC help us GUI-junkies who were still in cots when VMS and early Unix were being developed…

**Global Transport Settings** There are many places in Exchange 2007 where you can configure options such as message size limits. Even with the GUI-rich

Exchange 2003, we often experienced bounced messages because one of these options had been missed—usually the global settings. In Exchange 2007, these settings weren't obvious because of the lack of GUI accessibility—it's not easy to seek out all the available options via the shell.

Thankfully, SP1 provides access to the global transport settings via the GUI, accessible through Organization Configuration > Hub Transport > Global Settings (shown in Figure 1.6). The Transport Settings page accesses the options through the Get-TransportConfig and Set-TransportConfig cmdlets, which also includes Transport Dumpster and DSN message configuration.

**Figure 1.6** Global Transport Settings through the Lovely GUI

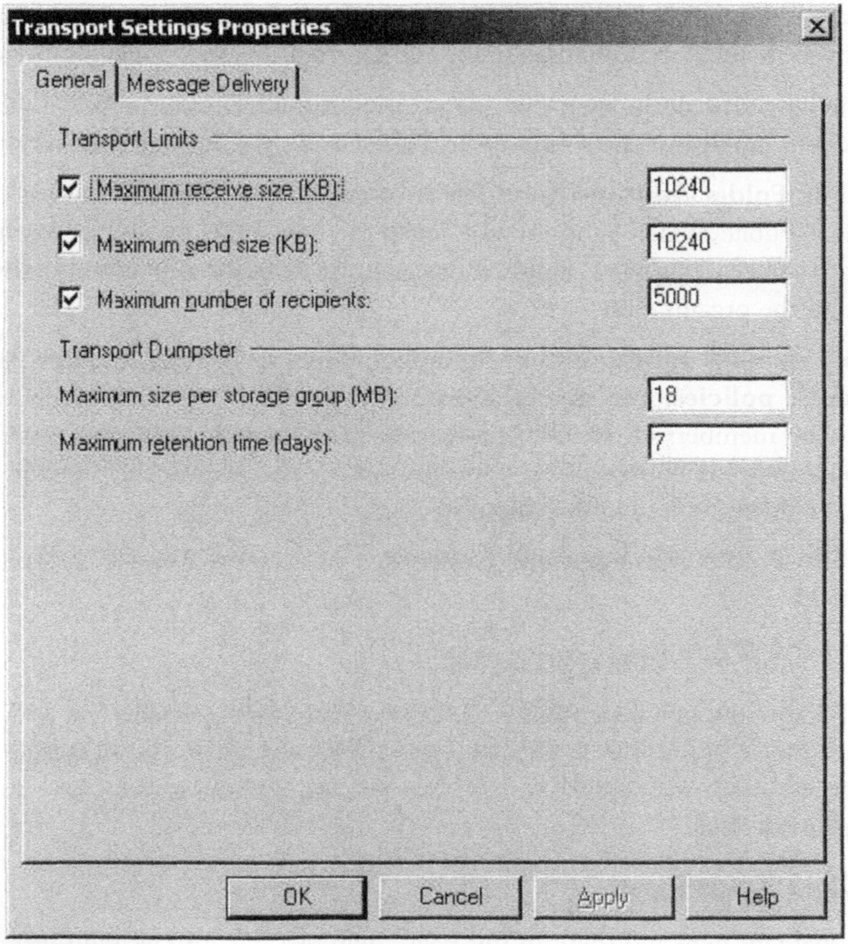

**Log Settings** Message Tracking, Connectivity and Protocol logging options have been added to the console. These are under the Properties of a server in the Server Configuration or Hub Transport windows (Figure 1.7).

**Figure 1.7** Viewing and Modifying Log Configuration Settings

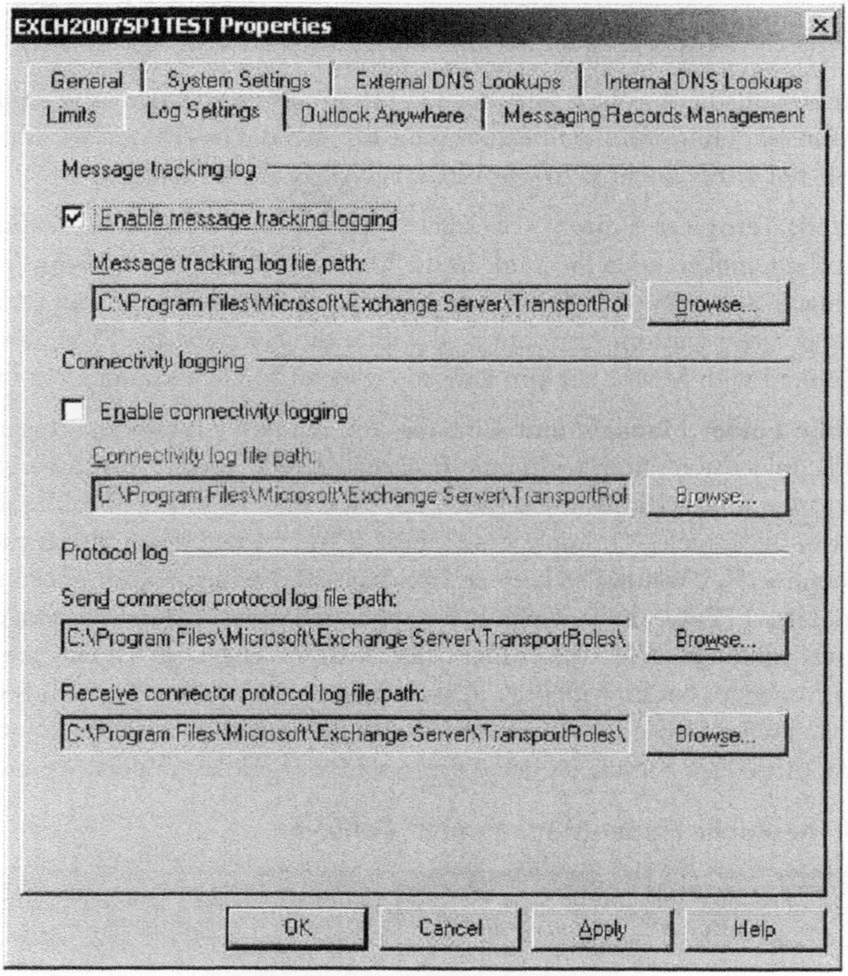

# Message Size Limits on AD Site
# Links and Routing Group Connectors

Setting a maximum size for messages sent internally is useful when WAN links are not good enough to realistically support a lot of email flow. SP1 allows you to set message size limits on both AD IP Site Links, which are used for Exchange 2007 mail flow, and Routing Group Connectors, which are used for communication with Exchange 2000/2003 servers.

To set the maximum message size on a Site Link to 10MB, use the shell command:

```
Set-AdSiteLink -Identity [SITELINKNAME] -MaxMessageSize 10MB
```

MaxMessageSize corresponds to the new delivContLength AD attribute, which can be viewed using ADSIEdit.

# Management

## Toolbox

In SP1, a number of additions have been made to the Toolbox, the area of the console where additional troubleshooting and modification tools are placed. They're not integrated into the console per se, but rather are links to open external MMC-based utilities.

**Details Template Editor** This addition to the Toolbox allows administrators to edit the templates used for items in the Outlook client address books (Users, Contacts, and Groups etc.). For example, you could modify the user template to incorporate a Custom Attribute used within the company. In RTM, this tool is registered with MMC, but you have to create an MMC console for it manually.

**Public Folder Management Console** You can now manage your organization's public folder stores from within the Exchange 2007 console. One of the issues Exchange admins had with Exchange 2007 was the lack of public folder admin support in the console—it simply wasn't there. If you wanted to administer public folders through a GUI, you had to keep an Exchange 2003 server in your environment or use a tool like PFDAVAdmin, which is also supported for use against Exchange 2007 servers (although DAV is also being deprecated). We guess this fell into the "didn't have time" category, but now it's back in and sitting in the Toolbox. Figure 1.8 shows the Public Folder Management Console. It lacks the administrative flexibility of previous versions; perhaps because it's being deprecated they put less importance on the tool.

**Figure 1.8** The Public Folder Management Console

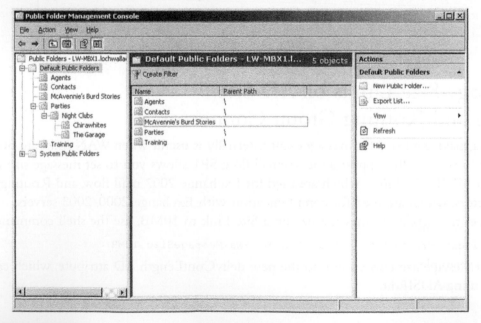

**Routing Log Viewer**  Similar to the WinRoute utility used with Exchange Server 2003, the Routing Log Viewer lets you look at the routing and server topology of your Exchange 2007 organization. The tool queries routing logs, which are generated by default by Hub Transport servers. Although this is likely to be useful to larger organizations (with, say, at least three sites), the "compare" feature of the tool is very useful for finding changes to the topology over a period of time. When comparing two log files, the tool highlights what has changed, so you can see exactly when a server, Send Connector, AD Site, etc., was modified.

# Messaging Records Management on Default Folders (with Std CAL)

Messaging Records Management (MRM) uses managed Outlook folders to manage email policies, such as item retention and deletion, to help organizations comply with legal obligations with regard to email. It does imply cooperation from the user fraternity to move relevant messages into their respective folders for processing. However, on a departmental basis, where users are doing similar work, it is relatively easy to implement with a little user coercion. To maintain parity with the equivalent feature of Exchange Server 2003—the Mailbox Manager—MRM can be used on default mailbox folders, such as the Inbox and Deleted Items, with the standard Exchange CAL. If you want to create your own folders for management, which, let's face it, is necessary for any meaningful management policy, an Enterprise CAL is required.

# Monitoring Online Defragmentation

The online maintenance tasks run by the System Attendant have always been a bit of a black box as far as administrators are concerned. Questions such as "When should I run online maintenance?" "How long should online maintenance be run for?" and "Will it interfere with the nightly backup?" are probably rarely answered because of the difficulty inherent in ascertaining the required information. Event Log entries 701 and 703 give basic information about when the online defragmentation (OLD) process starts and finishes. In SP1, the 703 event provides more information about the OLD process, including how long it took, how many pages were freed, and how many times the database has been defragmented.

# Management Console "Export List"

From the Exchange Management Console (and the Public Folder Management Console Queue Viewer and Details Templates Editor), you can export the list of items within the viewed scope into tab- or comma-delimited files for use elsewhere. In the case of Mailbox users, for example, you can specify the columns to view within the GUI and export this data into a format usable by tools such as CSVDE.exe. This can also be very useful for basic reporting (Figure 1.9).

**Figure 1.9** An Easy Way to Export Data from Exchange

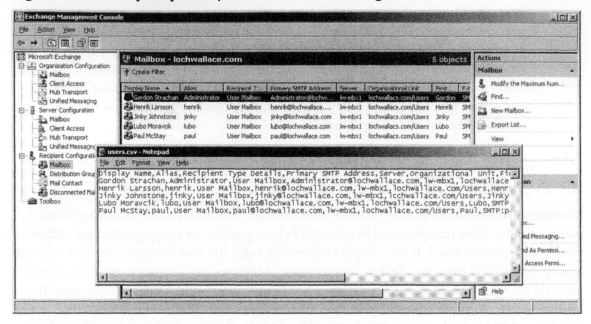

# Windows Server 2008 Support

Exchange Server 2007 SP1 is the first version of Exchange that can be installed on a Windows Server 2008 server. We'll cover the advantages of this later, but one of the primary advantages for high availability is the ability to implement CCR clusters across routed networks.

# IP Version 6

Exchange Server SP1 supports IPv6 running on Windows Server 2008 only, despite Windows Server 2003 also supporting IPv6. If you are running Exchange SP1 on a Windows Server 2008 server, you must leave IPv4 installed and enabled to support IPv6.

All the main functions of the Exchange server roles support IPv6, with the exception of the Unified Communications role, due to limitations with certain telephony and speech components.

We say "all the main functions" support IPv6 because they can all send/receive data and speak to clients, but some transport functionality does not support IPv6:

> **IP Allow and Block List Providers** Presumably because of lack of use, most providers don't support IPv6 addressing yet. However, provider information is input using FQDNs rather than IP addresses, so presumably Exchange will be compatible.

**Sender Reputation** The Protocol Analysis agent for Sender Reputation does not compute values for IPv6-originated emails. Presumably, this will be updated in a future version of Exchange.

**Incoming Message Rate Limits** Only global IPv6 addresses are supported when considering message rate limits (such as MaxInboundConnectionPercentagePerSource, MaxInboundConnectionPerSource, and TarpitInterval). Link local and site local IPv6 addresses are not affected. For more information on IPv6, go to http://technet.microsoft.com/en-us/network/bb530961.aspx.

**Unified Messaging** Because of limitations with some of the speech and telephony components, UM servers cannot communicate using IPv6.

## Virtualization

Windows Server 2008 brings in Microsoft's new "Hyper-V" virtualization technology, which will support 64-bit guest operating systems, and therefore very likely support production Exchange 2007 servers.

Until now, Microsoft's virtualization software (Virtual Server) has only been able to run 32-bit guests, whereas all the other major virtualization vendors have supported 64-bit for a while. Partly because of this, Microsoft has not officially supported running Exchange server on virtual machines (they will provide "best effort" support for virtualized environments). With Hyper-V, they are expected to officially support running Exchange Server 2007 on a virtual machine. This is good news for larger companies that want the flexibility virtualized environments provide, and the DR benefits of having easily imaged virtual servers.

You can find out more about Microsoft Hyper-V at www.microsoft.com/windowsserver2008/virtualization/default.mspx.

# High Availability

## Standby Continuous Replication

Standby Continuous Replication (SCR) is the big new feature for Exchange high-availability. Using the same continuous replication engine in LCR and CCR, SCR provides more DR options by bringing in site-resilience. Figure 1.10 demonstrates a many-to-one SCR deployment where a single server in a DR location is protecting the data for multiple production Exchange servers.

**Figure 1.10** Many-to-One Data Protection

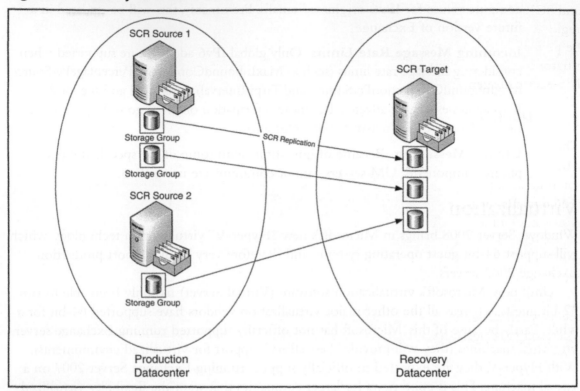

With Exchange Server 2003, standby clusters are used to get Exchange services up and running again quickly in the event of a disaster. In practical terms, SCR is a speedier way of doing the same thing, and leverages additional features such as the capability of Outlook to find its mailbox automatically from AD.

We discuss this topic in some detail in Chapter 5.

# Multi-Subnet Failover Clusters

By virtue of its support for Windows Server 2008, Exchange 2007 SP1 supports cluster configurations spread across routed subnets. Windows Server 2003 supports clusters only when the nodes are on the same IP subnet, but with Windows Server 2008, it is now possible to have geographically dispersed clusters using native tools.

Exchange clustering with Windows Server 2008 is covered in detail in Chapter 5.

# Cluster Monitoring/Reporting

SP1 introduces some new and some improved features related to cluster monitoring and reporting. The Get-StorageGroupCopyStatus cmdlet returns more information than previously and is more accurate thanks to a redesign of the underlying mechanisms.

A new cmdlet called Test-ReplicationHealth performs a series of tests on LCR, CCR, and SCR clusters, including checking the status of the nodes, networks, quorum and DNS registration, and how the replication and replay tasks are performing. Most of these tests can be performed manually, of course, but Test-ReplicationHealth makes it easier for the administrator to check all these things, and integrates tightly with the Microsoft Operations Manager management pack.

## I/O Performance on Passive Node

Thanks in part to some of the new replication technologies that came in as part of RTM, Microsoft noticed a number of differences in the way the Information Store behaved. In some situations, CCR clusters particularly, there are abnormally high memory and I/O requirements for some ESE operations, resulting in two to three times as much I/O on the *passive* node of a CCR cluster as on the active node!

Much tweaking of ESE has taken place in SP1, including disabled page dependencies and partial merges and caching improvements. As a result, performance has improved, and I/O on passive CCR nodes is down to more like 0.5—one times that of the active node.

It's worth mentioning that these changes have quite a marked effect on storage requirements when designing an Exchange environment, so get a hold of the latest version of Microsoft's Storage Calculator for Exchange, available from the Microsoft Exchange Team Blog (msexchangeteam.com).

## More Efficient Cluster Failover

In CCR environments, faster failover of the databases is achieved by removing the need to flush the database cache before taking the database offline, resulting in failover times of two minutes or less. SCC clusters now perform an opportunistic flush that allows clients to be still connected to the database. This means less downtime for clients when the failover is taking place.

## Continuous Replication over Redundant Networks

In Exchange 2007 RTM, all replication between nodes takes place over the public network. In a situation in which the nodes have been out of contact for a while and start a resynchronization, the flood of log file traffic has to contend with other public network traffic, which could lead to a depreciation in client service.

SP1 can use cluster "mixed networks" (networks that are configured for both heartbeat and client traffic) for seeding and log shipping. The Enable-ContinuousReplicationHostName command enables you to specify a mixed network for log shipping, and the Update-StorageGroupCopy command has been updated to enable you to specify networks for re-seeding of the databases.

In some organizations, private networks are sitting idle apart from heartbeat signals, and are woefully underused, so this is a welcome new feature.

# Client Access

## ActiveSync

In an effort to boost the functionality of Windows Mobile-based mobile devices, and to gain ground on other more feature-rich offerings from the likes of Research In Motion, Microsoft has introduced a number of new and enhanced features for its mobile platform. Some of these improvements require Windows Mobile 6.1, particularly the new policy settings for administrators.

## Mobile Device Policies

More than 30 new ActiveSync policies have been added, which require a future version of Windows Mobile (most likely 6.1). Some of these policies, primarily those that control the functionality of the device, require an enterprise Exchange CAL. These policies include Allow Bluetooth, Allow Consumer Email, and Approved/Unapproved Application Lists (Figure 1.11). However, in terms of enterprise device control, ActiveSync still lags behind the likes of RIM Blackberry. The new System Center Mobile Device Manager 2008 takes a much better and more comprehensive stab at enterprise device management, however.

**Figure 1.11** SP1 Provides Much Better Control of Mobile Devices

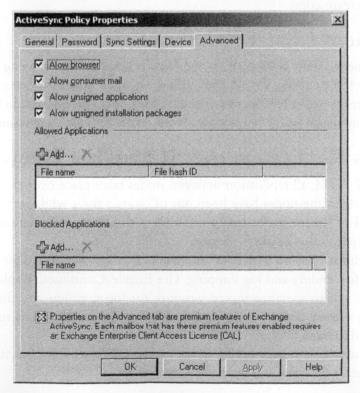

Microsoft supports over-the-air provisioning of mobile devices through Configuration Service Providers (CSPs), which are xml files with certain settings the device should apply. This is a method of enforcing settings on devices running against Exchange Server 2003 SP2 and later, and may provide a back-door method of achieving some of the control these new SP1 policies provide if you don't have enterprise CALs for your users.

## File Server Access via Windows Mobile

This isn't really new in SP1; rather it's a new feature of Windows Mobile 6.0 that was released after Exchange 2007 RTM so it's worth mentioning.

The heading is perhaps a little misleading, since direct access to UNC paths and Sharepoint servers is not possible on mobile devices. However, when you click on a link to a UNC path or Sharepoint server that is embedded in an email, Exchange proxies this request through ActiveSync (in a similar way to what OWA does when you open files on a file server) to deliver the document. Figure 1.12 shows screenshots of the process of opening a file on a file server that is referenced in an email using the internal UNC path.

**Figure 1.12** Opening an Internal Document from an Email in Windows Mobile

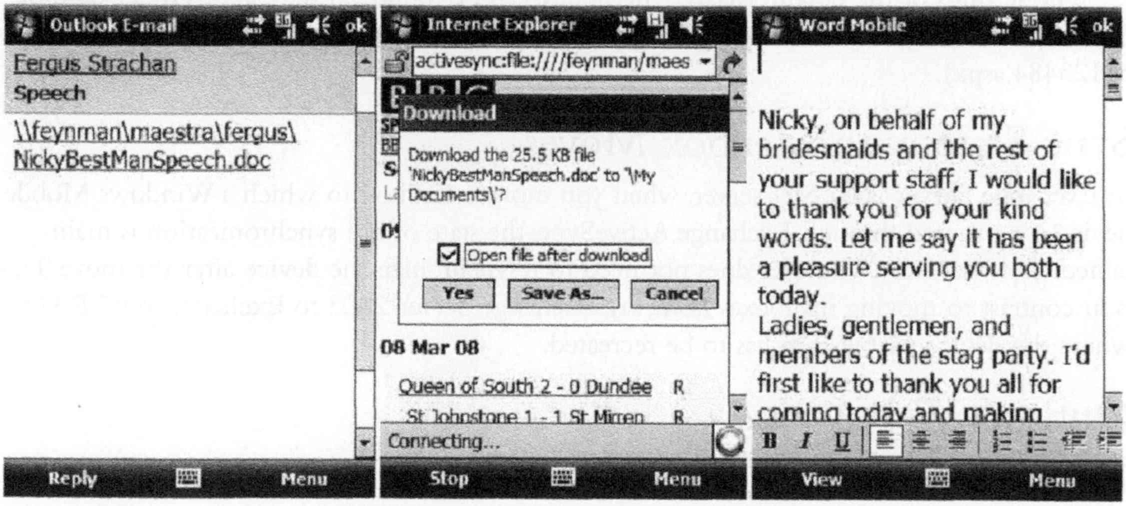

## Direct Push Performance Improvements

To further reduce the amount of traffic sent and received by mobile devices keeping their ActiveSync connection alive, Microsoft has managed to shrink the size of the HTTPS request and response headers. According to Microsoft's figures, they have achieved a 33% reduction in ActiveSync data in SP1.

In an environment where features such as streaming video are available on mobile phones, this would seem a relatively minor achievement, but it should save a bit of money for people still stuck on unreasonable data packages.

## Remote Wipe Confirmation

The Remote Wipe functionality in Exchange 2007 now has email confirmation built-in so you know the wipe has been successful. If the wipe is user-initiated, the user receives the confirmation; if the administrator performs the wipe, both the administrator and the user receive the confirmation.

You can also cancel a remote wipe job, useful for when you've been working too many nights and try to wipe the CEO's mobile device by mistake, or if you simply change your mind.

## ActiveSync Default Mailbox Policy

SP1 introduces a default ActiveSync policy for all users. Existing policies can be the default, but a policy will apply to all mailboxes after the application of SP1. If you have a lax environment for mobile users (e.g., no policy at all), be mindful of this when you are installing SP1.

The settings of the default ActiveSync policy can be found on the page "Understanding Exchange ActiveSync Mailbox Policies" (http://technet.microsoft.com/en-us/library/bb123484.aspx).

## Sync State with Mailbox Moves

In Exchange Server 2007 SP1 server, when you move a mailbox to which a Windows Mobile device is partnered through Exchange ActiveSync, the state of the synchronization is maintained after the move. The user does not need to resynchronize the device after the move. This is in contrast to moving mailboxes from, say, Exchange Server 2003 to Exchange 2007 RTM where the device partnership has to be recreated.

## Outlook Web Access

### WebReady Document Viewing Enhancements

WebReady document viewing is a feature of Exchange 2007 RTM that converts some Microsoft Office and PDF documents into HTML for viewing through Outlook Web Access. This is useful for clients that do not have the associated application installed (for example, in a kiosk scenario), and improves security by ensuring that the data in the document is not left on an unsecured OWA client machine.

SP1 has increased the scope of the WebReady document viewer to incorporate Office 2007 document formats (docx, xlsx, and pptx). You can also extend this to include file formats for which IFilters are available such as Visio or third-party formats (Figure 1.13).

**Figure 1.13** Some 2007 Office Format Documents Are Now WebReady

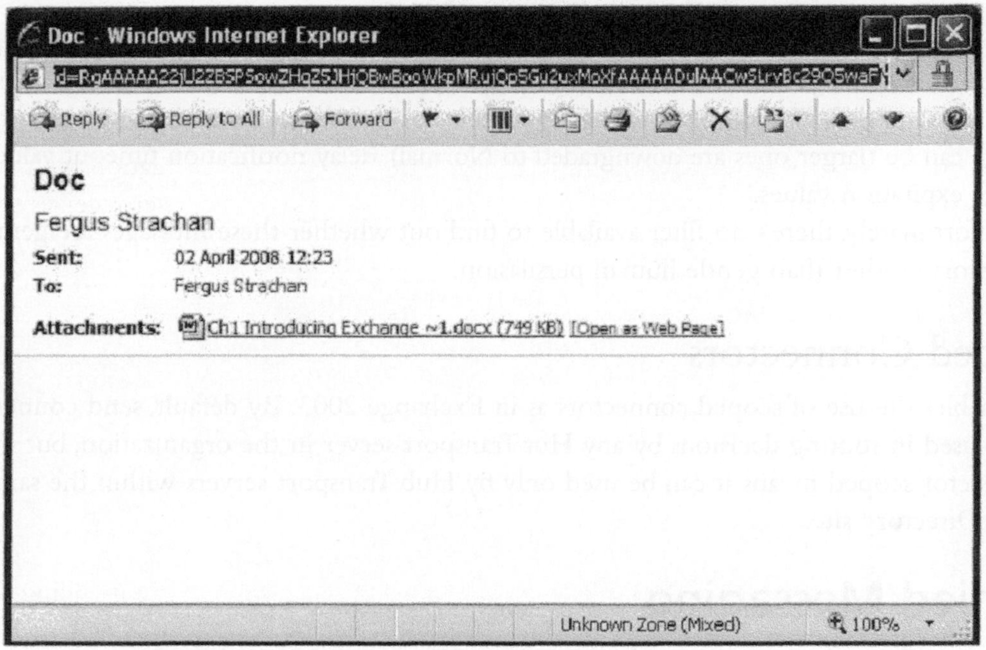

## Create/Edit Personal Distribution Lists

You can create and edit personal distribution lists through Outlook Web Access. These lists are maintained within your mailbox and can contain contacts from any shared address list such as the GAL and your mailbox contacts folders.

# Transport

## TransportConfig Object Cloning

In environments with multiple Edge Transport servers deployed in a load-balanced array, all the servers should have the same server-specific settings, which they store in an Active Directory Application Mode (ADAM) database. ExportEdgeConfig.ps1 and ImportEdgeConfig.ps1 scripts enable you to clone the configuration between servers to keep the rules, etc., the same.

The information cloned in this process includes Send- and Receive-Connector related information, accepted domains, and anti-spam configuration.

## Priority Queuing

For those who thought the small red exclamation mark on an email is just an annoyance from one of your self-important colleagues across the hall, now it actually has meaning above goading your colleagues into reading it first. Priority queuing is an option you can set on

Hub Transport and Edge servers to give priority to those messages marked "Important" so they reach their destination in a more timely manner.

Switched off by default, this feature is enabled by modifying the PriorityQueuingEnable parameter in the EdgeTransport.exe.config file (it's the same file on Edge and HT servers). There are a number of additional settings applicable, such as the maximum size a high-priority message can be (larger ones are downgraded to Normal), delay notification timeout values, and message expiration values.

Unfortunately, there's no filter available to find out whether these messages are genuinely high priority other than gentle human persuasion.

## Scoped Connectors

SP1 enables the use of scoped connectors as in Exchange 2003. By default, send connectors can be used in routing decisions by any Hut Transport server in the organization, but making a connector scoped means it can be used only by Hub Transport servers within the same Active Directory site.

# Unified Messaging

There are a few enhancements to the UM side of Exchange 2007 with SP1.

## Quality of Service (QoS) Using DiffServ

Exchange SP1 supports setting quality of service on packets using Differentiated Services (DiffServ). This enables an administrator to prioritize traffic such as phone calls higher than other traffic to help avoid degradation of service during network spikes.

DiffServ operates at layer 3 of the OSI model, so any layer 3 devices, such as routers and some switches, must support it.

## InBand Fax Tone Detection

Exchange can now detect fax tones and re-route calls accordingly. Normally, the PBX or IP gateway performs this function, but if these are unable to perform fax tone detection, you can configure the Exchange UM server to do so.

SP1 also provides some additions such as Secure Realtime Transport Protocol, more control through the Management Console, and inband fax tone detection.

## SP1 Features with Office Communications Server 2007

There are a number of enhancements to the unified messaging side of Exchange with SP1 when using it in conjunction with Office Communications Server, mainly addressing issues with voice calling quality, user experience, and ease of use.

There are no groundbreaking enhancements with the fax services as far as SP1 is concerned, and sadly, it is still good for only incoming faxes, not outgoing.

# Web Services

Good news for programmers is that the Web Services API has been opened up to allow access to features such as public folder access, folder-level permissions, and improved delegate access setting.

It's said, and hoped, that Web services will prove considerably easier to program than the likes of Outlook, the APIs and methods for which were largely undocumented and cause frustration among developers.

# System Requirements/Recommendations

System and domain requirements for Exchange Server 2007 SP1 are the same as for RTM with the following differences:

**Service Pack 2 for Windows Server 2003**  SP2 is a hard requirement for the server on which Exchange 2007 SP1 is being installed. SP2 also includes certain required components that would otherwise have to be downloaded separately.

**Global catalogs**  At least one Windows Server 2003 SP1 global catalog in each site with an Exchange server. Some GC operations require new features in SP1 for Windows 2003.

Other requirements for installing Exchange Server 2007 SP1, which it shares with the RTM version, follow.

## X64 Architecture-based Computer

**Memory**  2GB RAM plus up to 5MB per mailbox is the recommended amount, although Exchange can run (slowly) on less.

**Disk subsystem**  Recommended to have RAID10 across the board where feasible (although RAID1 for logs and RAID5 for databases are fine for small to medium organizations), with separate LUNs for logs, databases, and system files at least. When implementing Exchange on a high-end SAN that uses virtual RAID technology (where the relationship between disks and LUNs is blurred), you must determine how many spindles are required for the projected I/O profile of the server and configure disk groups accordingly.

**.Net Framework 2.0 SP1** (or .Net 2.0 with the update KB926776)

**Microsoft Management Console (MMC) 3.0**  The Exchange Management Console and tools are based on MMC 3.0.

**PowerShell 1.0** The Exchange Management Shell is based on PowerShell version 1.0.

**Domain functional level** Windows 2000 Server native domain functional level is required in domains where Exchange is installed or will host Exchange recipients.

**Forest functional level** Windows Server 2003 forest functional level is required if you need to use either cross-forest administration or cross-forest free-busy sharing. Otherwise, the forest must be Windows 2000 Server level.

**Writeable DCs** Writeable domain controllers and global catalog servers must be present in each site where Exchange is installed.

**Single-label DNS name** These are not recommended in an Exchange environment, although they are supported. It is expected that this support will not be there in the next version of Exchange Server.

# Windows Server 2008 Prerequisites

The prerequisites for Windows Server 2008 are similar to those of Windows Server 2003. Windows 2008 can be installed in a non-GUI mode called a "Server Core" installation, however, but Exchange does not support this kind of install, as it requires IIS, which is not available in core.

Windows Server 2008 has the same OS dependencies as previous versions of Windows, including IIS, the MMC console, and PowerShell, but installing these components is a little easier by using the command line. Following are lists of prerequisites for each Exchange Server role, installable through a command prompt on the server.

**All Roles**

ServerManagerCmd –i PowerShell (PowerShell 1.0 is included in the OS)

**Exchange Management Tools**

ServerManagerCmd –i Web-Metabase (IIS6.0 metabase compatibility)

ServerManagerCmd –i Web-Lgcy-Mgmt-Console (IIS6.0 management console)

**Client Access Server**

ServerManagerCmd –i Web-Server (IIS7.0 tools)

ServerManagerCmd –i Web-ISAPI-Ext (ISAPI extensions)

ServerManagerCmd –i Web-Basic-Auth (Basic Authentication)

ServerManagerCmd –i Web-Digest-Auth (Digest authentication)

ServerManagerCmd -i Web-Windows-Auth (Windows authentication)

ServerManagerCmd -i Web-Dyn-Compression (Dynamic Content Compression)

**Outlook Anywhere**

ServerManagerCmd -i RPC-over-HTTP-proxy

**Edge Server**

ServerManagerCmd -i ADLDS (Active Directory Lightweight Directory Services, formerly known as Active Directory Application Mode (ADAM))

**Mailbox Server**

ServerManagerCmd -i Web-Server (IIS Web server)

ServerManagerCmd -i Web-ISAPI-Ext

ServerManagerCmd -i Web-Basic-Auth

ServerManagerCmd -i Web-Windows-Auth

**Failover Cluster**

ServerManagerCmd -i Failover-Clustering (Failover Clustering—MSCS clustering)

To install the prerequisites for Windows Server 2008 for a particular role, you can simply copy the preceding lines that are required into a batch file and run all the install commands in sequence.

**Unified Messaging**

ServerManagerCmd -i Desktop-Experience (Unified messaging requires the Windows Media Encoder, Audio Voice Codec, and other components from the "Desktop Experience" feature.)

# Upgrading to Service Pack 1

Upgrading individual servers to SP1 is trivial. However, upgrading an organization isn't quite as easy as putting the CD into each server and clicking "GO"; servers should be upgraded in a particular order. Although the Exchange organization is unlikely to break if you do not adhere to the recommended order, you may have routing and client access issues during and possibly after the upgrade if you do not.

SP1 for Exchange is different from other service packs in that it is actually the whole Exchange product with SP1 included—a kind of streamlined install—rather than just a bunch of updated files to apply to the servers. Luckily, the download is not nearly as large as the RTM CD, as it omits a number of unified messaging-related files.

# Prepare Active Directory

## Schema

SP1 requires an extension to the Active Directory schema, so this is the first task to be undertaken. This will be done automatically by the setup program when you upgrade the first Exchange server, although the user must be a member of the Schema Admins and Enterprise Admins groups in the forest.

To update the schema in preparation for the upgrade, use the same method as for RTM— Setup /PrepareSchema.

## Active Directory

Some aspects of Active Directory must also be updated, as for RTM, by using the Setup /PrepareAD command. This will also be done as part of the first server upgrade providing the user is a member of the Enterprise Admins group.

## Domains

SP1 also requires changes to each domain in which Exchange items (users, contacts, etc.) are to be homed. This can be done beforehand using the Setup /PrepareDomain or /PrepareAllDomains switches. This requires membership of the Domain Admins group.

# Upgrade Order

As with previous versions of Exchange, the rule of thumb when upgrading is to first upgrade the servers that are first in the chain. For example, remote clients contact the Client Access servers, which handle requests along with the back-end mailbox servers. Therefore, the CAS servers (and hub transport for mail flow) servers are the first to be upgraded.

To avoid "potential service interruptions," use the following order when upgrading to SP1:

1. **Client Access (CAS) Servers**  If there are Internet-facing CAS servers, upgrade these first, followed by the internal CAS servers.

2. Unified Messaging servers

3. Hub Transport servers

4. **Edge servers**  Edge servers are not members of the domain, so require only local admin rights to upgrade to SP1. Exchange 2007 SP1 is incompatible with the RTM version of ForeFront. If the Edge servers have Microsoft ForeFront installed, they must be upgraded to ForeFront with SP1 before upgrading to Exchange 2007

SP1, as the prerequisites will fail during setup. For the Exchange SP1 install, disable all the ForeFront services and re-enable them after SP1 is installed.

5. **Mailbox servers**  Lastly, upgrade the mailbox servers. Clustered mailbox servers are a different prospect and are explained in the next section.

# Upgrading Clustered Mailbox Servers

The process of upgrading clustered mailbox servers is slightly different from standalone servers since they have additional dependencies and quirks. Only passive cluster nodes can be upgraded, and setup can be run only from the command line.

It's important to plan the upgrade of a cluster for it to run smoothly, properly, and with minimum downtime for clients. One of the advantages of clusters, of course, is that downtime can be minimized when performing upgrades and maintenance.

## Upgrading a Cluster

Upgrading SCC and CCR clusters to SP1 involve the same process. The difference is, a CCR cluster may have slightly different cluster services running on it and has only two nodes, whereas an SCC cluster can have up to eight nodes. Consequently, the number of times you have to perform a certain action may be different, but the actions are the same.

To upgrade a cluster to SP1:

1. **Move all cluster resources to the active node.**  The exception to this are the network-related cluster groups created on each node to facilitate replication over a redundant network. These resources are designed to stay on their respective nodes.

2. **Upgrade all the passive nodes first.**  SCC clusters can contain up to eight nodes.

3. **Start the Windows Firewall service on the nodes to be upgraded**, if not already started. This is so the setup program can add relevant exceptions for the Exchange services and will be disabled again after install.

4. Stop any performance counters including MOM agents.

5. Disable any file-level anti-virus agents.

6. **Restart the Remote Registry service**  This is a Microsoft recommendation, presumably so it is running smoothly and not in a hung state. This service must be running for the upgrade.

7. Run the SP1 upgrade program, Setup /m:upgrade (Figure 1.14).

**Figure 1.14** Upgrading the Node with Setup.com

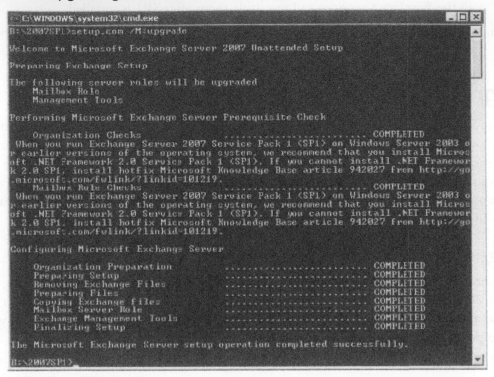

8. Stop and disable the firewall service (optional).

9. **Restart any MOM agents.** If they have not already restarted because of a reboot.

10. **Take the CMS offline.** Stop-ClusteredMailboxServer EXCHCLUS1 –StopReason "Upgrade". You need to take the CMS offline before moving it since it needs to be upgraded to SP1 while it is offline. An online move operation between nodes of different service pack versions is not possible since the target node must have an SP1 CMS to bring it online.

11. **Move the CMS to another (upgraded) node.** Move-ClusteredMailboxServer EXCHCLUS1 –TargetMachine NODE2.

12. **Upgrade the CMS.** Setup /upgradecms (Figure 1.15).

**Figure 1.15** Upgrading the Clustered Mailbox Server (SP1 Upgrade CMS.jpg)

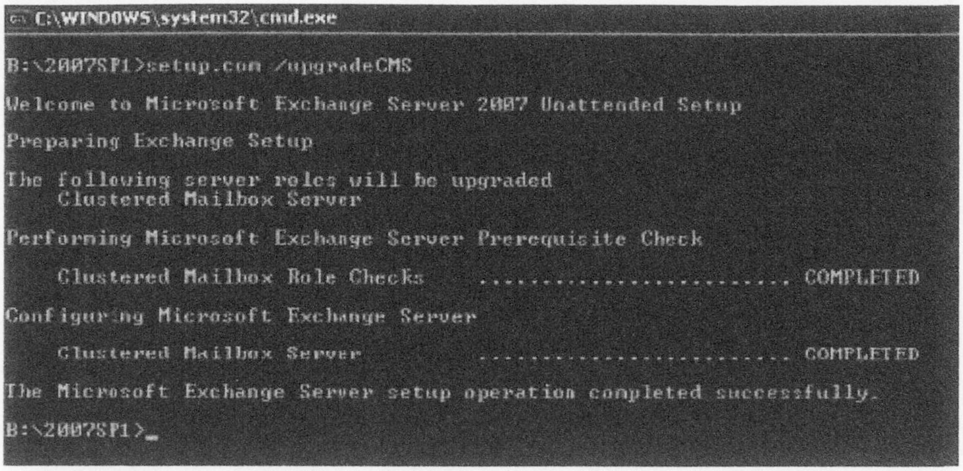

13.   Bring the CMS online.

14.   Upgrade the final node.

15.   **Move the CMS back to the original node.** This is of course an optional step, but you may wish to have the CMS running on the same node as at the start. Now that SP1 is installed, the EMC "Manage Clustered Mailbox Server" wizard can be used.

# Chapter 2

# Architecting an Exchange Server 2007 Solution

## Solutions in this chapter:

- **Using the Exchange Management Console**
- **Recipient Management**
- **Public Folder Management**
- **Storage Groups**
- **Server Role Management**
- **Server Roles Deployment**
- **Edge Transport and Hub Transport Servers**

☑ **Summary**

# Introduction

Microsoft Exchange Server is a viable collaborative tool that has been at the head of the industry for many years. The first public version, Exchange Server 4.0, was released in 1996. It is among the top 10 best-selling server applications in Microsoft's existence. Microsoft continually upgrades and adds new functionality and roles to enhance Exchange Server's capabilities. With the release of Microsoft Exchange Server 2007, an administrator should know how to take advantage of and manage the latest features for improved performance Exchange continues to deliver.

This chapter is designed to help you learn the best methods of managing these new features of Exchange 2007. It provides an overview of the capabilities and structure of Exchange Server, and discusses the major roles that require the diligent management of administrators when dealing with Exchange Server—in particular, how to deal with Recipient Management, Public Folder Management, and Server Role Management. It also offers great insight into some of the powerful new features of Exchange Server 2007. Although managing Exchange Server may seem daunting, this chapter guides you through the process and allows you the greatest benefit for your enterprise.

# Areas of Usage for Exchange Server 2007

The most basic question an administrator must ask, before preparing to manage an Exchange Server is, "What role does Exchange Server play in my company?" Ask three different administrators, and you will probably receive three extremely different answers. You might use it as a messaging system. You might use it as a groupware product. You might even employ it as a development platform. All of these are practical and not uncommon roles for Exchange Server. However, each requires different roles managed to accomplish maximum efficiency.

Exchange Server 2007 acts as a fully functioning messaging system. It represents the highest standard of reliability, scalability, and performance. Over the past couple of decades, electronic messaging has become one of the dominant methods of business communication, and Exchange Server is one of the most popular messaging systems in the world. It is a total solution for any deployment situation.

In the 1980s, the term *groupware* was created to encompass products that could be used as collaborative applications for people to share access to a group of centralized resources. Since then, the terminology has grown much less formal and is referred to simply as *collaborative software*. If you were involved in IT 25 years, ago you remember the term *groupware*. Luckily, Exchange Server 2007 allows you the ability to store or share just about any kind of document within its system. As a backup system, Exchange Server will automatically send copies of documents to different physical information stores. This allows for much more efficient automated backup and storage of shared documents across an organization.

As we mentioned, Exchange Server has also become increasingly popular as a development platform. By this, we mean that Exchange Server is being used as a basis for creating customized applications and systems that can address the needs of your specific organizations. It can be used to create forms that change or expand upon those of simple messages. These forms can also contain application logic so that when configured, Exchange Server can route these forms accordingly. In addition, once Exchange Server routs the forms, the forms can undergo further modification.

As you can see, Exchange Server is a very advanced and complex product that requires proper diligent management in several key areas. In the remainder of the chapter, we cover several key elements of Exchange Server 2007.

# Using the Exchange Management Console

Those familiar with older builds of Exchange Server are probably accustomed to the Exchange System Manager. This was the standard interface for Exchange Server 2002/2003. Previous versions used the Exchange Administrator program and had many limitations in both design and application. Exchange Server 2007 introduces an updated GUI management console that replaces the Exchange System Manager of previous versions. Exchange Management Console is a Microsoft Management Console (MMC) 3.0 snap-in, similar to Exchange System Manager. MMC does not provide any management functionality. The MMC environment allows for a common basis for integration between snap-ins, allowing administrators to have access to custom management tools. You as an administrator can select the tools you have created for later use. You can also share them with other administrators and users, allowing you to distribute specific tasks and delegate responsibilities by creating specific tools that contain the exact level of complexity for the user who will perform the tasks.

MMC 3.0 and Exchange System Manger use standard GUI elements that include a navigation tree, result pane, action pane, wizards, property pages, and dialogs. There have been significant improvements to the GUI design that simplify the console experience when compared to its predecessor. Those experienced with previous versions of Exchange Server will appreciate these changes, along with the fact that the new Exchange Management Console has not undergone a complete paradigm shift. The console provides an intuitive interface with a simplified learning curve while allowing for an organized management experience. Although the Exchange Management Console contains a graphical view of many resources and components, several tasks still must be performed via the Exchange Management Shell that exists in an Exchange organization. Regardless of how large your server configuration is, it can be easily managed from a single Exchange Management Console window. You use both container and leaf objects to administer an Exchange organization. Most objects in the Exchange Management console window—both container and leaf—have a property sheet that allows you to configure various parameters for that object to best serve the organization's needs. This section is a brief overview of the console frame and the three main aspects on the navigation tree.

# Main Aspects of the Exchange Management Console

Familiarizing yourself with the Exchange Management Console should be simple if you have worked with other versions of Exchange Server. For those who are new to Exchange Server or would like a fresh overview, begin by opening the Exchange Management Console:

1. Click **Start**.
2. Select **All Programs**.
3. Select **Microsoft Exchange Server 2007**, and then click **Exchange Management Console**.

In Figure 2.1, the Exchange Management Console is separated into a few main aspects:

- **Console tree:** On the left is the console tree. The tree is organized by containers that represent the hierarchy of the Exchange organization. This list of containers will differ based on the server roles that are installed when you view the console tree. By selecting a container in the console tree, you display the results of that selection in the Results pane.

- **Results pane:** In the center of the main console is the results pane. The Results pane displays the objects that reflect the container you have selected in the console tree. This is useful, for example, to view individual mailboxes inside the Recipient Configuration container. The Results pane displays these details.

- **Work pane:** At the bottom of the Results pane is the Work pane. The Work pane is only displayed when you select objects under the Server Configuration container, such as Mailbox, Client Access, or Unified Messaging. Objects based on the server role that is selected in the Server Configuration container can be found in this pane.

- **Actions pane:** On the right side of the console is the Action pane. This pane displays the actions you may perform in regard to the object selected in the other areas of the Exchange Management Console. These actions correspond to the actions available to you by right-clicking the object.

**Figure 2.1** Exchange Management Console Overview

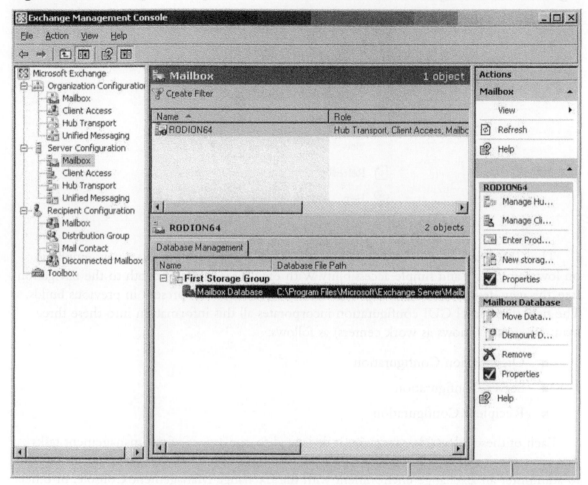

The fundamentals of the console don't differ much from Exchange System Manager. The newest addition is the Action pane, which acts as an extension of the right-click menu. This pane allows visual discovery of available actions at a glance without having to right-click. For those who prefer to use the right-click menu, it is still available. The administrator can choose to turn off the Action pane completely by going to the View menu and choosing **Customize** as shown in Figure 2.2.

**Figure 2.2** Disabling the Action Pane in the View Menu

The GUI interface For Exchange Server 2007 is still familiar but has a new emphasis on low complexity and simple accessibility. With only three levels of depth to the navigation tree, the new design has done away with the myriad of sublevels present in previous builds. The new three-level GUI configuration incorporates all this information into these three main categories (knows as work centers) as follows:

- Organization Configuration
- Server Configuration
- Recipient Configuration

Each of these selectable categories is dedicated to one aspect of the management tasks that were previous much less concise. You must be logged on to Active Directory to be able to administer an Exchange environment with the Exchange Management Console. In other words, a domain user account with administrative privileges must be active to administer the Exchange organization.

As we move forward in the chapter, we discuss in detail the aspects of each of these three groups and the functionality they offer administrators. We break down each level and discuss in detail the aspects of their functionality.

By selecting the Organization Configuration container, you can display a list of all users configured as Exchange administrators. This allows you to configure administrative access roles for all users and groups and delegate access privileges. To do this, you must be a member of the Exchange Server Administrators group. This will allow you access to the Organization Configuration container and allow you to change the roles assigned to users.

The organization work center is designed for global- or system-wide configuration data. From here, you can access features like E-mail Address Policies, formerly called Recipient Policies in previous versions. From here, you can also access Address Lists and Accepted Domains.

All of this work center's subnodes are broken down by server role, which allows for easy access and organization. This is helpful to the administrator because configuration data can both be server-level and organization-wide. The server-role grouping provides an effective method to organize both server and organization configuration work centers. It also grants quicker access to all the configuration data for a particular server-role. The top-level node of the work center "Organization Configuration" is used for general global data that doesn't map to a specific server role; for instance, managing your Exchange Administrator roles is found on this top-level node.

Exchange administrator roles function similarly to Windows Server security groups. Administrator roles allow you to assign sets of permissions to users with ease. This also includes assigning most common administrative functions in Exchange Server. Here are some of the Exchange administrative roles:

- **Exchange Server Administrators** By selecting this role, you can gain access to local server Exchange configuration data. This includes data, both in the Active Directory or on the physical computer on which Exchange Server 2007 is installed. The permissions granted by this role allow users who are members of the Exchange Server Administrators role to administer a particular server. They do not, however, have permission to perform operations that have global affects in the Exchange organization. Here is a list of the access granted by this role:

  - Members are made owners of all local server configuration data. As owners, members of the role have full control over the local server configuration data.

  - Members are granted administrative authority on the computer on which Exchange is installed.

  - Members are made members of the Exchange View-Only Administrators role.

- **Exchange Organization Administrators Role** This role provides administrators with full access to all Exchange properties, including all objects in the Exchange organization. In addition, members assigned this role are granted the following permissions:

  - Members are granted ownership of the Exchange organization in the configuration container of Active Directory. As owners, these members of the role are granted full control over the Exchange organization data in the configuration container in Active Directory. This also includes the local Exchange server Administrator group.

  - Members are granted Read access to all domain user containers in Active Directory. This permission is granted by Exchange during setup of the first Exchange Server 2007 server in the domain. This is true for each domain in the organization. These permissions are also granted by being a member of the Exchange Recipient Administrator role.

- Members are given Write access to all Exchange-specific attributes in all domain user containers in Active Directory. Exchange Server 2007 grants this permission during setup of the first Exchange Server 2007 server in the domain, for each domain in the organization. These permissions are also granted by being a member of the Exchange Recipient Administrator role.

- Members are made owners of all local server configuration data. As owners, these members have full control over the local Exchange server. Exchange Server 2007 grants this permission during setup of each Exchange server.

- **Exchange Recipient Administrators Role**  This role has permissions that allow modification to any Exchange property on an Active Directory user, contact, group, dynamic distribution list, or public folder object. Members of this role are granted the following:

  - Members are given Read access to all the Domain User containers in Active Directory that have had Setup/PrepareDomain run in those domains.

  - Members are given Write access to all the Exchange-specific attributes on the Domain User containers in Active Directory. This includes those that have had Setup /PrepareDomain run in those domains.

  - They are automatically granted membership in the Exchange View-Only Administrator role.

- **Exchange View-Only Administrators Role**  The Exchange View-Only Administrators role has Read-Only privileges to the full Exchange organization tree in the Active Directory configuration container. This also includes read-only access to all the Windows domain containers that have Exchange recipients.

# Organization Configuration

Now let's take a closer look at the organization configuration tree and see how each aspect's functionality can help to better administrate the Exchange environment. The Organization Configuration container contains the following containers, which all function on an Organizational level:

- **Mailbox**  The Mailbox container allows for management of Mailbox server role settings that apply to the entire Exchange organization. This means you can create and manage address lists, custom folders, messaging records management (MRM) mailbox policies, and offline address books (OABs). This is discussed in detail later in this chapter.

- **Client Access**:  The Client Access container allows for the creation and management of Exchange ActiveSync mailbox policies for mobile users. These policies apply common sets of security settings or policies to collections of users.

- **Hub Transport**: The Hub Transport container allows for the configuration of the features of the Hub Transport server role. The Hub Transport server role is responsible for all internal mail flow. It also applies organizational message routing policies, and handles the delivering of messages to a recipient's mailbox.

- **Unified Messaging**: The Unified Messaging container allows management of Unified Messaging (UM) server role settings that directly apply to the entire Exchange Server 2007 organization. This allows the maintenance of existing or creation of new UM dial plans, UM IP gateways, UM mailbox policies, and UM auto attendants.

# Server Configuration

The server configuration work center is the hub for server-centric data, and possesses features like database management and protocols. It is similar in layout to the organizational work center and has subcategories based on server roles. The top-level node of this work center—"Server Configuration"—provides an unabridged view of all Exchange 2007 and higher servers. This is true regardless of server role. This can help an administrator who wants to search for a specific server by filtering without having to choose a role. The admin can then select the server and navigate to the correct subnode to manage the settings for that server. The Results pane for this work center uses a Work pane that allows us to show child objects for the server, and has tabs to group similar features.

The Server Configuration container can be used to view a list of all the servers in your Exchange organization. IT can also perform tasks specific to server roles. By selecting the Server Configuration container, you can view the role, version, edition, product ID, cluster status, last modified time, and site for each server in the Results pane.

A number of containers appear under Server Configuration. Each shows only the Exchange servers that have a particular server role installed. Here is a list of the containers contained within the Server Configuration role that all function at a Server level:

- **Mailbox** The Mailbox container can display a list of all servers in the organization that have the Mailbox server role installed. It includes the ability to perform actions specific to that server role. The Database Management tab in the Work pane lists all the storage groups and databases that exist on the selected server.

- **Client Access** The Client Access container provides access to the settings for Microsoft Outlook Web Access (OWA), Exchange ActiveSync, and the offline address book (OAB). From here, you can view or maintain any of these aspects.

- **Hub Transport** The Hub Transport container provides a display list of all servers in the organization that have the Hub Transport server role installed. It also allows you to perform actions specific to that server role.

- **Unified Messaging** The Unified Messaging container allows configuration of voice messaging, fax, and email messaging so users can access them from a telephone or a computer. Exchange Server 2007 Unified Messaging allows you to integrate Microsoft Exchange with telephony networks. This allows you to bring the Unified Messaging features to the core of Microsoft Exchange.

# Recipient Configuration

The Recipient Configuration container allows you to perform a variety of recipient management tasks. From it you are able to view all the recipients in your organization. You can also create new recipients and manage existing mailboxes, mail contacts, mail users, and distribution groups.

The recipient work center is for management for all types of recipients. As stated, this includes mailboxes, distribution groups, and mail-enabled contacts. The functionality that used to belong to Active Directory Users & Computers is now present in the Exchange Management Console within the recipient work center. You must manage Exchange 2007 recipients from the 2007 UIs and not via ADUC. The subcategories are similar and based on recipient types. For example, the Mailbox node will show user mailboxes, linked mailboxes, resource mailboxes, and practically anything that has to do with mailbox configuration. The top-level node of this work center—"Recipient Configuration"—provides an overview of all recipient types. You can use the "Disconnected Mailbox" node to manage mailboxes that have been disconnected from the Active Directory user account and remain in the mailbox database. This node is specifically used to reconnect the mailbox to an AD user account.

The Recipient Configuration container contains the following containers:

- **Mailbox** At the recipient level, the Mailbox container allows you to manage all mailbox users and resource mailboxes. The term *Resource mailboxes* refers to room and equipment mailboxes. From this node, you can create new mailboxes and remove, disable, or move existing mailboxes. You are also able to configure mailbox properties, enable and disable Unified Messaging (UM), and manage mobile devices from this area.

- **Distribution Group** The Distribution Group container enables you to manage mail-enabled distribution groups (including security groups) and dynamic distribution groups. You are able to create new distribution groups and remove, disable, or configure existing distribution groups.

- **Mail Contact:** The Mail Contact container enables you to manage mail contacts. You are able to create new mail contacts and delete or configure existing mail contacts.

- **Disconnected Mailbox:** The Disconnected Mailbox container enables you to view and connect disabled mailboxes. Disconnected mailboxes are retained based on the configured mailbox database limits. Only the mailboxes disconnected within the retention period specified for the mailbox database will be present and visible here.

# Toolbox

The Toolbox work center is a launching site for the additional tools needed to manage Exchange. These are mostly tools for troubleshooting, diagnostics, and analyzing your Exchange system.

The Toolbox is a very useful collection of tools that are installed with Microsoft Exchange Server 2007. The Toolbox provides a central location for diagnostic, troubleshooting, and recovery activities using various Exchange tools.

The tools in the Toolbox are divided into the following categories:

- **Configuration Management Tools** This category contains only the Exchange Server Best Practices Analyzer, which automatically examines an Exchange Server 2007 deployment and determines whether the configuration is in line with Microsoft best practices. Run the Exchange Server Best Practices Analyzer after installing a new Exchange server or after making any configuration.

- **Disaster Recovery Tools** This category contains two tools: Database Recovery Management Tool and Database Troubleshooter. Both work through a set of troubleshooting steps to help identify and resolve database issues.

- **Mail Flow Tools** This category contains the following three tools:

  - **Mail Flow Troubleshooter** This tool allows you to troubleshoot common mail flow problems. After selecting a symptom of the mail flow problems you are experiencing (such as delays or nondelivery reports), the tool attempts to find a solution and then provides advice to walk you through the correct troubleshooting path. It shows an analysis of possible root causes and provides suggestions for corrective actions.

  - **Message Tracking Tool** This tool lets you view a detailed log of all message activity as messages are transferred to and from an Exchange Server 2007 server that has the Hub Transport server role, the Mailbox server role, or the Edge Transport server role installed. You can use message tracking logs for mail flow analysis, reporting, and troubleshooting.

  - **Queue Viewer** This tool allows you to monitor mail flow and inspect queues and messages. You can also perform actions to the queuing databases such as suspending or resuming a queue, or removing messages.

- **Performance Tools** This category contains two tools: Performance Monitor and Performance Troubleshooter. You can configure Performance Monitor to collect information about the performance of your messaging system. Specifically, you can use it to monitor, create graphs, and log performance metrics for core system functions. Performance Troubleshooter helps you locate and identify performance-related issues that could affect an Exchange server. You diagnose a problem by selecting the symptoms observed. Based on the symptoms, the tool walks you through the correct troubleshooting path.

# Using the Exchange Management Shell

The Exchange Management Shell, shown in Figure 2.3, is based on Microsoft Windows PowerShell. This means that it provides a powerful command-line interface for executing and automating administrative tasks. With the Exchange Management Shell, you can manage every aspect of Exchange Server 2007. By taking advantage of the Exchange Management Shell's capabilities, you are now able to create new email accounts, configure store database properties, and conduct just about every other management task associated with Exchange Server 2007.

**Figure 2.3** Exchange Management Shell

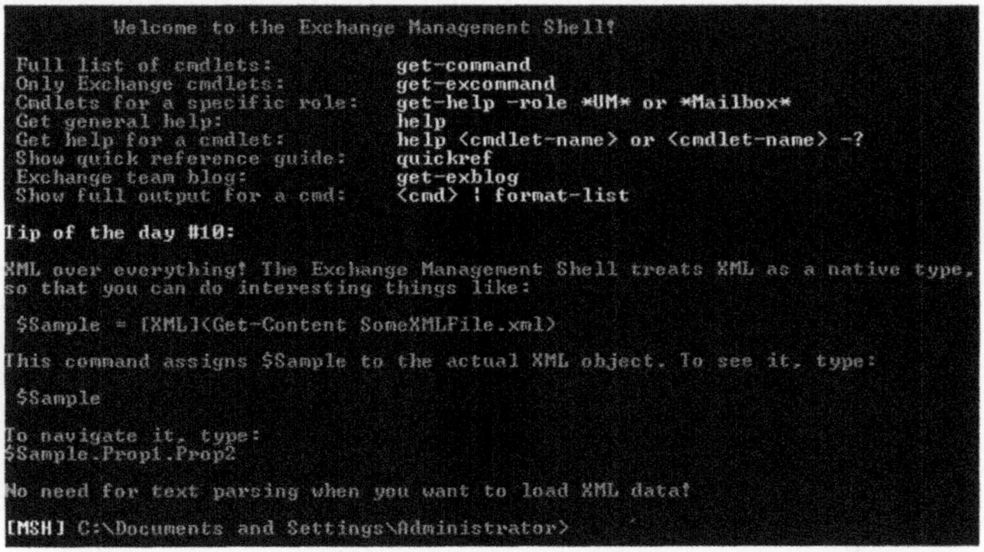

More precisely, you can use the Exchange Management Shell to conduct every task available in the Exchange Management Console. This also includes a number of tasks that cannot be performed in the Exchange Management Console. Think of it this way: The Exchange Management Console provides a graphical interface for most of the functionality of the Exchange Management Shell. When you run a command in the Exchange Management Console, the Exchange Management Shell is called upon to perform the command. When you perform a command in the Exchange Management Console, the graphic interface often shows you the proper associated commandlet. Think the Exchange Management Shell as the engine responsible for executing all commands in Exchange. The Exchange Management Console is merely a remote control for that engine.

So why use the shell instead of the console? Aside from the fact that some commands (such as those used to manage public folders) are available mostly as shell commands, the shell offers flexibility that can speed up and simplify common operations. You can also use ESM to manage the 2007 PFs if you still have a server with the ESM system tools installed. In addition, there are custom PS scripts for PF management in the Scripts folder. For example, with a single shell command, you can get a list of recipients, filter that list according to a set of criteria, and then perform a function on only the filtered list of recipients.

The Exchange Management Shell also provides a robust and flexible scripting platform that can reduce the complexity of current Microsoft Visual Basic scripts, thereby improving the efficiency of the tasks being run. Tasks that previously required many lines in Visual Basic scripts can now be done by using as little as one line of code in the Exchange Management Shell. The Exchange Management Shell provides this flexibility because it does not use text as the basis for interaction with the system. Instead, it uses an object model that is based on the Microsoft .NET platform. This particular object model enables the Exchange Management Shell cmdlets to apply the output from one command to subsequent commands when they are run.

# Recipient Management

Sending and receiving information is the foundation of most major businesses in some respect or another. Messaging, groupware, and, of course, Microsoft Exchange Server 2007 are designed with this goal in mind. The message transfer process within an Exchange system is very important. Exchange Server 2007 is based on a multitude of messaging components and may seem overtly complex to someone without an understanding of its workings. However, with some analysis it becomes apparent how these components interact to create an enterprise-wide messaging system.

Recipients, defined simply, are objects in the Active Directory directory service. These objects are capable of referencing resources that can receive messages through interaction with Exchange Server 2007. Such a resource might be a mailbox in the mailbox store. This mailbox may be one in which one of your users receives email, or a public folder in which information is shared among many users.

Regardless of where a resource exists, a recipient object for that resource is always created within Active Directory on your network. One of the main tasks of an administrator is to create and manage these recipient objects. Therefore, in addition to discussing mailboxes and message transfer, this section explains how to create and manage various types of messaging recipients.

## Identifying Different Types of Recipients

There are many trains of thought when dealing with recipients in Exchange Server. Thinking of a recipient as a mailbox or simply as an object that can receive a message is common philosophy. As you administer your organization, it might seem convenient and even helpful to take that view. Bear in mind that it is important to understand the ways in which the underlying architecture affects how you work with recipients in Exchange Server.

Contrary to the preceding train of thought, in Exchange Server, a recipient object does not receive messages; it is in fact a reference to a resource that can receive messages. This is a small but important distinction. Recipient objects are contained in and maintained by Active Directory. The resources that recipient objects reference could be found anywhere, despite what may be indicated by Active Directory. One resource might be a mailbox for a user in your organization. A mailbox resource would be contained in the mailbox store of a particular Exchange server and therefore be maintained by that server. Another resource might be a user on the Internet. In cases like this, the recipient object would possess a reference to that resource. This includes rules governing the transfer of messages to the Internet.

Five types of recipient objects are available in Exchange:

- **User** A user is any individual with logon privileges on the network. The types of users in Active Directory with regard to Exchange Server can be a mailbox user, a mail-enabled user, or neither. A mailbox user has an associated mailbox on an Exchange server. This means that each user mailbox is a private storage area. This allows an individual user to send, receive, and store messages. All mail-enabled users have an email address and can receive, but not send, messages.

- **Resource mailbox** A resource mailbox represents a conference room or a piece of shared equipment. Users can include resource mailboxes as resources in meeting requests, providing a simple way to schedule resource availability for an organization. The two types of resource mailboxes in Microsoft Exchange Server 2007 are room and equipment. Room mailboxes are delegated to a meeting location, such as a conference room. Equipment mailboxes are linked to a resource that is not location specific, such as a projector or company car.

- **Mail contact** A mail contact is essentially an indicator that points to a mailbox in an external messaging system. It is most likely used by a person outside the organization or from a remote location. This type of recipient points to an address that will be used to deliver messages sent to that person and to any properties that will govern how those messages are delivered to that recipient. Contacts can be frequently used to connect your organization to foreign messaging systems, such as Lotus Notes or the Internet. An administrator creates contacts so that frequently used e-mail addresses are available in the Global Address List as real names. This makes it easier to send e-mail because users do not have to guess at what cryptic e-mail address a frequent contact may have.

- **Distribution group** A distribution group is a mail-enabled group object in Active Directory. Messages sent to a group are redirected and distributed to each member of that group. Groups can contain any combination of the other types of recipients, including other groups. Distribution groups enable users to send messages to a variety of multiple recipients without having to address each recipient individually. This allows for mass messaging to frequent contacts. A typical group is "Everyone." The "Everyone" group includes all Exchange members. This means that when a public announcement must be made to all members of an organization, the sender of the announcement simply selects the "Everyone" group. This way, the sender is not forced to select every user's mailbox from the Global Address List.

■ **Public folder**  A public folder is a public storage area, and is typically open to all users in an organization. Users can post new messages or reply to existing messages in a public folder, allowing them to create an ongoing forum for discussion of topics. Public folders can also be used to store and provide access to just about any type of document. The concept of a public folder as a recipient is sometimes difficult to grasp because the repository for information is shared.

Although a public folder is a type of recipient, it performs many more functions than just transferring or receiving messages. It is an abstract subject that requires a good deal of review. Consequently, we will discuss most of public folders' features, functions, and administration requirements separately.

# Public Folder Management

Sharing information is a requirement today, and is possibly the single most important tool available to any business. Sharing information is a powerful means of facilitating workgroups and teams. When members of a team are located in geographically distant locations around the world, the ability to share information becomes even more important. Microsoft Exchange Server 2007 offers that powerful groupware foundation through its implementation of public folders.

In Exchange Server 2007, public folders have a lowered emphasis compared to previous versions of Exchange Server. While you can create and manage public folders using the Exchange Management Shell, there is no provision for doing so in the Exchange Management Console. It is likely that this de-emphasis is due to the growing popularity and power of Microsoft SharePoint Server, which like the public folder feature of Exchange Server offers centralized document storage. In addition, SharePoint Server offers sophisticated document management, versioning, and tracking features public folders lack. This makes for a better overall system of accomplishing the same activities.

If all users in your organization are using Microsoft Office Outlook 2007, there is no need for public folders unless you want to use them for centralized storage. If users in your organization are still using previous versions of Outlook, public folders will be required, as they provide offline address book distribution, free/busy information, and Outlook security settings.

During the initial installation of Exchange Server 2007, you will be asked whether you have any users running Outlook 2003 or previous versions of Outlook. If you do, Exchange Server 2007 enables public folders during installation. If you do not, public folders will be disabled by default, and you must add a public folder database later.

Public folders can be excellent tools. They can provide a centralized storage area for virtually any type of document or message. They also can allow controlled access by any user in the organization. To effectively conduct the primary management of public folders, you will need to use the Exchange Management Shell. You can use the Exchange Management Console to perform a few database-related tasks. You can also use the Microsoft Outlook client to create and access public folders, and to perform limited administrative duties from that end.

A public folder is essentially a specific kind of mailbox. Like all other mailboxes, public folders can be mail-enabled or mail-disabled. In addition, like other mailboxes, public folders may contain a hierarchy of folders inside the top-level folder. The major difference with public folders is that they are publicly available to all the users in the organization.

When you create a public folder, that folder becomes located in the public folder database of a particular Exchange server. Any Exchange server with a public folder database can host a public folder. A public folder is initially created in the public folder database of only one server. This public folder can then be replicated to the public folder databases of multiple additional servers. In most organizations, the public folders do not all exist on one server, but are distributed across several servers.

Within a public folder tree, the folders at the first level are referred to as top-level public folders. When a user creates a top-level public folder, it is placed in the public folder store on that user's home server. When a user creates a lower-level public folder, it is placed in the public folder store containing the parent folder in which the new folder is created. Additionally, each public folder can then be replicated to other servers in the organization. This situation can become very confusing and quite complicated. It is important for you as the administrator to understand that public folders exist on different servers. Some public folders may have instances on multiple servers as well.

# Managing Public Folders with Outlook 2007

The Outlook 2007 client can be used to create public folders and manage certain public folder properties. This section covers both topics. You can also create and manage public folders using previous versions of the Outlook clients. Although this section focuses on the use of Outlook 2007, most of the techniques described work with these other clients as well. Be sure to consult appropriate source material when dealing with these clients.

Creating a public folder using Microsoft Outlook is simple:

1. Make sure the Public Folders object (or the folder inside which you want to create the new folder) is selected.

2. Choose **New Folder** from the File menu.

3. In the Create New Folder dialog box, enter the name of the public folder you wish to create.

4. Choose the type of items that folder should contain.

5. Select the folder in which it should be created, and click **OK**.

From this point, you can then set the types of messages that can be posted in a new folder. This includes calendar items, notes, tasks, contacts, and email items. The default is the type of item that can be posted in the parent folder.

After you create a public folder, you can configure it in several ways. The management of a public folder occurs in two places: the Outlook client and the Exchange Management Shell. Users can create public folders, so it is to your benefit to allow them certain managerial duties. This is why some management can occur in the client.

When a user creates a public folder, that user automatically becomes the folder's owner. The owner of the folder is responsible for the folder's basic design, including its access permissions, rules, and association of electronic forms. To conduct this management, the user can simply open the Properties sheet for a particular public folder in Outlook.

# Public Folder Databases and the Exchange Management Console

If during Exchange Server 2007 installation, you indicated that your organization did not contain versions of Outlook previous to Outlook 2007, public folders will not be activated by default. You will therefore need to create a new public folder database to use public folders. You may want to create multiple public Folder databases based on the size of your public folder infrastructure and individual needs.

You can create a new public folder database using either the Exchange Management Console or the Exchange Management Shell. To create a new public folder database using Exchange Management Console:

1. In the console tree of the Exchange Management Console, expand the **Server Configuration** node.

2. Click the **Mailbox** subnode located within the **Server Configuration** node.

3. Locate the **Results** pane and click the server on which you want to create the new public folder database, as shown in Figure 2.4.

**Figure 2.4** The Server Configuration Node

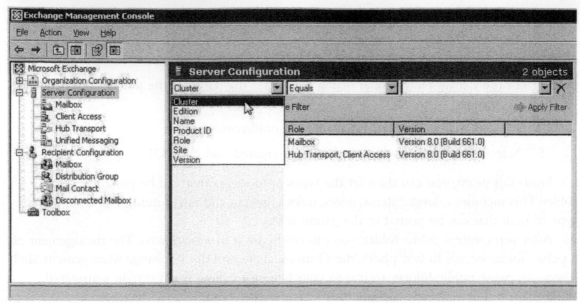

4.  In the **Work** pane, click the storage group in which you want to create the new public folder database.

5.  In the **Actions** pane, click **New Public Folder Database**.

6.  On the **New Public Folder Database** page of the **New Public Folder Database Wizard**, shown in Figure 2.5, type the name of the new public folder database. If you want to specify the location of the public folder database files, click **Browse**, and then type the name and location of the new Exchange database file (.edb) for the public folder. By default, the new database is mounted right after creation. If you want to mount it manually later, clear the **Mount This Database** check box. When you finish, click **New.**

**Figure 2.5** The New Public Folder Database Wizard

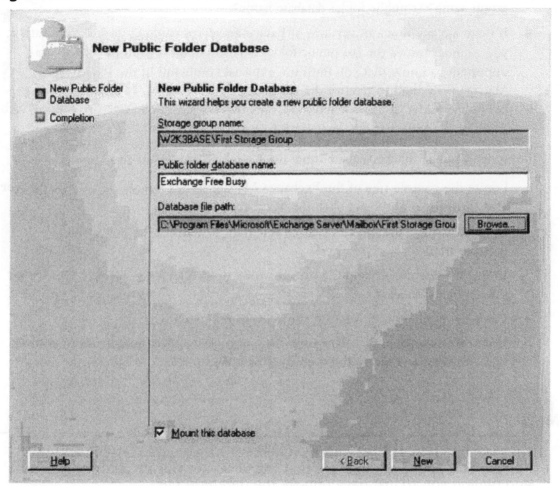

7.  On the **Completion** page, click **Finish**.

It's possible to remove a public folder database that is no longer in use. Before doing so, be aware of the following:

■  You cannot remove a public folder database that contains any data. You must first delete or move the public folders in the database to another database before removal.

■  You cannot remove a public folder database if any mailbox databases are associated with it. If any mailbox databases are using the public folder as their default database, they must be assigned another default database.

■  When a public folder database is removed, the database file is not deleted from the disk; you must delete the file manually. By default, the location for a public folder database file is C:\Program Files\Microsoft\ExchangeServer\Mailbox \<storage group name>\<public folder database name>.

■ If there are any previous versions of Exchange Server running in the organization, you cannot remove the last public folder database in an organization. It is also important to know that you must use a special command in the Exchange Management Shell to remove the last public folder database. In addition, once the last public folder database is removed, only users of Outlook 2007 or Outlook Web Access can connect to the organization

To remove a public folder database using the Exchange Management Console:

1. Locate the console tree of the Exchange Management Console, expand the **Server Configuration** node, and click the **Mailbox** subnode.

2. In the **Results** pane, click the server you want to remove the public folder database from.

3. In the **Work** pane, expand the storage group from which you want to remove the public folder database.

4. Click the public folder database you want to remove.

5. In the **Action** pane, click **Remove**. A message will appear asking you to confirm that you want to remove the database. Click **Yes**.

**NOTE**

Upon completion of the removal, a Microsoft Exchange Warning page will appear. This page with indicate that the database was successfully removed and remind you to manually remove the database file.

Exchange Server 2007 originally lacked public folder management features, so administrators had to install Exchange Server 2007 Service Pack 1 (SP1) to perform such tasks as managing public folder replicas. Be sure your version of Exchange Server 2007 has SP1 installed on it. After downloading SP1, it may appear that nothing has changed within the Exchange Management Console.

In the Tools container is a link to the Public Folder Management Console. When attempting to connect to a server, the console will only allow you to connect only to Exchange servers containing public folder stores. Consequently, you won't be able to use the Public Folder Management Console to create a public folder store. You must use the Exchange Management Console or the Exchange Management Shell for this task as described earlier. You can then use the Public Folder Management Console to create public folders once the store exists.

Once you have connected to an Exchange server, the console displays two containers:

- Default public folders
- System public folders

The public folders you created will appear in the Default Public Folders container and can be managed as follows:

1. Select this container, and all public folders beneath it will appear in the Details pane.

2. Right-click on an individual public folder

3. From here you can delete it, update the folder's contents, mail-enable the public folder, or access its Properties sheet.

4. Right-click on a folder and select **Properties**. This will allow you to view three tabs:

    - The General tab gives you a few statistics on the folder's size, and lets you maintain per-user read information for the folder.

    - The Limits tab lets you set quotas on the folder.

    - The Replication tab lets you control folder replication.

Unlike Exchange Server 2003, you cannot click **Add** to access the list of servers to create folder replicas on.

By clicking **Add**, you gain access to a list of individual public folder stores across the Exchange organization. This simplifies the process of creating folder replicas because you can pick the store for which you want to create the replica.

By default, public folders data will be replicated according to the store's replication schedule. You can create your own custom replication schedule:

1. Deselect the **Use Public Folder Database Replication Schedule** check box.

2. Choose either a preset replication schedule or the **Use Custom Schedule** option from the drop-down list.

The last option in the Replication tab is Local Replica Age Limit. A frequently used public folder's contents may potentially deplete server disk space. To help prevent this from happening, the Exchange Management Console allows you to define a specific age limit for data in the public folder. Posts older than the age specified will be purged from the folder.

Remember, public folders provide centralized storage of virtually any type of document or message and allow controlled access by any user in the organization. By now, you have learned what you need to know to create and manage a public folder system in your Exchange organization.

# Storage Groups

In terms of Exchange, a *store* is the location in which user mailboxes are located. A store also has its own associated database file in which mailbox contents can be saved. Storage groups are not a new concept and were first introduced in Exchange 2000 Server. They were designed as a way to achieve more defined and reasonable scalability. In essence, they are collections of individual stores. The level of utilization of storage groups in your organization will be primarily based on the version and edition of Exchange Server in use. Over the various builds of Exchange since Exchange Server 2000, significant changes have taken place in Exchange's inner workings when it comes to store and storage group support.

In the workplace currently, it is not uncommon to find massive Exchange databases. Many will be exceeding or approaching 100 GB or more, and can even reach 200 GB when using CCR, as this is the maximum recommended size in a CCR scenario. Backup time for these databases can exceed several hours. The problem with this is not the time it takes to back up the database, but the time it takes to restore such a large database. During the restoration process, your users' productivity with regard to email will be highly affected and usually at a standstill. In Exchange database planning, it is important to plan for the worst, so you can achieve the best results. Prudent use of storage groups helps you succeed during disaster recovery.

# Using Storage Groups

As you have learned, in implementing storage groups and allowing multiple databases per Mailbox server, Microsoft has made some tremendous changes to the Extensible Storage Engine (ESE) database architecture since Exchange Server 2003. When compared to Exchange Server 5.5 the changes are even more dramatic. Overall, the changes significantly enhance recoverability and maximize productivity when an Exchange database becomes corrupted or inoperable. In addition, storage groups offer several key benefits:

- The number of users per server has increased.
- Databases can now be backed up and restored individually.
- Multiple businesses can be hosted per server.
- Special mailboxes that may require different limits than users in other stores can be set up.

One of the greatest benefits of storage groups in Exchange Server 2007 is that it allows you to spread users across databases and storage groups on the same Exchange Server 2007 server. This scenario offers three distinct advantages:

- More users per single server can be supported than in earlier versions of Exchange. This is very apparent when you look at the way Exchange Server 2007 is architected.

The 64–bit capability of Exchange Server 2007 allows significantly more memory to be available. This only furthers to increase the number of potential users per server.

■ Downtime from database corruption is greatly reduced. By breaking up your users into separately managed groups, it is possible to keep the overall database size lower for each individual group. This helps to reduce the time it takes to restore after a failure.

■ You now have the ability to host more users on a single Exchange server because you can keep your databases to a manageable size. The more storage groups you create, the more they become separately managed entities. This allows for individual backup and restore of each. This way, if a single database becomes corrupt, you affect fewer users.

Within a storage group, you can have up to 50 databases. Each server can house up to 50 storage groups. However, each server can have a maximum of 50 databases, regardless of how many storage groups you may create. These numbers reflect Exchange Server 2007 Enterprise Edition. The Standard Edition has lower limits, which should be verified before using the OS.

There are some good arguments concerning why to refrain from creating the maximum number of databases possible in a single storage group. First, a simple log file problem could bring down all the databases in that storage group, resulting in an horrible situation for your help desk to deal with. Second, when you run the Information Store Integrity Checker (Isinteg.exe) on a database, you must dismount that individual database's information store. In addition, Isinteg.exe needs a second database for temporary use while the tool does its thing. This means that if you have five databases operating in a given storage group on a Standard Edition server; you will be forced to dismount a second database so Isinteg.exe can run properly. By limiting the total number of operating databases to less than the maximum for a storage group, you will always have room to run Isinteg.exe without having to dismount a second store.

## Multiple Databases

Having multiple databases can limit downtime for your users, although you should consider using HA functionality to protect the databases. Having your users spread out across multiple databases means that only a subset of your users is affected if one of your databases goes offline for some reason; all the other users are free to continue working because their databases are unaffected. Remember that an offline database is considered dismounted. Its icon will appear with a down arrow in the Exchange Management Console. Further, the database's status will be displayed as Dismounted.

Each individual database is capable of being mounted or dismounted. You can take advantage of this to back up and restore databases individually while other databases in the same storage group are mounted and running.. If one of the storage groups becomes corrupted, the others can remain mounted while you restore the corrupted store from backup and then mount it again. You are not required to dismount all the stores in a storage group to restore one of them. Moreover, if one store becomes corrupted and cannot be mounted, it does not stop other stores in the same storage group from being mounted and available to users.

It is also possible to manage email for multiple businesses, and is fairly simple to host them on a single server. You can create an individual store for each business, or even devote a storage group to a business if needed. Regardless, Exchange Server 2007 keeps the information for each business separate in its respective store.

Another advantage of multiple databases is scheduling. Separate, distinct stores will help you to set up different administrative schedules for the businesses, allowing you to cater to the preferences of your organization. Some administrators might want to have full backups performed every day. Other administrators might need only weekly full backups. Others still may want to have each department hosted in a separate store or want to house all their users in the same store. You will find that this flexibility makes it easier to meet your customer's needs and manage your databases fluidly.

Through creative use of storage groups and stores, you can isolate special mailboxes and keep them in their own store. This could be useful for users who need to receive copies of all appropriate emails in your organization to ensure compliance with local laws or industry-specific regulations—a popular practice in the Quality Assurance industry. Another case would be a project team that is working with highly sensitive and mission-critical company information, which might warrant the use of a separate store.

The use of proper planning will benefit both your short- and long-term goals and will result in less downtime later regardless of whether you are dealing with an old or new installment. It's not possible to overstress the fact that poor planning will lead to poor implementation. Consequently, this will lead to increased administration over the long term. It would not be incorrect to estimate that at least 50 percent or more instances of extended downtime could be avoided with better planning and implementation. Anyone with experience in the industry knows that IT pros are overwhelmed when it comes to workload. However, spending a little extra time planning your Exchange Server 2007 storage needs will reap huge rewards down the line.

Once you understand your disk space needs, consider how many storage groups you will require and the varying priorities of the work your users do. Always assume that 20 of every 300 users perform critical work—people who take orders over the phone or process customer orders that are placed in a public folder exposed on your Web site. If these users are down for even 15 minutes, your company losses will be in excess of $50,000. For this type of situation, you should consider splitting these users into two groups. Each group should be hosted in its own mailbox and public folder store. Hosting them in their own storage group would not always be necessary. However, as a reference Microsoft recommends that you maintain a 1:1 ratio between stores and storage groups whenever possible. Because with Exchange Server 2007 you have 50 storage groups at your disposal, you would be well advised to consider doing so.

The reasoning behind this recommendation is that if the other databases become corrupted, these users can continue to operate without disruption because you can dismount and restore one or any combination of stores while another store runs in the same storage group. If one group's database needs to be restored, a fast restore would be possible because it would be much smaller than the company-wide database. Because these users are spread over two databases, the other half of the group can continue to work and remain productive. This is why you should plan your storage groups with disaster recovery in mind more than disk space usage considerations.

As was the case with previous versions of Exchange, Exchange Server 2007 provides full management capability for dealing with storage groups. This includes creating, modifying, and deleting these store containers. In Exchange Server 2007, storage groups are a function of the Mailbox Role Server and are managed using either the Exchange Management Console or the Exchange Management Shell. In this section, you learn how to manage storage groups.

# Creating Storage Groups

Before you create a new storage group, verify that you have adequate physical disk space available and that it corresponds to your Exchange storage master plan. To create a storage group:

1. From the **Mailbox** server on which you intend to install the new storage group, start the **Exchange Management Console**. In reality, you can choose to do this from any server. Some administrators may choose to work directly on the server they intend to manage.

2. Expand the **Server Configuration** container.

3. Select the **Mailbox** server on which you want to create the new storage group.

4. From the **Action** pane, click on **New Storage Group**. This will begin the **New Storage Group wizard** that helps you to complete the procedure.

The wizard consists of a single screen as shown in Figure 2.6. Once open, it will ask you to provide some information, and to name the new storage group. The rest of the information is optional, unless you want to change the location of the log and database files. You can also choose to enable local continuous replication for your new storage group by selecting the check box next to **Enable Local Continuous Replication For This Storage Group**. Click **Browse** to direct each item to a particular location. It is recommended that you always create a specific subdirectory for each storage group. No matter how you create the new storage group, it appears in the Exchange Management Console window, as shown in Figure 2.7. You may notice a difference in certain icons, which indicates that local continuous replication is enabled for these storage groups.

**Figure 2.6** The New Storage Group Wizard

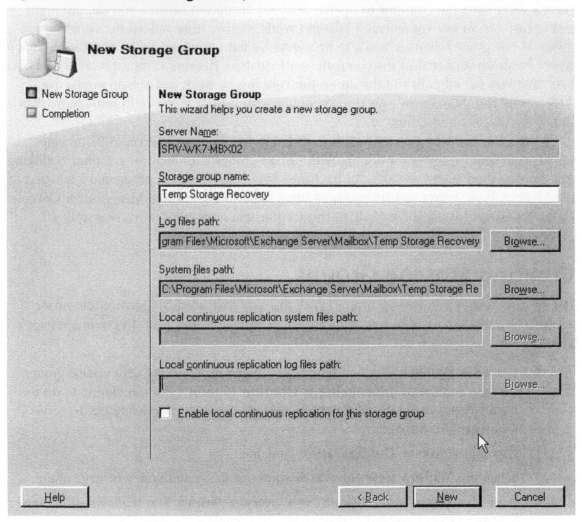

**Figure 2.7** The New Storage Group in the Exchange Management Console

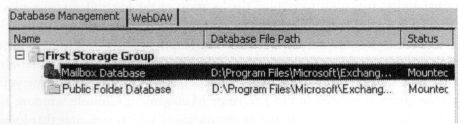

# Managing Storage Groups

Once created, your storage group may require modifications to the new object. For example, you may want to enable features such as circular logging for a particular storage group. As with most things Exchange, the Storage Group Properties page gives you the opportunity to make these changes. Storage group configuration changes are handled in a couple of different ways, depending on what you're trying to modify.

Here's a list of what is modifiable from the Sample Storage Group Properties page, which is accessed by right-clicking an existing storage group and choosing **Properties**:

- **Rename The Storage Group** The top of the Properties page contains the name of the storage group. If you want to rename this storage group, just overwrite the contents of this field with the desired name.

- **Enable Circular Logging** The Enable Circular Logging option allows circular logging for the storage group. This basically reduces the number of transaction logs that are stored on the disk, with some drawbacks. Consider enabling this feature only for those storage groups that do not hold mission-critical data. With circular logging enabled, it is possible to recover only to the last full backup. Carefully consider the full implications of losing the most recent data in your Exchange databases before selecting this option.

- **Local Continuous Replication** If you enable local continuous replication, a tab by the same name is available on the Properties page. This tab contains no configurable information, but is a status update instead.

# Server Role Management

Exchange Server 2007 introduces a new Exchange term: *server role*. Server role is a logical concept used to organize Exchange Sever 2007 services and features across one or more servers. While Exchange 2003 provided primitive server roles called BackEnd server and FrontEnd server, Exchange 2007 has more granular divisions.

The division of Exchange features among several server roles has numerous advantages to past versions:

- **Flexible deployment topology** This benefits small or medium companies that have only a few hundred mailboxes and all users are centralized. This allows the customer to install all required roles on one physical server. For a large enterprise where tens of thousands of mailboxes span multiple physical locations, the customer can choose to deploy each role on a separate server or even multiple servers per role to provide better performance and fault tolerance.

- **Improved hardware utilization and scalability** Because of the granular division, each role only installs binaries and runs services for a specific feature set. Older versions of Exchange allowed the configuring of a server that has only one or two roles to reduce memory, CPU, and disk space requirements for the server—that is no longer the case. In addition, all the individual roles are scalable so administrators can load balance work of one role to multiple servers.

- **Simplistic maintenance** In the past, upgrading, applying hotfixes, or other server changes could cause server outages. Server roles allow isolation of only one server role, thereby reducing maintenance downtime and end-user impact. Administrators can also install or uninstall roles on a server as needed.

You are probably curious about what these new roles are exactly and how they will change the way Exchange is managed. During the beta releases of Exchange 2007, there were six planned roles: Mailbox, Public Folder, Client Access, Edge, Bridgehead, and Unified Messaging. As Exchange Server 2007 development progressed, the Public Folder role was merged into the Mailbox role since they share Extensible Store Engine and MAPI access. Additionally, the Bridgehead role was renamed to "Hub Transport" to more clearly illustrate its functionality. If anyone is familiar with the Exchange Server 2007 beta, this will help clear up any confusion that may exist.

The release version of Exchange Server 2007 has the following server roles:

- **Mailbox (MB)** The Mailbox server role is responsible for hosting mailbox and public folder data. This role also provides MAPI access for Outlook clients. There is also a variation of this role called Clustered Mailbox role, for use with high-availability MSCS clustering of mailbox data. When Clustered Mailbox role is selected, other server roles cannot be combined on the same physical server.

- **Client Access (CA)** The Client Access server role provides the other mailbox server protocol access apart from MAPI. This role is very similar to Exchange 2003 Front-end server. It enables users to use an Internet browser (OWA), third-party mail client (POP3/IMAP4), and mobile device (ActiveSync) to access their mailbox.

- **Unified Message (UM)** This role enables end users to access their mailbox, address book, and calendar using telephone and voice. IP-PBX or VoIP gateway needs to be installed and configured to facilitate much of the functionality of this server role.

- **Hub Transport (HT)** The Hub Transport role handles mail by routing it to the next hop, usually another Hub Transport server, Edge server, or mailbox server. Unlike Exchange 2003 Bridgehead that needs Exchange admin defined routing groups, Exchange 2007 Hub Transport role uses AD site info to determine the mail flow.

- **Edge Transport (ET)**  Edge Transport is the last hop of outgoing mail and first hop of incoming mail, acting as a "smart host." It is usually deployed in a perimeter network configuration. Edge Transport provides mail quarantine and SMTP service to enhance security. One advantage of this role is that is does not require Active Directory access, which means that it can function with limited access to the corporate network for increased security.

# Server Roles Deployment

For Exchange Server 2007, Microsoft has eliminated the redundant routing group architecture. You may be wondering what is meant by "redundant." In the simplest terms possible, your legacy routing group topology should basically mimic your network structure or Active Directory topology. In older versions of Exchange Server, administrators were forced to add an additional routing layer used only by Exchange Server. Exchange Server 2007 has eliminated the need for this additional layer by using a structure that must already be in place and working in an organization, the Active Directory site topology. In this way, to support coexistence between a legacy routing group and an Exchange Server 2007 environment, you can use a routing group connector.

Before getting too deep into a transport discussion, here are definitions for a couple of terms and concepts important to this discussion:

**Send Connector**  A Send connector is a representation of a logical gateway through which outbound messages can be sent from an Exchange Server 2007 Hub Transport server or Edge Transport server. Most Send connectors have complementary Receive connectors. This is, of course, with the exception of a Send connector created to send mail to the Internet. No explicit SMTP Send connectors are created upon installation of Exchange Server 2007. It is important to note that implicit and invisible Send connectors are created based on the structure of your Active Directory site topology. SMTP Send connectors are used to route mail between Hub Transport servers in your Active Directory site. Send connectors created on servers with the Hub Transport role installed are stored in Active Directory. These Send connectors are then made available to all Hub Transport role servers in the organization.

**Receive Connector**  An SMTP Receive connector acts as the inbound connection point for SMTP traffic into a particular Hub Transport server or Edge Transport server. Receive connectors will actively listen for connections that specifically match the connector's parameters. This includes the originating IP address and port. A Receive connector is valid only on the server on which the connector is created.

**Foreign Connector**  The Foreign connector allows Exchange Server to send messages to a local mail system that does not use SMTP for its communication mechanism.

# Creating SMTP Connectors

SMTP connectors are created in Exchange Server 2007 in three ways:

- **Manually/explicitly** As the Exchange Server administrator, you can intentionally create an SMTP connector.

- **Implicitly** This method of creating SMTP connectors in Exchange Server 2007 is based on the Active Directory site topology. These types of connectors do not show up in the Exchange Management Console or in the Exchange Management Shell.

- **Automatically** During the setup process and the subscribing of an Edge Transport server to the environment, SMTP connectors are created that enable end-to-end mail flow.

It is very possible for you to go through your entire Exchange Server 2007 administration career and never need to touch the SMTP connector configuration in your Exchange environment. If you use an Edge Transport server and aren't required to perform any cross-forest mail transfers, Exchange Server 2007 provides a complete end-to-end routing scenario for you.

# Message Routing

In Exchange Server 2007, all message routing is handled using a direct-relay method. This means that the Hub Transport server will first establish a direct IP connection to another Hub Transport server. The second Hub Transport Server will, in turn, connect to a Mailbox server and then complete message delivery. In doing so, Hub Transport servers strongly rely on the capability of the underlying IP network's capability to reroute in the event of a network failure.

In Exchange Server 2003, link state tables were the only way individual servers knew whether the links between routing groups were alive. This is the meaning behind the term *link state routing*. In Exchange Server 2007, Hub Transport servers use deterministic routing and no longer rely on these link state tables. Because of this, Exchange Server 2007 doesn't make use of any link state information. Deterministic routing means that the transmission route is determined before transmission occurs.

Exchange Server 2003 and Exchange 2000 Server relied heavily on routing groups as a critical component of the overall transport architecture. These same routing groups are still supported in part in Exchange Server 2007. To provide better interoperability with legacy Exchange environments, Exchange Server 2007 has accounted for the creation of a single legacy routing group. This group's sole purpose is to create a connection between your legacy Exchange routing groups and your new Exchange Server 2007 environment.

Whenever possible, Exchange Server 2007 will route messages using the physical IP network. It may also opt to use your already configured Active Directory sites to find a path by which to deliver messages, if it exists. Hub Transport servers attempt to make connections directly to Hub Transport servers in the destination site. This helps to avoid intermediate relay sites that add no value and in general just slow the process. The use of the Active Directory site topology by Exchange Server 2007 will help make it easier for administrators because there is no redundant routing topology to worry about or manage. For the most part, Exchange Server 2007 automatically configures its routing topology and creates default connectors based on your existing Active Directory topology.

# Transport Protocols

Depending on the communication entities involved, the following list outlines the communication method used:

- Communication between Mailbox servers and Hub Transport servers is accomplished via MAPI/RPC.

- Communication between Mailbox servers and Client Access servers is also accomplished via MAPI/RPC.

- Communication between Hub Transport servers in different sites is accomplished via SMTP.

- Communication between a Hub Transport server and a legacy Exchange server accessible via a routing group connector is accomplished via SMTP.

- Communication between Hub Transport servers in the same site is accomplished via SMTP/TLS.

- Communication between Hub Transport servers and Edge Transport servers is accomplished via SMTP/TLS.

Clients, as it is to be expected, use a wide variety of communication protocols, including HTTP, HTTPS, MAPI, POP3, IMAP, and RPC over HTTP/S.

Also, try to bear in mind the following points:

- All e-mail is routed by a Hub Transport server, regardless of whether an e-mail is destined for a mailbox on the same server as the sender.

- A Mailbox server will have a preference and attempt to use a Hub Transport server that is installed on the same server. However, the Mailbox server will use any Hub Transport server it can find in the local site.

- The Hub Transport server role will automatically load balance at the local site. This prevents a single server from holding up mail delivery.

# Edge Transport and Hub Transport Servers

The two newest modifications to how Exchange Server 2007 handles message routing are Edge and Hub Transport servers, the two primary roles that handle message routing in Exchange Server 2007. As discussed previously, the Hub Transport server handles the brunt of the work, but the Edge Transport server also has its uses.

## Edge Transport Deployment and Management

In short, the Edge Transport server provides the following services:

- Connection filtering
- Content filtering
- Sender filtering
- Recipient lookup
- Recipient filtering
- Sender ID lookup
- Header filtering
- Rules processing
- Attachment filtering
- Virus scanning

The Edge Transport server has some unique and requirements and recommendations. First, the Edge Transport server is a standalone role. Basically, you can't deploy the Edge Transport server on an Exchange Server 2007 server on which you've installed other roles. You cannot deploy it on a server you intend to install other roles either. The reason for this oddity is that the Edge Transport server is intended to protect your Exchange environment by running outside your firewall or in your perimeter network. Because of this, segregating this role on its own hardware that lies outside your network helps to ensure that you run less risk of an infected message wreaking havoc in your organization.

To further its isolation, Microsoft recommends that you install the Edge Transport server onto a computer that is not a part of your Active Directory domain. The obvious question about this recommendation would be, "How can the Edge Transport server communicate with your other Exchange servers if the Edge Transport server isn't a part of your Active Directory infrastructure?" You might think that a server designed to handle mail coming in to and out of the organization would require pretty tight communication with the rest of your network.

It may seem like your Edge Transport server sits alone and isolated from everything else on the network. While this is mostly factual, the Edge Transport server needs a means of contact to your Active Directory to achieve some of its goals. After all, you wouldn't want the Edge Transport server sitting in your perimeter network forwarding mail to users that aren't present in Active Directory. The solution to this conundrum is the Edge Transport server's use of an Active Directory tool, called Active Directory Application Mode (ADAM), along with a component called EdgeSync. EdgeSync runs on a separate server that has the Hub Transport role installed on it. From here, EdgeSync performs regular one-way synchronization of recipient and configuration information from Active Directory to the ADAM instance running on the Edge Transport server.

In this way, the Edge Transport server sees every message that comes in to and goes out of your organization. Your domain's external DNS Mail Exchange (MX) record should point to this server. In addition, Exchange will automatically route outgoing mail through this service as well after you take the necessary steps to install the Edge Transport server.

## Installing Active Directory Application Mode

The Edge Transport server role uses ADAM to store configuration and recipient information. Make sure you install ADAM on the intended server before you install the Edge Transport server role. During the ADAM installation, accept all the default settings. The Exchange Server 2007 installer configures ADAM during the installation of the Edge Transport server role.

Deployment is complete once you install ADAM and the Edge Transport server role on its own server. In addition, you must install at least one Hub Transport server from which you will then subscribe the Edge Transport server. Once these steps are taken, the deployment is considered complete. This subscription process automatically creates all the SMTP connectors necessary for end-to-end mail flow to be operational in your environment.

## Deploying the Edge Transport

To deploy an Edge Transport server into your organization's Exchange Server 2007:

1. Using information gained about the hardware and storage requirements of your organization, create a deployment plan for the other Exchange Server 2007 roles and deploy them on other servers in your organization.

2. On a server that is not a member of your Active Directory domain, install the Exchange Server 2007 prerequisites. These include the .NET Framework 2.0, Microsoft Management Console (MMC) 3.0, and PowerShell 1.0. Ideally, this server should be located inside your company's perimeter network or outside the firewall. It's highly recommended that you deploy the Edge Transport server in a perimeter network so it has some protection.

3. Make sure the new server has an appropriate DNS suffix.

4. Make sure any firewalls between the Exchange Server 2007 organization and the Edge Transport server are configured to pass appropriate traffic. See the following section for necessary configurations.

5. Install ADAM, which is available for download at www.microsoft.com/downloads/details.aspx?familyid=9688f8b9-1034-4ef6-a3e5-2a2a57b5c8e4&displaylang=en.

6. Install the Exchange Server 2007 Edge Transport server role.

7. Subscribe the Edge Transport server to the Exchange Server 2007 organization.

8. Be sure you have changed external DNS MX records to point to the Edge Transport server.

## Verifying the Edge Transport Server's DNS Suffix

Unless you join a Windows Server 2003 computer to a domain or assign a DNS suffix via DHCP, the default primary DNS suffix of the server is normally blank. As a rule, the Edge Transport server services in Exchange Server 2007 cannot be installed on a server with a blank primary DNS suffix. Before you can continue, make sure your server's primary DNS suffix is configured:

1. From the server's desktop, right-click **My Computer**.

2. From the shortcut menu, choose **Properties** to open the System Properties window.

3. Click the **Computer Name** tab.

4. Click **Change.** This will open the Computer Name Changes window.

5. Click **More** to open the DNS Suffix and NetBIOS Computer Name window.

6. Enter the DNS suffix for your domain.

7. Click **OK** until you're asked whether you would like to restart the computer.

8. Restart of the computer for the computer name changes to take effect.

It is a strongly recommended that you place a firewall between your Edge Transport server and your Hub Transport server to limit the potential breadth and depth of the damage that can be caused by a successful attack on your Edge Transport server. Bear in mind that doing so requires that you make sure that certain traffic can pass unfettered between the two servers.

## Subscribing the Edge Transport Server to the Exchange Server 2007 Organization

Before we you continue, let us take a moment to review exactly where we are. You should now have an Exchange Server 2007 organization that is sitting in isolation, sort of like an island.

On a separate island, you have your Edge Transport server you just installed. The problem here is that you will need to take active steps to allow communication between these two islands of information. There are two options you can use to allow communication between your Exchange Server 2007 organization and the Edge Transport server:

- **Manually creating SMTP send and receive connectors** Doing this on a Hub Transport server in your organization and on the new Edge Transport server will allow communication. Bear in mind that the only servers in your organization that can pass mail are Hub and Edge Transport servers. The main downside to this process is that you are unable to take advantage of powerful edge services, such as recipient lookup features or safe-list aggregation. Recipient lookup verifies that a user actually exists in your Active Directory organization before any messages are sent to that user. Safe-list aggregation collects data from each user's Safe Recipients Lists, Safe Senders Lists, and Outlook contacts, and makes this information available to the Edge Transport server. All these features seriously help to reduce false positives, because incoming mail destined for these safe addresses is not subjected to spam tests. Because both services rely on the Edge Transport server's capability to have an understanding of your Active Directory organization, you must establish some way for the Edge Transport server to be able to query Active Directory.

- **Subscription** The subscription process, which is the preferred and recommended method, is a multistep process. This process provides one-way recipient synchronization from the Active Directory domain to the Edge Transport server. This is the only way to take advantage of the Edge Transport server's power and efficient recipient lookup feature and safe-list aggregation features. The subscription method also offers easier management options. It allows you to perform configuration tasks on the Hub Transport server and push them out to the Edge Transport server. This helps in lessening the amount of administrative overhead required to manage your organization.

For the subscription method to be successful:

1. Export an Edge Subscription file on the Edge Transport server.
2. Copy this Edge Subscription file to the Hub Transport server.
3. Import the Edge Subscription file on the Hub Transport server.
4. Verify that synchronization is completed successfully.

As mentioned earlier, many of the configuration needs are handled automatically. The following actions take place during subscription and provide end-to-end mail flow for your Exchange organization:

- An implicit Send connector is created from the Hub Transport servers that are in the same forest to the new Edge Transport server.

- A Send connector is created from the Edge Transport server to the Hub Transport servers in the Active Directory site to which the Edge Transport server is subscribed.

- A Send connector from the Edge Transport server to the Internet is created.

# Exporting an Edge Subscription File on the Edge Transport Server

During the subscription process, recipient and configuration information is copied to the Edge Transport server from Active Directory to the Edge Transport server's ADAM incarnation. EdgeSync, as mentioned earlier, handles this synchronization. It handles the job of copying the information that is required for the Edge Transport server to perform anti-spam and message security tasks. It also handles the information about the connector configuration that is required to enable end-to-end mail flow.

The first step in the subscription process is performed on the Edge Transport server. It involves exporting an .xml file from your Edge Transport server for use on the Hub Transport server. This file is called the Edge Subscription file, which contains the authentication and authorization credentials used for LDAP communication between the ADAM instance on the Edge Transport server, and the Active Directory's directory service. The export process can be accomplished only from the Exchange Management Shell. In other words, the GUI-based Exchange Management Console does not support this feature. To accomplish the export process:

1. Log on to the Edge Transport server using an account that is a member of the local administrators group.

2. Start the Exchange Management Shell.

3. Issue the following command through the Exchange Management Shell:

   ```
   new-edgesubscription -filename "<Location of .xml Information file>"
   ```

You *must* include the path information. Be aware of the warnings that indicate that all manually created accepted domains, message classifications, remote domains, and Send connectors will be deleted by proceeding. After the subscription process is complete, all these items are managed from Hub Transport servers. From here, the Hub Transport servers then synchronize the information out to the Edge Transport server.

# Copying the Edge Subscription File to a Hub Transport Server

This step is self-explanatory: simply copy the file you created in the previous step to your Hub Transport server. After you complete the copy, it is recommended by Microsoft that you delete the .xml file from the Edge Transport server.

# Importing the Edge Subscription File on a Hub Transport Server

With the Edge Subscription file copied to a Hub Transport server, you must initiate the new subscription. This means that you must indicate to the Hub Transport server that the new subscription should be initiated. To do this you must import the .xml file you copied from the Edge Transport server into the Exchange organization. The necessary SMTP Send and Receive connectors are silently created on the Hub Transport server during the import process. This will enable end-to-end mail flow from your clients to the Internet and vice versa.

To import the Edge Subscription file:

1. Log on to the Hub Transport server with an account that has Exchange Organization Administrator rights.

2. Start the Exchange Management Console.

3. Click on and expand **Organization Configuration**.

4. Click on and select the **Hub Transport** option.

5. From the Actions pane, click the **Edge Subscriptions** tab.

6. In the Actions pane, choose **New Edge Subscription**. This action starts the New Edge Subscription Wizard (Figure 2.8).

**Figure 2.8** The New Edge Subscription Wizard

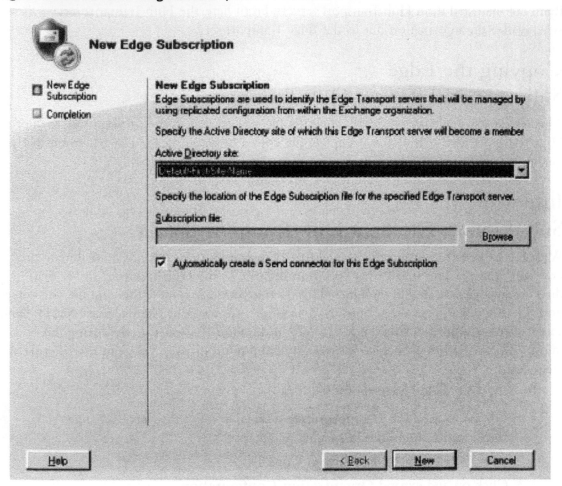

7. On the first page of the wizard, choose the Active Directory site for which this edge subscription will apply.

8. Also on the first page, click **Browse** and locate the .xml file we discussed earlier that you copied to the Hub Transport server.

9. Click **New**.

10. When the process is complete, click **Finish**.

## Management Shell Management

From this point, you must take proactive steps to complete the Edge subscription process. This step will create and enable SMTP Send and Receive connectors on both the Hub Transport and Edge Transport servers. Further, this subscription process makes it possible to manage the environment from the Hub Transport server. Any configuration changes made on the Hub Transport server will be automatically synchronized to the Edge Transport server.

From the Exchange Management Shell, use the *new-edgesubscription* command to complete the subscription process.

```
new-edgesubscription -filename "Location of .xml Information file"
-site "Default-First-Site-Name" -createinternetsendconnector $true
-createinboundsendconnector $true
```

## Verify Synchronization Success

Once you complete the subscription process on the Edge Transport server, verify the synchronization process. To do so you must view the Edge Subscriptions.

Follow these steps to locate them:

1. Open the Exchange Management Console.
2. Under the Organization Configuration, select **Hub Transport**.
3. In the Work pane, choose **Edge Subscriptions**.

You can also verify on the Edge Transport server that the process is successful by doing the following:

1. From the Exchange Management Console on the Edge Transport server.
2. Select **Edge Transport**.
3. From the Work pane, click the **Send Connectors** tab.

## Force Synchronization

Let us say you a large-scale group of new usernames. In this case, you may want to force the EdgeSync synchronization process to take place immediately. In the preceding example, you will want the initial synchronization process to start immediately. To force synchronization to take place, from the Exchange Management Shell on the Edge Transport server, issue the command:

```
start-edgesynchronization
```

This command does not require any parameters.

# Forefront Client Security

Forefront Client Security acts as a first line of defense for your Exchange server. It can be installed on the Edge Transport and Hub Transport server roles to provide additional anti-virus and anti-spam scanning of messages. This happens as they enter or transit the messaging domain. These types of transport scans conducted at the peripheral and routing servers allow for messages that are clean when they arrive at the Exchange Mailbox server. This reduces the need for mailbox database scanning. The advantage of this is that it allows you to spread the scanning load among several servers to decrease the workload on individual servers. This helps to reduce or completely get rid of the need for scanning at the mailbox database. This is the specific design goal of Forefront Security for Exchange Server. Forefront can help to greatly improve the security of your Exchange Server, and is recommended by Microsoft as a unified anti-spam/anti-virus solution. It also is interoperable with Microsoft SharePoint Portal Server. By design, Exchange Server 2007's anti-spam security features are intended to work in conjunction with Forefront Security. Forefront can be used with both Hub and Edge Transport servers, but is recommended to be used specifically with Edge Transport Server role. Some of the security features offered by Forefront include:

- Forefront provides layered protection through Multiple Scan Engine Management to secure messaging systems.

- Forefront also offers sophisticated scanning options for added value and flexibility. These options include:
    - "In-memory" scanning that minimizes impact on Exchange servers for optimum protection and efficiency.
    - Real-time, scheduled, and on-demand scanning of multiple storage groups and databases.
    - Full protection of Outlook Web Access.
    - SMTP and Exchange Information Store scanning for reinforced protection and performance.
    - MTA message scanning for all messages routed through Exchange MTA Connectors (X.400, MS Mail, CC Mail, etc.).
    - Includes Microsoft-approved virus scanning API integration for Exchange 2000 and 2003.

In addition, Forefront offers these features:

- Minimizes worm-generated spam and safeguards the Information Store through Forefront Worm Purge.

- Identifies all messages with unwanted attachments through flexible file-filtering rules.

- Diverts infected attachments into a quarantine repository with Forefront Quarantine Manager.

- Automatically uploads the latest virus signatures.

- Notifies administrators of virus incidents and scan events through e-mail, event logs, and SMTP pagers.

- Includes customizable multiple disclaimers for outbound messages based on sender, recipient, and domain name criteria set by administrators.

If you do decide to add Forefront Security to your organization's security, you will find that most of the features and GUI interface commands are very similar and compatible in design with Exchange Server 2007's interface.

Because of the obvious space restrictions, we will not discuss the intricate details of setting up and managing every detail of Forefront. Instead, know that Forefront allows for very advanced security policy enforcement that can be highly customized to the needs of any organization or individual.

This is accomplished using policy creation. The design similarities compliment the setup of the Edge Transport Server role's Content Filtering and Anti-Spam security features. Let us now look at how these features have been improved in this version of Exchange Server 2007.

# Managing Anti-Spam Features of Exchange Server 2007

The Edge Transport server is the foundation on which the messaging protection features of Exchange Server 2007 rest. Most email administrators pray for the day when spam no longer exists. Until that utopian vision happens, Exchange Server 2007 provides a number of ways in which an administrator can fight spam. It should be noted that although most of the information in this section applies to the Edge Transport server, most of these examples also work on a Hub Transport server and accomplish the same goals. Microsoft recommends, but does not require, that you use an Edge Transport server to maintain the highest level of security in the organization.

## Content Filtering

Microsoft introduced the first version of the Content Filter in Exchange Server 2003 under the name Exchange Intelligent Message Filter. Now, the newly renamed Content Filter acts differently from previous versions by evaluating inbound messages and determining the likelihood of whether a message is spam. This method uses a statistically significant sample of messages to make its determination, which will help decrease the chance for mistakes. The result of this analysis by Content Filter produces a spam confidence level, in essence a number between 0 and 9 that is then assigned to each message. The higher the spam confidence level is, the more likely a message is spam.

There are four specific actions the Content Filter can take, based on the spam confidence level assigned to a message:

- **Allow** the message.

- **Delete** the message. When this occurs, no notification is sent back to the sender.

- **Reject** the message. When this happens, the sender is notified that the message was rejected.

- **Quarantine** the message.

Depending on your organization and quantity of spam, you might decide that messages with a particularly high spam confidence level should be immediately deleted. On the other hand, messages with a lower level may need to be quarantined until further review.

To change the specific action taken by Content Filter:

1. From the Edge Transport server, open the **Exchange Management Console**.

2. Select the **Edge Transport** option.

3. From the Work pane, select the **Anti-spam** tab as shown in Figure 2.9.

4. From the Work pane's lower window, right-click **Content Filtering**.

5. From the shortcut menu, choose **Properties**.

6. In the Content Filtering Properties dialog box, click the **Action** tab.

7. On this page, select options that are in line with your organization's policies. From here, you can select the spam confidence level at which messages should be deleted, rejected, or quarantined. If you choose to quarantine messages, be sure to provide a mailbox address to which quarantined messages can be sent.

8. Once finished, click **OK**.

There are two other ways you can manage how content filtering works in your organization. There might be some users for whom content filtering is not a desirable way to combat spam. In these instances, exclude the user from content filtering by clicking the **Exceptions** tab. On the **Exceptions** tab, provide the email address that should be excluded from the service, and then click **Add**.

**Figure 2.9** The Anti-Spam Tab

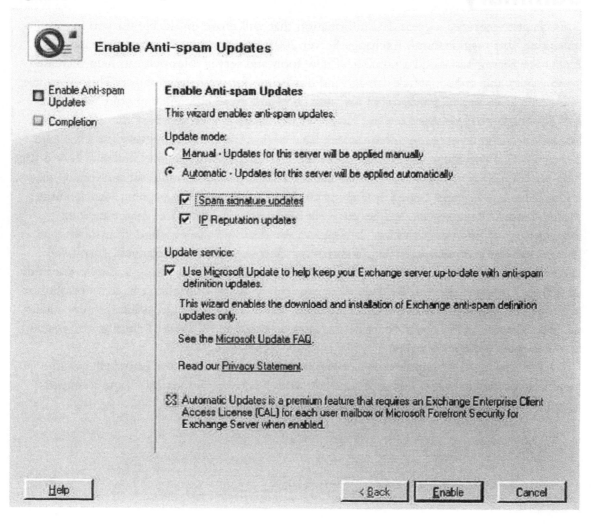

# Summary

This chapter provided a great deal information that will prove invaluable for you in managing you organization's Exchange Server 2007 environment. This latest release of Exchange Server has added a number of new tools and server roles that can help increase productivity and reduce attack damage and downtime for your organization. This, of course, will result in increased productivity for your users and more efficiency in your workplace.

To summarize, we discussed the history of Exchange Server and how the management features available to you, the administrator, have been changed and improved in Exchange Server 2007. From there, we learned about the Exchange Management Shell and how it can help accomplish any task the GUI interface for Exchange can accomplish, ands many others. From there, we learned a good deal about the inner workings of Recipient Management, Public Folder Management, and Server Role Management—the three major areas of management in your organization. In addition, we discussed the pros and cons of storage groups and the recommended requirements for their setup and management. Lastly, we talked about the new server roles in Exchange Server 2007 with a strong focus on the Hub and Edge Transport servers. We then went into the in-depth configuration and subscription of Edge Transport servers to the Hub Transport server. Finally, we discussed the new added security features of Forefront Security and how to configure Content Filtering and enable the anti-spam security features.

After reading this chapter you should have a fairly comprehensive knowledge of the new features and management tools available with Exchange Server 2007, and a renewed confidence with managing Exchange servers in general.

# Chapter 3

# Guarding Microsoft Exchange Server and Outlook Web Access

## Solutions in this chapter:

- **Introduction to Microsoft Forefront Server for Exchange**

- **Implementing Microsoft Forefront Server for Exchange**

- **Configuring Microsoft Forefront Server for Exchange**

- **The Importance of Securing Outlook Web Access**

- **Publishing Outlook Web Access in the Internet Application Gateway**

- **Securing the Outlook Web Access Interface**

☑ **Summary**

# Introduction to Microsoft Forefront Server for Exchange

Microsoft Forefront Server for Exchange (FSE) is a tool that will help companies deal with the threats associated with e-mail service. Microsoft Exchange is used in a large number of businesses for e-mail services. Microsoft FSE was not always so widely used, but its integration with Active Directory (starting with Exchange 2000) made it a more viable product for companies to use. The number of threats written to compromise these systems has increased as more companies implement Microsoft FSE in their infrastructure.

The importance of e-mail to productivity in most companies is the reason that extra security mechanisms, like Microsoft FSE, need to be in place. Attachments and phishing scams pose serious threats to companies. The Microsoft FSE gives companies extra mechanisms to filter attachments and scan for viruses.

The Microsoft FSE server allows network administrators to centrally manage the security of the exchange servers. Administrators using FSE can conduct filtering, scanning, and job scheduling of e-mail-related attachments from a central management console. Reports can give the security professional using FSE indication of what the real problems are and help them to discern from where they are originating. Using FSE can help companies effectively deal with security issues related to e-mail.

# Implementing Microsoft Forefront Server for Exchange

When you are implementing FSE you should ensure that you carefully plan your deployment to ensure that the additional load placed on your FSE servers does not negatively impact performance and that you do not inadvertently block legitimate messages.

Due to the filtering abilities of FSE, it is very easy to block legitimate messages. This causes inconvenience for the recipient of the message, but also creates more work for administrators who either have to provide an alternative method of *sending* files to people or retrieve the files from quarantine and forward them to the recipient. Depending on the amount of legitimately blocked attachments, you may have to dedicate significant resources to review and deliver quarantined attachments.

It is common within companies to block executable attachments from being sent and received. This is done to protect the company's infrastructure from programs, which could potentially cause problems, and also prevent potentially dangerous attachments being sent to third parties. While this will help to protect your infrastructure, it can easily cause legitimate messages to be blocked causing inconvenience to the sender and the recipient.

# Planning a FSE Deployment

The complexity of your FSE deployment will vary depending on the complexity of your FSE infrastructure and the types of message filtering you want to implement. In order to help with your planning it is recommended that you split this into two components, Antivirus (AV) scanning and message filtering.

When you are planning the deployment of FSE, it is important to understand the FSE infrastructure. It is assumed in the course of this chapter that an FSE 2007 infrastructure is being used.

In FSE 2007, the functionality has been split into five roles:

- **Client Access Server** Allows clients to access FSE.
- **Hub Transport Server** Transports messages between mailbox servers and to edge transport servers.
- **FSE** Stores users mailboxes.
- **FSE** Provides unified messaging capabilities.
- **FSE** Allows messages to be sent and received from external sources.

The first four roles can all be installed on a single server for small deployments. The Edge Transport Server has to be installed on its own server as it usually resides in a perimeter network.

This chapter will refer to different roles when indicating where to install or how to configure FSE. It is assumed that these are installed on separate servers.

## Antivirus Scanning

FSE allows you to virus scan messages as they enter and transit through your FSE infrastructure. When they are in the user's mailbox, this is done by deploying FSE on your Edge and Hub Transport roles and on the Mailbox role.

It is recommended that you deploy AV scanning on all of your servers running the FSE. This ensures that messages are virus-scanned providing for a safe FSE infrastructure. You can use up to five AV engines to scan each message and then attempt to clean the message, remove the attachment, or log that a virus was detected, When messages are cleaned or removed, they can be quarantined allowing you to retrieve the files if required. You can specify different AV engines for each of the three Scan Job types—*Transport, Real Time,* and *Manual*—although it is recommended that you keep them the same.

On servers running the edge and hub roles, you can choose to scan internal, incoming, and outgoing messages. It is recommended that you choose to scan all three. This allows you to ensure that no virus-infected messages enter or leave your organization and that internal machines are not sending viruses to your own users. By default, FSE only virus scans a message once, which allows for the best use of resources across your FSE infrastructure. This means that if a message is scanned on an edge role, it will not be re-scanned on the hub role used to relay the message through your organization.

On servers running the mailbox role, you have more control over which messages are virus-scanned. You can perform real time scanning which allows for messages to be scanned as they are accessed. This will, by default, only scan messages that have not been scanned for viruses before. These are usually public folder posts, calendar appointments, and messages in folders like Sent Items, as these messages do not pass through the hub role. While there is an overhead to scanning messages as they are accessed in terms of both resources and a delay to the end user, the impact should be minimal due to the small amount of messages that will be scanned.

You can also configure messages to be background scanned. Background scanning allows you to re-scan messages that have been received or created within the last $x$ days by re-scanning. It is likely that new AV definitions will have been released, meaning that any new viruses will be detected. This is the only AV scan that will, by default, re-scan messages that have been previously virus-scanned. Running this scan is a considerable overhead, so you should set it to run in off-peak hours.

The final option is to perform a *manual* scan, which can be scheduled to run at a specific time. This is most commonly used when you first install FSE, to allow you to scan and stamp all existing messages, ensuring that your infrastructure is virus free. AV stamping is used to indicate that a message has already been virus-scanned. This stamp is placed in the message header when it is being routed through the FSE infrastructure. Once the message have been accepted into a users mailbox, the AV stamp is converted into a MAPI property of the message.

For each of the Scan Jobs on the Mailbox Role, you can choose which mailboxes they scan. This can be useful if you have a large number of mailboxes and you want to use the Manual Scan Job to scan these in batches. For the Real Time Scan Job, it is recommended that you scan all mailboxes, which will ensure that your entire infrastructure is protected.

Once a message is detected as containing a virus, the recommended action is to delete the attachment. While you can opt to clean a message, this uses considerable resources and most attachments containing viruses are usually unsolicited. Therefore, there is no point in trying to clean them. Unsolicited messages are also known as spam. These messages usually have a commercial content where the recipient has not requested this information. It is common for these messages to contain misleading attachments that contain viruses.

When you are planning your AV protection, you should ensure that all of your messages are scanned at least once to ensure that they are free from viruses. You should do this not only for incoming messages, but also for outgoing and internal messages. By scanning these messages you are ensuring that you are not sending viruses to other companies and that your entire infrastructure remains virus free.

If you opt to quarantine detected viruses you should ensure that you clean out the quarantine area on a regular basis to prevent the quarantine database from being filled up and that disk space does not run out. You can opt to automatically purge this information after a number of days. It is recommended that you enable this and purge messages after 30 days. The purge setting will also affect messages quarantined due to messages filtering.

# Message Filtering

Message Filtering in FSE allows you to filter messages based on attachments, message content, keywords, and who is sending the message. This filtering is in addition to filtering performed by the Exchange Edge role and is performed after the FSE filtering. Therefore, it is likely that a large amount of unsolicited e-mail will have been rejected by this stage.

FSE Message Filtering is a lot more flexible than the filtering offered in Exchange, and allows you to quarantine the messages you filter. This allows you to recover deleted messages and attachments if required, along with being able to create highly complex and customized filters to meet your company's requirements.

It is vital that you plan your filtering correctly, otherwise you could end up filtering messages that you never intended to. The Transport Scan Job allows you to filter messages based on their attachments and the contents of the message body. You can specify senders that you always want to receive e-mails from; these are known as *safe senders*. If you enable filtering on Real Time and Manual Scan Jobs, you can filter messages based on their attachments and against the contents of the Subject and Senders Domain.

It is recommended that you restrict all file filtering to the Transport Scan Job. This way messages are only scanned once before they are submitted for delivery. The reason for this is that if you enable filtering for executable files in the real time scan and a user attempts to send a message with an executable file attached, the message will be modified while it sits in the Drafts folder. This will result in an error when the user tries to send the e-mail. These error messages can cause confusion for the sender and may result in an increased number of calls to your Helpdesk.

By moving the file filtering to the Transport Scan Job, users will be able to send e-mails, but they will be checked during transit. This allows for the message to be filtered and for a notification e-mail to be sent if configured. While this has the same end effect as the message being filtered, the end user has a better experience.

When you configure file filtering you can do this based on extension, type, and file size. This provides you with a large amount of flexibility when configuring the file filters. It is recommended that you filter by file type wherever possible, as this prevents people from changing a file extension to bypass the filter. An example of file filtering will be provided in the configuration section of this chapter.

Once you have planned your file filtering, you will need to plan any other filtering methods you plan to use. If you need to check the body of the message for certain phrases, this can be done using the Transport Scan Job. Also known as *keyword* filtering, this filter provides more control than the content filter in FSE.

When you create a keyword filter you can configure logical operators. Logical operators allow you to specify that multiple words have to be in the message body or that words have to appear multiple times. Using this technique allows you to create complex filters.

The final set of filters you can create are *content* filters. These are available in the Real Time and Manual Scan Jobs and allow you to specify sender domains. This allows you to filter messages from certain e-mail addresses or domains. While you can perform the same functionality using sender filtering on an FSE Edge server, this filter has the added ability to quarantine messages and can be used if you have not deployed an Edge server.

Using the *content* filter you can also filter messages based on their subject. This allows you to filter on common unsolicited e-mail subjects, which may be useful if you are not running an FSE Edge server.

When you start to plan you FSE filtering, you should ensure that you are not duplicating workload if you are using the anti-spam filters on an FSE Edge server. You should not duplicate their work in FSE, as this places an additional work load on your servers. You should ensure that you test your filters before deploying them to make sure they only filter e-mail you want to filter (e.g., if you are only filtering incoming executables and not ones sent between internal recipients).

You should be aware that the more filtering you add, the higher the load on your servers. If you are using real time filtering this will also affect the access time for users when accessing messages.

## Designing & Planning...

### Exchange Hosted Service

When you are planning the protection for your FSE Infrastructure, you should also review Exchange Hosted Services (EHS). EHS provides a similar service to FSE, but on a hosted basis and only for incoming and outgoing e-mail.

EHS provides the same features as FSE, but does not provide for the proactive scanning of mailboxes or for the scanning of internal-only messages. By using a hosted solution, you can remove a considerable processing overhead from your own infrastructure.

Many companies use the two systems together, using EHS to remove a large amount of messages with viruses and obvious unsolicited e-mail, and then using FSE to process the remainder of the e-mail which is more likely to be legitimate and also have the added advantage of being able to proactively scan internal e-mails.

# Installing Forefront Server for Exchange

When you install FSE you can either install it locally on each machine or by performing a remote install. Remote installs are performed within the Forefront installer. When possible, it is recommended that local installations are performed. This section will take you through performing both a local and a remote installation along with how to install FSE on clustered mailbox servers.

When you install FSE you have the option to perform a full installation. This can be performed on Exchange servers running the Edge Transport, Hub Transport, and Mailbox roles or a Client Installation, which installation allows you to install the Forefront Server Administrator onto administration machines and can only be installed locally.

If you have clustered mailbox servers using either Single Copy Cluster (SCC) or Cluster Continuous Replication (CCR), the installation process will differ slightly to installing on other FSE servers. The process is different for both SCC and CCR clusters. If you are using Local Continuous Replication (LCR), the installation of Forefront Server for Exchange should be the same as a normal install.

If you are using Standby Continuous Replication (SCR), you should not install FSE unless this server becomes active. Once the server is made active, you will then need to configure it as required. Fortunately, to speed up the configuration, you can use configuration templates.

When performing a local installation you should be logged into the machine as a user that has administrative rights on the machine. As part of the installation, you may be required to restart some of the FSE services; therefore, it is recommended that installation is performed during off-peak hours.

To perform a local install:

1. Run the FSE Installer.

2. Click **Next**.

3. Accept the **License Agreement**.

4. Enter **User Name** and **Company Name** and click **Next**.

5. Select **Local Installation** and click **Next**.

6. For a full installation, select **Full Installation** and click **Next**.

7. Select **Secure Mode** or **Compatible Mode** and click **Next**. When you select Secure Mode, AV scan and filter messages are forwarded from quarantine. When you select Compatible Mode, AV scan messages are forwarded from quarantine.

8. Select up to four AV engines (see Figure 3.1) and click **Next**.

9. Click **Next**.

10. If you need to use a Proxy Server for updates, enter **Address** and **Port** and click **Next**. (If you need to use a username and password you can specify this under General Options once FSE is installed.)

11. Choose the **Installation Location** and click **Next**.

12. Choose the **Programs Folder** and click **Next**.

13. Review the **Installation Options** and click **Next**.

14. You may be asked if you want to restart Exchange Transport Service. If you want to restart this now click **Next**; if you want to restart this later click **Skip**.

15. If you choose to restart the service, click **Next** once the service has restarted.

16. You may be asked if you want to restart FSE Information Store. If you want to restart this now click **Next**; if you want to restart this later click **Skip**.

17. If you choose to restart the service, click **Next** once the service has restarted.

18. Click **Finish**.

19. For a Client installation **Select Client – Admin** console only and click **Next**.

20. Choose the **Installation Location** and click **Next**.

21. Choose the **Programs Folder** and click **Next**.

22. Review the **Installation Options** and click **Next**.

23. Click **Finish**.

**Figure 3.1** Selecting the AV Engines

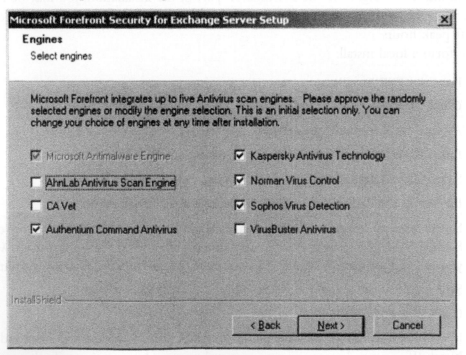

When performing a remote installation, the destination machine and the machine that you are to perform the install from need to be in the same domain. You should be logged in as an administrator of the remote machine. File sharing also needs to be enabled on the remote machine in order to allow for installation files to be copied over. The installation may also require you to restart some of the FSE services; therefore it is recommended that the installation is performed during off-peak hours.

To perform a remote install:

1. Run the FSE Installer.

2. Click **Next**.

3. Accept the **License Agreement**.

4. Enter **User Name** and **Company Name** and click **Next**.

5. Select **Remote Installation** and click **Next**.

6. Enter the **Server Name** and **Share Name** (see Figure 3.2).

7. Select **Secure Mode** or **Compatible Mode** and click **Next**. When you select Secure Mode, AV Scan and Filter messages are forwarded from quarantine. When you select Compatible Mode, AV Scan messages are forwarded from quarantine.

8. Select up to four AV engines and click **Next**.

9. Click **Next**.

10. If you need to use a proxy server for updates, enter **Address** and **Port** and click **Next**. If you need to use a username and password you can specify this under General Options once FSE is installed.

11. Enter the Installation Location into the Destination Directory field, enter the **Programs Folder** into the **Folder Name** filed, and click **Next**. This will start the installation.

12. You may be asked if you want to restart Exchange Transport Service. If you want to restart this now click **Next**; if you want to restart this later click **Skip**.

13. If you choose to restart the service, click **Next** once the service has restarted.

14. You may be asked if you want to restart FSE Information Store. If you want to restart this now click **Next**; if you want to restart this later click **Skip**.

15. If you choose to restart the service click **Next** once the service has restarted.

16. Click **Next** to perform another remote installation or click **Cancel** to exit.

**Figure 3.2** Specifying Remote Server and Path

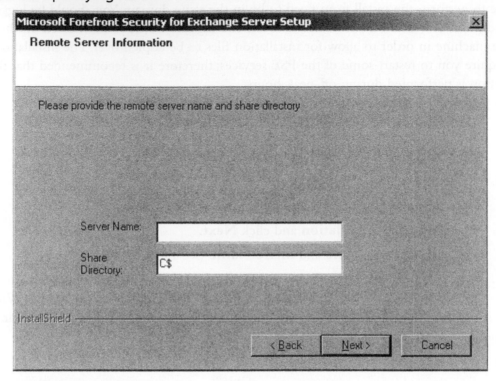

To install FSE on a CCR mailbox cluster you will need to install the FSE on to the Active node first and then, once the installation is complete, you will need to install FSE on to the Passive node. Each installation should be done locally.

To install FSE on a CCR node:

1. Run the FSE Installer.

2. Click **Next**.

3. Accept the **License Agreement**.

4. Enter **User Name** and **Company Name** and click **Next**.

5. Select **Local Installation** and click **Next**.

6. Select **Full Installation** and click **Next**.

7. Select **Secure Mode** or **Compatible Mode** and click **Next**. When you select Secure Mode, AV scan and filter messages are forwarded from quarantine. When you select Compatible Mode, AV scan messages are forwarded from quarantine.

8. Select up to four AV engines and click **Next**.

9. Click **Next**.

10. If you need to use a proxy server for updates, enter **Address** and **Port** and click **Next**. If you need to use a username and password, you can specify this under General Options once FSE is installed.

11. Choose the **Installation Location** and click **Next**.

12. Choose the **Programs Folder** and click **Next**.

13. Review the **Installation Options** and click **Next**.

14. You will now be asked if you want to restart the Clustered Mailbox Server (CMS). If you want to restart this now click **Next**; if you want to restart this later click **Skip**.

15. If you choose to restart the CMS, click **Next** when the CMS has stopped, and click **Next** again when the CMS has started. Click **Next**.

16. Click **Finish**.

You should now perform the same procedure on the passive node. You should ensure that the CMS has not failed over. Any configuration information you enter such as proxy server, details will be overwritten with the configuration from the Active node.

To install FSE on a SCC Mailbox cluster you will need to install the FSE on to the active node first, and then once the installation is complete you will need to install FSE on to the passive node. Each installation should be done locally.

To install FSE on a SCC node:

1. Run the FSE Installer.

2. Click **Next**.

3. Accept the **License Agreement**.

4. Enter **User Name** and **Company Name** and click **Next**.

5. Select **Local Installation** and click **Next**.

6. Select **Full Installation** and click **Next**.

7. Select the **Cluster Drive** from the **Shared Cluster Volume List**, enter a Cluster Folder, and click **Next**.

8. Select **Secure Mode** or **Compatible Mode** and click **Next**. When you select Secure Mode, AV scan and filter messages are forwarded from quarantine. When you select Compatible Mode, AV scan messages are forwarded from quarantine.

9. Select up to four AV engines and click **Next**.

10. Click **Next**.

11. If you need to use a proxy server for updates, enter **Address** and **Port** and click **Next**. If you need to use a username and password, you can specify this under General Options once FSE is installed.

12. Choose the **Installation Location** and click **Next**.

13. Choose the **Programs Folder** and click **Next**.

14. Review the **Installation Options** and click **Next**.

15. You will now be asked if you want to restart the CMS. If you want to restart this now click **Next**; if you want to restart this later click **Skip**.

16. If you choose to restart the CMS, click **Next** when the CMS has stopped and click Next when the CMS has started. Click **Next**.

17. Click **Finish**.

---

**NOTE**

When you are installing Forefront Server for Exchange on a SCC, you are required to select the Cluster Drive, which is the shared volume used by the Cluster Service. If the drive you require is not listed, you will need to exit the installer and re-run it specifying the following. It is assumed the drive letter is S:
*forefront_setup_file.exe* /c S:
You should now be able to select the drive from the **Shared Cluster Volume** List.

---

You should now perform a standard local installation on the passive node. You should also ensure that the CMS has not failed over. Any configuration information you enter during the passive installation such as proxy server details, will be overwritten with the configuration from the active node.

# Configuring Microsoft Forefront Server for Exchange

Once you have installed FSE, you will need to configure the various settings to ensure that messages are processed as required for your business.

There are two ways to configure FSE. The first option is to use the Forefront Server Security Administrator (FSA), which allows you to configure each server running FSE on an individual basis using the tool locally or remotely. The other option is to use Forefront Server Security Management Console (FSSMC), which allows for Forefront servers to be centrally administered (The Management Console is an additional product and is not included with FSE.) For this reason, this section will focus on the FSA as the method used to configure FSE.

While the configuration information is stored in a number of different locations, the majority of the information is stored in a series of FDB files, which are located in the FSE installation directory. This information can also be stored in templates to allow for settings to be copied across servers. The remainder of the information is stored in the registry. This information is usually server specific, and the majority of the settings can be modified through the FSA.

When you are running clustered mailbox servers you should ensure you connect FSA to the Exchange Virtual Machine. The one exception to this is if you need to release quarantined files from a passive node. In that case, you should connect FSA directly to the passive node. All configuration information is replicated between the active and passive nodes ensuring that if a failover occurs the configuration information is available.

# Settings

The Settings section allows you to configure the AV scanning options and server configuration for FSE along with the ability to create new configuration templates. Throughout this section there will be up to three available Scan Jobs for which you can modify settings. The Scan Jobs available are dependent on the Exchange Roles installed on the server.

If the server is running the Edge Transport or Hub Transport role, the Transport Scan Job will be available. If the server is running the Mailbox Role, the Real Time Scan Job and Manual Scan Job will be available. If you add roles to the server, you will need to re-run the FSE installer for the relevant Scan Jobs to be made available. Scan jobs are automatically removed if you install a role.

## Scan Job

The Scan Job section allows you to configure which messages and mailboxes will be processed by the jobs (see Figure 3.3).

**Figure 3.3** Scan Jobs

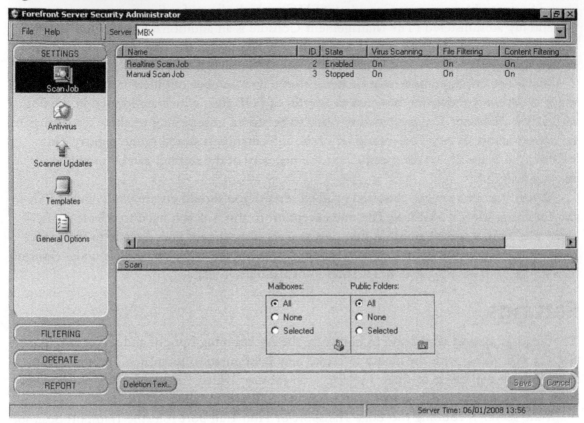

For each of the Scan Jobs, you can specify the deletion text that is used when an attachment is removed and replaced with a text file containing the specified text. To allow for e-mail-specific information to be entered, there are a number of keyword substitution macros available.

Keyword substitution macros can be inserted by right-clicking in the Edit Text field and selecting **Paste Keyword**, and then selecting the Macro to insert.

## Transport Scan Job

The Transport Scan Job is used to process messages on servers running the Edge or Hub Transport Roles. This can be configured to process inbound, outbound and/or internal e-mail. The option to scan internal messages is available on servers running the Edge role, even though Internal mail should not reach the Edge.

The other configurable option is the *tag text,* which is used when keyword filtering is enabled for the Scan Job. Tag text allows for a subject line text and header tag text to be specified. These are applied to an e-mail when it triggers a keyword match, and the action is set to tag the message.

## Real Time and Manual Scan Jobs

The Real Time and Manual Scan Jobs are used to process messages on the servers running the mailbox role. These will process messages that have not previously be scanned. This is particularly important for messages that do not use a hub transport server, including messages in sent items, public folder posts, and calendar messages.

The real time scan processes messages as they are accessed by a client; this is also known as an *on access* scan. By default, this will only process messages that have never been scanned before and are within a certain time range. This range in the first release of FSE is within the previous 24 hours but can be changed. If you are running FSE for Exchange 2007 Service Pack 1, this value is fixed to be every day since FSE was installed. Settings specified for the real time scan are also used for the background scans.

The manual scan can either be run on a manual basis or on a schedule. This is usually used to scan specific mailboxes or to clean up a mail server after a virus outbreak.

For both of these scans you can configure which mailboxes and public folders are scanned. There are three available options for each:

- **All** Scans all current and future mailboxes or public folders
- **None** Does not scan any mailboxes or public folders
- **Selected** Scans only the selected mailboxes or public folders

If you select *Selected* you will need to select which mailboxes or public folders to scan:

1. Select **Selected**.
2. Click on the **Mailbox** or **Public Folder** icon.
3. Check the mailboxes or public folders you want to scan; you can select an entire *store*. If you select a store, then only current mailboxes will be included. Any new mailboxes will need to be added as required. (See Figure 3.4.)
4. Click on the **Back Arrow** to exit the Selection List.
5. Click **OK** to save the changes.

**Figure 3.4** Selecting Mailboxes

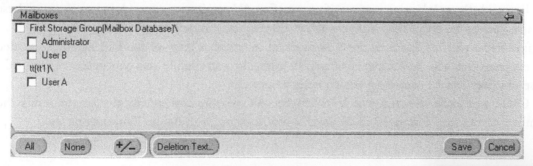

It is recommended that you leave the real time scan set to "All" as this will ensure that messages that have not been scanned are scanned to ensure they do not contain viruses.

# Antivirus

The AV section allows you to configure which AV engines are used when scanning messages, how many engines need to be used for each message, and the action to take if a virus is detected (see Figure 3.5).

**Figure 3.5** Antivirus Settings

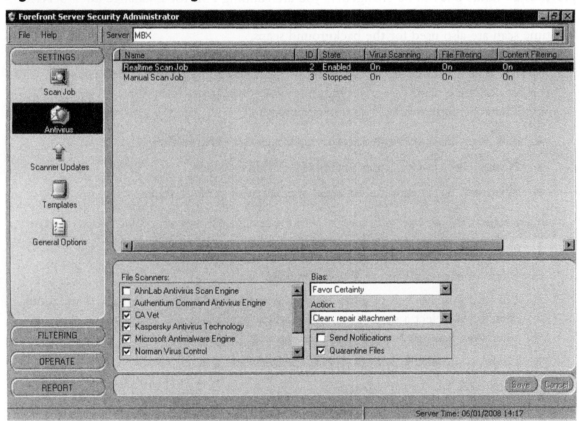

For each Scan Job, you can specify up to five AV engines to use. However, one of these engines has to be the *Microsoft Antimalware Engine.* You can select any of the four other engines from the list. Each of these engines are licensed as part of the FSE licenses, so select the engines that you feel most comfortable using. It is advisable that you research each of these engines before choosing which ones to use.

Once you have selected which AV engines to use you can specify the *bias*, which is the number of engines that need to be used when scanning a message. The options are:

- **Max Certainty** Use all selected engines. If an engine is not available, queue e-mail until all the engines are available.

- **Favor Certainty** Use all selected engines. If an engine is not available, continue to process e-mail with available engines,

- **Neutral** Scan each e-mail with at least half of the selected engines,

- **Favor Performance** Scan each message with between one and one-half of the available engines.

- **Max Performance** Scan each message with one engine.

The choice you make depends on your environment and requirements, but it is recommended that *Favor Certainty* is chosen. Favor Certainty produces the best results in terms of virus detection and also keeps e-mail flowing if an engine becomes unavailable. Engines become unavailable when their virus definitions are updated. Since each engine can be updated several times a day, this could cause significant interruption to e-mail flow if you use *Max Certainty*.

You will need to select what action to take when a virus is detected. There are three possible options:

- **Skip: Detect Only** This option leaves the infected file in the e-mail and places an entry in the logs.

- **Clean: Repair Attachment** This option attempts to repair the attachment. If a repair is not possible, the attachment is removed and replaced with a text file containing the *deletion text*.

- **Delete: Remove Infection** This options removes the attachment and replaces it with a text file containing the deletion text.

There is an exception to the above if in *General Settings* the following options are set. The attachments will be deleted if they match the setting:

- Delete Corrupted Compressed Files

- Delete Corrupted Uuencoded Files

- Delete Encrypted Compressed Files

The final two options are to *Send Notifications* and to *Quarantine Files*. The Send Notifications option allows for notification e-mails to be sent if a virus is detected. These e-mails are configurable and will be covered later in this section. The Quarantine Files option allows you to specify if attachments are quarantined when a virus is detected; this will occur no matter what you set the Action to be.

# Scanner Updates

The Scanner Updates section allows you to configure the update source for the AV engines and how often they are updated. By default, all of the engines are updated on an hourly basis at 5-minute intervals of each other; this includes engines that are currently not being used.

For each of the engines, you can specify a primary and secondary update location. This can either be left at the default (which is the Microsoft Update Web site) or can be changed to point to an internal distribution server. Any FSE server can be set to be a redistribution server (covered later in this section). Alternatively, FSSMC can be used to distribute updates.

The choice of where to download updates from depends on your requirements. If your servers are able to access the Internet either directly or through a proxy server, then you may wish to leave the update location to be the Microsoft Update Web site.

To configure a Proxy Server:

1. Select **Settings** followed by **General Options**.
2. Check **Use Proxy Settings**.
3. Under **Proxy Server Name/IP Address** enter your **Proxy Server Name** or **IP Address**.
4. Under **Proxy Username** enter an **Account Username**, if required.
5. Under **Proxy Password** enter an **Account Password**, if required.
6. Click **OK** to save the changes

If you choose to receive updates using a Redistribution Server you will need to enter the UNC path into the Network Update path. This will need to be done for each AV engine. If you have multiple redistribution servers you can enter a secondary Update Path by clicking on **Secondary** and entering the **UNC path**. Alternatively, the secondary Update Path could point to the Microsoft Update Site.

If you need to configure credentials in order to access the Update Path:

1. Select **Settings** followed by **General Options**.
2. Check **Use UNC Credentials**.
3. Under **UNC Username** enter an **Account Username**.
4. Under **UNC Password** enter an **Account Password**.
5. Click **OK** to save the changes.

The update interval for the AV definitions can be configured on a per-engine basis and can be performed once, every $x$ hours per day, daily, weekly, and monthly. The start time for the updates can also be specified. This should be staggered for each engine to ensure that updates do not occur at the same time. It is recommended that you update the definitions once per hour, which is the default setting. This helps to ensure that you are running the latest definitions. By not updating the definitions regularly, you run the risk of detectable viruses not being detected.

It is also possible to configure updates to occur when FSE is started. This is useful if you have specified a long update window. If you use the default setting of hourly updates, then this is usually not required.

This can be configured by:

1. Select **Settings** followed by **General Options**.
2. Check **Perform Updates at Startup** (see Figure 3.6) .
3. Click **OK** to save the changes.

If you want to be notified of update actions such as Update Success, Failure, and No Updates Available, these updates can be sent to the *Virus Administrator*. The address of the Virus Administrator is configurable and is covered later in this section. To enable notification:

1. Select **Settings** followed by **General Options**.
2. Check **Send Update Notifications**.
3. Click **OK** to save the changes.

**Figure 3.6** Scanner Updates and General Settings

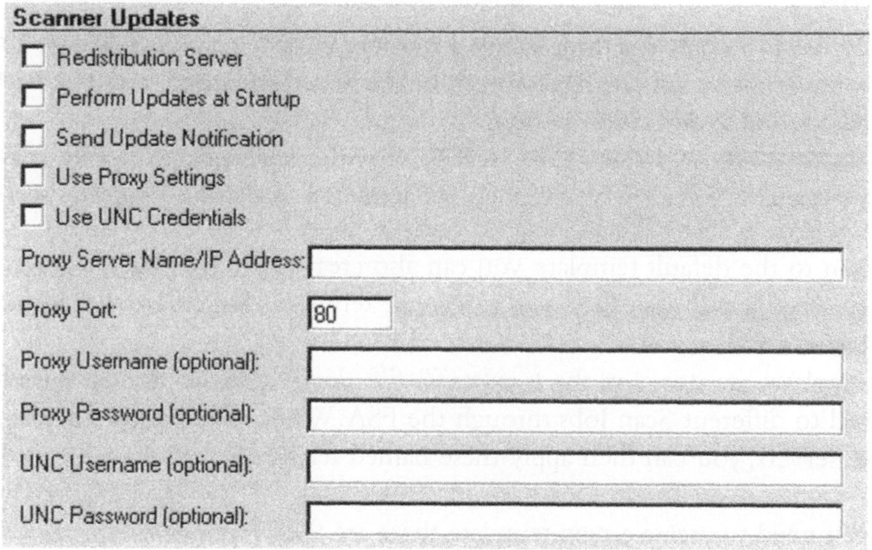

The remaining options are to force an update using the *Update Now* option and to disable updates for AV engines. This can be useful it you do not use some of the engines or do not want to keep up-to-date definitions for them. If you choose to change AV engines for Scan Jobs at a later time, you will need to ensure you enable updates.

**WARNING**

If you are using a proxy server or redistribution server and usernames and/or passwords become invalid, updates will fail. As a result, you could become vulnerable to new viruses.

### Redistribution Server

A Redistribution Server allows a Forefront Server for Exchange Server to redistribute AV definitions to other FSE servers. This allows for updates to only be downloaded once from the Internet. This means that other FSE servers do not need access to the Internet. To configure an FSE Server to be a Redistribution Server:

1. Share the **Engines** folder located, by default, at C:\Program Files (x86)\Microsoft Forefront Security\Exchange Server\Data.

2. In FSA, Select **Settings** followed by **General Options**.

3. Check **Redistribution Server** (see Figure 3.6).

4. Click **OK** to save the changes.

## Templates

Templates are used to control settings across a number of FSE servers. A default template exists that controls the initial settings for each of the Scan Jobs along with the Antivirus, Scanner Updates, and Notification settings.

By default, templates are hidden from view. To view the templates, go to **File | Templates | View Templates**. This will allow you to view the templates under the Templates section and under other sections in FSA, allowing you to configure them.

In addition to the default template, you can also create new templates, known as *named templates*. By using named templates, you can create templates for different scenarios or for groups of different FSE servers.

These templates are stored in the *template.fdb* file along with the default templates, and can be applied to different Scan Jobs through the FSA. When you deploy the *template.fdb* file to other FSE servers, you can then apply these named templates to Scan Jobs on that FSE server.

When you need to create a new template there are four types of templates you can create. These are:

■ Transport

■ Real time

- Manual
- Filter Set

The first three templates are for each of the Scan Job types and the Filter Set template is used to create a set of filters. The Filter Set can then be applied to any of the Scan Job types, allowing for a single set of filters to be applied to both real time and manual Scan Jobs. For example:

To create a new named template, this can be seen in Figure 3.7:

1. Go to **File | Templates | New**.

2. Select the type.

3. Enter a template name.

4. Click **OK**.

**Figure 3.7** Creating Templates

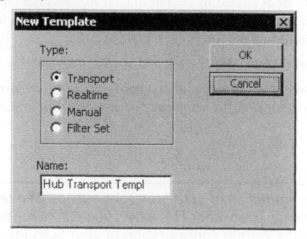

You can also rename and delete the templates by going to **File | Template** and choosing the appropriate option. If you are renaming the template, you will be asked to enter a new name. If you are deleting a template, you will be asked to confirm the deletion.

Once you have configured a template, you will need to apply it to a Scan Job. To apply a template in the Templates section, select the Scan Job, then select the template from the drop-down list under **Templates**. Once you have selected your template, click **Load From Template**. If you also need to apply a filter set, you can do this by selecting the Filter List from the drop-down list under **Filter Sets** (see Figure 3.8).

**Figure 3.8** Applying Templates to Scan Jobs

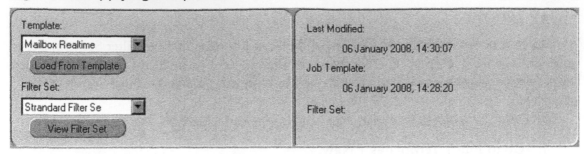

If you have applied a filter set to a Scan Job, these settings will be used first, followed by settings for the Scan Job.

Once you have configured your templates you will need to copy them to the other FSE servers. This can be done by either using FSSMC or by using the command line *FSCStarter.exe*.

To apply the templates to another FSE server, you should first copy the *template.fdb* file to the FSE server. This file is located by default in C:\Program Files (x86)\Microsoft Forefront Security\Exchange Server\Data. Once you have copied this file, you should run the following at the command prompt:

```
"C:\Program Files (x86)\Microsoft Forefront Security\Exchange Server\FSCStarter" t
```

This command forces FSE to re-load the template file that you have just copied over. If you do not run this command, the templates will not be made available in FSE.

**TIP**

If you have configured all of your Scan Jobs outside of a template but want to copy the settings to another FSE server, you can re-create the default template based on the current configuration of your Scan Jobs.

This can be performed by deleting the *Template.fdb* file from C:\Program Files (x86)\Microsoft Forefront Security\Exchange Server\Data. Then, restart the FSC Controller service. This will re-create this file based on your current Scan Job settings. This will only re-create the default template. If you have any named templates, these will be lost.

## General Options

The General Options section allows you to configure settings specific to the server. These settings are stored in the registry and include diagnostic and event logging along with additional configurations for scanning. (The Scanner Updates section was covered previously in this chapter).

## *Diagnostics*

The diagnostic logging allows for additional logging information to be written to the *programlog.txt* file. The additional logging can be useful when trying to troubleshoot issues related to FSE. This logging should only be turned on when necessary, as it can generate large amounts of information and degrade performance (see Figure 3.9).

**Figure 3.9** Diagnostic Logging

As part of diagnostic logging, you also have the option to archive messages. This option is only available on FSE servers with the Transport Scan Job. You have four options when configuring this:

- No Archive
- Archive Before Scan
- Archive After Scan
- Archive Before and After Scan

E-mails are archived into two folders—In and Out for inbound and outbound messages. By default, these folders are located at C:\Program Files (x86)\Microsoft Forefront Security \Exchange Server\Data\Archive. If you choose to archive messages before scanning, the messages may contain viruses. Be aware of the consequences to storing these e-mails. The archiving of e-mails can use up a significant amount of disk space and degrade performance. You should only enable this option when required.

You can opt to send notification to the Virus Administrator whenever the *Internet Scanner* starts. The Internet Scanner is used by the Transport Scan Job to process messages. It is recommended that this should only be enabled on servers running the Transport Scan Job if you wish to receive these notifications.

The final option is the Critical Notification List, which allows you to specify a list of addresses that Critical Notifications should be sent. A Critical Notification is defined as the failure of the FSE Services. Failure of these services would result in AV Scanning and Message Filtering failing. However, e-mail would continue to flow through FSE.

## Logging

The Logging section allows you to choose which information is logged. It is recommended that these default settings be utilized, as this allows for basic logging of FSE activities along with Virus and Filter Notifications. The available settings are shown in Table 3.1. Settings marked with an * are dependent on which FSE Server Roles have been installed.

**Table 3.1** Virus and Filter Notifications

| Setting | Description |
| --- | --- |
| Enable Event Log | FSE writes basic information to the Application Event Log, such as engine updates and Scan Jobs not running. These events can be monitored from systems like System Center Operations Manager |
| Enable Performance Monitor and Statistics | Performance and statistics information can be made available to Performance Monitor; if these are not required this can be disabled. |
| Enable Forefront Program Log | The Program log provides information on FSE starting along with AV engine updates; this provides basic trouble-shooting information. This file is located in the Forefront Data folder and is called *ProgramLog.txt*. |
| Enable Forefront Virus Log | The Virus log allows for the logging of detected virus Infections to a text file *VirusLog.txt*. It is recommended that this be left disabled. |
| Enable Incidents Logging – Transport* Enable Incidents Logging – Real Time* Enable Incidents Logging – Manual* | Incident logging allows for the actions taken on detecting viruses and filter matches to be logged into a database. This is covered later in this chapter. It is recommended that these options are not disabled. |
| Max Program Log Size | The Program Log file can grow to be large, especially if debugging is left turned on for any period of time. Inworder to ensure that it does not use up all the available disk space, a maximum size can be set the value is in KB with a minimum of 512. If you do not want to set a max size, enter a value of 0. |

## Scanning

This section allows you to modify settings relating to the virus scanning of messages. For the majority of companies, these default settings can be used. Due to the large amount of settings, only the most common are covered, as seen in Table 3.2. The FSE Help File provides extensive details on all settings. Settings marked with an * are dependent on which Exchange Server Roles have been installed.

**Table 3.2** Virus Scanning Settings

| Setting | Description |
|---------|-------------|
| Body Scanning – Manual* <br> Body Scanning – Real Time* | Enables the scanning of the message body instead of just the attachments. Transport scans always scan the body. |
| Delete Corrupted Compressed Files <br> Delete Corrupted Uuencoded Files | If files are corrupt, virus scanning cannot always detect viruses. The safest option is to delete these files from the message. Since corrupted files are of no use to the recipient, there should be no issues with removing them. |
| Delete Encrypted Compressed Files | Encrypted compressed files cannot be virus scanned. Allowing these through poses a significant risk. These files will be quarantined so they can be manually retrieved if required. |
| Scan Doc Files As Containers – Manual* <br> Scan Doc Files As Containers –Transport* <br> Scan Doc Files as Containers – Real Time* | This setting is relevant to Office Documents up to the 2003 release. These documents can contain embedded files. Enabling this will ensure that these files will be virus scanned. |
| Optimize for Performance by Not Scanning Messages That Were Already Virus Scanned – Transport* | When messages are virus scanned, an AV Stamp is placed in the message header during transport, then stored in the MAPI Properties of the message. If this is detected, the message will not be re-scanned. If you disable this option, the message will be re-scanned. If this tag exists, this can add considerable load. It is recommended that this be left enabled. |

**Continued**

**Table 3.2 Continued.** Virus Scanning Settings

| Setting | Description |
| --- | --- |
| Scan on Scanner Update* | This setting indicates that messages should be re-scanned if newer AV definitions are available. This only effects the On-Access scanning on the Mailbox servers. If you run Outlook Clients in Cached Mode, an On-Access event will not be triggered when accessing cached items. If an update occurs when a background scan is running, this will be restarted. This could continue to restart if updates keep occurring. It is recommended that this setting is not enabled as it can add a considerable load to your servers. |
| Enable Forefront Security for Exchange Scan | This gives you the option to enable only parts of FSE. You can Disable All, Enable Store Scanning, Enable Transport Scanning, and Enable All. By configuring this option, you can prevent the scanning process from being loaded allowing for resource saving. You need to restart FSE after modifying this setting. |
| Transport Process Count*  Real Time Process Count* | You can specify how many processes are available to process messages. This setting can be between 1 and 10. It is recommended that you do not enable more than 2 for each processor core in the server. There is also a large memory overhead for each process. For most companies four processes will suffice. |
| Quarantine Messages | When messages are quarantined due to content or file filters, they can be stored as an EML file, which keeps the attachment and message in a single file. Or, the attachment and message can be stored separately. If you store messages as an EML file you will need an application that is capable of viewing them. |

**Continued**

**Table 3.2 Continued.** Virus Scanning Settings

| Setting | Description |
| --- | --- |
| Deliver From Quarantine Security | This setting controls how messages are handled when they are delivered from quarantine. If this is set to Compatible, messages will be virus scanned. If this is set to Secure, messages will be virus scanned and filters will also be applied. |
| Internal Address | In this field you should enter all of the domain names hosted on your FSE servers. This will be used to indicate who internal notifications should be sent to. You do not need to enter sub-domains. Domains should be separated by semicolons with no spaces. |
| Transport External Hosts | You should enter the Internet Protocol (IP) address of each of your Edge Servers. Addresses should be separated by semicolons with no spaces. |

## Background Scanning

Background Scanning is only available on servers running the Mailbox Role. This allows for messages to be re-scanned based on their age. This also allows for scanning with updated AV definitions, ensuring that new viruses are detected. This scan in enabled as a Scheduled Job and is covered later in this chapter (see Table 3.3).

**Table 3.3** Scanning Enabled

| Setting | Description |
| --- | --- |
| Enabled Background Scan if 'Scan On Scanner Updated Enabled' | This setting is conditional on "Scan on Scanner Update" being enabled. |
| Scan Only Messages With Attachments | By scanning only messages with attachments, you reduce the total number of messages to scan. |
| Scan Only Unscanned Messages | Scan only un-tagged messages. This setting is not recommended as it prevents new viruses from being detected. |
| Scan Messages Received Within The Last x Days | The available time intervals are Anytime, 4, 6, 8, 12, and 18 hours, and 1, 2, 3, 4, 5, 6, 7, and 30 Days. |

By default, the scan interval is set at 2 days. For most companies, this should be sufficient to ensure that the job completes within a number of hours. If you host a large amount of mailboxes on your Mailbox server and receive large amounts of messages daily, you should reduce the interval to a value appropriate for your company.

# Filtering

The filtering section allows you to configure message filters for each of the Scan Jobs.

When you configure the filters, you are able to select the *action* to take if the filter matches. While the options vary depending on the filter type, there are four available:

- **Skip: detect only** This option leaves the attachment in the message and places an entry in the logs.
- **Delete: remove contents** This option removes the attachment and replaces it with a text file containing the deletion text.
- **Purge: eliminate message** Remove the entire message.
- **Identify: tag message** Place a tag in the subject and/or message header.

You will also be able to choose if the files or messages should be quarantined. If you enable this option, the file will be quarantined if you choose the Delete or Purge action. You will also be able to enable Notifications, which will allow you to send notifications to the sender and/or recipients.

# Content

Content filters allow you to filter messages based on the Sender or the Subject Line. These filters can be used by the Real Time and Manual Scan Jobs. When setting up a Subject Line filter, it will only match against the entire subject unless you use wildcards. For example, if you specify *make money* as the subject line it will only match if "make money" is the subject. If you specify "*make money*," it will match as long as "make money" appears somewhere in the subject. If "you can make money now" is the subject, it will be a match and that message will be filtered. Similar wildcards can be used for the Sender Domain, for example, *testuser@fse.syngress.local* or *\*@fse.syngress.local*.

When you create a Content filter, you can either enter the Sender Details or Subject Lines directly into the filter, or you can use a Filter List. It is recommended that you use Filter Lists because this allows you to put a meaningful name against the list. Using Filter Lists makes things easier when you are reviewing your settings at a later time.

To create a Content filter (not using a Filter List):

1. Go to **Settings** | **Filtering** | **Content**. If this is grayed out, select the **Scan Job** or **Template** first.

2. Select the **Scan Job** or **Template**.

3. Select **Sender-Domains** or **Subject Lines** from **Content Fields**.

4. Click **Filters**.

5. Click **Add**.

6. Enter the **Subject Line** or **Sender E-mail Address** or **Sender Domain** you want to match.

7. Under **Filter** select **Enabled**.

8. Select the required **Action**.

9. Select if you want to **Send Notifications** or **Quarantine Files**.

To create a Content filter using a Filter List, you first need to create the Filter List. To do this, refer to the Filter List section. Once you have created the Filter List you can create the Content Filter (see Figure 3.10):

1. Go to **Settings | Filtering | Content**. If this is grayed out, select the **Scan Job** or **Template** first.

2. Select the **Scan Job** or **Template**.

3. Click **Lists**.

4. Select the **Filter List**.

5. Under Filter select **Enabled**.

6. Select the required **Action**.

7. Select if you want to Send Notifications or Quarantine Files.

Each Content filter can be disabled by selecting **Disabled** from the Filter List. If you need to edit or delete a Sender-Domain or Subject Line, you can do this by selecting it and clicking **Edit** or **Delete**.

**Figure 3.10** Configuring Content Filter

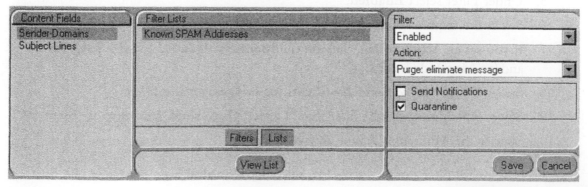

# Keyword

Keyword filters are used by the Transport Scan Job to process the body of a message. If the message body matches the criteria of the filter, the defined action will be applied to the message.

When you create a Keyword filter you first need to create a Filter List. This Filter List can contain multiple items, and each item should be the word or sentence you want to match against.

This filter can contain logical operators that allow for more control over the matching. These are (there must be a *space* between the word and the underscore):

- ■ *word1_AND_word2* Logical AND operator, message must contain *word1* and *word2*.

- ■ *word1_NOT_ word2* Logical NOT operator, message must contain *word1* but not *word2*.

- ■ *word1_ANDNOT_word2* The same as _AND__NOT_.

- ■ *word1_WITHIN[#]OF_word2* *word1* has to be within # words of *word2*, where # is a number.

- ■ *_HAS[#]OF_ word* The body has to contain # of the word, where # is a number.

The filter will match if a single item in the list is matched. You can increase this by changing the *minimum number of matches required*.

To create a Keyword filter, you first need to create the Filter List. To do this, refer to the Filter List section. Once you have created the Filter List, you can create the Keyword filter (see Figure 3.11):

1. Go to **Settings | Filtering | Keyword**. If this is grayed out, select the **Scan Job** or **Template** first.

2. Select the **Scan Job** or **Template**.

3. Select **Message Body** under **Keyword Fields**.

4. Select the **Filter List**.

5. Under Filter select **Enabled**.

6. Select the required **Action**.

7. If you set an Action of Tag, click on the **Identify** tab and check the **Subj Line** and/or **Msg Hdr** boxes.

8. Select if you want to **Send Notifications** or **Quarantine Files**.

9. Select which messages the filter should effect; **Outbound**, **Inbound**, or **Internal**.

10. Specify the Minimum Unique Keyword Hits.

Each Keyword filter can be disabled by selecting **Disabled** from the Filter List.

**Figure 3.11** Configuring Keyword Filter

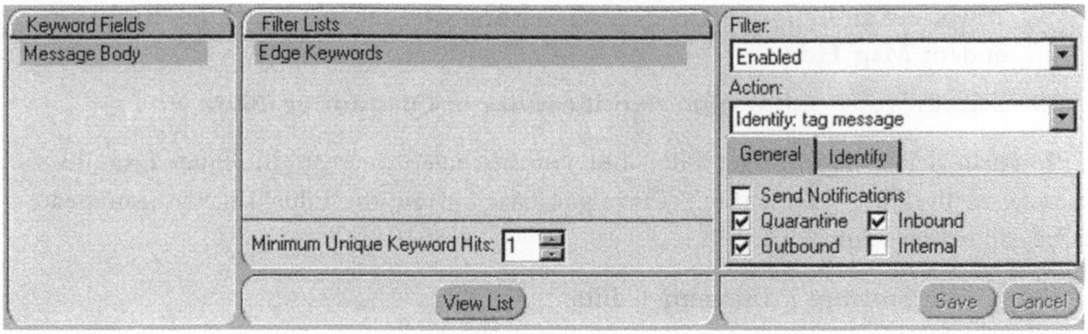

# File

File filters are used to control the types of files sent through your FSE infrastructure. These filters can be applied on any of the Scan Jobs, but it is recommended that you do not use File filters on the Real Time Scan Jobs.

When you create a file filter, you can either enter file names directly into the filter or you can use a Filter List. It is recommended that you use Filter Lists, because this allows you to put a meaningful name against the list and when reviewing settings later, this can make things clearer.

For each of the entries, you need to specify an extension. Extensions can include wildcards, along with a file type and an action to take. You can also specify if the filter should be applied to inbound and outbound messages, and if it should only affect files of a certain size.

To limit the effect of a filter, it can be preceded by either *<in>* or *<out>*. This will limit the filter to either inbound or outbound messages. To limit the filter by size, you should place a comparison operator followed by the size. For example:

```
<in>*.exe>500KB
```

This will limit the filter to inbound files with an *.exe* extension that is over 500 Kilobytes in size.

To create a File filter (not using a Filter List):

1. Go to **Settings | Filtering | File**.

2. Select the **Scan Job** or **Template**.

3. Click **Names**.

4. Click **Add**.

5. Enter the **Extension** along with any limitations.

6. Under File Filter select **Enabled**.

7. If you need to choose specific file types, uncheck **All Types**, accept the warning, and check the **File Types** required.

8.  Select the required **Action**.

9.  If you set an Action of Tag, click on the **Identify** tab and check the **Subj Line** and/or **Msg Hdr**.

10. Select if you want to **Send Notifications** or **Quarantine Files**.

To create a File filter using a Filter List, you first need to create the Filter List. (To do this, refer to the Filter List section.) Once you have created the Filter List you can create the File filter (see Figure 3.12):

1.  Go to **Settings | Filtering | File**.

2.  Select the **Scan Job** or **Template**.

3.  Click **Lists**.

4.  Select the **Filter List**.

5.  Under File Filter select **Enabled**.

6.  If you need to choose specific File Types, uncheck **All Types**, accept the warning, and check the **File Types** required.

7.  Select the required **Action**.

8.  If you set an Action of Tag, click on the **Identify** tab and check the **Subj Line** and/or **Msg Hdr**.

9.  Select if you want to **Send Notifications** or **Quarantine Files**.

**Figure 3.12** Configuring File Filtering

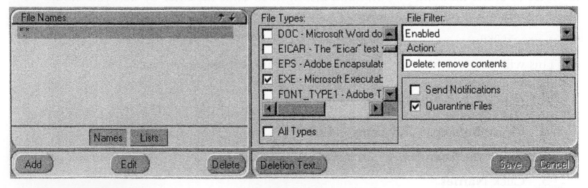

Each File filter can be disabled by selecting **Disabled** from the File Filter List. If you need to edit or delete an extension from the File Names List, you can do this by selecting the **filename** or **extension** and clicking **Edit** or **Delete**. If you need to modify the order that the Files Filters are evaluated, you can use the up and down arrows to change the order. Filters higher up the list are evaluated first. Once a match has been made, no other filters will be evaluated.

For example, if you wanted to disable the ability for users to receive incoming executables you would configure the following:

1. Create a Filter List called **Executables**.
2. Add an item to that filter as **<in>\*.\*** This will check all incoming attachments irrelevant of name or extension.
3. Go to **Settings | Filtering | File**.
4. Enable the **Executables** Filter List for the **Transport Scan Job**.
5. Specify a File Type of **EXE – Microsoft Executable File**.
6. Set an action of **Delete: remove contents**.
7. Under the **General** tab select **Quarantine Files**.

By configuring the above, you have told FSE to scan all incoming attachments to see if it contains an executable file, and if it finds one to delete it from the e-mail and place it in quarantine. When the end user receives the e-mail, it will contain a text attachment explaining that the file had been removed. If you choose to modify the Deletion Text you could instruct them to contact the Helpdesk for their attachment.

---

**NOTE**

This will also remove executable attachments in ZIP files. If you wanted to allow these, you would need to create another entry above the one to remove executables that has an action of *Skip: detect only* and has a *File Type* of *ZIP – Compressed file created by* PKZip.

---

## Allowed Senders

The Allowed Senders tab allows you to specify that messages from specified senders should not be subject to Keyword, File, or Content filtering. This could be useful if you generally block Visual Studio source files, but you need to ensure you receive them from a development company.

Before you configure the Allowed Senders, you need to create a Filter List. To do this, refer to the Filter List section.

Now that you have created the Filter List, you can enable it for a Scan Job. You can also specify which filters should be skipped when messages are from the specified senders:

1. Go to **Settings | Filtering | Allowed Senders**.
2. Select the **Scan Job** or **Template**.

3.  Select the **Sender Filter List** from Sender Lists.

4.  Under **List State** select **Enabled**.

5.  Under **Skip Scanning**, select the **Filters** you want to skip.

If required, you can enable multiple Allowed Senders for each Scan Job, or they can be disabled by selecting **Disabled** from the **List State**.

## Filter Lists

Filter Lists are used to create groups of settings for the filters. These lists allow for settings to be created under a meaningful name. This also means that the same list can be used by multiple Scan Jobs. Filter Lists are all created, edited, and deleted in the same manner as when you add items to a Filter List. There is no checking performed on the entries to ensure that they are valid; therefore, if you are creating an Allowed Sender List, you are able to enter invalid e-mail addresses, such as addresses missing the @ symbol. If you find that a filter is not acting as you would expect, you should ensure that you have not entered any information incorrectly.

To create a Filter List:

1.  Go to **Settings | Filtering | Filter List**.

2.  Select a **List Type**.

3.  Click **Add**.

4.  Enter the list name, which should be something meaningful.

Once the list has been created, you can delete it by selecting the list from List Names and clicking **Delete**. Adding items to a Filter List is done through editing the list.

To edit a Filter List:

1.  Select the **List Type** followed by the **List Name**.

2.  Click **Edit**.

3.  An Edit Filter List window should open.

4.  Under **Include in Filter** click **Add**.

5.  Enter the item text (e.g., an e-mail address or a file extension).

6.  To add multiple items click on **Add** again. If you need to **Edit** or **Remove** an item, select it from the list and click the appropriate button.

7.  Click **OK**.

## Operate

The Operate section allows you to choose which Scan Jobs are enabled along with settings related to these jobs. You can also specify schedules for scans and initiate a quick scan.

# Run Job

The Run Job section allows you to:

- Enable or disable Scan Jobs
- Specify if the Scan Job scans for viruses or filters messages
- View logs for each Scan Job

By default, each of the Scan Jobs are enabled. If you need to disable them for any reason, it can be done by selecting the Scan Job and selecting **Bypass** (see Figure 3.13). You can re-enable the job by selecting **Enable**.

**Figure 3.13** Enabling Scan Jobs

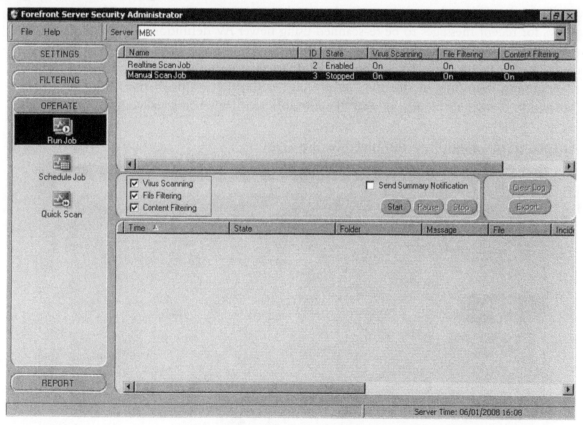

For each of the Scan Jobs, you can also specify if the job carries out virus scanning and filtering. This is configured through a series of checkboxes. For Transport Scan Jobs, you can enable or disable File and Keyword filtering. For Real time or Manual Scan Jobs, you can enable or disable file and content filtering. These settings take effect immediately, and affect the job even if it is running.

You are also able to view the incidents for each Scan Job. This information is the same as the incident information shown in the Report section, but is specific to the selected Scan Job. You also have the option to export the incident information or to clear the log, or you can also delete individual log entries if required.

## Schedule Job

Scheduled jobs are only available on servers running the Mailbox role. There are two jobs that can be scheduled. The first is the Manual Scan Job, which can be run on a one time, daily, weekly, or monthly basis. This can be useful if you want to scan mailboxes that are not covered by a real time scan or you want to use different settings or AV engines. This could also be useful to run after an outbreak to ensure that no mailboxes are infected and can be scheduled to run during off-peak hours.

The other Scheduled job is the Background Scan Job (see Figure 3.14). This Scan Job allows for recent messages to be re-scanned using newer AV definitions. This helps to ensure that new viruses are located and removed. While this can be configured to run one time, daily, weekly, or monthly, it is recommended that you run this daily during off-peak hours. (Background Scan Jobs are discussed in greater detail earlier in this chapter.) You also have the ability to enable, disable, and stop these Scan Jobs; these settings take effect immediately.

**Figure 3.14** Scheduling the Background Scan

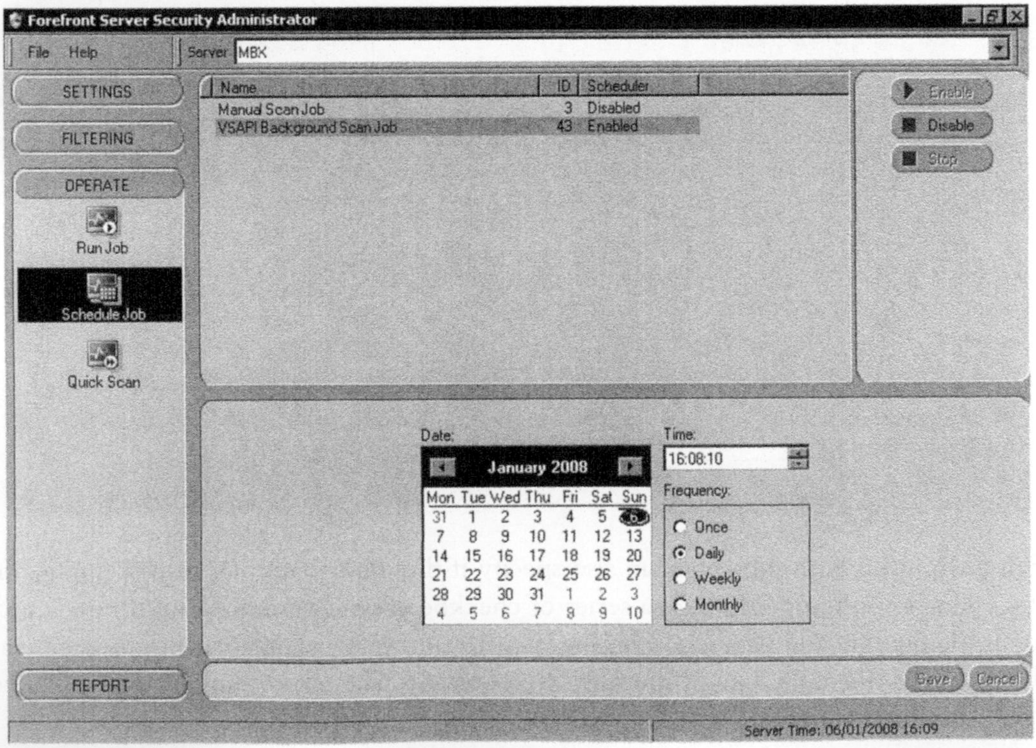

# Quick Scan

A Quick Scan allows for the ad-hoc scanning of mailboxes and public folders, and is available only on servers running the Mailbox role. This is configured in the same manner as other Scan Jobs in terms of AV engines to use along with the bias and actions.

You can specify which mailboxes and public folders are scanned. This allows you to select mailboxes that you suspect have been infected. For example, a Quick Scan can only perform AV scanning and cannot be used to apply filters to messages. Depending on the number of messages within the selected mailboxes and public folders running, a Quick Scan could put a considerable load on the server. It would be wise to be careful to ensure that this does not adversely affect performance for day-to-day operations.

# Report

The Report section allows you to view the Incident Logs and the Quarantined Messages. You can also configure E-mail Notifications.

# Notification

The Notification section allows you to configure who receives e-mail notifications, along with the contents of the e-mails. Most of the e-mails have pre-defined recipients and contents, If needed, these notifications can also be enabled and disabled (see Figure 3.15).

**Figure 3.15** Enabling Notifications

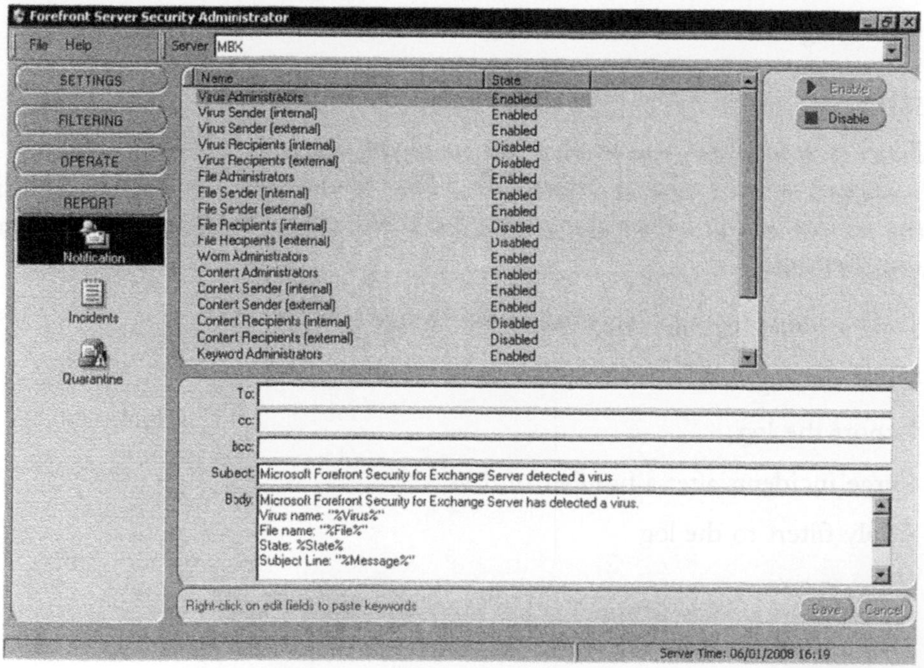

The notifications you should modify are the Administrator e-mails, as these are used to notify you of issues. They are also used to notify you of viruses and filter matches if notifications for these have been enabled. You should specify whom these are sent to. This could be individual recipients or distribution lists (multiple addresses should be separated by semicolons).

The other available notifications are for alerting either the sender or recipient that there was an issue with a message. These notifications are further separated into external or internal parties. By default, only the sender is notified. Recipient e-mails are disabled but you may choose to enable or disable these depending on the requirements for your company. By allowing different messages for external and internal parties, you can tailor messages to the intended audience (e.g., an internal recipient may be instructed to contact the IT Helpdesk).

The final part to consider is the sender of the Notifications. By default, this is Forefront ServerSecurity@*ServerName*.com. It is recommended that this be changed to something more meaningful (e.g., the postmaster address for your company or the address for your IT Support desk).

These settings are configured through the registry:

1. Go to **Start | Run**, enter **regedit**, and click **OK**.

2. Navigate to **HKEY_LOCAL_MACHINE\SOFTWARE\Wow6432Node\ Microsoft\Forefront Server Security\Exchange Server**.

3. Locate the **ServerProfile** key.

4. Modify the key and enter an e-mail address.

5. Close **regedit**.

# Incidents

The Incidents section allows you to view the incidents that have occurred. Incident entries are created when a virus is detected or a filter is matched. The information displayed includes the recipients and sender along with the action taken. It is possible to perform the following actions:

- Delete individual incidents (using the Delete key)

- Clear the log

- Export the log

- Purge incidents after a number of days

- Apply filters to the log

- View statistics

- Clear statistics

The incident log is stored in an Access Database and has a file limit of 2 GB. If the Notification Log grows to more than 1.5 GB a notification will be sent daily to the Virus Administrator. To clear the log you can click the **Clear Log** button. This command will be queued and the messages will be cleared when the database is compacted which is at 02:00 daily.

An alternative to this is to automatically purge messages when they reach a certain age. For example, after 30 days the rate at which incidents are generated depends on how busy your e-mail servers are and how many viruses or filter actions are received. Configure this to match the requirements for your company.

# Quarantine

The Quarantine section allows you to view the messages that have been quarantined. You can also choose to deliver these messages to the intended recipients. While this may not be of use for viruses, it can be useful for messages that have been quarantined due to matching a message filter. It is possible to perform the following actions:

- Delete individual messages (using the Delete key)
- Clear the log
- Export the log
- Save attachments to the file system
- Deliver messages to the intended recipient
- Purge messages after a number of days
- Apply filters to the log

If you choose to save attachments to the file system, this will allow infected files to be saved. Therefore, you should ensure that you have a current virus scanner running on the machine and that you understand the consequences of doing this.

If you want an attachment to be delivered to either the intended recipient or to another address, this can be done using the Deliver option. When you select this option, you will be given the option to send to the original recipients and/or to new recipients (see Figure 3.16). If you have selected a virus to be delivered, you will be warned that the file is infected but you will still be able to submit the message for delivery. This message will be treated the same as any other new message and will be subject to the same AV scanning as any other new message. This may result in the message being quarantined again.

**Figure 3.16** Delivering a Quarantined Message

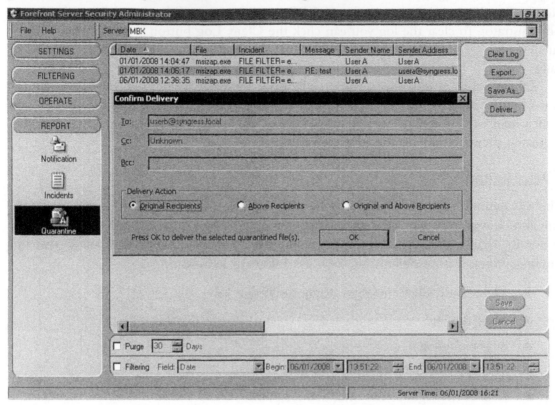

If you choose to deliver a message that was quarantined due to a filter match, this will be handled in one of two ways depending on the Deliver from Quarantine security setting. If this is set to Secure Mode, messages will be processed against the message filters. If this setting is set to Compatible Mode, messages will not be checked against filters.

---

**NOTE**

If you are often in a position where you need to deliver legitimate files that have been quarantined due to a filter match, you will either need to set the *Deliver from Quarantine Security* to Compatible Mode to deliver them through e-mail, or use an alternative method by saving them to the file system and then transporting them to the recipient.

---

The Quarantine database has the same limitations as the Incidents database, and only the log details are stored in the database. The actual messages are stored as individual files on the file system.

# The Importance of Securing Outlook Web Access

More and more, users rely on e-mail in today's busy world. Unfortunately for many administrators, users have turned e-mail into a critical file storage repository as well as a preferred method of communication. However, with an inability to function without e-mail, and with the ever increasingly mobile workforce, administrators have been forced to provide remote access to e-mail. Numerous protocols exist for providing this functionality including:

- Post Office Protocol 3 (POP3)
- Simple Mail Transfer Protocol (SMTP)
- Internet Message Access Protocol (IMAP)
- Hypertext Transfer Protocol (HTTP)

Traditionally, POP3 and IMAP have been the most widely used standard protocols for providing remote mailbox access. However, with the introduction of OWA in Exchange 5.5, OWA has been an appealing option. It is fairly simple to deploy, and for organizations already opening port 80 for other Web services, it does not require exposing new protocols to the public. Many organizations began using OWA as an easy way to fix the functionality issue, allowing users to access their e-mail over a service they already allow and monitor.

# The Security Problem

As many of you know, Microsoft's OWA has some serious security issues that hackers love to exploit. Exchange administrators worry daily over these possible security breaks. One of the security issues dealt with the fact that an OWA user's cached credentials can easily be used to gain unauthorized access to an Exchange mailbox from the local Internet browser. Another problem was that because an OWA session does not time out if the user forgets to logout and close the browser window, an intruder can gain access to the Exchange mail system simply by browsing to the open OWA session. Finally, OWA user ID's and passwords are stored in the browser cache for subsequent use, and remain in the cache as long as a browser session is active.

Most organizations know to use SSL to encrypt data transferred to and from the OWA client and the Exchange server, thus making it impossible to "sniff" the contents of a user's e-mail. But what some organizations do not understand is that SSL will not prevent an intruder from gaining access to the Exchange server via an OWA session. If SSL is used in conjunction with other security products such as the IAG, this reduces the risks by introducing policies that are related to certain rules that are created by the corporate security practices.

> **NOTE**
>
> Windows NT Challenge/Response (NTLM) is the authentication protocol utilizing the integrated single sign-on mechanism, also known as the Integrated Windows Authentication.

With the Integrated Windows Authentication, the user name and password (credentials) are hashed before being sent across the network. When you enable Integrated Windows Authentication, the client browser proves its knowledge of the password through a cryptographic exchange with your Web server, involving hashing. However, all of the information transmitted over HTTP is sent in the clear, and OWA is no exception.

The problem is that most information contained within an organization's e-mail system is sensitive and confidential and should be encrypted. The username and password are just the tip of the iceberg.

Users simply do not understand that e-mail is a fundamentally insecure communication method. In my experience as a System Engineer, I have witnessed users sending sensitive information such as their credit card information and social security numbers over e-mail, and then argue with System Administrators when they tried to inform them that e-mail was not secure method for transmitting such information. This type of activity also exposes security concerns on a company-wide level that a diligent hacker could use to their advantage. Some of the consequences could include stealing great deals of sensitive proprietary company information, including information about employee salaries, disciplinary actions, terminations, and company intellectual property information. In this day and age, it is difficult to believe sensitive information would be transmitted in clear text.

While securing an OWA deployment certainly will not solve every security issue related to e-mail, it can address those related to providing remote access to e-mail. With any remote e-mail access solution, the organization should be primarily concerned with connections from public networks, especially those from public wireless access points. A few places that are inherently problematic to have users connecting from include coffee houses, Internet cafés, technical conferences (kiosks), and international airports, all breeding grounds for sniffers. The logon credentials and all e-mail messages transmitted in these environments can easily be sniffed and captured by malicious eavesdroppers.

Similarly, there are situations where some corporations do not maintain a local Exchange Mail system on site, choosing to lease e-mail systems from local Internet Service Providers (ISPs), but still use OWA or other remote access methods to access their e-mail when on the road. Some people prefer OWA over the regular Outlook clients.

Users may also use remote e-mail access from their homes. While this seems private enough, there are plenty of users who have turned on and deployed unencrypted wireless access points in their homes. Even those connecting over hard-wired connections may be susceptible to snooping, especially if they receive service from their cable company, and are on a shared connection with several of their neighbors.

The threats to remote e-mail access are numerous because of the vast amounts of organizational data e-mail presents.

Some of the following threats will likely consider e-mail a prime target for attack:

- Entities engaged in corporate and industrial espionage
- Entities engaged in extortion
- Curios hackers
- Phishing Scams
- Worst-case hackers using e-mail to crash servers, thus stifling the corporation's communication

# The Security Solution

In short, e-mail is potentially the most appealing target in your organization. Additionally, it is a requirement to provide remote access to the service; however, it provides an attack means for hackers, and there is no shortage of hackers who have the motivation, resources, and skills to penetrate the security of the network and e-mail system. Therefore, it is absolutely essential that when implementing OWA, the entire remote access session is encrypted.

Since OWA is a Web-based application, it makes sense to use SSL, which is also referred to as Transport Layer Security (TLS), which came out with Windows 2003 Server to provide the confidentiality and security required.

## Configuring & Implementing…

### SSl/TlS

So what exactly is SSL/TLS? The Secure Sockets Layer (SSL) protocol v.3 and Transport Layer Security (TLS) protocol, v.2 are the same protocols with a new name. The protocol is based on public key cryptography. SSL/TLS is used to authenticate servers and clients and then encrypt messages between the authenticated parties. In the authentication process, a SSL/TLS client sends a message to a SSL/TLS server, thus responding with the information that the server needs to authenticate itself. The client and server perform an additional exchange of session keys, ending the authentication dialog. When authentication is completed, secured communication can begin between the server and the client using the symmetric encryption keys that are established during the authentication process.

## Securing Your OWA Connection

- OWA sessions aren't encrypted by default, and the communication between the Exchange server and the end-user browser is in clear text. Adding SSL to your OWA sessions ensures end-to-end encryption for the duration of the session.

- Use the SSL/TLS support that is built into most current Web-browsers. If the user has access to a Web browser and an Internet connection they can connect securely.

- Establish an SSL connection between the OWA client and the ISA server firewall.

- Establish an SSL connection between the ISA server firewall and the OWA server.

# Publishing Outlook Web Access in the Internet Application Gateway

One day you are minding your own business at your desk and your IT director approaches you and asks you to clarify why the company should consider using the IAG and why should they choose it over ISA 2006?

### Designing & Planning...

#### OWA Server Placement

Although the main goal in this chapter is to show you how to use the IAG feature in ISA Server 2006 to secure OWA, it is important to consider the other aspects of securing the deployment. You should make sure you put your OWA server in a demilitarized zone (DMZ) separate from your mail servers and other systems. As with any service or application you are making public, you want to provide separation from your internal systems. This can be an especially sensitive consideration for an application that provides Web-based access to your organization's e-mail store.

Your comments should be easily explained by setting up a basic planning explanation. ISA server should be used when you need:

- Branch office gateway for site-to-site connectivity and security

- Data center Internet access control and Web caching

- Advanced security with inbound and outbound firewall

- Publishing, securing, and pre-authenticating access to specific Web services such as Microsoft Exchange server and Microsoft SharePoint server (when more advanced client options aren't required)

- Full network connectivity for managed PCs (via Virtual Private Network [VPN])

- High-security client access via Windows 2000 or Windows XP that needs host checking and quarantine and Internet Protocol Security (IPSec) (or other) encryption and authentication

To augment and enhance the ISA server, it recommended adding the Intelligent Application Gateway when you need to do the following in the corporate world.

- Browser-based clientless access with granular policy control of data and application components

- More advanced security and manageability control over the client when accessing Web- and non-Web-based resources

- Remote access to a broader range of third-party and line-of-business applications

- Access from unmanaged PCs or mobile devices on unknown networks

- Strong endpoint security verification

- No IPSec VPN clients available for the target host platform

- Extend policy-based access to partners and customers if warranted

# Adding OWA to the IAG (Portal)

The first step before adding the OWA to the IAG is to verify that your portal Web site is up and operational. If not, you will not be able to proceed with the OWA installation. Creating the portal Web site is out of the scope of this chapter.

## IAG 2007

Microsoft offers the Intelligent Application Gateway (IAG) 2007 as a high-performance application access and security appliance integrated with ISA Server 2006. IAG 2007 provides SSL VPN, a Web application firewall, and endpoint security management that enables access control, authorization, and content inspection for a wide variety of line-of-business applications. These technologies provide remote workers with easy and flexible secure access from a broad range of devices and locations including PCs and mobile devices. IAG also enables IT administrators to enforce compliance with application and information usage guidelines through a customized remote access policy based on device, user, application, or other business criteria. See Figure 3.17 for a basic idea of how the IAG could fit within your environment.

**Figure 3.17** Infrastructure Cloud

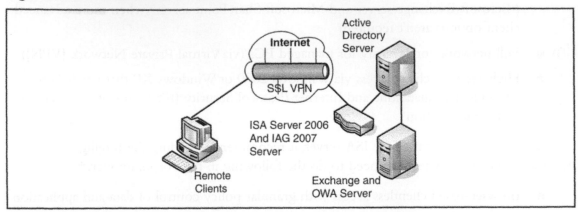

The following configuration steps provide you with a step-by-step process to add the OWA to the IAG gateway, otherwise known as the IAG Portal.

**NOTE**

Some assumptions need to be understood before the following steps can be implemented.

In adding to the following steps, it is understood that the IAG gateway is configured and running within your infrastructure. Only the following steps are needed to add the OWA.

## Server Roles

Table 3.4 represents the server names and roles used as my examples for the successful install.

**Table 3.4** Table of Computer Names Used in Demonstration

| Computer Name | Role |
| --- | --- |
| "HQ" | Represents a Windows 2003 server R2 DC for the demo.com domain, and an exchange/OWA server |
| "SRV1" | Represents a Windows 2003 server R2, IAG 2007 and ISA 2006 |
| "Client" | Represents a client computer on the internet; note that a client authentication certificate is installed |
| "Portal1" | Represents your company's infrastructure portal name |

1.  On the SRV1 computer, in the IAG Configuration console, under **HTTPS Connections**, select **Portal1** (see Figure 3.18).

**Figure 3.18** IAG Configuration Console

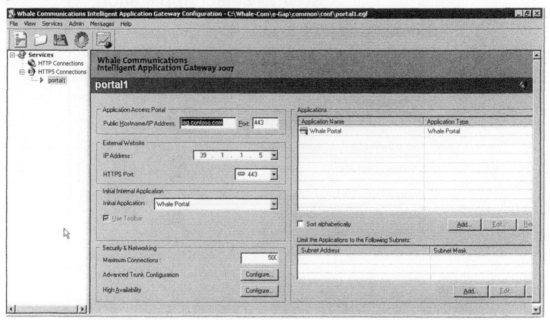

2.  In the right pane, in the **Applications** section, click the top **Add** button. Note that depending on the window size, you may have to scroll through the IAG configuration pane to see the Add button.

3.  On the Step 1–Select Application page in the **Web Applications** drop-down box, select **Microsoft Outlook Web Access 2007** and then click **Next** (see Figure 3.19).

**Figure 3.19** Add Application Wizard-Select Application

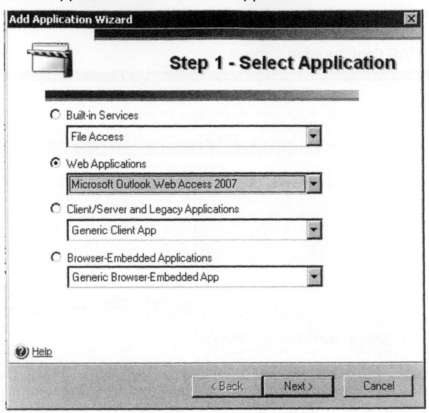

4. IAG contains application-specific settings for many well-known applications.

5. On the Step 2-Application Setup page, in the **Application Name** text box, type **OWA2007** and then click **Next** (see Figure 3.20).

**Figure 3.20** Add Application Wizard-application Setup

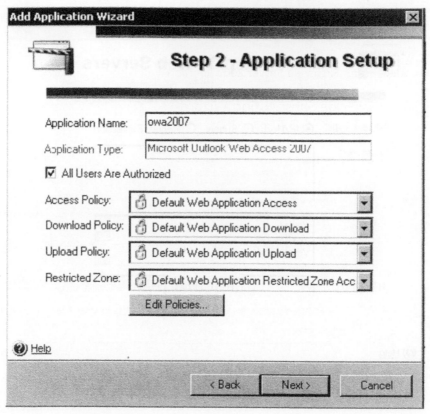

6.  On the Step 3–Web Servers page, notice that IAG has already preconfigured the paths that OWA 2007 uses (see Figure 3.21).

**Figure 3.21** Add Application Wizard-Web Servers

7. On the Step 3-Web Servers page, double–click the first row in the **Addresses** text box, and then in the new text box, type **hq.demo.com**, press **Enter**, and then click **Next** (see Figure 3.22).

**Figure 3.22** Add Application Wizard-Web Servers

8.   On the Step 4–Authentication page, click **Add**.

9.   In the Authentication and User/Group Servers page, select **AD**, and then click **Select**.

10.   IAG will authenticate requests for the OWA2007 application against the AD authentication server.

11.   On the Step 4–Authentication page, click **Next**.

12.   On the Step 5–Portal Link page, in the **Application URL** text box, change the URL to use HTTPS instead of HTTP - **https://hq.demo.com/owa/**, and then click **Finish** (see Figure 3.23).

**Figure 3.23** Add Application Wizard-Portal Link

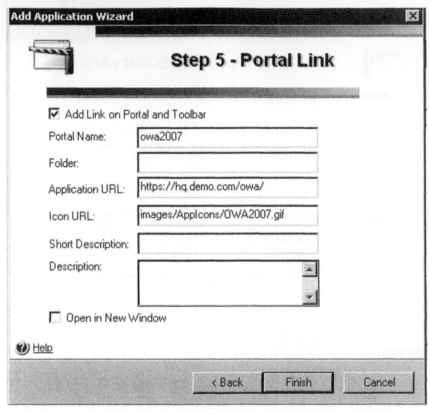

The revised URL will appear under the Portal Link tab in the Application Properties (Microsoft Outlook Web Access 2007) page (see Figure 3.24).

**Figure 3.24** Application Properties (OWA 2007)

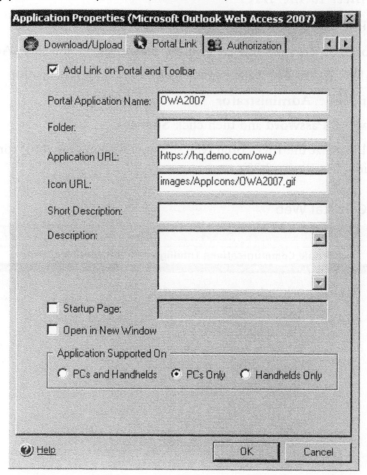

13. Later in this exercise, you will create a Redirect Trunk, which will automatically forward non—secured request to http://hq.demo.com and to https://hq.demo.com.

14. A window with an application-specific note for OWA 2007 appears.

15. Close the **Note** window.

# Activating the Configuration

1. On the **File** menu, click **Activate**, or on the toolbar, click the gear icon.

2. In the **Passphrase** dialog box, type **password**, and then click **OK**.

3. On the Activate Configuration page, click **Activate**. (wait a few moments for the configuration activation to complete)

4. On the Configuration Activation Completed page, click **OK**.

## Client to Connect to the IAG

The following represents the steps on the client computer:

1. Open Internet Explorer, and then on the **Favorites** menu, click **IAG Portal**.

2. On the IAG logon Web page, complete the following information:

   - User Name: **Administrator**

   - Password: **Password** and then click **Submit**.

3. You will see that the IAG Portal Web site now contains an entry for the OWA2007 application (see Figure 3.25).

**Figure 3.25** IAG Portal Web

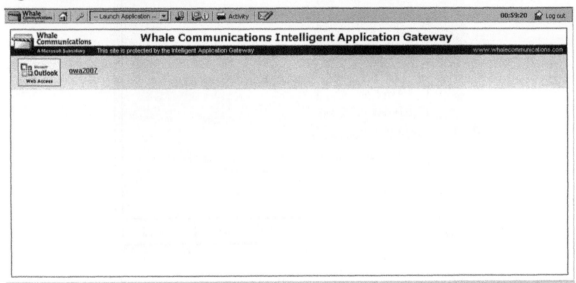

4. In the IAG Portal Web site, click **OWA2007**

At this point, you should notice that you do not have to authenticate again when connecting to the OWA Web site. IAG handles the single-sign-on authentication.

> **NOTE**
>
> The first time any OWA Web site is opened, it may take a few seconds before the OWA screen appears and the OWA displays the inbox of Administrator.

5. On the IAG toolbar, click the home icon to go back to the IAG Web portal. Close the IAG portal Web site.

## IAG Portal Web

In the next tasks, you will configure the IAG portal Web site to automatically redirect HTTP requests to the HTTPS trunk. This allows users to use the address http://iag.demo.com, and still connect to the HTTPS portal Web site.

Now let's attempt a connectivity test. In your Web browser connect to the IAG Portal Web site at **http://iag.demo.com**. (Remember do not use https.)

1. Open Internet Explorer, and then in the **Address** text box, type **http://iag. demo.com**, and then press **Enter**. You should see the browser attempt to connect to the IAG portal Web site, without using HTTPS. After a few moments, the browser will display an error page as shown in Figure 3.26. (The page cannot be displayed).

**Figure 3.26** HTTP Error Status Page

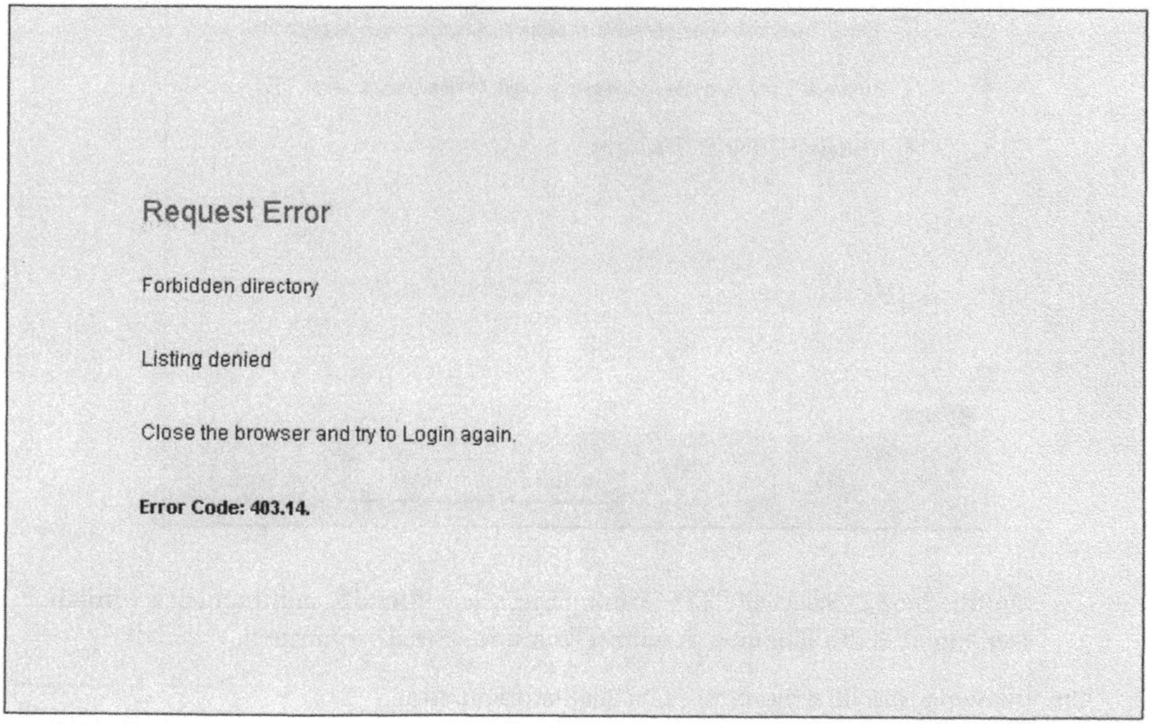

Request Error

Forbidden directory

Listing denied

Close the browser and try to Login again.

**Error Code: 403.14.**

2. Close Internet Explorer.

## Redirect the Trunk on SRV1

On the SRV1 server, create a Redirect Trunk for **Portal1**.

1. On the SRV1 Server, in the IAG Configuration console, right click **HTTP Connections**, and then click **New Trunk**.

2. On the Step 1-Select Trunk Type page, select **Redirect HTTP to HTTPS Trunk**, and then click **Next** (see Figure 3.27).

**Figure 3.27** Create New Trunk Wizard - Select Trunk Type

3. On the Step 2-Select HTTPS Trunk page, select **Portal1**, and then click **Finish** (see Figure 3.28). The new Redirect Trunk for Portal1 is created.

The following should activate the Changed configuration.

**Figure 3.28** Create New Trunk Wizard- Select HTTPS Trunk

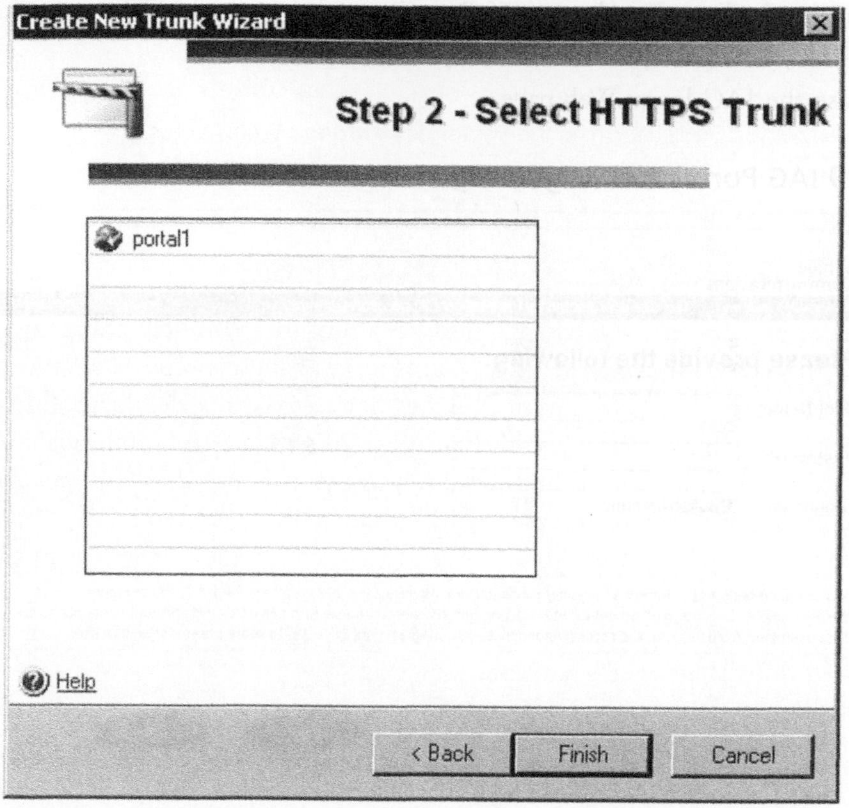

4.   On the **File** menu, click **Activate**, or on the toolbar, click the gear icon.

## "Client" to Connect to the IAG

The following represents the steps on the client computer. Also, the first time a client PC attempts to connect to the IAG portal Web site, some client computers may require components to be installed. Don't forget to click the Information Bar and then Click **Install ActiveX Control** and install when and if prompted.

1.   On the Client computer, connect to the IAG portal Web site at http://iag.demo. com (Remember do not use HTTPS.)

2.   On the Client computer, open Internet Explorer, and then in the **Address** text box, type **http://iag.demo.com**, and then press **Enter**.

3.   Internet Explorer connects to http://iag.demo.com. The IAG server responds with HTTP status code 302-Object moved, and informs Internet Explorer to reconnect to https://iag.demo.com.

4.  The IAG logon Web page opens, using an HTTPS connection. This result confirms that the Redirect Trunk successfully redirected the initial HTTP request to the HTTPS trunk (see Figure 3.29).

5.  Close the IAG logon Web page.

**Figure 3.29** IAG Portal Web Logon Page

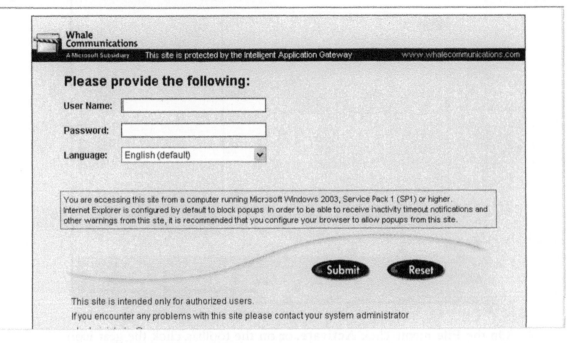

You have just successfully installed the OWA Web application.

# Examining the Rules Added to the ISA Configuration

Any time the IAG has a configuration change and when the "activate the configuration" button is depressed, IAG will update the related ISA firewall rules.

In our demonstration for this chapter, both ISA 2006 and IAG 2007 are installed on the same server (SRV1). In the process of adding the OWA application and configuring the IAG, some 13 new rules are created on the ISA 2007 server. Also, additional "ALLOW RULES" are created when you update the portal trunk configuration.

## ISA Rules

One newly created firewall rule on the ISA server called AUTH#001, allows network traffic from the IAG server to the domain controller. This new rule is for authentication purposes only.

The next rule, Trunk#001, allows network traffic from client computers to the IAG server on HTTPS port 443, which is the IAG portal Web site.

These rules and many more can be reviewed in the ISA Server Manager console.

# Securing the Outlook Web Access Interface

Securing the OWA is straightforward with no hidden complicated procedures, and can be accomplished in approximately 5 minutes or less in most circumstances.

In this demonstration, you will define endpoint policies. "Endpoint policies" is another term for client computers. Endpoint policies allow you to specify required security configuration settings on the client computers. The IAG Client Components verify these client-side configuration settings when a user connects to the IAG portal Web site.

At this stage, you will define the criteria for your clients to be allowed to enter the portal Web site. Only if the client computer(s) meet certain configuration criteria will it be allowed access to the IAG portal Web site.

## *IAG Server*

On the IAG server, session policies are needed to be configured to allow the corporate client PC's to connect to the AIG portal.

1. On the SRV1 server, in the IAG Configuration console, under **HTTPS Connections**, select **Portal1**.

2. In the right pane, in the **Security & Networking** section, after **Advanced Trunk Configuration**, click **Configure** (see Figure 3.30).

**Figure 3.30** IAG Configuration Console - Security & Networking

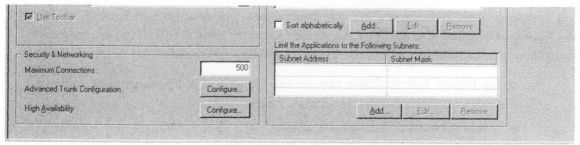

3. In the **Advanced Trunk Configuration (Portal1)** dialog box, on the **Session** tab, click **Edit Policies** (see Figure 3.31).

**Figure 3.31** Advanced Trunk Configuration - Session Tab

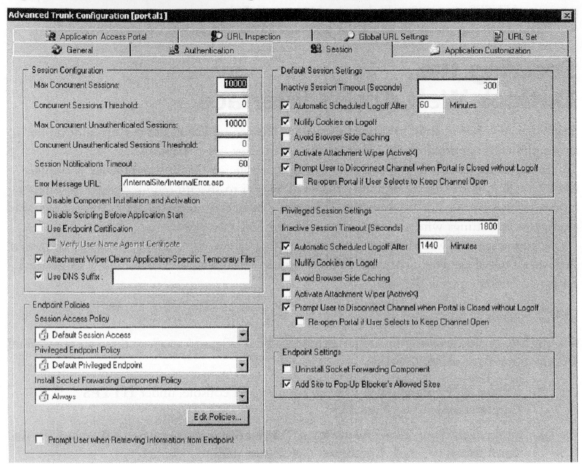

4. In the **Policies** dialog box, click **Add**.

For demonstration purposes, you will create a new policy definition to verify whether the Windows Firewall is enabled on the client computer. Instead of creating a new policy definition, you can also use any of the predefined policy definitions.

5. In the **Policy Editor** dialog box, on the General Policy Settings page, complete the following information (see Figure 3.32):

- **Policy Name:** Firewall is enabled
- **Category:** Policies
- **Explanatory Text:** Windows Firewall must be enabled on network connection.

**Figure 3.32** Advanced Trunk Configuration - General Policy Settings Editor

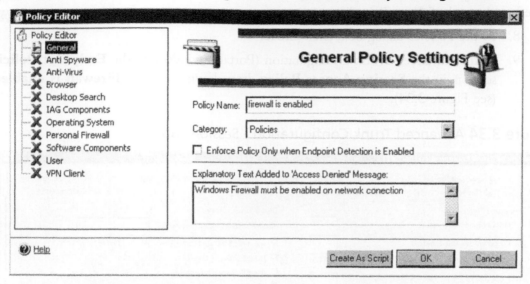

6.  On the left side, select **Personal Firewall** (see Figure 3.33).

7.  On the right side, on the **Personal Firewall** page, complete the following information:

    ■ **Enable Group:** enable

    ■ **Windows XP SP2 Personal Firewall:** enable

    ■ **Windows 2K3 SP1 Personal Firewall:** enable and then click **OK**.

**Figure 3.33** Advanced Trunk Configuration - General Policy Settings - Personal Firewall

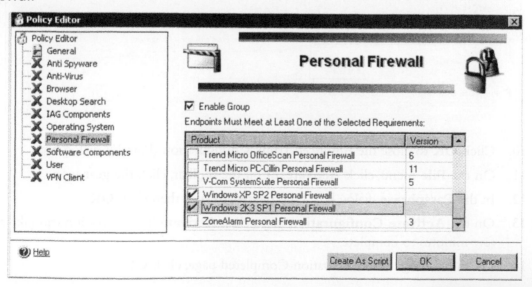

You have just added a new policy definition named "Firewall," which is enabled and is added to the end of the policies list.

8. In the Policies dialog box, click **Close**.

9. In the Advanced Trunk Configuration (Portal1) window, in the **Endpoint Policies** section, in the **Session Access Policy** drop-down list, select **Firewall is enabled** (see Figure 3.34).

**Figure 3.34** Advanced Trunk Configuration - Session Tab

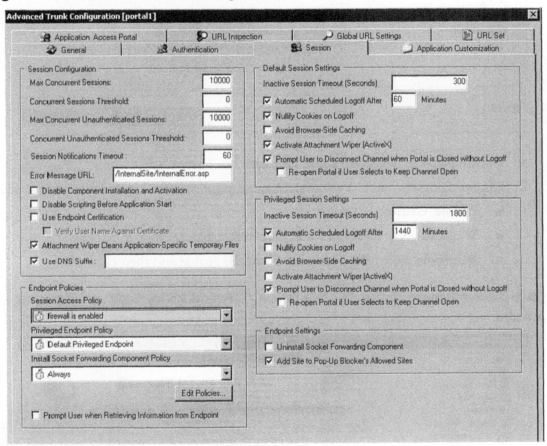

10. Click **OK** to close the Advanced Trunk Configuration (Portal1) dialog box.

11. On the **File** menu, click **Activate**, or on the toolbar, click the gear icon.

12. In the **Passphrase** dialog box, type **password**, and then click **OK**.

13. On the **Activate Configuration** page, click **Activate**. This activation can take a few minutes to complete.

14. On the Configuration Activation Completed page, click **OK**.

15. On the "client" computer, open your browser., and then on the **Favorites** menu, click **IAG Portal**, or type **https://iag.demo.com**.

   ■ At this point, IAG checks the client compliance with the access policies. Because Windows Firewall is not enabled on the client computer, the user cannot access the IAG portal Web site (see Figure 3.35).

**Figure 3.35** IAG Portal Web Warning Page

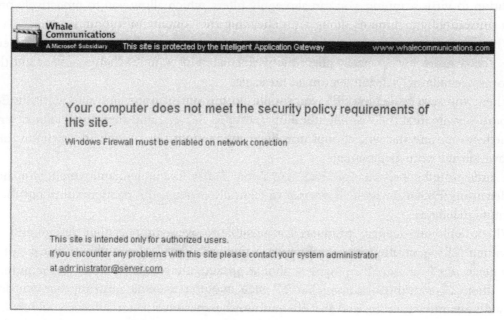

16. Close Internet Explorer.

Now to verify the connection with the firewall turned on, go the **Start** menu, click **Control Panel**, and then click **Windows Firewall**.

17. In the **Windows Firewall** message box, click **Yes** to confirm that you want to start the Windows Firewall/ICS service.

18. In the **Windows Firewall** dialog box, select **On**, and then click **OK**. Windows Firewall is enabled on the "Client."

19. Now having the Client firewall enabled, open Internet Explorer, and then on the **Favorites** menu, click **IAG Portal**.

Because Windows Firewall is enabled, the client computer meets the access policy, and IAG allows access to the portal Web site. Connection complete.

20. Close the IAG logon Web page.

# Summary

With the increasing number of viruses being circulated through e-mail, it is becoming more important to ensure that your FES infrastructure if fully protected against viruses and other threats that threaten your infrastructure.

FSE allows you to virus scan messages as they transit through you FSE infrastructure and when they are in the user's mailbox, ensuring that your infrastructure remains virus free. In addition to virus scanning, you can also apply filters, which allow you to proactively protect against unwanted attachments, along with checking the contents of the messages.

When you are considering deploying FSE, you should carefully plan your deployment to ensure that you do not adversely affect the performance of your Exchange servers and that you do not accidentally delete legitimate messages.

When you start to deploy FES, you should do this out of hours and start with the Edge Transport Servers first, followed by the Hub Transport Servers and then the Mailbox Servers. This helps to ensure that you do not introduce any new viruses to your infrastructure once you have started your deployment.

In order to effectively manage FES across your entire Exchange deployment, you should consider using FSSMC, which allows you to centrally manage the configuration and the quarantine databases.

When deploying security products, it is possible to over-engineer their design and deployment. This can often cause unforeseen issues and a level of complexity that is not always necessary. Your initial deployment should provide the basics for what you require. You should then add additional scanning and filtering as required while ensuring that you do not overload your infrastructure, and that the end user's experience is not adversely affected.

We've also given you a better understanding of how to install the Microsoft Outlook Web Access mail program through the newly acquired IAG 2007 appliance, that was turned into a software form of a gateway by Microsoft within the past year. The IAG is a comprehensive and secure remote access gateway that augments an ISA 2006 security, providing a SSL protection with endpoint security to protect all Web-based applications such as Microsoft OWA.

# Chapter 4

# Publishing Exchange 2007

## Solutions in this chapter:

- Lab Configuration

- Why Use ISA Server 2006?

- Security and Authentication

- Publishing for Resilience

- A Typical Certificate Infrastructure

# Introduction

In terms of the technology, Exchange Server 2007 is a marked departure in many ways from Exchange Server 2003 and previous versions. Exchange Server 2003 brought in many features for users that are highly visible and that users and finance directors can appreciate in terms of flashy lights and "Ooh, cool!"—features users can show to others and finance people can feel a contented glow that their money was well spent.

However, in many ways the advent of Exchange Server 2007 has meant less to the users than it has to the administrators and IT bosses of the world. It's hard to quantify the advantages to the users, who already have a pretty good Outlook Web Access feature, and are able to synchronize their mobile devices and laptops with Exchange without any fangled virtual private networks (VPNs) getting in the way. The main advantages are arguably in high availability and scalability. These features are less visible to finance directors and therefore harder to sell.

One aspect of that hard sell is that you may find yourself spending more time configuring your new Exchange environment to suit your needs. This is particularly true when it comes to security and publishing Exchange to the Web. Two particular aspects of Exchange 2007 need special attention, and therefore more planning and implementation time:

- Certificate infrastructure
- The Autodiscover service

Exchange Server 2007 has introduced us, for many for the first time, to subject alternative name (SAN) certificates; certificates that can validate traffic against a server with not just one fully qualified domain name (FQDN) but many, using the same certificate. This has great advantages in some applications since they enable you to hold encrypted conversations for multiple domains names using the same server and IP address. Exchange 2007 uses these certificates extensively internally, and indeed, when you install Exchange the server assigns itself a self-signed SAN certificate to get you going with a minimum of fuss. (Note that Microsoft recommends you don't carry on using these self-signed certificates indefinitely, but create them yourself using a Microsoft Certificate Authority.) Exchange must talk internally using SSL/TLS and relies on SSL certificates to do it. Because of this, the certificate infrastructure in the domain must be in proper working order.

When companies started migrating from Exchange 5.5 to Exchange 2000 and Exchange 2003, it was very common to go into these companies with a view to designing their new Exchange environment but coming out with a remit for a whole Active Directory audit. Well, with Exchange 2007 it's somewhat similar—it relies heavily on Active Directory (even more so than previously), and you might end up having to audit their entire PKI infrastructure. That's enough to make some Exchange consultants quake in their boots.

The Autodiscover service is another big departure from previous versions. Internally it pretty much works and you can run an Exchange environment without knowing too much about it. However, don't ignore it, because it'll come and bite you on the bum, especially if you're publishing Exchange to the Internet.

As we'll see in this chapter, the Autodiscover service introduces a number of variables when designing an infrastructure, and there are many, many ways to get the same result. Because of this, and the time involved in making sure you have the right design, be ready for a series of long and detailed discussions about how you're going to configure your mobile workforce.

This chapter is concerned primarily with ISA Server 2006, Exchange Web Services (including the Autodiscover service), and certificate security. If you are testing some of these scenarios, build the test environment and try to set up the configurations described. Otherwise, you can use this chapter to read about the possibilities open to you when implementing a published Exchange Server 2007 environment.

# Lab Configuration

In this chapter, we discuss a number of Exchange network and server configurations, many of which have been demonstrated on various forums and Web sites. When writing this book we took the view that we didn't want to go over old ground, so detailed drill-downs of how to configure these environments are not included, with an exception or two when we couldn't find relevant "how to" on the Internet. Even in these cases, we assumed a higher level of competency than many books do, so the details of the configurations are there if not the actual steps involved in setting them up.

The lab environment used to demonstrate these configurations and to take screenshots is shown in Figure 4.1. It is a relatively simple environment, but there are a number of similar configurations we use with the same servers, particularly with regard to the ISA server.

**Figure 4.1** The Standard Lab Environment for This Chapter

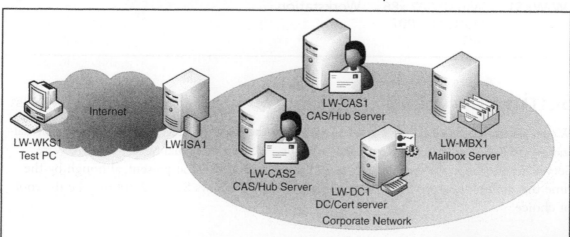

When we discuss a back-to-back firewall configuration, this is more of a theoretical setup since the ISA box is sitting at the back of that pair, and so the front server is just any old firewall, so to speak. We therefore don't recreate it. (See Table 4.1.)

**Table 4.1** Server Configuration

| Name | Software | Roles | NIC 1 | NIC 2 |
|------|----------|-------|-------|-------|
| LW-DC1 | Win2003 Std SP2 x64 | Domain controller Ent Root Cert Server | IP: 192.168.7.150 GW: 192.168.7.110 DNS: 192.168.7.150 | |
| LW-ISA | Win203 Std SP2 x86 ISA Server 2006 Std | ISA 2006 Standard | IP: 192.168.7.110 DG: DNS: 192.168.7.150 | IP: 192.168.1.5 192.168.1.6 (DG: 192.168.1.111) DNS: |
| LW-CAS1 | Win2003 Std SP2 x64 Exch2007 Std SP1 x64 | Client Access Hub Transport | IP: 192.168.7.151 GW: 192.168.7.110 DNS: 192.168.7.150 | |
| LW-CAS2 | Win2003 Std SP2 x64 Exch2007 Std SP1 x64 | Client Access Hub Transport | IP: 192.168.7.152 GW: 192.168.7.110 DNS: 192.168.7.150 | |
| LW-MBX1 | Win2003 Std SP2 x64 Exch2007 Std SP1 x64 | Mailbox server | IP: 192.168.7.153 GW: 192.168.7.110 DNS: 192.168.7.150 | |
| LW-WKS1 | WinXP SP2 x86 Outlook 2007 SP1 | Workstation | | |

# Setting up a Lab

When setting up this lab you'll want to virtualize the servers. There are a number of virtualization packages freely available on the Internet—Microsoft Virtual Server and VMWare Server are probably the most widely used for this sort of thing at present, although by the time this is published the Hypervisor included with Windows Server 2008 may be the tool of choice.

To save yourself from setting up a number of servers from scratch, use a parent disk if supported—this allows you to set up a single virtual hard disk with a generic copy of the server operating system, and set it as read-only. For each single virtual server you then create a difference disk that keeps the changes from the original disk on its own, much smaller disk.

If this is not available (for example, in VMWare Server), you can configure a Windows server disk and Sysprep and reseal it. For each new server you wish to create, make a copy of this virtual server, and when you boot into Windows it will make necessary changes to the SIDs, etc. on the OS to make it an individual server. This method is still quite easy but takes much more disk space on the host machine.

# Why Use ISA Server 2006?

This book is primarily concerned with publishing Exchange using Microsoft ISA Server 2006, for the simple reason that it is developed with this function squarely in the mind of the developers. ISA provides excellent security for Exchange Server, and is easy to configure advanced firewall and filtering capabilities through a series of wizards.

Having said that, applications that employ wizards extensively to get themselves up and running tend to bypass the knowledge required to maintain and troubleshoot such an installation, as the person setting it up doesn't necessarily need to know what each option does. It's important to learn the basics of ISA and what it is capable of in which situations.

On the subject of troubleshooting, another gripe to be had at ISA is its logging and troubleshooting capabilities. Despite the introduction of the "ISA Server 2006 Supportability Update," which adds better troubleshooting functionality, it still falls down in its usability and particularly when faced with problems using Outlook Anywhere. Troubleshooting ISA Server is still very much a hit-and-miss affair that requires a logical mind and a lot of patience.

## The Benefits of ISA Server 2006

ISA Server 2006 is an integrated security gateway that helps protect company networks from external threats while providing authorized users with access to internal resources.

**Defend against Internet threats** ISA Server helps protect the company network with a hybrid proxy-firewall architecture, packet inspection and verification, granular policies, and monitoring and alerting capabilities. Standard firewall rule sets combine with packet inspection to filter which ports traffic can enter and what kind of traffic, and whether it must be authenticated to the internal network beforehand.

**Connect and secure branch offices** ISA Server can be used to integrate company branch offices by combining site-to-site VPNs, content caching, and HTTP compression with its application layer filtering capability.

**Securely publish internal resources** ISA Server is an intelligent, application-layer gateway that can securely publish information such as Web applications, Exchange Server, and any other internal resource users need access to from the Internet or from other company sites. Using pre-authentication and packet inspection, it prevents unauthorized data from entering the network and drastically reduces the risk of intrusion.

ISA Server 2006 is one of the most secure firewalls out there. It has been approved for certification of Common Criteria Evaluation Assurance Level 4+, which is the highest level mutually approved by all participating countries. Since ISA Server 2004 came out there have been no security bulletins issued for ISA Server 2004 and ISA Server 2006, and instances of ISA servers being compromised in the wild are extremely rare if they exist at all.

# Web Publishing Rules

The main feature of ISA Server 2006, certainly from the point of view of Exchange Server, is its capability to securely publish Web sites and other servers to the Internet. When used as a reverse-proxy server in this way, it has a whole host of tools to bring to bear when it comes to providing access to internal services while preventing unauthorized access and attacks from the Internet.

ISA Server Web publishing rules are, among other things, used for publishing Exchange services such as Outlook Anywhere, Outlook Web Access, and Exchange ActiveSync. Some of the features of ISA Server Web publishing rules relevant to publishing Exchange are:

**Reverse-proxy access to sites** When publishing, or reverse-proxying sites on internal servers, ISA Server's Web proxy filter deconstructs and reconstructs client to server communication. In contrast to many hardware-based firewalls, this allows ISA to perform inspection on the traffic, even SSL-encrypted traffic, to check the validity and harmfulness of the packets. It also allows for reverse Web caching and other features.

**Pre-authentication of users** ISA Server's pre-authentication feature allows you to ensure that any traffic reaching your internal servers has been authenticated and authorized by your access policy. This helps stop attacks on your servers based on unauthenticated connections using known weaknesses in server applications such as IIS, the likes of which are being patched on a monthly basis. When publishing Exchange Web protocols, OWA, Outlook Anywhere, and ActiveSync connections can be authorized at the ISA server before being let in to the Exchange Client Access servers. Using delegation of user credentials, the ISA server can then authenticate with the Exchange server on the user's behalf, preventing the need for the user to log in twice. If the delegation fails (the Exchange server rejects the connection), the client connection is dropped at the ISA server.

**RADIUS and LDAP authentication methods** In situations where you don't want to make the ISA server a member of the domain—for example, when it is the Internet-facing firewall in a back-to-back arrangement—you can still authenticate users against the Active Directory database by using RADIUS or LDAP. RADIUS is a standard authentication protocol across the industry and is the default method for many devices and operating systems, and so may be the best option where a RADIUS infrastructure and policy is already in place. However, LDAP authentication, which is new in ISA Server 2006, gives you benefits beyond RADIUS:

- There is no additional component to install (such as IAS on a Windows server)—it works against a DC out of the box since AD is an LDAP database.

- LDAP can leverage AD groups for authorization, unlike RADIUS.

- ISA Server 2006 has also added a second two-factor authentication protocol—RADIUS One Time Password (OTP).

**Delegation of user credentials** Pre-authenticating users is a great feature of ISA Server, but if the published server also requires authentication it's not great if the user is faced with a prompt for credentials twice. ISA Server can answer the published server's call for credentials by forwarding the credentials obtained through pre-authentication to the server in question. There are a number of methods by which ISA can send these credentials, and we discuss some of them in this chapter (Figure 4.2).

**Figure 4.2** Delegation Can Happen Using a Number of Methods

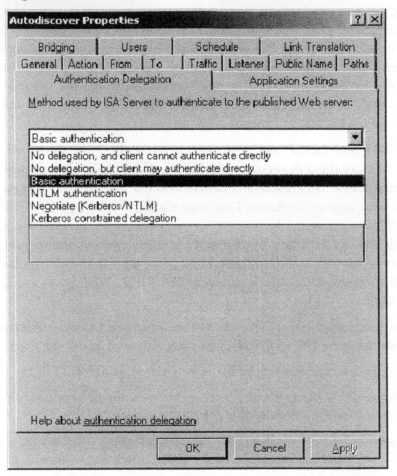

**Single Sign On** ISA Server allows you to specify that once a client has authenticated with ISA to access a service within the network, it can access further services within the same network without having to re-enter credentials. For example, if a user accessing Outlook Web Access on https://mail.lochwallace.com/owa and then opens a page to the published SharePoint site on https://sharepoint.lochwallace.com/, ISA Server can seamlessly use the user's already provided credentials to authenticate him with the SharePoint server, and the user isn't asked for his username and password. For this to work, single sign on must be configured on the ISA server for *.lochwallace.com, and both sites must be published using the same listener.

**Application-layer inspection** ISA Server's HTTP Security Filter is used to inspect traffic going across its border and apply rules on the HTTP traffic. Almost every aspect of HTTP communication can be specified using this filter, from maximum payload length, HTTP methods/verbs, file extensions, Request and Response headers, and executable content (Figure 4.3). Using SSL bridging, ISA decrypts, inspects, and then encrypts traffic destined to internal servers. Because of this bridging, it is also possible to redirect SSL traffic to an FQDN not specified in the original traffic. This HTTP filtering is done on a per-rule basis.

**Figure 4.3** Many Filter Settings Can Be Applied to a Rule

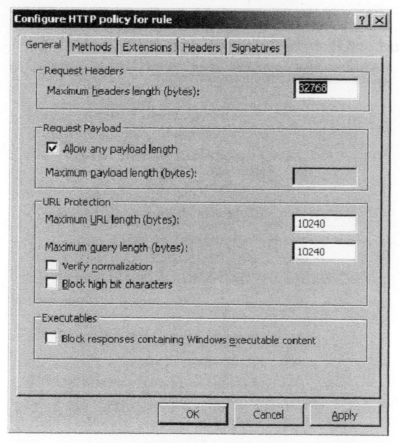

**Path redirection** ISA Server allows you to redirect connections to different paths and even different internal servers based on the path in the URL. For example, requests to https://mail.lochwallace.com/owa and https://mail.lochwallace.com/Autodiscover come into the same IP address on the ISA server, but can be redirected to different internal Exchange servers. In addition, a Web publishing rule can redirect traffic to a different URL directly, as in the Autodiscover example later in the chapter where requests to https://autodiscover.lochwallace.com/ are redirected to https://mail.lochwallace.com/.

**Port and protocol redirection**  Using port redirection, ISA Server can listen to incoming requests on port 80, for example, and forward the traffic to a different port on the internal Web server. This is useful if the internal server is published on a nonstandard port but you want to publish it to Internet users using standard port 80. It is also the method by which you terminate an incoming SSL connection at the ISA server and forward the traffic unencrypted (Figure 4.4).

**Figure 4.4** Port and Protocol Translation Is Set on the Bridging Tab

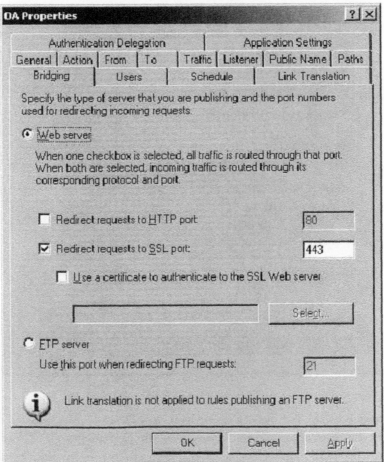

HTTP to FTP protocol redirection is supported by the Web publishing rules. This enables FTP sites to be published using Web publishing rules, as it transforms an HTTP GET command to an FTP GET command when it flows across the firewall.

**Rule scheduling** ISA Server allows you to put schedules on when users are allowed to access resources published through the publishing rules. This is useful if you want workers accessing sites only during working hours, or high-bandwidth applications you want people to access only during network "trough" times (Figure 4.5).

**Figure 4.5** You Can Set Exactly when to Allow Access to Resources

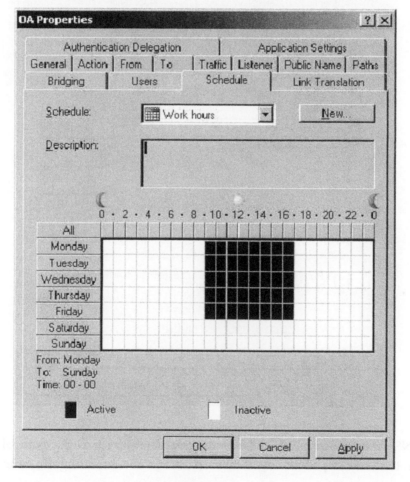

**Multiple Web site publishing through a single IP address** ISA Server can publish multiple Web sites on a single IP address by inspecting the host header in the packet and applying the rule that corresponds to the Web site requested. For example, to publish webserver.lochwallace.com and mail.lochwallace.com on the same IP address, you can simply create twp publishing rules and apply the same Web listener to both. Each rule specifies the Public Name of the server it is publishing, and as long as the name is in the request's host header, ISA server will pick it up and send it to the correct internal server (Figure 4.6).

### Figure 4.6 Publishing Multiple Web Sites

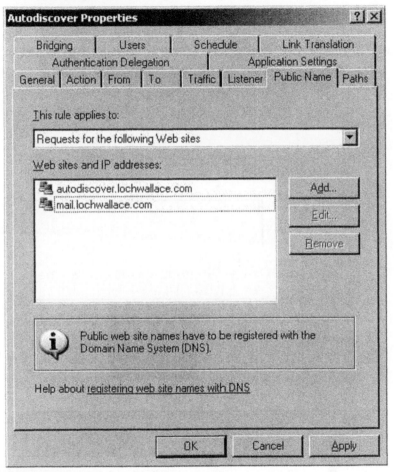

Public DNS must resolve the FQDNs of the published servers to the external IP address of the ISA server. It is easy to publish any number of servers this way using the same IP address.

**Link translation** Internal servers often publish links to other URLs using the NetBIOS name of the server since they are geared toward internal communication. External users accessing this information will receive broken links when they try to follow them since they need an FQDN to traverse the Internet through the ISA server and to the published server (Figure 4.7).

**Figure 4.7** Global Link Direction Mappings

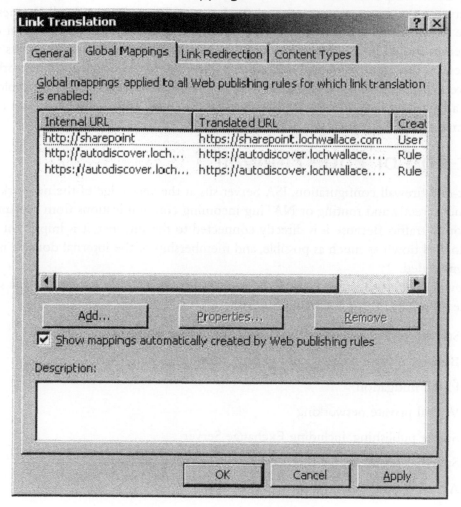

Link mappings can be set globally or on a per-rule basis.

# Typical ISA Server Configurations

There are a number of particular situations and configurations in which ISA Server 2006 can be used in corporate networks. Because of its comprehensive feature set, ISA can function as a simple firewall, a publishing and filtering proxy server, a branch office VPN device, and many others. In terms of publishing Exchange Server 2007 we are interested mainly in its firewall and proxying functionality and therefore in the Internet-facing configurations set out here.

Many small companies have a single gateway to the Internet comprising one security device between the company network and the Internet. Often this is a Small Business Server where the ISA software is on the main server itself. Preferably, from a security point of view, the ISA server should be a different box, and larger companies may configure it this way. Corporates, on the other hand, will undoubtedly have at least one perimeter network where some servers that are published to the Internet lie. In these situations, they may deploy ISA Server as a back-end firewall between the corporate network and a DMZ, and as a member of the domain to provide increased security and flexibility.

# Front-end or Edge Firewall

In a front-end firewall configuration, ISA Server sits at the very edge of the network facing the Internet directly and routing or NATing incoming communications from the Internet and outbound traffic. Because it is directly connected to the Internet, it is important that the server is locked down as much as possible, and membership of the internal domain is usually not recommended.

However, ISA Server offers many features common firewalls do not, and in this situation, it can take advantage of the following features:

- Stateful packet inspection* and application layer inspection
- Built-in intrusion detection and protection
- Flood mitigation
- Virtual private networking
- Server publishing, including Exchange Server
- Speedy firewall engine that works at speeds of up to Gbps
- Access control based on users and groups

Stateful packet inspection, or *dynamic packet filtering*, refers to a method of tracking and controlling traffic through a firewall. *Static filtering* examines the packet header to determine source and destination, etc., and applies the firewall rules to the traffic to allow or deny its passage. Dynamic filtering is a more proactive method that keeps track of the state of the connection between parties and examines the packet sometimes right up to the application layer to determine whether it's traffic appropriate to the context established by prior packets that have passed across the firewall (Figure 4.8).

**Figure 4.8** Using ISA Server as a Front-end Firewall

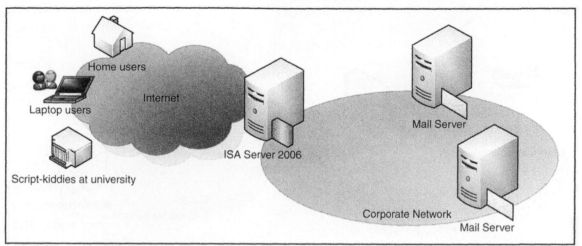

In this configuration, the ISA server has an interface on the Internet side and one on the corporate network. In many cases, the ISA server can act transparently to users, inside and out, as traffic is forwarded to internal servers according to publishing rules, and outbound traffic is intercepted and inspected without clients being aware of it.

## Back-end Firewall

For larger companies that already have high-end firewalls at their perimeter, it is often attractive to supplement their high-speed packet filtering capabilities with ISA Server's publishing and application layer inspection features. ISA Server can also augment the features of the existing firewall; it's a common requirement in corporate to have multivendor firewalls to better protect their assets by covering more bases. If one firewall has a deficiency or vulnerability, the other may well offer the protection needed against such a problem.

When deployed in a back-end configuration as in Figure 4.9, ISA Server can be used to its full extent, publishing internal servers, pre-authenticating clients, and performing packet inspection.

Features likely to be used by ISA Server in a back-end configuration include:

- Secure publishing of Exchange Web services such as Outlook Anywhere, Outlook Web Access, and Exchange ActiveSync

- User- and group-based access to internal resources

- Site-to-site VPNs

- Packet filtering and application layer inspection

**Figure 4.9** Using ISA Server as a Back-end Firewall

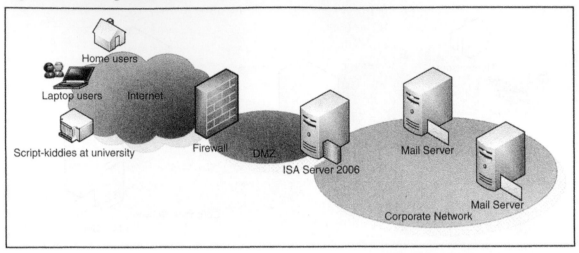

In this configuration, ISA Server is more likely to be a member of the internal domain*, and can therefore take advantage of features such as Kerberos Constrained Delegation, required for pre-authentication of Outlook Anywhere clients using NTLM authentication. Domain membership also provides you with full support for the firewall client, user certificate authentication, monitoring through System Center Operations Manager and Group Policy management, and many others.

> **NOTE**
>
> To the subject of domain membership of ISA servers: There is a lot to read out there on isaserver.org and other places about the merits, and otherwise, of domain membership of ISA servers in various configurations. We're not going to enter this argument here—people will implement ISA as they see fit, and we are not suggesting a preference. Clearly, however, domain membership has its advantages, and when using any Kerberos protocols it is a requirement.

# Configuration Options/Requirements

ISA Server 2006 can be deployed in a number of situations and configurations, according to the features you wish to use. There are three main deployment options we might be interested in for publishing Exchange: single-homed, dual-homed, and multihomed. These configurations correspond loosely to the network templates in ISA Server 2006, which allow you to set the server up in one of these configurations with minimum fuss and configuration. The templates include starting points for rule sets, such as "Deny All" or "Allow Limited Web Access" and so on, which should be modified according to your particular needs.

The Edge Firewall, Front Firewall, and Back Firewall configurations in ISA Server 2006 correspond to the dual-homed server discussed in this section. The network configuration is the same, with the Internal and External networks, but configuration such as firewall rules may differ.

# Single-Homed ISA Server

Typically, you would use an ISA server with a single network card when you already have a heavy investment in packet filtering firewalls and want to simply publish Web servers to the outside world. A typical configuration for this is to place the ISA server in an existing DMZ or in the internal network if there is no DMZ present. This supports the following scenarios:

- Web publishing
- Web proxying and caching

It doesn't sound like a lot, but the single-homed configuration retains the very powerful Web Proxy Filter functionality, which gives you the application-level filtering for HTTP, HTTPS, and FTP over HTTP. (FTP is not supported in this configuration; only FTP over HTTP—Figure 4.10.)

**Figure 4.10** ISA Server 2006 in a Single Network Card Configuration

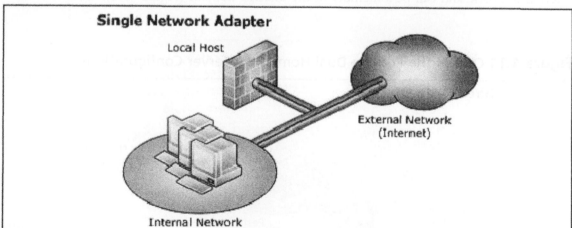

Because this server has only one network card, it has no concept of multiple networks (only the Internal network and the Local Host), so the following features are not available:

**Multinetwork firewall policy** The server has no concept of an External network—everything comes from and goes to the Internal network—so the only firewall policy applied is in terms of the local host, since ISA protects itself by default in every configuration.

**Server publishing** You cannot publish servers since there is no NAT functionality with a single NIC. The exception here is of course the Web Proxy Filter, which is a special case.

**Firewall and secure-NAT clients** Internal clients use ISA's Firewall service and route traffic through the ISA server to the outside world. Because the Firewall service is not available in this configuration, these clients are not supported and will not function.

**Application layer inspection** Application layer filtering does not function in this scenario, with the exception of the Web Proxy Filter, which gives powerful filtering functionality for Web protocols and FTP over HTTP.

**Virtual private networking** VPNs are not supported in a single-NIC configuration.

## Dual-Homed ISA Server

With a dual-homed server, you can take advantage of the full feature set of ISA Server 2006, particularly the routing and NATing functionality and firewall policy. Typically, this kind of setup is used as a back-end firewall where there is already a firewall in place on the perimeter of the network. In this situation, the ISA server routes/NATs between the DMZ and the internal network, and can be a member of the internal domain (Figure 4.11).

**Figure 4.11** One of the Possible Dual-Homed ISA Server Configurations

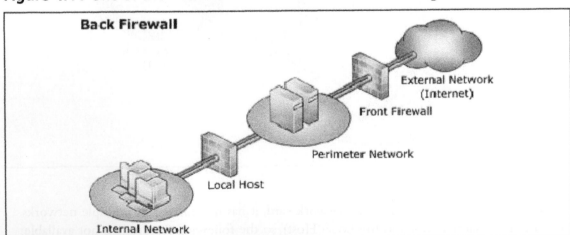

Alternatively, ISA can be deployed as a front-end firewall, with another firewall device behind it, or as the sole firewall on the network, which is the case in many small network deployments. Small Business Server is an example of this, although in this scenario the ISA server is also the domain controller, file server, Exchange server, etc.

## Multihomed ISA Server

Another configuration option in ISA Server 2006 is the three-leg perimeter network. This utilizes the ISA server to provide the protection of a dual-homed server (either front- or back-end) while using a third network card to create a perimeter network, or DMZ, on which you can place other Internet-facing servers to be published (Figure 4.12).

**Figure 4.12** A Three-NIC ISA Configuration

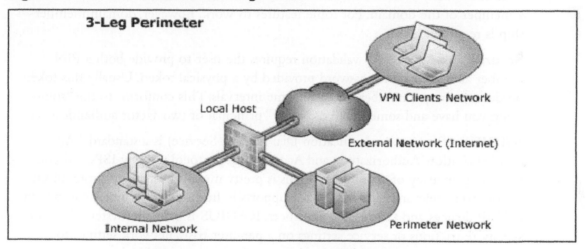

This configuration is slightly more complicated than the dual-homed setup, as it requires a little more thought in terms of networking (when the server should NAT traffic and when to route etc.), but the network templates make the initial setup very simple.

# Security and Authentication
## User Validation Methods

ISA Server 2006 gives you the choice of a whole array of credential validation methods that should cover any application and connectivity requirements you might have:

**Active Directory** Being a Windows-based server, ISA Server can also authenticate directly against a domain controller. However, it must be a member of the same domain, or a trusted domain, for this to be an option. Active Directory authentication is necessary for ISA Server arrays (against AD or ADAM (Active Directory

Application Mode), which we cover later in this chapter. Password management features are available when authenticating using AD.

**LDAP (Lightweight Directory Access Protocol)** LDAP is the directory protocol on which Active Directory is based, so using this protocol to authenticate users requires no additional input—you simply point it toward a domain controller. This is a new method to ISA Server 2006 and provides similar functionality to Active Directory based validation without having to install a RADIUS server on the domain such as Microsoft IAS Server. Using LDAP authentication you can enable password management features of ISA, which allows users to change their passwords after logging on through an HTML form and warns them when their password is near expiry. You can also specify AD groups against which to configure your allow/deny rules. LDAP validation is especially useful if the ISA server is not a member of the domain. For some features to work, however, domain membership is required.

**SecurID** RSA's SecurID validation requires the user to provide both a PIN number and a one-time password provided by a physical token. Usually this token produces a unique number at certain time intervals. This conforms to the "something you have and something you know" principal of two-factor authentication.

**RADIUS** (Remote Authentication Dial In User Service) is a standard AAA (Authentication, Authorization, and Accounting) protocol used by ISPs and companies using an array of technologies. This is pretty much the standard protocol since almost every relevant network device supports it, from 802.11 wireless equipment to VoIP devices and Cisco ASA appliances. RADIUS is a flexible system that can specify restrictions or service settings on a per-user basis, network settings for clients (such as static IP address), and connection parameters like log-on times and duration. It is also extensible, meaning vendors can implement their own extended versions of RADIUS to fit their needs. Using RADIUS authentication doesn't allow any password management through ISA Server and can't leverage pre-existing AD groups when used against IAS.

**RADIUS OTP (One Time Password)** OTP is a RADIUS-based authentication method similar to SecurID. Each user has a token that generates a number at a certain frequency that matches up to numbers generated by the server component, which is usually installed on a RADIUS server. The number is used in conjunction with the username to gain access. This is presumably not quite as secure as SecurID, since a username would be easier to ascertain than a pin code.

Which method you choose depends on a number of factors:

**Functionality** Are the ISA servers in an array? Do you require the password management functionality of ISA Server?

**Domain membership**  If the ISA server is a member of the domain, this is the easiest method to use. Some administrators and security specialists, for one reason or another, prefer to have an ISA server in its own workgroup rather than in the domain, especially if it is directly facing the Internet or sitting in a DMZ.

**Existing infrastructure**  There may already be an infrastructure in place for authentication via other remote access devices, most likely taking the form of RADIUS servers. There may well be reasons for using the existing infrastructure and lowering administrative cost.

# Pre-Authentication

One of the biggest security features of ISA Server is its capability to pre-authenticate client requests before passing the traffic onto the published server on the LAN. By authenticating the client before allowing any traffic from it through to your published server, you can reduce the likelihood of certain attacks such as SYN and DoS attacks, or at the very least find out who's sending the malicious code and block off that account! Along with the application filters ISA Server provides, this makes for a difficult barrier to any nasties out there on the Internet trying to break your internal machines. Compare this with a standard hardware firewall that simply opens ports or forwards traffic to internal machines, and you have a much more secure system.

## The Pre-Authentication Process

The client pre-authentication process works as shown in Figure 4.13. The ISA server takes care of the authentication transparently, so the client doesn't know it's being authenticated by something other than its destination server.

**Figure 4.13** The Client Pre-Authentication Process

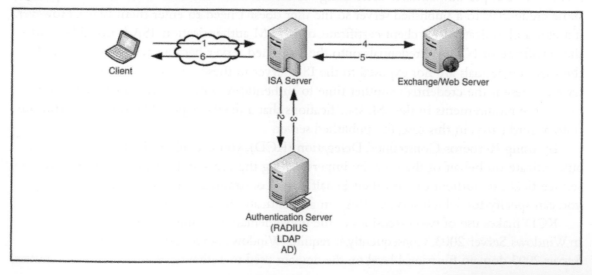

**Step 1** The client sends its credentials to the ISA server, either via a standard log-in box in the case of Outlook Anywhere, or via the forms-based authentication method used for Outlook Web Access.

**Step 2** ISA Server uses these credentials to authenticate the user against the authentication server. Depending on domain membership and other factors, this may be a RADIUS service, LDAP, or an Active Directory domain controller.

**Step 3** The authentication provider sends acknowledgment of the credentials and gives the ISA server a green light to let the user in.

**Step 4** ISA server sends the original client request to the Web server and uses authentication delegation to present the client's credentials for validation. The form the credentials take is not dependent on how it was presented by the client. (For example, the client may provide credentials by NTLM, but if the Web server requires Basic authentication, the ISA server can present those credentials to the Web server using Basic auth.)

**Step 5** The Web server sends a response to the client, which is intercepted by the ISA server. (Actually, depending how the publishing rule is set up, the ISA server may *be* the client as far as the Web server is concerned.)

**Step 6** The ISA server forwards the response to the client.

Later in this chapter, we explore different methods of publishing Exchange Server 2007 with ISA Server 2006 and dependencies on certificates, and making the Autodiscover service available to Outlook Anywhere clients.

# Kerberos Constrained Delegation

ISA Server can pre-authenticate users using the likes of Basic authentication and then pass those credentials to a published server so the user doesn't need to enter them twice. However, if a user authenticates by a client certificate, or NTLM authentication, ISA is not able to pass the certificate or NTLM credentials onto the published server because with these methods, the user's credentials are not exposed to the ISA server in these scenarios. The user would have to present the credentials another time to authenticate with the published server. It is one of the requirements in the SSL specifications that a device is not able to pass a certificate onto a third party; in this case, the published server.

By using Kerberos Constrained Delegation (KCD), you can allow the ISA server to authenticate on behalf of the users by impersonating the users and obtaining a Kerberos service ticket to authenticate on their behalf. The "constrained" part comes in because you can specify for which services ISA can authenticate the users; for example, HTTP.

KCD makes use of two extensions to the implementation of the Kerberos v5 protocol in Windows Server 2003. Consequently, it requires Windows Server 2003 and Windows Server 2003 domain functional level on the domain used to authenticate the users or computers.

**Protocol transition** The protocol transition extension allows a service that uses Kerberos to obtain a Kerberos service ticket on behalf of a user (or computer) without requiring the user to authenticate to the KCD first. Instead, a user with credentials such as a client certificate that aren't acceptable for Kerberos authentication first authenticates with the server (ISA Server in this case) using another appropriate authentication method. The server then creates a user token and impersonates the user to gain access to services on the target server. To do this, the service must have the necessary impersonation privileges on the target server.

**Constrained delegation** The constrained delegation extension allows a service access to a restricted list of services running on network servers after it has been presented with a service ticket, which in this case is a service ticket obtained through protocol transition. This allows administrators to restrict the actual services for which delegation can be allowed.

ISA Server 2004 is able to delegate credentials to internal servers, but only when they are presented using either Basic or Forms-Based authentication. By employing Kerberos Constrained Delegation, ISA Server is also able to delegate credentials for Integrated, SSL client certificate, and two-factor authentication.

# Pre-Authenticating Using NTLM and Certificates

The advantage of KCD is that ISA Server 2006 can pre-authenticate users using NTLM or client certificates without the users having to re-enter their credentials. Without KCD, it is possible, for example, to configure ISA Server so that users of Outlook Anywhere don't have to enter their username and password when they open Outlook (as long as they're logged on using the cached credentials of their domain account), but this requires you to switch off pre-authentication at the ISA server and have them authenticate directly with the Exchange Client Access Server. This is not a good idea, as it negates one of the main advantages of having ISA in the first place—preventing anonymous connections directly into the network.

Later in the chapter, we discuss using Kerberos Constrained Delegation with Outlook Anywhere and NTLM, and with Windows Mobile devices and client certificates.

One of the big new features in ISA Server 2006 is its capability to authenticate users by Kerberos after the ISA server has verified them using non-Kerberos authentication methods. Kerberos authentication directly across the Internet is not possible in most situations, so being able to authenticate users at the ISA server using Integrated authentication or user certificates and use Kerberos to pass those credentials onto the published server has a great benefit. Using this method, ISA Server pre-authenticates users using Certificates or Integrated authentication, and then authenticates these users internally using a different method (KCD), without requiring additional input from the user.

# Using Certificates

More so than any previous version of Exchange Server, Exchange 2007 relies on SSL-encrypted communication, between servers and between client and server. When an Exchange 2007 server is installed, the setup process looks for an appropriate SSL certificate on the server, and if it doesn't find one, it creates its own self-signed certificate. This certificate has the server's NetBIOS name as the common name, and the FQDN in the Subject Alternative Name (SAN) field.

To see the properties of this self-signed certificate, open an MMC console and add the Certificates snap-in (Figure 4.14).

**Figure 4.14** Opening the Certificates Snap-in in the MMC Console

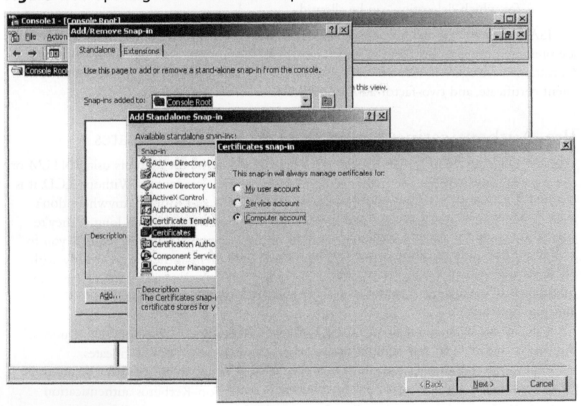

In the Personal certificate store, you will find the self-signed certificate with the name matching the NetBIOS name of the server. In the Subject Alternative Name field is the FQDN, or full DNS name of the server (Figure 4.15).

**Figure 4.15** Examining the Subject Names of the Self-Signed Exchange Certificate

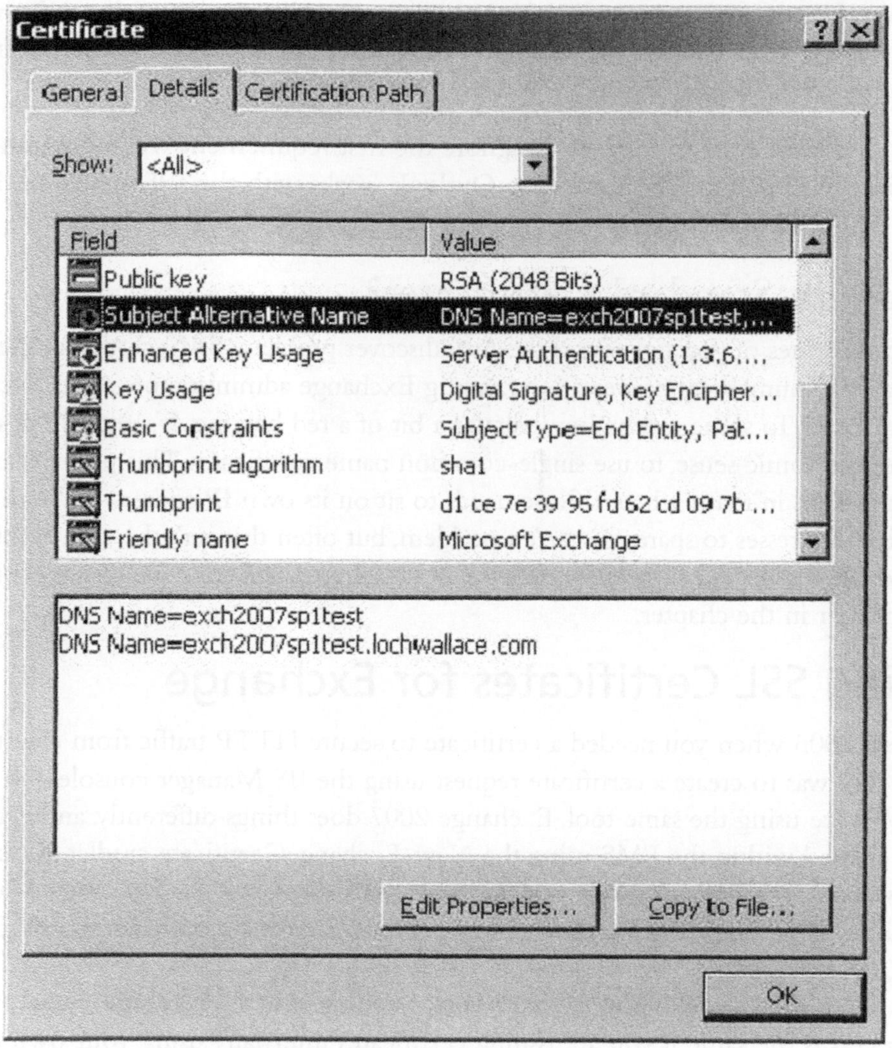

A SSL certificate must pass three tests to be valid:

- The certificate chain can be followed up from the certificate to a trusted root. Okay, so if you're opening up Outlook Web Access and the certificate isn't trusted, you can always bypass the certificate warning page by clicking the "Yeah yeah, I don't care" button, but where the negotiation process is less transparent, such as with Outlook Anywhere and ActiveSync, you don't have that option and they will fail.

- The certificate subject name (or one of the subject alternative names) matches the FQDN of the server with which the client is communicating. Likewise, with OWA this can be bypassed, but not with Outlook Anywhere or ActiveSync.

- The certificate date is valid; i.e., it has not expired. I guess this is a no-brainer, but if you spend your time making your own certificates internally and giving them 20-year lifetimes, you have to be aware of the fact that commercial certificates have a definite lifetime and you need to renew them!

In fact, Outlook 2007 is designed to ignore the first requirement when communicating in a domain environment. This is solely so Outlook works with the self-signed certificates of Exchange 2007 out of the box.

## What about Standard Certificates?

Because of the issues of getting around the Autodiscover problem, SAN certificates are the subject of a large number of conversations among Exchange administrators since Exchange 2007 was released. To some extent, however, it's a bit of a red herring. It's entirely possible, and often makes economic sense, to use single-common name certificates. This presents an additional requirement in that each certificate needs to sit on its own IP address. If you have plenty of external IP addresses to spare, this isn't a problem, but often this isn't the case. Another option is to use a wildcard certificate, which also has its pros and cons. We discuss both of these topics later in the chapter.

## Creating SSL Certificates for Exchange

In Exchange 2003 when you needed a certificate to secure HTTP traffic from client to server, the easiest way was to create a certificate request using the IIS Manager console and assign it to the Web site using the same tool. Exchange 2007 does things differently, and certificates should be created within the EMS using the New-ExchangeCertificate cmdlet. Of course, you can use other methods to create and transport certificates, but the Exchange Management Shell is a little more flexible in that you can import and enable a certificate in a single command, for example.

In this section, we assume that the certificate is being issued by a commercial provider, but the process is the same if you are issuing certificates internally using your own certificate authority. For now, we assume that somebody else will pick up the certificate request and deliver us a nice new certificate and we don't need to do a thing.

As we know, Exchange 2007 creates self-signed certificates for each server and enables it for each installed server role, but Microsoft recommends replacing these certificates with commercial or internal PKI-signed certificates. The reason for this seems to be to have a contiguous certificate structure and namespace in and outside the organization, and better central control of the certificate infrastructure. Although domain-connected Outlook clients will find the Autodiscover service through Active Directory, it, along with external OWA, ActiveSync, and Outlook clients, still needs to connect to Web services using a trusted certificate. Using the same connection points and certificates for internal and external clients makes things easier in the long run.

It's perfectly feasible to retain the self-cert certificates in the long term as long as the distinction is made between internal and external clients, which is sometimes not so easy to do.

You need to watch out for a number of things when going through the certificate process—the creation of the certificate and the planning.

# Organization Name

One of the fields in an X.509 certificate you may not always worry about (if you're used to issuing your own) is the Organization field. When you use your own internal CA, the only fields that really matter are the domain names, but when you are purchasing a "proper" official certificate, it's important to get this right. The issuing authority will insist that the organization named on the certificate request actually owns the domain name. This means that your WHOIS registration details should be correct and up to date. It may be possible to obtain a registration by proxy, if the owner of the domain name verifies and approves the certificate, but this can be a lengthy process, so it's best to keep them the same.

So, if your common name (CN) looks like *C=GB, O=Lochwallace, CN=lochwallace.com*, make sure "Lochwallace" is the owner of the lochwallace.com domain.

# Subject Alternative Names

As discussed previously, one sticking point with Exchange Server 2007 is the issue of Subject Alternative Name certificates. Most X.509 certificates refer to a single Web site address (e.g., www.microsoft.com), and so are used on a per-FQDN basis for securing Internet traffic. Exchange 2007, specifically the Autodiscover service, introduces a complication in which Internet hosts may need to contact two separate Web addresses (FQDNs) on the same IP address. With the single IP to certificate restriction, this introduced the need to use a certificate with SANs, or a Unified Communication Certificate, as Microsoft likes to call it.

This is great in a way because now we can publish a whole load of Web sites through ISA Server using just a single IP address, and you don't need to pay exorbitant ISP prices for additional IPs. Moreover, consolidating IPv4 addresses may delay further the introduction of the horrendous IPv6, which can't be a bad thing! However, ISA Server 2006 RTM and previous versions of ISA Server do not support SAN certificates, so we need to find a way around that.

# Creating the Certificate Request

To create the certificate request, use the New-ExchangeCertificate cmdlet in the Exchange Management Shell. New-ExchangeCertificate can be used either for creating a new self-signed certificate for use internally or for generating a request to send to the commercial provider. When generating a new certificate request, the following parameters are required or recommended:

**GenerateRequest** Tells the command to generate a certificate request rather than creating a (self-signed) certificate. The request file is used to create the certificate either by sending it to a commercial issuer or using it against your internal CA to complete the request.

**DomainName** The Subject Alternative Name field. Enter all the alternative FQDNs, such as "owa.lochwallace.com, autodiscover.lochwallace.com, mail. lochwallace.com."

**SubjectName** Not strictly required to create a certificate, as the default value for this field (entered automatically if you don't include this switch) corresponds to the first address you specify in the –DomainName field (in the format "cn=mail.loch-wallace.com"). It's customary to enter this in the format "c=uk,o=Lochwallace,cn=mail.lochwallace.com" and it's important to format it correctly if you're sending the request to a commercial issuer, since they will check the organization against the Internet domain name via WHOIS.

**Path** Specify the file where you want to save the request. Typically, the path is c:\certreq.txt.

**PrivateKeyExportable** If you want to be able to export the certificate along with the private key, you must specify "-PrivateKeyExportable:$True". This is important if you are going to import it onto another server—for example in an NLB cluster scenario—or onto a publishing ISA server.

Another interesting switch is the -*IncludeAutodiscover* switch. According to the Exchange help, this switch "adds the prefix, 'autodiscover' to each domain name that is generated for the resulting certificate," but what it does is add FQDNs to the Subject Alternative Name field of the resulting certificate based on the authoritative domains of the Exchange organization.

For example, if your Exchange organization is set up with "lochwallace.com" and "lochwallace.com" as its Accepted Domains, as in Figure 4.16, this switch will add "autodiscover.lochwallace.com" and autodiscover.lochbruce.com" to the SAN field.

**NOTE**

The IncludeAutodiscover switch is available only if you run the request from a Client Access server.

**Figure 4.16** The Accepted Domains for the Organization

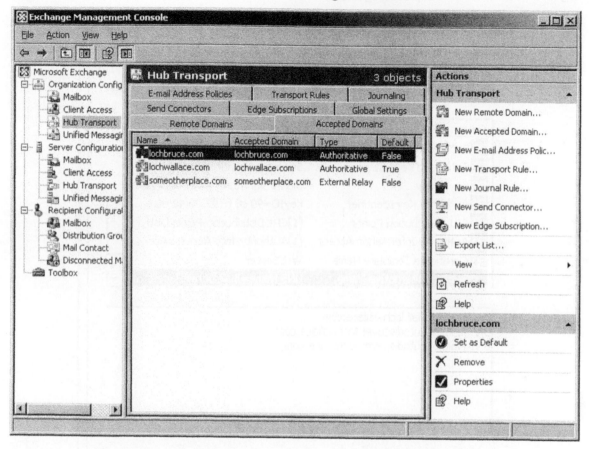

Running the following command in the shell creates the certificate:

```
New-ExchangeCertificate -GenerateRequest -DomainNamemail.lochwallace.com-SubjectName
"c=GB,o=MyCompany Ltd,cn=mail.lochwallace.com" -PrivateKeyExportable:$True -
IncludeAutodiscover -Path "c:\certreq.txt"
```

The certificate generated includes the autodiscover addresses for the Accepted Domains
in the Organization (Figure 4.17).

**Figure 4.17** The Corresponding Autodiscover Addresses Have Been Added

**NOTE**

This does not apply for accepted domains that are relayed elsewhere (internally or externally), which makes sense as these people will not have mailboxes on your servers and therefore will not need autodiscover service in your organization.

**NOTE**

**NetBIOS names:** The self-cert SAN certificates created by Exchange setup contain the NetBIOS name of the server and the FQDNs. This is not a technical requirement, but may be useful if you have internal OWA users who want to use the NetBIOS name in Internet Explorer, or other requirements for SSL connections to Exchange such as third-party applications.

# Importing the Certificate

When you receive the certificate, it is in the form *certnew.cer or certnew.p7b*. Note that this certificate does not include the private key—this is retained on the server on which you created the request. Therefore, you must import the certificate into the original requesting server.

The Import-ExchangeCertificate cmdlet imports the .cer file into the correct certificate store on the server. The only switch you need is to tell it where the certificate is:

Import-ExchangeCertificate –Path c:\certnew.cer

You then have to enable the certificate for use with Exchange services. The Enable-ExchangeCertificate commandlet does this, and you specify in the command which services the certificate should be associated with—SMTP, IIS, POP, and IMAP. To enable a certificate that is already imported, you must specify the Thumbprint switch, which is shown when you import the certificate or by using a command such as

```
Get-ExchangeCertificate |fl FriendlyName,Subject,Thumbprint
```

The following command enables the certificate for all services:

```
Enable-ExchangeCertificate -Thumbprint -Services IIS, SMTP, POP, IMAP
```

You can streamline the whole import and enable procedure by piping the result from one into the other. So the command

```
Import-ExchangeCertificate -Path c:\certnew.cer | Enable-ExchangeCertificate -Services
IIS, SMTP, POP, IMAP
```

imports and applies the certificate in one fell swoop. No need to use these daft thumbprints at all.

# Transporting the Certificate

If you're publishing your Client Access server with ISA Server or clustering your Client Access servers using NLB, you'll have to transfer the certificate to another server. You can do this using the *Export-ExchangeCertificate* cmdlet or by the standard methods of the Certificates MMC snap-in or IIS Manager. Either method is good, as both export the intermediate certificates as well.

Use the following command to export the certificate to a .pfx file:

```
Export-ExchangeCertificate -Thumbprint [certificate thumbprint] -Password
(Get-Credential).password -Path c:\certificate.pfx
```

The Export-ExchangeCertificate cmdlet exports the certificate (or certificate request) in the appropriate format. In the case of the certificate, it is exported into a PKCS #12 certificate that holds the private key.

To import the certificate to an ISA server, you can use the Certificates MMC snap-in (in Figure 4.18), since the Exchange Powershell extensions are not present.

### Figure 4.18 The Certificates MMC Snap-in

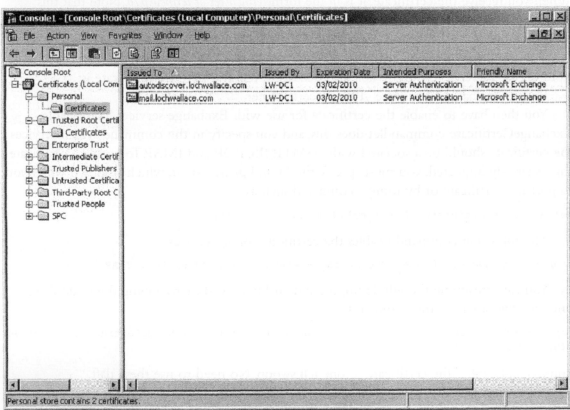

When you use the Certificates MMC snap-in to import a certificate, make sure you deal appropriately with any included certificates from intermediate certification authorities. By default, the import mechanism will place these certs in the same place as the server certificates, but you want to move these to the Intermediate Certification Authorities folder instead so the server can follow the certificate chain up to the root.

# The Autodiscover Service

Certificates play a central role in an Exchange organization since they are used to encrypt much of the traffic that flows within the LAN and with clients and servers outside the network or organization. One particular service we have to consider when working out the certificate infrastructure is the Autodiscover service because it is so central to the connection of clients such as Outlook and Windows Mobile devices.

Autodiscover is a new service in Exchange 2007 that provides configuration information to clients such as Outlook 2007 and mobile devices. It fulfills two main functions: providing profile configuration information to Outlook 2007 clients, and publishing the URLs of servers that provide Exchange Web services—Offline Address Book (OAB), Availability (free/busy info), Out of Office (OOF), and Unified Messaging. Configuring Autodiscover correctly is therefore crucial to a working Exchange environment.

The Autodiscover service is implemented on every Client Access server in an Exchange organization. When a CAS server is installed, the setup program creates a Service Connection Point (SCP) in Active Directory that points to the FQDN of the new server (e.g,., CAS1.lochwallace.com). An SCP is kind of a domain version of a DNS SRV record in that it helps domain-connected clients locate services on the network. In this case, the SCP holds the addresses of all Exchange servers with the Autodiscover service (all CAS servers).

The SCP information for each CAS server can be found using ADSIEdit or another LDAP querying tool. Figure 4.19 shows the SCP data for one of the CAS servers.

**Figure 4.19** Exposing the Service Connection Point Data for a Client Access Server

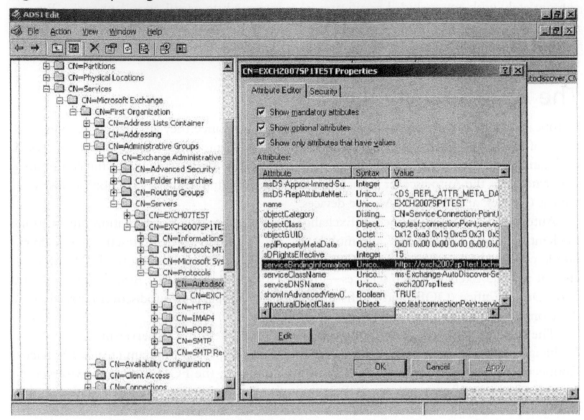

You shouldn't need to configure the SCP information using an LDAP tool since the Exchange Powershell cmdlets will take let you do that while protecting you from making errors, which ADSIEdit or LDP will not do.

# Outlook and Autodiscover

In previous versions of Outlook, when you create a new profile you have to tell it that you're using Exchange Server, provide your mailbox name and mailbox server, verify it is correct, and then proceed. Creating a profile in Outlook 2007 is more of an automatic process; when you log on to a workstation using a mailbox-enabled domain account, and start creating a new Outlook profile, it enters the required fields for you. If everything's configured correctly, you don't need to enter any information at all. Outlook sends an

LDAP query to Active Directory for your mail-related information—after all, it's all there to be gotten if you give it your username and password—and then configures Outlook automatically. Autodiscover uses the domain account or the email address to provide the following information:

- Display name
- Mailbox server
- Outlook Anywhere settings
- Internal and external connection settings
- URLs of servers providing Web services (availability, OAB, etc.)

Outlook invokes the Autodiscover process when you create a new profile, but it also invokes it in other situations:

- **When the application starts** Outlook queries Autodiscover every time it starts up to check for any changes.

- **When it can no longer connect** If Outlook loses connectivity with the mailbox or Web services, it queries Autodiscover for any changes. Note that this will also happen if you move a user's mailbox in Exchange; if the user is logged on, Outlook automatically reconfigures itself and carries on working.

- **Periodically** Outlook polls the Autodiscover service every six hours for any changes

Outlook goes through a number of lookups. The first is the AD lookup, and if it's successful, it stops there since it has the information it needs. If the AD lookup fails (for example, in an Outlook Anywhere scenario), it goes through a number of further lookup attempts, which we will explore.

# Internal Autodiscover Process

To split the process into "internal" and "external" is perhaps a little misleading. Outlook goes through the same process wherever it is; what distinguishes them is where the process succeeds. Once Outlook finds the Autodiscover service, the process is the same inside and out.

The process Outlook goes through to find Autodiscover internally is demonstrated in Figure 4.20.

**Figure 4.20** The AutoConfiguration Process for Internal Clients

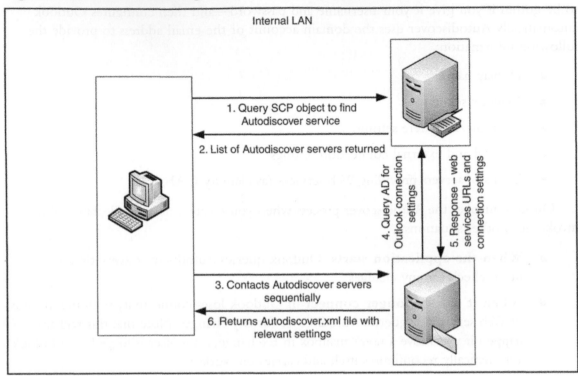

If you have a copy of Outlook running against Exchange 2007, open it and then right-click the Outlook icon in the system tray while holding the Ctrl key. Select **Test Email-AutoConfiguration**. Enter your email address and password, uncheck the Guessmart checkboxes (these are used for POP3/IMAP4), and watch what happens on the Log tab.

1. Outlook sends an LDAP query to an Active Directory server for the Service Connection Point information for the Autodiscover process.

2. The information returned by the DC contains a list of servers that are running the Autodiscover service. Outlook sorts these into two lists, one in its own site and one for those in other sites.

3.  Outlook goes through the first list (the in-site list) and contacts the CAS servers sequentially until one responds. One would hope it would be the first one, but of course, this is for resilience. Outlook provides the user's domain credentials along with the request.

4.  The CAS server uses the credentials to query AD for the user's details listed previously, such as the mailbox server. It returns this information, along with the URLs for other Web services, in an xml file named Autodiscover.xml. Outlook uses this file to configure the profile and ultimately connect to Exchange.

You may wonder why it has to go through all this palaver if the server providing all the services (Autodiscover, Availability, OOF, etc.) is the Client Access server. The CAS server can have any number of FQDNs, internal and external, which may be changing either through reconfiguration or installing/uninstalling servers. In addition, you want to have some amount of load balancing across a larger organization, which adds to the transient nature of the data returned by the Autodiscover service.

The other thing you start to understand during this process is that connecting to Exchange is no longer as simple as pointing Outlook to an Exchange server; Outlook potentially connects to many servers all providing different services.

**NOTE**

For additional considerations when configuring Autodiscover in larger, more complex Exchange deployments, see Chapter 2.

# External Autodiscover Process

When the Outlook client is outside the LAN—in an Outlook Anywhere scenario—it can't connect directly to AD to find the SCPs for Autodiscover, so it has to guess. Actually, the developers had to decide on a few URLs that are able to be published to the outside world or may already be reachable, and so Outlook has a list of URLs it tries when the AD route fails.

The process for finding Autodiscover services is the same, although obviously the outcome is different (Figure 4.21).

**Figure 4.21** The AutoConfiguration Process for Outlook Anywhere Clients

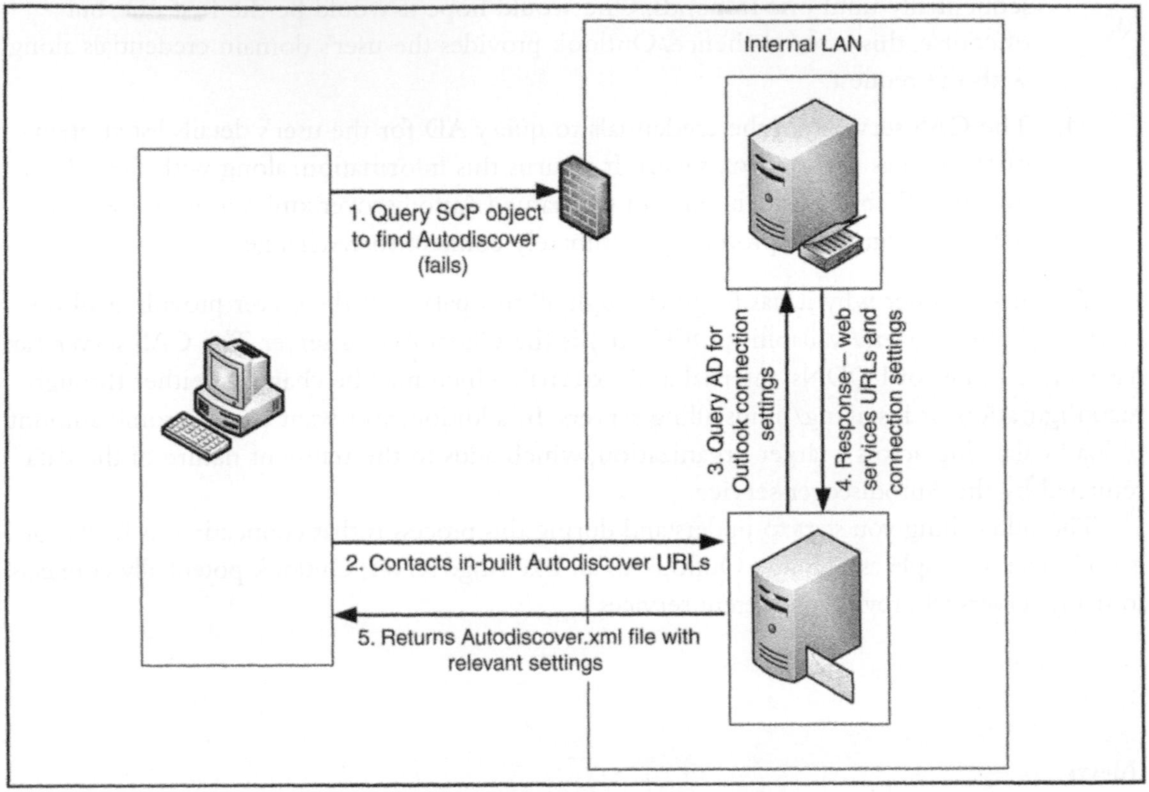

The difference with the external discovery process is that Outlook can no longer use Active Directory to find the URLs of the Autodiscover service. It therefore attempts to contact it by using a number of pre-defined URLs made up from the user's primary SMTP domain.

When a user with the primary email address gordon@lochwallace.com configures Outlook, it will search for the Autodiscover process in the following order:

1.  https://lochwallace.com/autodiscover/autodiscover.xml

2.  https://autodiscover.lochwallace.com/autodiscover/autodiscover.xml

3.  Local autodiscover

4.  http://autodiscover.lochwallace.com/autodiscover/autodiscover.xml

5.  SRV record lookup (a new feature in Outlook 2007 SP1 and the hotfix in KB939184)

> **NOTE**
>
> For internal Outlook 2007 clients it's worth creating the DNS records for the Autodiscover service and for external clients. This way, if Outlook can't find the information via the LDAP lookup (maybe the SCP data is incorrect or not present), it can fall back to the DNS discovery method. Bear in mind, however, that you might want to build some resilience into the process—the SCP process has it built in since it returns the names of a number of servers, whereas a single host (A) record in DNS will point all the Outlook clients to the same server.

## Autodiscover Scalability

The Autodiscover process is quite intelligent in that it will provide URLs to the Web services that correspond to the site the client is attached to. However, when looking up Autodiscover URLs (through the Service Connection Points in Active Directory), Outlook 2007 isn't too clever and randomly selects one of the possibly many Autodiscover servers in the organization. This can be rectified by setting Site Affinity on each Service Connection Point (SCP).

However, whereas internal clients receive a list of possible Autodiscover servers, external Outlook clients, depending on the publishing method, point toward a single URL, for example https://Autodiscover.lochwallace.com/Autodiscover. In environments with thousands of external users, this connection to the Exchange organization must be resilient and able to manage the traffic this produces.

The Autodiscover publishing sites (where external clients connect to the service from the Internet) can be scaled out if there are multiple SMTP domain names in use. Autodiscover. lochwallace.com and Autodiscover.lochbruce.com can be hosted in different geographical regions according to the geographical spread of the users and companies. If all Autodiscover traffic is coming through the same site, a good option is to use the Web farm load-balancing method with ISA Server 2006 described later in the chapter.

## Publishing Autodiscover to the Outside World

These discovery methods have implications on the way you publish Exchange to the Internet. Ideally, you will want to publish the Autodiscover service through either https://lochwallace. com/autodiscover/autodiscover.xml or https://autodiscover.lochwallace.com/autodiscover/ autodiscover.xml, but it's not always as easy as that.

We've seen how Outlook 2007's Autoconfiguration process works, whether inside or outside the firewall perimeter; the methods Outlook uses to search for the Autodiscover servers and the other Exchange Web services. Inside the LAN, there is no need for special configuration and publishing of this data. (Actually, you may want to configure the Web services internally to provide a more efficient and resilient service, but it does work out of the box.) However, outside the perimeter the process is more manual, and the cause of many a headache for Exchange administrators.

Again, it all revolves around the Autodiscover service. This is the first point of call for Outlook 2007, and as long as Outlook obtains this Autodiscover.xml, you can point it to any published Web service at any address. Before we discuss different methods of publishing the Autodiscover service, however, let's see by what methods Outlook can find it when sitting out in the wild wild Web.

As discussed previously, when outside the company LAN, Outlook uses the following methods to find the Autodiscover service:

- **Pre-defined URLs** Outlook looks to two pre-defined URLs based on the primary SMTP domain of the user (https://domain.com/autodiscover/ autodiscover.xml, etc.).

- **SRV records, using the Outlook hotfix** It is possible to implement an SRV record in Internet DNS, which Outlook will search for when furnished with this hotfix.

- **Local Autodiscover xml file** A manual configuration method, Outlook can be configured to look to an autodiscover.xml file stored locally on the client machine. This is applicable to Internet email such as Web, POP3, and IMAP4, as opposed to Exchange.

There are a number of ways to make it available to Internet clients. It seems to be the case that the easiest methods cost the most money, and the sneakiest, more interesting methods involve more administrative pain. We'll explore each method and its advantages and drawbacks.

# Methods of Publishing Outlook Anywhere and Autodiscover (with ISA Server 2006)

"With ISA Server 2006" is in brackets because most of this discussion—and indeed the book—concerns ISA Server 2006. For all its advantages and excellent features, ISA is the weakest link in the chain when it comes to this subject, and the reason we are discussing all of these publishing methods.

The first method is the easiest—using a certificate with Subject Alternative Names (SAN). However, ISA Server does not yet support SAN certificates, so the rest of the list is methods that get around this fact.

- **Use a Subject Alternative Name certificate** This allows you to publish multiple services on a single IP address as it does away with the single IP-to-FQDN relationship when using SSL.

- **Use unencrypted HTTP** Perhaps not the most secure or politically attractive method, but possible nonetheless.

- **Use an Autodiscover SRV record** Relies on a DNS lookup by Outlook to find the address of the Autodiscover service.

- **Autodiscover service with redirection** This neat method enables you to redirect Outlook to an alternative FQDN of your choice in order to pick up the Autodiscover information.

- **Publish Autodiscover on a separate IP address and listener** This is preferable if you have IP addresses to spare since it simplifies the setup in the configuration stage and makes it easier for others to understand how it has been configured.

- **Use a wildcard certificate** An alternative to the SAN certificate method is to use a wildcard certificate that is valid for all FQDNs with the same domain name.

- **Publish everything using autodiscover.lochwallace.com** Although nice and simple to implement, politically not the best option.

## Use a Subject Alternative Name Certificate

Using an X.509 v3 certificate with additional domain names specified in the SAN field enables you to publish multiple domain names through a single IP address with applications and appliances that support them. Unfortunately, ISA Server does not yet support this, and there is no word on when it might.

## Unencrypted HTTP

It is of course possible to publish Autodiscover using an unencrypted channel. Without the restrictions inherent in using an SSL certificate, you can publish almost as many Web sites as you want on a single IP address. Because the Autodiscover service requires authentication, this would likely mean the transport of your credentials in plain text, which would be a hard one to get past the security guys. It may be possible to use NTLM authentication, which does not exchange the actual password, but the Autodiscover information would still be unencrypted.

## SRV Record-based Autodiscover

To alleviate some of the problems with publishing the Autodiscover service, Microsoft came out with a (pre-SP1) hotfix for Outlook 2007 that introduces a new method for Outlook to find Autodiscover—a DNS service record. An Outlook 2007 installation with this hotfix applied will check for the standard URLs, and check Internet DNS for a SRV record relating to Autodiscover for that domain. Specifically, it checks for the entry _autodiscover._tcp.lochwallace.com to find a pointer to the server providing the service. To provide the record for Outlook, you use the following parameters in the lochwallace.com zone:

**Service:** _autodiscover

Protocol: _tcp

Port Number: 443

**Host:** mail.lochwallace.com

Outlook ascertains from this record that it should look to the following address for autodiscover:

https://mail.lochwallace.com/autodiscover/autodiscover.xml

Pointing Outlook to the same FQDN as the Outlook Anywhere connection allows you to publish both Autodiscover and Outlook Anywhere through the same single IP address. The one drawback to this process is that because it is essentially a Web redirect, Outlook will warn and check with you that it is okay to do so, by means of a dialog box. The user can, however, specify that the warning should not appear again, which eases the pain for the end user (Figure 4.22).

**Figure 4.22** The User Is Presented with a Confirmation Dialog Box

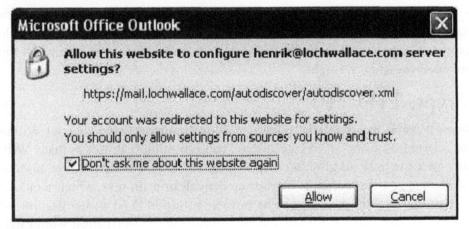

This method of Autodiscover comes under the bracket of "If you are able to use it" rather than "If you want to." There are a number of potential show-stoppers with this method:

- **Your DNS provider or ISP may not support SRV records** It is quite common, especially with free DNS services, that you are provided with Host, MX, and CNAME records only through your Internet DNS host. One option would be to change this host.

■ **Proxy clients have problems resolving SRV records** Particularly CERN proxy and earlier SOCKS proxy clients will not be able to resolve SRV records. This poses a major problem for the traveling workforce if they are using a customer's wireless LAN connection, for example, as this will likely be served behind a proxy server over which you have no control. And who knows what kind of proxy arrangements mobile providers have for their walled gardens!

# Autodiscover HTTP Redirect

The Exchange Product Team must have predicted the hassle there was going to be around publishing Exchange, particularly around certificates, because they threw us a lifeline—the HTTP redirect. Among all of the checks Outlook makes for https-this and https-that, it also has a little look to see if anything is listening on http-port 80. You may be thinking that it's not a very secure method of doing anything, particularly in a secure world such as Exchange publishing, but read on.

This little check for an unencrypted Web site gives us a lot of flexibility, and here's how: When configuring Outlook Anywhere publishing in ISA Server 2006, only one certificate can be assigned to an IP-address/port pair (for example, you might configure port 443 on 192.168.1.5 and assign a certificate with the name mail.lochwallace.com on this address). Since usually the main publishing rule is going to be something like "mail.lochwallace.com" since it's a nice easy name for users to remember, when it comes to publishing "Autodiscover. lochwallace.com" you need to assign it a second IP address, since it's looking for this on port 443.

You could assign "autodiscover.domain.com" the same IP address as "mail.domain.com," but this would fail because of the certificate dependencies. You can also create a second IP address and certificate and do it that way, as discussed previously. However, we can also redirect this request to http://Autodiscover.lochwallace.com/ to somewhere more meaningful— https://mail.lochwallace.com/.

The process goes like this:

1. Outlook checks the secure Web sites (https://lochwallace.com... and https:// Autodiscover.lochwallace.com...).

   ■ The connection fails.

2. Outlook checks the unsecured Web site (http://Autodiscover.lochwallace.com).

   ■ Outlook is redirected to https://mail.lochwallace.com/Autodiscover/ Autodiscover.xml

   ■ The connection succeeds.

Outlook doesn't mind going to a different address to reach the Autodiscover service, and sending it to the same address where the RPC, ActiveSync, and possibly OWA connections are served makes a lot of sense since this site is already configured with a certificate and will accept the connection.

In the Lochwallace environment, mail.lochwallace.com is published under 192.168.1.5 and with its certificate named "mail.lochwallace.com." Port 443 is being used on this address, but port 80 isn't so we want to point "Autodiscover.lochwallace.com" to the same IP address as mail.lochwallace.com and open port 80. Figure 4.23 shows the process involved.

**Figure 4.23** Outlook Is Redirected to Someone Who'll Listen

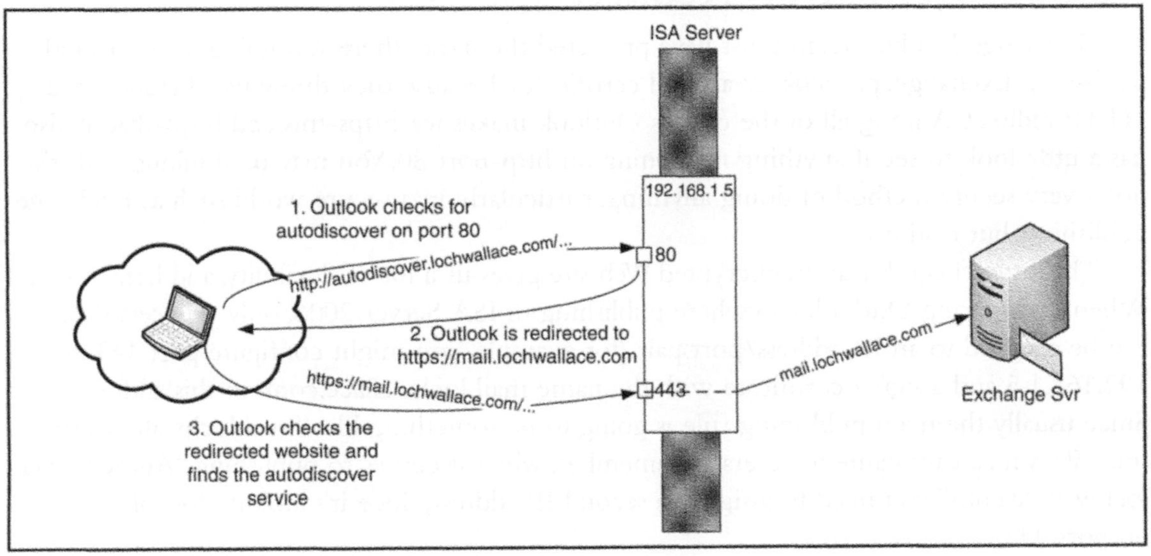

The trick is that the DNS records for mail.lochwallace.com and autodiscover.lochwallace.com point to the same IP address (192.168.1.5) so it's just a port-redirection in effect.

## Creating the Autodiscover Redirect

To create the Web redirect in ISA Server 2006 is relatively straightforward:

1. Create a Deny rule using the Web Publishing Rule Wizard with the following settings:

| Action | Deny |
|---|---|
| Connection Security | Non-secured (port 80) |
| Internal Site Name | This doesn't matter (it's not directing requests to an internal site) |
| Path | /Autodiscover/Autodiscover.xml* |

**Continued**

| Action | Deny |
| --- | --- |
| Domain Name | Autodiscover.lochwallace.com |
| Web Listener | IP Address—192.168.1.5<br>Port 80<br>No Authentication |
| Delegation | None |

\* You only need to specify a path if you are publishing other sites on this address; otherwise, leave it blank.

2. Open the new rule, and on the Action tab select **Redirect HTTP requests** and enter the new URL—**https://mail.lochwallace.com/autodiscover/ autodiscover.xml** (Figure 4.24).

**Figure 4.24** Configuring the Redirect URL

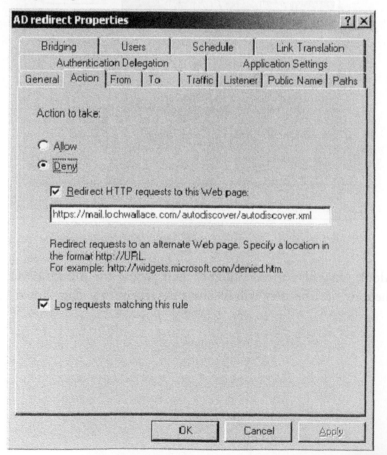

3.  Add the required extra "path" parameter to the existing mail.lochwallace.com publishing rule (Figure 4.25).

**Figure 4.25** Getting the Rule to Respond to /Autodiscover/* Requests

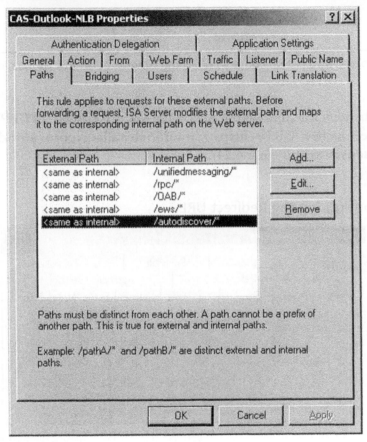

When Outlook Anywhere users configure their profile, the Autodiscovery process will be redirected to the new site and they will receive the security warning shown in Figure 4.26.

**Figure 4.26** Outlook Warns You that You're Going to a Different Web Site

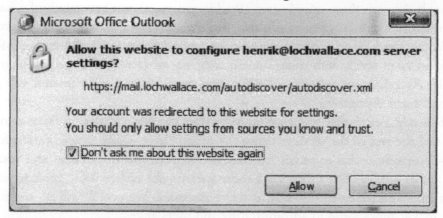

So users do not have to click **Allow** every time they open Outlook, or any other time Outlook checks with the Autodiscover service, you can tell it not to warn you again about that particular Web site. Just as well, as if this wasn't an option we suspect it wouldn't be a very inviting prospect for most users!

## Redirects for Additional Domains

Your organization may have more than one SMTP address acting as the primary address for users, particularly if you are hosting Exchange for many companies. In this case, if you need to make Autodiscover available for the lochbruce.com users as well, you simply add them to the same redirect rule. Moreover, you can have any number of domains on the single redirect.

To add additional Autodiscover domains:

1. Create a DNS record to point Autodiscover.domain.com to the external address of the ISA server.

2. In the Autodiscover redirect rule, add Autodiscover.domain.com to the list of addresses to which the rule will respond (in the Public Name tab).

With the HTTP redirect, it is possible to publish all of the Exchange Web protocols and Autodiscover for multiple domains on a single IP address. Great if you're hosting your and your brother's email domains on your home ADSL connection, for example!

## Using a Separate IP Address and Listener

Despite fears that the IPv4 address range has until around 2011 to survive until all the addresses are gobbled up, in most cases a company will be able to utilize two public IP addresses for use with publishing Exchange services. If they need any gentle persuasion, remind them what they are getting—Outlook Web Access, Exchange ActiveSync, and

Outlook Anywhere. In addition, with ISA it is easy to publish IMAP, POP, SMTP, and many other protocols through these miserly two IP addresses, so it's not too much of a hardship.

In this section, we discuss publishing the "big three" (OWA, Outlook Anywhere, and Exchange ActiveSync) using a few configurations around the two IP address method since we are, in most cases, stuck with using two IP addresses externally. The only ways out of that are to use the Autodiscover redirect or SRV record methods, and to be honest you probably want to avoid them if possible.

In the following examples, we're going to publish the Autodiscover service using one IP address, and the rest of the services using the other. There is one simple reason for this: the Autodiscover service has to sit on "autodiscover.yoursmtpdomain.com" and you want to publish the other services like OWA on a more meaningful address like "mail.domain.com."

Okay, it doesn't have to be this way, as we've discussed, but you'll find it's much easier and usually makes more sense to administrators and users alike.

## Using Two Publishing Rules

Consider Figure 4.27. Here we use two publishing rules to publish everything we need. Mail.lochwallace.com (the one with the name that makes sense to users) takes care of the connections where the user is likely to have to enter the FQDN, such as OWA and possibly Exchange ActiveSync. The second rule, autodiscover.lochwallace.com, is determined by the default Outlook Autoconfiguration settings, although luckily the user should never need to know about it.

**Figure 4.27** Publishing Exchange through Two Publishing Rules

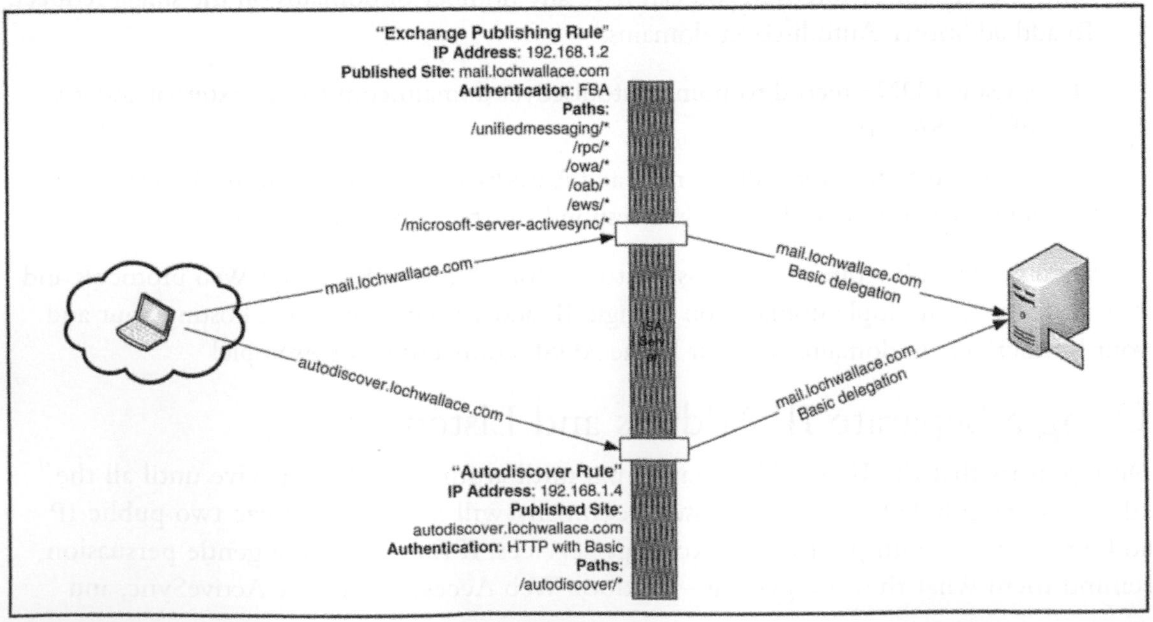

This configuration is set up using standard Exchange publishing rules. One rule uses one listener that has one certificate attached, making it relatively easy to set up, and more importantly easy for somebody else to understand. Simple configurations are good in ISA, as it's sometimes very difficult to go onto a server that somebody else has set up and figure out what is going on.

The rule settings are listed here.

| Rule | Exchange Publishing Rule |
|---|---|
| To | mail.lochwallace.com (Published Site) |
| Public Name(s) | mail.lochwallace.com |
| Paths | /rpc/*<br>/owa/*<br>/OAB/*<br>/microsoft-server-activesync/*<br>/ews/* |
| Auth Deleg | Basic Authentication |
| **Listener:** | |
| Networks, Certificates | 192.168.1.2<br>mail.lochwallace.com |
| Authentication | FBA with Windows (Active Directory) |

| Rule | Autodiscover Rule |
|---|---|
| To | autodiscover.lochwallace.com (Published Site)<br>mail.lochwallace.com (Computer Name) |
| Public Name(s) | Autodiscover.lochwallace.com |
| Paths | /autodiscover/* |
| Auth Deleg | Basic authentication |
| **Listener:** | |
| Networks, Certificates | 192.168.1.4<br>autodiscover.lochwallace.com |
| Authentication | Basic |

# Using a Single Publishing Rule

Although two IP addresses and two certificates are required for this setup, you can also consolidate the published services into a single rule. Figure 4.28 shows the configuration for such a rule.

**Figure 4.28** Publishing Autodiscover and Other Services through a Single ISA Rule

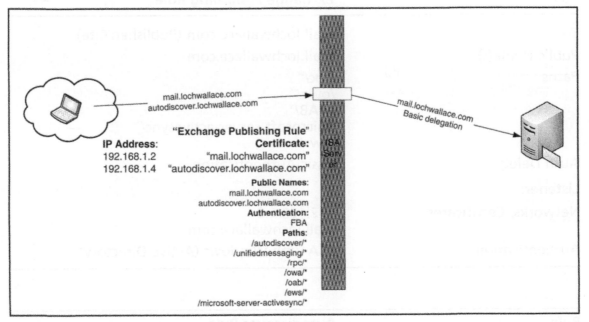

The rule settings are:

| Rule | Exchange Publishing Rule |
| --- | --- |
| To | autodiscover.lochwallace.com (Published Site)<br>mail.lochwallace.com (Computer Name) |
| Public Name(s) | Autodiscover.lochwallace.com<br>Mail.lochwallace.com |
| Paths | /rpc/*<br>/owa/*<br>/OAB/*<br>/microsoft-server-activesync/*<br>/ews/*<br>/autodiscover/* |
| Auth Deleg | Basic Authentication |

**Continued**

| Rule | Exchange Publishing Rule | |
|------|--------------------------|---|
| **Listener:** | | |
| Networks, Certificates | 192.168.1.2 mail.lochwallace.com | 192.168.1.4 autodiscover.lochwallace.com |
| Authentication | FBA with Windows (Active Directory) | |

---

**NOTE**

The "Published Site" value can correspond to any one of the server names listed under "Public Name."

---

This setup works just as well as that with two ISA rules and looks slightly tidier in the ISA Rule Set page—just one rule to publish all of your Exchange services, neat. However, it is slightly more complex and potentially confusing for other administrators.

The difference here from a standard two-rule setup is in the Autodiscover rule. In this example, we are publishing Autodiscover using the same CAS server as for mail.lochwallace.com, so the traffic to both listeners is going to the same internal server. Hence, we use the mail.lochwallace.com certificate to encrypt the traffic from the Autodiscover listener to the published server (Figure 4.29). When you configure the Autodiscover rule, direct the traffic to an alternative internal server; in this case, mail.lochwallace.com. The FQDN you insert here must correspond to the certificate on the CAS server; otherwise, Autodiscover will fail and will return a generic 0x80004005 error in Outlook's "Test E-mail AutoConfiguration" utility.

**Figure 4.29** Redirecting Traffic

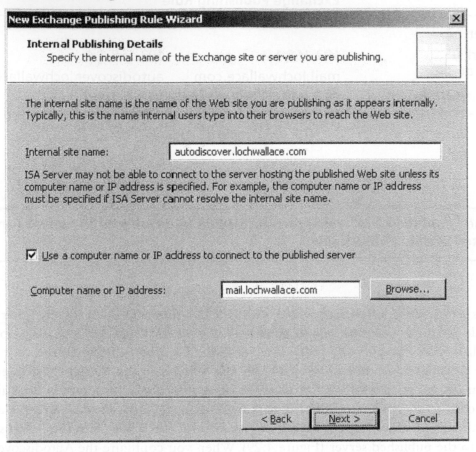

In the ISA rule configuration pages, this translates to Figure 4.30.

**Figure 4.30** "Autodiscover" Redirected to "Mail"

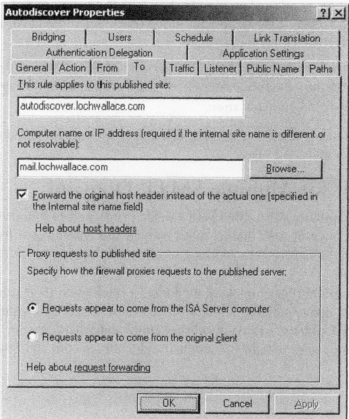

Besides ease of use, there are a number of additional reasons you might have for splitting the services into separate rules:

**SSL offloading versus bridging** SSL offloading terminates the SSL connection at the ISA server, and the traffic between ISA and the published server is unencrypted. Most security specialists will tell you this is a bad idea, unless the internal traffic is encrypted using another method; for example you are using IPsec across your network. Bridging is the standard method where the ISA server decrypts, inspects, and then encrypts the traffic again using the published Web server's certificate.

**The destination (published) server is different** If your internal Exchange server configuration is such that each CAS server is providing a specific service, you might need to forward Autodiscover traffic to CAS1, ActiveSync to CAS2, etc. This may be the case in larger environments where you want to specify roles or even just separate traffic for some reason.

**Different client authentication (or validation) method** Because the client authentication method is tied to the listener, if you want to break out, say, Outlook

Anywhere to use NTLM authentication, you will need to put it on its own rule/listener/IP. As mentioned previously, there isn't the same conflict between FBA and Basic, as ISA 2006 is clever enough to recognize when the client can't use forms and default to Basic for those clients.

**Authentication delegation** Not all services accept all the available types of authentication. Exchange ActiveSync, for example, accepts only Basic and Certificate-based authentication.

There are of course a few other reasons such as user groups and schedule, which are easily visible in the publishing rules.

# Autodiscover for Multiple SMTP Domains

So, what about organizations that don't have a single primary SMTP domain configured? How about those big companies that have just merged and consolidated Exchange orgs while still providing lochbruce.com addresses to some employees and lochwallace.com addresses to the rest?

At present, the Lochbruce employees are going to crack open their spanking new 3G-enabled laptops, open Outlook 2007 for the first time, create a new profile by entering their primary SMTP address "fergus@lochbruce.com," and what happens? Outlook's Autodiscovery process goes straight to autodiscover.lochbruce.com and obviously doesn't find it.

**NOTE**

When referring to the FQDNs Outlook looks up using the Autodiscovery process, we refer only to "https://autodiscover.domain.com" rather than "https://domain.com" because in practice it is much more likely that you will be publishing Autodiscover through the former address. Bear in mind that there are a number of addresses Outlook attempts to contact, and therefore a number of options for you, as detailed earlier.

Because the organization now handles additional primary SMTP domains, these domains have to be added to the Autodiscover publishing infrastructure. For each additional SMTP domain, we require:

- An FQDN (autodiscover.newdomain.com)
- An IP address corresponding to the FQDN
- A certificate with the Subject Name corresponding to the FQDN

Thanks to the wonders of the ISA 2006 listeners, we can create a single listener to respond on multiple IP addresses with a different certificate for each IP, as in Figure 4.31. This means that potentially we can use a single listener and a single Web publishing rule to listen on all three of the required addresses:

- mail.lochwallace.com

- autodiscover.lochwallace.com

- autodiscover.lochbruce.com

This has the potential to be messy…

**Figure 4.31** Configuring All IP Addresses on the Same Listener

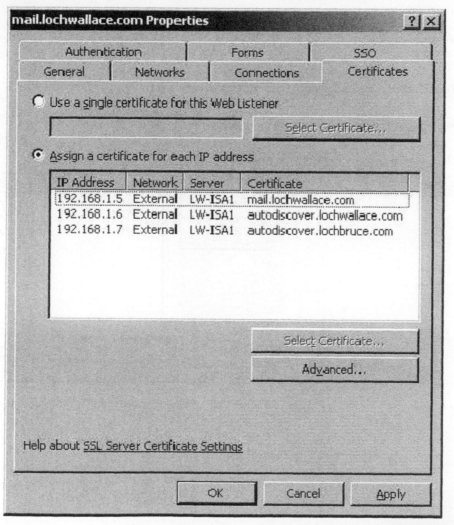

In fact, it is relatively simple to have the main Web publishing Web site (mail.lochwallace. com) and the autodiscover addresses (autodiscover.lochwallace.com and autodiscover. lochbruce.com) on the same listener and rule. From the starting point of the consolidated rule we discussed earlier, we simply need to add the second autodiscover address to the mix.

First, we have to assign the IP address to the ISA Server as in Figure 4.32 (you may have to reboot for it to take effect), add the FQDN "autodiscover.lochbruce.com" to DNS, and create a certificate with the Subject Name "autodiscover.lochbruce.com."

**Figure 4.32** First You Have to Add the New IP Address to the Listener

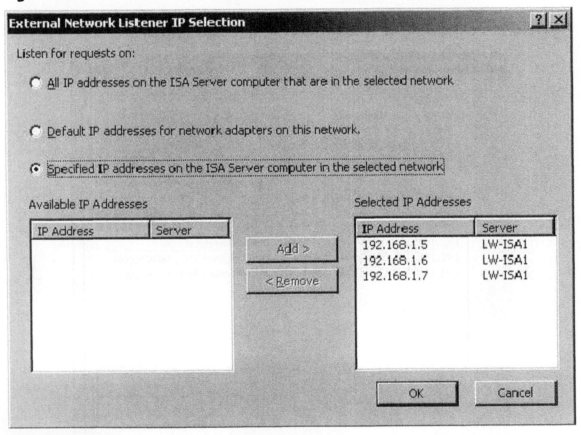

Importing the certificate into the ISA server will allow us to assign it to the 192.168.1.7 address. The only remaining thing to change is to add the new address to the "Public Name" tab on the rule. This will ensure that it picks up requests to that FQDN (Figure 4.33). You can of course configure the rule to listen to all requests—to listen on any address/FQDN—but you then have to disable link translation.

**Figure 4.33** Add the New Autodiscover FQDN to the Rule

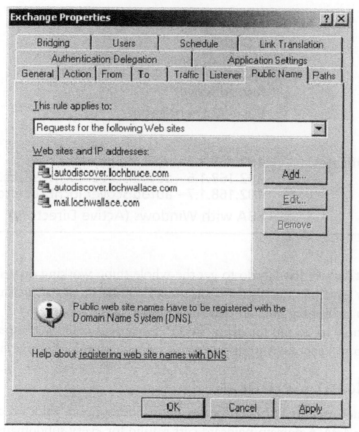

In summary, the rule will have the following settings:

| Rule | Exchange Publishing Rule |
| --- | --- |
| To | autodiscover.lochwallace.com (Published Site)<br>mail.lochwallace.com (Computer Name) |
| Public Name(s) | Mail.lochwallace.com<br>Autodiscover.lochwallace.com<br>Autodiscover.lochbruce.com |
| Paths | /rpc/*<br>/owa/*<br>/OAB/*<br>/microsoft-server-activesync/*<br>/ews/*<br>/autodiscover/* |
| Auth Deleg | Basic Authentication |
| **Listener:** | |
| Networks, Certificates | 192.168.1.5 - mail.lochwallace.com<br>192.168.1.6 - autodiscover.lochwallace.com, and<br>192.168.1.7 - autodiscover.lochbruce.com |
| Authentication | FBA with Windows (Active Directory) |

That's it. That's all we have to do to get the whole thing working on a single listener and rule. We now have one rule listening on three IP addresses and using three certificates to serve the main publishing site and two autodiscover sites.

Now, if you have to do this for many SMTP domains, it could get quite complicated, so it's a good idea to keep the Autodiscover sites separate, running on one or more rules.

## Use a Wildcard Certificate

ISA Server may not support SAN certificates, but it does support wildcard certificates such as the one in Figure 4.34. A domain wildcard cert is valid for every subdomain you care to use, so an ISA server with a certificate named "*.lochwallace.com" will accept connections to mail., autodiscover., and anything else you care to throw at it.

**Figure 4.34** A Wildcard Web Server Certificate for Publishing with ISA Server

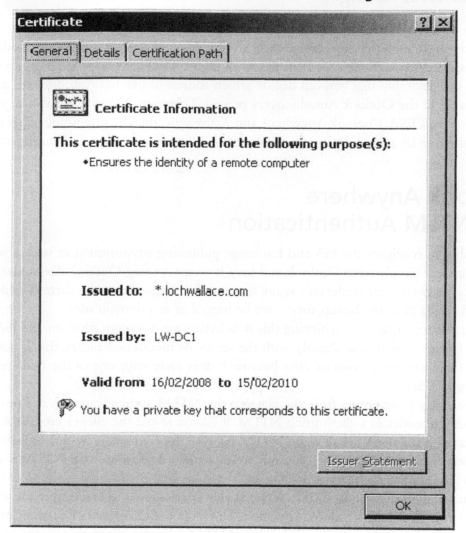

Wildcard certificates are easy to create using your internal certification authority, so if you are employing solely internal certificates in your environment it may be a viable option. However, they tend to be rather expensive when purchased from a commercial authority.

Unfortunately, Windows Mobile 5.0 and earlier does not support wildcard certificates. However, you can work around this by disabling certificate checking on the device (which also enables the use of self-signed certificates), but this is not recommended in production environments.

## Publish Everything
## Using autodiscover.domain.com

Possibly the least attractive available method would be to publish all of the services through autodiscover.lochwallace.com, for example. With the FQDNs for OWA and ActiveSync, you have the flexibility that you can decide which address to use, but Autodiscover is rather fixed because of the Outlook Autodiscovery process. Therefore, it's quite possible to use this address also for OWA, Outlook Anywhere, and ActiveSync, thereby publishing all of them through the one IP address. This may not be terribly attractive to users and management, however.

# Outlook Anywhere
# and NTLM Authentication

It is possible to configure the ISA and Exchange publishing environment in such a way that laptop users can simply open Outlook and have it connect using Outlook Anywhere, without having to enter their credentials again. Because this method uses the cached credentials they used to log in to the laptop, they must be logged in as a domain user.

The previous method of achieving this is to bypass pre-authentication on the ISA server and have clients authenticate directly with the server. As mentioned earlier, this is not the best idea from a security point of view because it does away with one of the main reasons for having ISA Server.

The sticking point comes from the fact that the NTLM authentication is not proxyable. When ISA authenticates a client using NTLM, it cannot re-use the client's credentials to then authenticate on the user's behalf using NTLM because the credentials are never disclosed to the ISA server using NTLM. The only way to implement delegation with NTLM is to use Kerberos Constrained Delegation (KCD).

Authentication delegation in ISA Server is rule-specific, so you can simply use an additional rule to publish Outlook Anywhere. However, the client authentication method is listener-specific, and because it needs to use NTLM with the client, this means creating a new listener and an additional IP address.

To configure Outlook Anywhere with NLTM and KCD, you have to configure the environment:

1. **Configure ISA Server 2006 to use Kerberos Constrained Delegation as the authentication delegation method** The ISA server must use KCD to impersonate the authenticated user and authenticate on his behalf. The SPN specified must match one of the SPNs for which ISA is trusted for delegation (Figure 4.35).

**Figure 4.35** Easy to Set Up, Hard to Troubleshoot

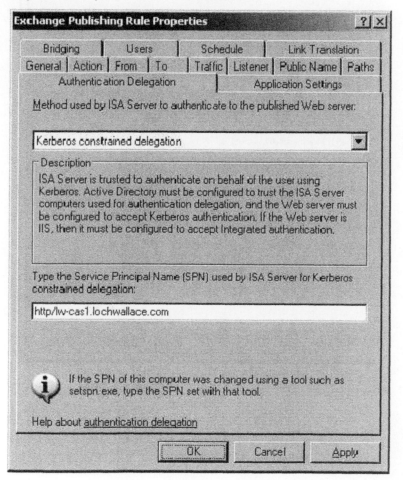

2. **Configure Outlook Anywhere on the CAS server** Exchange allows you to specify NTLM and/or Basic as the client authentication method for Outlook Anywhere. You must specify NTLM in the Outlook Anywhere properties of the CAS server (Figure 4.36).

**Figure 4.36** If These Settings Are Not Correct...

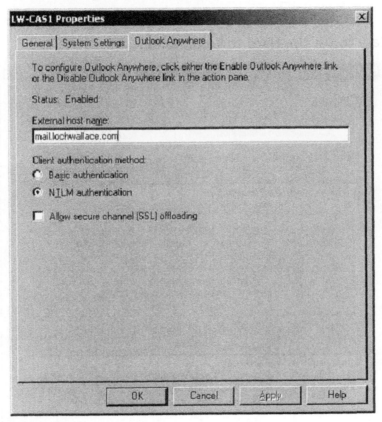

3. **Register the SPN records for the Client Access servers** Check that the SPN for the target service (HTTP) has been registered in Active Directory using the SetSPN tool (included in the Support Tools on the Windows Server 2003 CD). Normally, Exchange setup will register the Service Principal Name for the client access server at install time. If not, you can use SetSPN to register the appropriate services and names. Figure 4.37 shows a query of registered services on the server LW-CAS1.

**Figure 4.37** Verify the SPN Entries

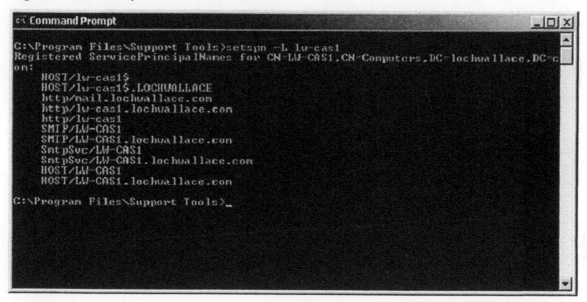

The SPN is used in by ISA Server 2006 for requesting a Kerberos service ticket for delegation.

4. **Configure delegation trust for the ISA server** The ISA server must be configured in AD as trusted for Kerberos constrained delegation, and restricted (constrained) to the SPN of the target service on the Client Access server. This is done in Active Directory Users and Computers as shown in Figure 4.38.

**Figure 4.38** Configuration Delegation Trust for the ISA Server

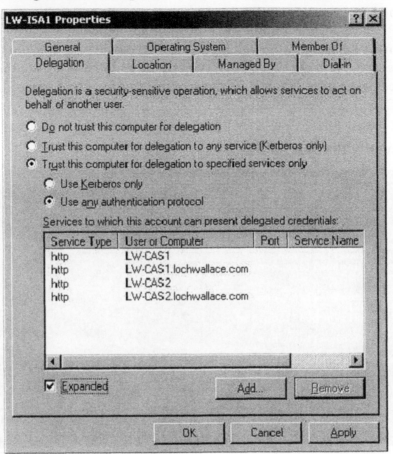

5. **Configure Outlook to use NTLM authentication**  In the Exchange account settings in Outlook you must specify NTLM as the authentication method (Figure 4.39).

**Figure 4.39** The Method on the Client Must Correspond with that on the Server Side

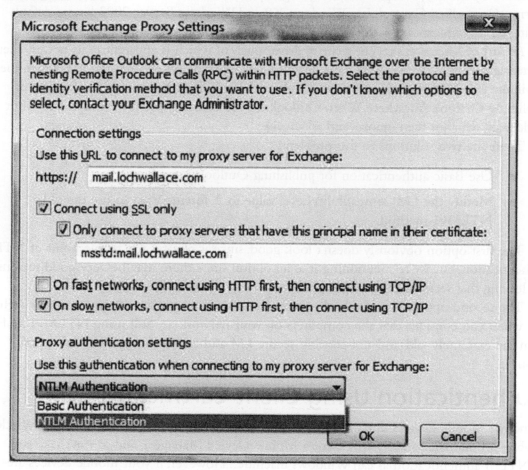

Other requirements for KCD to work include:

- The user must have a valid AD account.
- The ISA server must be in the same domain as the target CAS server.
- The AD domain must be set to Windows Server 2003 functional level. The test environment will be in Windows 2000 functional level when first created.

# Windows Vista and NTLM Security

You can tell from the silly window transparency that Figure 4.39 is from a Windows Vista client. There is one more important thing to mention when configuring NTLM authentication with Windows Vista clients: LanManager Compatibility (LMCompatibilityLevel).

Windows clients behave differently when passing NTLM-based credentials, which is governed by the LMCompatibilityLevel registry key that sits in HKLM\SYSTEM\ CurrentControlSet\Control\Lsa. Windows XP and Windows Server 2003 have a default setting of "2," which means the client will use NTLM authentication only.

As part of Microsoft's recent security drive, much of which is apparent in its newest client operating system, Windows Vista has a default LMCompatibilityLevel setting of 3, which means it will use *only* NTLMv2. This is all well and good, but it doesn't work in our situation of publishing Outlook Anywhere. When Outlook tries to connect, you are prompted for your credentials, which it then ignores and asks again.

There are two solutions to this problem:

- Use Basic authentication for publishing Outlook Anywhere.

- Modify the LMCompatibilityLevel value to 2, forcing Vista to use the older NTLMv1 method.

The first option obviously doesn't look good, since it negates the whole point of NTLM authentication, but we're mentioning it as an option since there may be very good reasons for leaving that security registry entry alone.

The second option is probably the favored option. Sure, you're lowering security slightly, but when you consider that the computers on your network are still using NTLMv1 and even the extremely-old-and-not-terribly-secure LM authentication, you needn't worry about it.

# Authentication Using Client Certificates

Windows Mobile devices don't act as members of the domain (unless you are using Windows Mobile 6.1 and later and System Center Mobile Device Manager), and so can't take part in NTLM authentication as can Windows machines. However, if your mobile devices are running WM5.0 with the Microsoft Security and Feature Pack (part of AKU2) or higher, you can implement better security by using client certificates. With this method, mobile devices authenticate using user SSL certificates instead of the username and password method.

This provides a number of security advantages over Basic authentication:

- **Reduced risk of credentials being compromised** Users cannot loan their passwords on other devices, and credentials are protected by a hash and SSL encryption by default. Keyloggers on public kiosks, for example, are therefore unable to steal the credentials.

- **Device control** Certificates enable you to control which devices can connect to the system, thereby specifying that only managed devices can take part.

- **Provides mutual authentication when using SSL/TLS**  Mutual authentication is a two-way trust between client and server. In one-way authentication, the server provides a certificate the client trusts because the issuing root is in its Trust store. In two-way authentication, the client also has a certificate the server must trust using the same method.

- **Administrator-determined key strength**  The key length can be determined by the administrator, and Windows Server and Windows Mobile support up to 2048-bit keys.

Client certificates can be user or machine certificates stored in the local certificate stores, embedded in a smart card or one used by a mobile device.

To provide the greatest security level possible, the connections should be terminated at the ISA server as before. When delegating credentials provided in client certificates, as with NTLM, the ISA server must use Kerberos Constrained Delegation to authenticate with the published server.

## Client Certificates

The client certificate provides the server with proof of the identity of the connecting user. The certificate may be installed on the device itself or embedded on a smart card, and either method should employ additional protection such as requiring the user to enter a PIN number. In the case of Windows Mobile devices, when used without a certificate but rather just user credentials, these credentials are usually stored within the device by telling the device to save the username and password. The device should therefore be protected by security policy that specifies that the device should lock itself after a period of inactivity. You should also implement this when using client certificates, in case an untrusted party gets a hold of the device.

## Public or Private Certificates

Whether to use a public or private certification authority for distributing client certificates for mobile devices is different from that for published Web servers, for example. When publishing Web servers such as for Outlook Web Access and ActiveSync, the server certificates should be trusted by the client (*must* be trusted in the case of ActiveSync and Outlook Anywhere). Since many clients will be Internet kiosks, for example, which are not members of your domain, using public certification authorities that are trusted by default by the versions of Windows you are using makes a lot of sense.

When distributing client certificates, however, two main factors should be considered:

- **Finance**  Each privately provided certificate costs money. Certificates deployed by an internal Microsoft PKI infrastructure do not.

- **Flexibility** Using an internal CA, the certificates and certificate structure can be changed, clients added when required, and security is increased because of the central control of certificates and certificate roots. An internal CA is usually the best route when you can maintain some control over the mobile devices.

Maintaining a publicly issued certificate on the ISA server and private certificate for ISA to CAS traffic usually offers the best flexibility and cost benefit. This allows you to make changes internally on the ISA and CAS servers without having to reconfigure mobile devices. If you want to use an internal certificate for the ISA server as well, you must install the internal enterprise root certificate on each mobile device. This may be a simple task of opening the certificate on the device, which automatically installs it. However, some mobile operators lock down the operating system to prevent you from installing certificates and running unsigned applications.

**NOTE**

The server certificates on the ISA and CAS servers used to encrypt traffic can be from a public issuing authority, but client certificates must be issued by an internal Microsoft certification authority on the domain in order to provide the required user to certificate mapping.

# Configuring Certificate Security for Mobile Devices

In this section, we'll go through what's required to configure certificate authentication using Windows Mobile 6.0 devices. Without going too deep into the procedures (some of which have been covered earlier in the chapter anyway), we'll discuss the prerequisites and required design aspects of such a configuration.

## Infrastructure

The servers required are included in the lab set up for this chapter. It shares the Kerberos Constrained Delegation requirements with the previous section for NTLM and Outlook Anywhere, so if this has been configured already it is mainly a case of configuring and distributing the certificates (Figure 4.40).

**Figure 4.40** The Configuration for Certificate-based Device Authentication

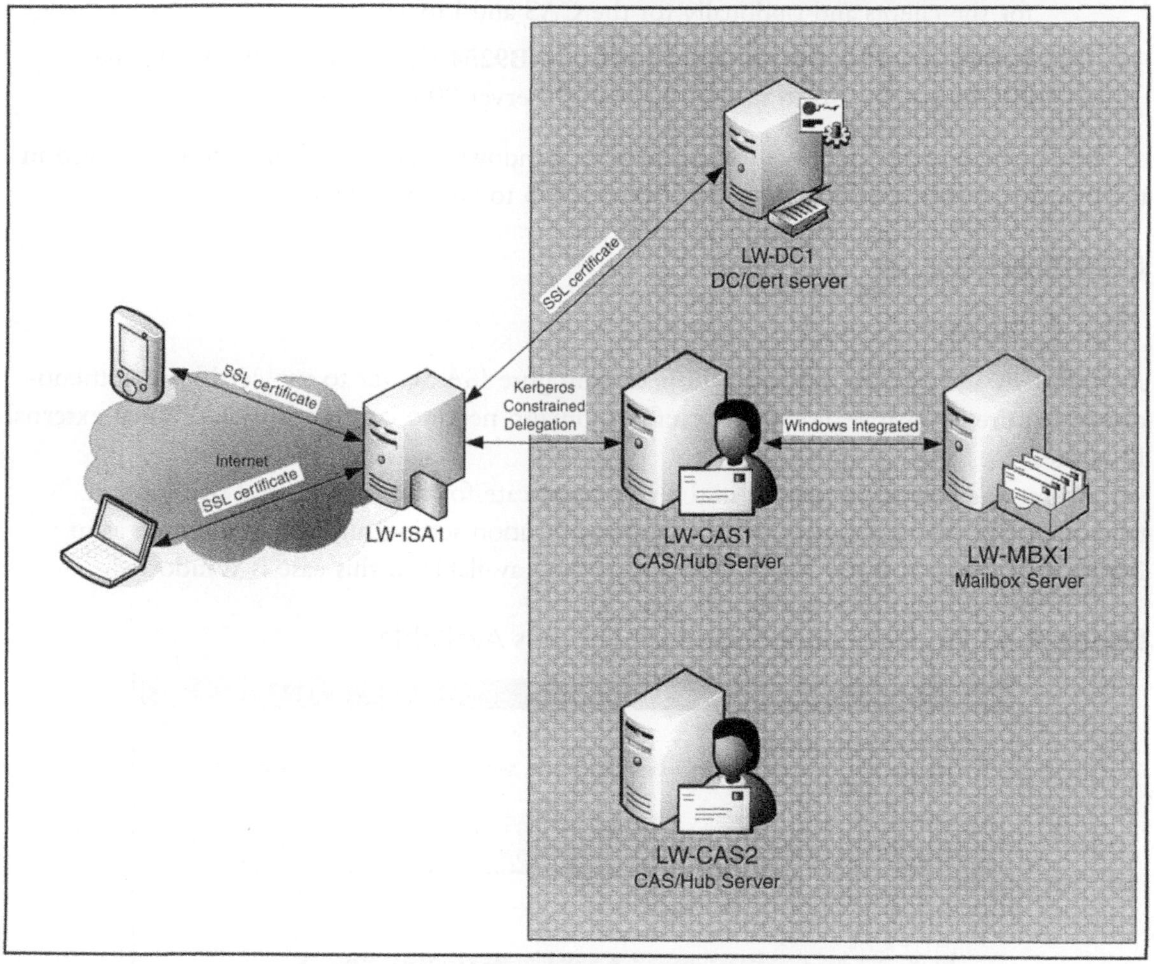

## Prerequisites

Before configuring certificate-based authentication on Windows Mobile devices, check that the existing infrastructure is able to support it. There are a number of prerequisites, most of which are the same as the NLTM-based Outlook Anywhere authentication discussed previously.

1. **Configure the ISA server as a member of the domain**  For KCD to work, the ISA server (as all machines in this scenario) must be in the same domain as the published Exchange servers. ISA Server 2006 supports Kerberos constrained delegation only within a domain boundary.

2. Ensure the domain is in Windows Server 2003 Functional Level.

3. **Implement a PKI infrastructure** This is required to issue internal certificates, for the clients and optionally for the CAS and ISA servers.

4. **Install the ISA Server 2006 hotfix (KB925403)** to update the Exchange Publishing Wizard to include Exchange Server 2007.

In addition, since KCD is a feature new to Windows Server 2003, all servers involved in the process must be running Windows Server 2003 to take part in KCD.

# Configuration

## *Web Listener*

As with ISA and NTLM authentication, to configure ISA Server to use certificate authentication requires a separate listener. Therefore, you also need to configure an additional external IP address for ISA.

Assign an external IP address and server certificate for the listener, and configure it to require SSL secured connections. The authentication setting must be configured as in Figure 4.41. Note that the only validation method available in this case is Windows.

**Figure 4.41** Plenty of Authentication Options Available

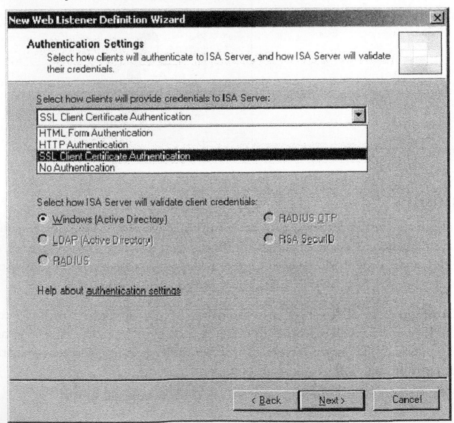

When you finish creating the listener, you receive a warning shown in Figure 4.42. By default, when using client certificates ISA Server will check the incoming certificate against a certificate revocation list (CRL) which is likely hosted on your Enterprise Root CA. To reach the CRL, ISA must have a rule configured to allows that particular type of access (HTTP) to the CRL server. Since it doesn't know what that server is, as such, this enables a system rule that allows HTTP access from the ISA server to all networks. You can narrow this down by editing the system policy to specify the particular hosts or networks you want ISA to be able to access for these CRLs.

**Figure 4.42** Warning about Certificate Revocation List Access

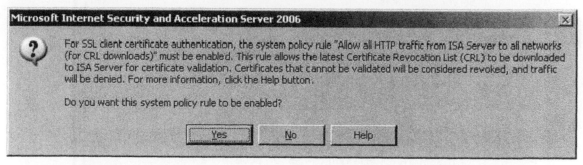

By default, ISA Server 2006 checks a CRL for incoming client and server certificates (Figure 4.43). If it discovers that the certificate is revoked, the connection is denied. Additionally, as the warning tells you, the certificate will also be denied in the event it doesn't find the CRL against which to check, so this is an important aspect to configure correctly.

**Figure 4.43** The Default Revocation Verification Settings

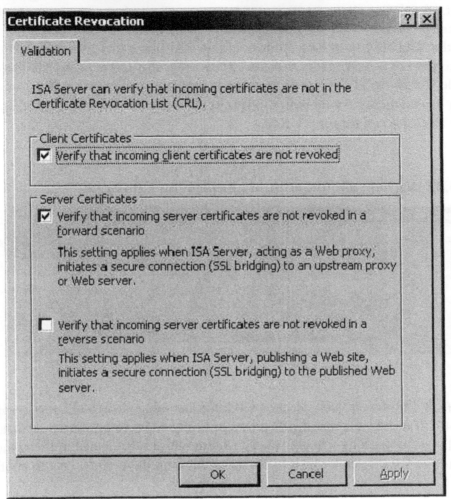

## Publishing Rule

Use the New Exchange Publishing Rule Wizard to create a publishing rule for Exchange ActiveSync. Since the wizard allows you to create the rule for only one specific service, if you want to publish OWA using the same method you can add the appropriate Path tab on the rule after the wizard completes.

When it comes to Authentication Delegation, choose Kerberos constrained delegation. The Service Principal Name you specify here must be correct. When publishing a Web farm (LW-CAS1 and LW-CAS2), enter **http/\*** to specify any of the CAS servers (Figure 4.44).

**Figure 4.44** Setting the Authentication Delegation Properties

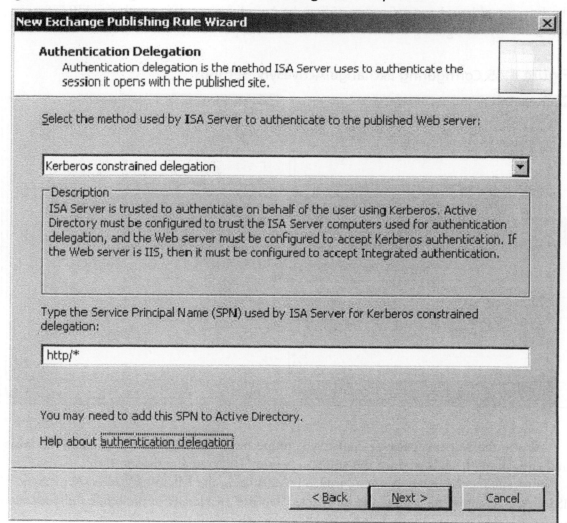

# Kerberos Delegation

To configure the Kerberos delegation part, refer to the previous section detailing NTLM authentication and KCD. The service to configure for delegation (HTTP) is the same as for that of Outlook Anywhere.

# Client Access Server Configuration

The ISA server, when it receives the client certificate, collects a Kerberos ticket for authenticating with the back-end (published) Web server. It then attempts to authenticate with that server using Windows Integrated authentication, so the published server must be configured to accept it.

The External URL field should reflect the address of the CAS server as reachable from the Internet, although apart from providing the Autodiscover service with this URL for automatically configuring mobile devices, it doesn't appear to do much (Figure 4.45).

**Figure 4.45** Configuring Exchange ActiveSync Settings

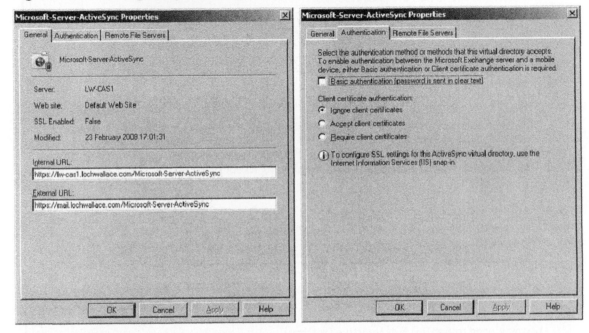

Also in the Microsoft-Server-ActiveSync properties for the CAS server, disable the Basic authentication check box, since this solution is using Integrated authentication.

Integrated authentication is not enabled by default on the Microsoft-Server-ActiveSync ISS virtual directory, so it must also be enabled. Do not enable any of the other authentication methods unless required internally by another service.

# Enrolling Mobile Device Client Certificates

To enroll a Windows Mobile client device and transfer the certificate onto the device, you must use Microsoft ActiveSync (the desktop version). It's not possible to deploy certificates over the air using just Exchange and ISA Server, although it is possible with Microsoft System Center Mobile Device Manager and Windows Mobile 6.1.

To enroll the device you must first connect it to your Windows desktop PC on the domain. The certificate enroll process is done through ActiveSync as follows:

1. With the WM device cradled, under Advanced Tools, start the device certificate tool (Figure 4.46).

**Figure 4.46** Retrieving a Client Certificate Using ActiveSync

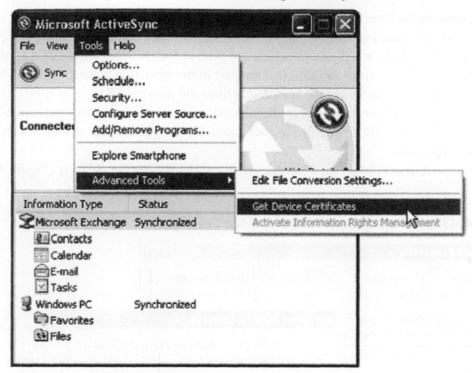

2. Select a User Certificate from the list of Certificate types from Active Directory.

3. Approve and install the certificate from the mobile device and finish the enrollment on the desktop machine.

The process installs the user certificate in the device's certificate store, and the root certificate and any intermediates required to follow the chain up to the root.

---

**NOTE**

Because issuing a certificate from the internal authority also installs the root certificate, if the ISA server is using a server certificate from the same authority, you don't need to distribute the root certificate to the clients separately.

---

## Restrict the Certificates Clients Can Present

For extra security, or if you have a perversely complex security infrastructure that isn't using internal certificates, you can specify that ISA Server allows only certificates issued by certain trusted roots. By default, it will accept certificates from any authorities whose root certificates are in ISA's store. This consists of those that are part of the operating system (such as Microsoft, VeriSign, and the likes) and any root certs added from the internal PKI.

ISA enables you to put further granular restrictions on certificates based on Issuer, Subject, Extensions, and Object ID, so you can restrict access based on certificate authorities and individual certificates.

Certificate restrictions are on a per-listener basis, not per-server, or array (Figure 4.47).

**Figure 4.47** Restricting Certificates by Root Certification Authority

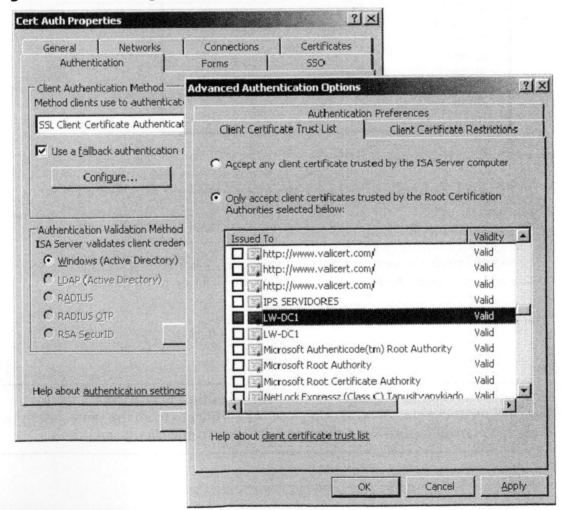

## ActiveSync Policies

Creating and applying an Exchange ActiveSync policy is not necessary in the procedure, but is certainly recommended. ActiveSync policies can enforce password length, device lock timeouts, and other important security settings. ActiveSync policies are created at the Organization level in the console, but are applied to mailbox-enabled users. The console doesn't give you a way to enable a policy for multiple users, so you have to drop down into the shell to do that (Figure 4.48).

**Figure 4.48** You Should Set at Least a Password Policy for ActiveSync

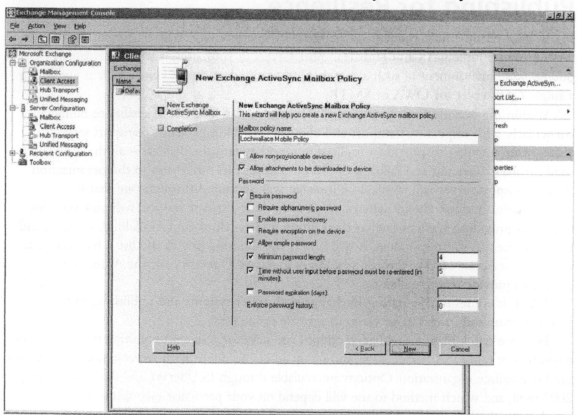

One of the nice features of Windows Mobile 6.1 and Exchange Server 2007 together is the Autodiscover process, which works in much the same way as with Outlook Anywhere. Using this method, a user can provision a device over the air without going to the office to do so. The Exchange server applies the policy, such as password settings, and the ISA server mediates the connection between client and server. No input is required from the administrator apart from perhaps adding the user to whatever list of mobile users they have, but Exchange can provide this information and no interaction is required with the user.

While certificate authentication on mobiles provides greater security, it does require the device to be connected via ActiveSync to a desktop that is a part of the domain. This could of course be a laptop connected via VPN, but it's not quite as flexible as the standard method of using simply a username and password.

Besides bringing the mobile devices into the domain and applying flexible group policy, Microsoft System Center Mobile Device Manager enables over the air (OTA) certificate provisioning, which makes multiple-handset provisioning considerably easier, particularly for larger companies.

# Publishing for Resilience

If you have set up a fully resilient Exchange 2007 environment, with clustered mailbox servers and multiple CAS and Hub Transport servers in your sites, it would be daft to publish your environment in such a way that leaves a single point of failure such as publishing a single CAS server for OWA or SMTP.

Within the organization, Exchange 2007 has a certain amount of resilience built-in, particularly with respect to transport and client access. Multiple Hub Transport servers in a site group together to provide a resilient transport system for that site—all the servers are used for load balancing and fallback of SMTP transport to other sites in the organization. If one transport server is unavailable, a message will be routed through one that is.

Similarly, Outlook clients, when querying the Autodiscover service, will pick up a list of servers providing services such as the Offline Address Book and Availability services, and if one of them is not responding, it will simply use the next one in the list it has received. Each Client Access server registers its services in Active Directory for the Autodiscover service to provide to these clients.

When it comes to integrating Exchange with other systems and publishing to the Internet, extra steps need to be taken to provide resilience.

Here we will look at a number of options you have for resilient publishing of the Exchange environment using ISA Server 2006, and set up an environment with server-resilience based on the Lochwallace organization. Options are available through ISA Server and through Exchange 2007 itself, and which method to use will depend on your particular environment.

## ISA Server Enterprise

Since we're talking about publishing your entire Exchange 2007 environment using ISA Server 2006, we should start by making the ISA layer resilient. There are a number of ways to provide resilience with ISA Server without setting up resilient ISA, as it were. For example, you may have two routes into the organization, as you may well do for SMTP traffic. It is also possible to configure Network Load Balancing with ISA Server Standard servers, although it is not supported and suffers from a limited feature set.

ISA Server 2006 Enterprise, however, allows you to set up an array of servers to work together providing resilience, load balancing, and common configuration. The following are some of the features of ISA Server Enterprise.

## Firewall Arrays

Firewall arrays are a collection of ISA firewall servers that act as a single logical firewall. All the members share the same configuration data, held in the Configuration Storage Server (CSS) database. This allows administrators to configure a policy that will automatically be distributed to each member in the array. The CSS is stored in an Active Directory Application Mode (ADAM) database. This single repository enables you to easily remove and add servers to the array.

You can install the CSS on each ISA server or on a number of separate servers for resilience (Figure 4.49).

**Figure 4.49** Installing the CSS

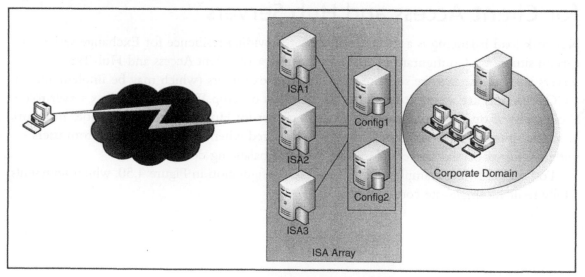

## Network Load Balancing

An array wouldn't be much good without some sort of load balancing. In a dual-homed server configuration, for example, ISA Server Enterprise provides network load balancing (NLB) on both the internal and external interfaces, so both incoming publishing rule traffic and outgoing Web proxy traffic is shared across the array. If one of the nodes becomes unavailable, the rest of the array picks up the traffic with hopefully little or no interruption. The advantage of NLB is that you can publish an Exchange service using a single Internet IP address, but avoid a single point of failure. Of course, if you have other devices in the way, such as Cisco firewalls, you would want to have more than one of them as well. We are not going to delve into NLB for ISA servers here, but you can read about NLB on the ISA Server site (www.microsoft.com/technet/isa/2006/nlb.mspx).

## Enterprise and Array Policies

Enterprise and array policies apply to each member of the array. Like configuration of a cluster resource, you have to modify a rule only once for each ISA server to pick it up and apply it. This centralized administration makes the configuration much easier.

In-depth information on ISA Server 2006 Enterprise can be found on the Microsoft ISA Server Web site (www.microsoft.com/isaserver). For the purposes of publishing Exchange, the configuration is the same as with an ISA Server Standard server, except for the additional networking configuration with an array.

## Network Load Balancing for Client Access and Hub Servers

Network load balancing is a great candidate for providing resilience for Exchange servers in certain situations. Configurations that have a number of Client Access and Hub Transport servers in your site that are separate from the mailbox servers (which may be implemented as a CCR cluster) are a perfect candidate for this kind of setup. When the mailbox server role is also employed on the server running an NLB cluster for Hub Transport, NLB does not work properly since the local server will always be preferred when sending messages from users with a mailbox on that server. Therefore, true load balancing does not occur.

For the following examples, we will use the configuration in Figure 4.50, which represents a fully resilient, single-site configuration.

**Figure 4.50** A Nice Resilient Single-Site Exchange Organization

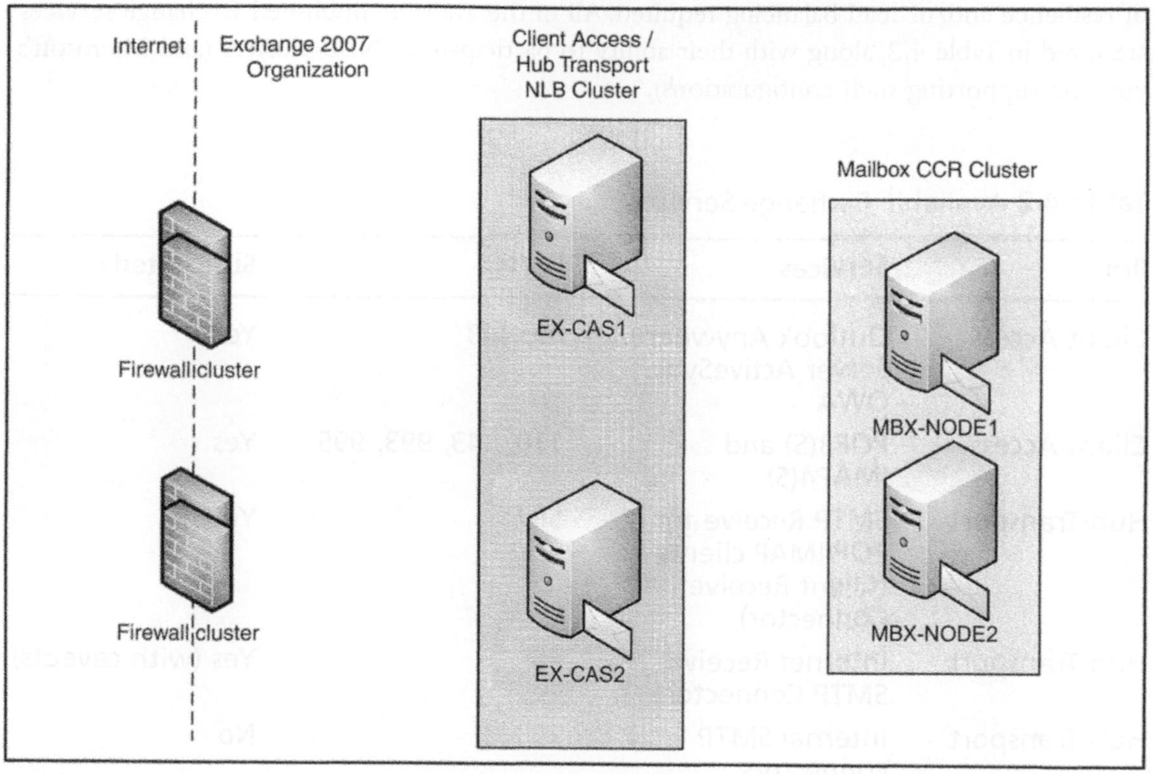

The mailboxes are contained within a dedicated Continuous Cluster Replication (CCR) cluster server at the back. Depending on the environment, CCR clusters may be preferable to Single Copy Cluster (SCC) clusters, as they should provide extra protection against database corruption. (We say, "should" since database corruption can sneak up on you over a number of months or years, and we doubt that CCR would help in this case. In the case of hardware failure or loss of data through a RAID cache or so—immediate corruption—it may help.)

The Client Access and the Hub Transport roles are present on two servers that are also running Network Load Balancing. Services can either participate in the NLB cluster or run standalone—if a service is not specified in the NLB configuration, the servers will run that service as they do in a single server configuration. The services we will include in the NLB configuration depends on other factors that we will look at in this section.

The firewall component is set up to represent two separate points of entry into the organization. The fact that the firewalls are themselves clustered is just to look good and not necessarily required. Clearly, if there is only one point of entry (which is one of the scenarios here), it's better to have clustered firewalls of some sort.

Let's look at each of the services we would like to publish and determine the best form of resilience and/or load balancing required. All of the available published Exchange services are listed in Table 4.2, along with their ability to participate in NLB clusters (and Microsoft's view on supporting such configurations).

**Table 4.2** Available Exchange Services

| Role | Services | Ports | Supported? |
| --- | --- | --- | --- |
| Client Access | Outlook Anywhere, Server ActiveSync, OWA | 80, 443 | Yes |
| Client Access | POP3(S) and IMAP4(S) | 110, 143, 993, 995 | Yes |
| Hub Transport | SMTP Receive for POP/IMAP clients (Client Receive Connector) | 587 | Yes |
| Hub Transport | Internet Receive SMTP Connectors | 25 | Yes (with caveats) |
| Hub Transport | Internal SMTP connectors | 25 | No |

# NLB for Exchange Services, and Their Supportability

Before looking at each Exchange service group and how best to publish these services resiliently, we need to check out what is supported and what will or will not work. Microsoft support for load-balancing Hub Transport servers has changed since SP1 was released, and there is some confusion over what is possible and supported.

Client Access and Hub Transport servers have built-in resilience for certain aspects of their feature-set—some of the protocols they handle have multiple delivery methods built in to the Exchange software. One of these, as we discussed, is SMTP. For protocols such as HTTP, however, there is no in-built resilience, and Web traffic is sent to a single host, which if unavailable, the connection is lost.

Network Load Balancing (NLB) is a feature included in every version of Windows Server 2003 and is used to intelligently distribute traffic between server hosts to balance load and provide failover in case of a server outage. Certain features of the Client Access and Hub Transport roles are supported in an NLB array, and some are not. Table 4.1 shows which services are supported and able to be load-balanced.

# Configuring an NLB CAS and Hub Cluster

Depending on what you want to achieve with the NLB cluster, there are a number of ways to configure it; for example, whether to use dual-network cards, unicast or multicast, etc. For publishing Exchange CAS and Hub servers, however, use the following guidelines:

**Use an additional network card for host-to-host communication** If the cluster is running in unicast mode, because both NLB NICs share the same MAC address, the nodes will not be able to communicate with each other unless they each have a separate NIC for this purpose. It's not ideal to have two Exchange servers that are not able to communicate with each other, so use two network cards.

**Use unicast mode** It isn't a requirement to use unicast over multicast for Exchange; indeed, there don't seem to be any specific recommendations for which mode to use, but unicast is slightly easier to set up. Which mode to use depends more on your network configuration and hardware than anything else.

**Affinity** Assuming we use multiple-host filtering (which allows all the NLB members to service the traffic to a particular port), for our purposes we generally want to use single affinity. Single affinity essentially creates an affinity between a single client IP address and an NLB node. When the first request comes in from the client, it is serviced by a node as determined by the NLB service. Further traffic between the cluster and this client address is serviced thereafter by the same host.

Alternatively, class-C affinity can be employed. Class-C affinity is similar to single affinity, but maps the cluster node with the class-C address range from which the traffic comes. If a client site has multiple proxy servers, traffic traversing the ISA server may come from different source IP addresses, which could break IP-affinity. Assuming all these proxy servers are sitting on the same class-C subnet, clients will keep the same session even if the source address changes.

When you use Outlook Web Access with forms-based authentication, you must use single or class-C affinity. Likewise, with Outlook Anywhere, affinity helps reduce overhead for negotiating SSL connections.

## Notes on Unicast and Multicast

An NLB cluster must be configured as either unicast or multicast. The main difference is in the way MAC addresses are implemented.

**Unicast** Each node uses a shared virtual MAC address for listening to inbound traffic, corresponding to the cluster rather than the node (which has its own MAC address). This can cause a problem because with two or more servers connected to a switch with the same MAC address, the switch no longer knows where to send the packets destined to that MAC, so it falls back to hub-type behavior and sends the packet to every port on the switch. This can cause switch flooding, and means that the nodes cannot talk to each other unless you configure an additional NIC specifically for inter-node communication (Figure 4.51).

**Figure 4.51** Two Servers with the Same MAC Address Present a Problem for the Switch

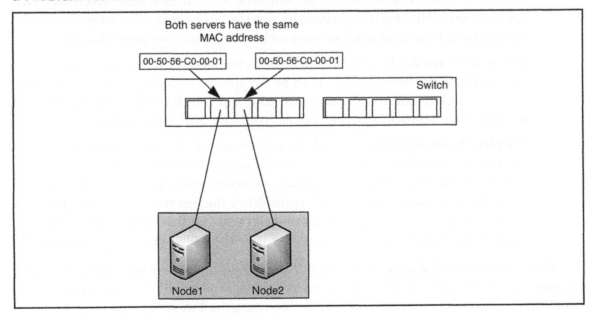

**Multicast** Each node is given an additional MAC address for its NIC, so they end up with their real MAC and an NLB-generated one. With multicast, you can create static ARP entries in the switch so that packets are sent only to the members of the cluster, which prevents the switch flooding from happening.

Solutions to switch flooding:

- Using unicast, the cluster members can be attached to a hub hanging off the switch. This way, the switch has a one-to-one mapping for MAC to IP address and sends traffic only to the port associated with the hub.

- Use multicast and create static ARP entries/mappings so the flooding happens only on the ports associated with the cluster (which is, after all, the intended behavior).

- Use IGMP on the routers (and network cards).

These additional methods have been suggested as well, although success may depend on the behavior of the switch hardware itself:

- Use port mirroring (Switched Port Analyzer in Cisco terms), which is a function of a switch where traffic destined to a port is also sent to a second port, usually for analysis such as packet sniffing. This would require some tampering of the MAC mappings to avoid switch confusion and therefore switch flooding.

- Configure a VLAN and configure all the cluster traffic to travel over the VLAN and not the entire switch(es).

There is a lot of confusion and incorrect information out there regarding NLB, pretty much all of it to do with the network cards and network traffic. Often, when installing an NLB cluster, people will take the same approach as with an MSCS cluster—with these clusters, there is a main LAN network card (NIC) for the LAN traffic, and a secondary NIC for the heartbeat traffic that lets each node know that the other is still there and responding. In MSCS, you specify what traffic is to run across which NIC, so typically the heartbeat NIC is for heartbeat traffic only, and the main NIC is for LAN traffic and heartbeat as well (for resilience).

Best practice dictates that in an NLB cluster you should, generally speaking, add a secondary NIC so the nodes can communicate with each other. So, taking the configuration we have in an MSCS cluster and translating it to an NLB cluster, we get a configuration such as shown in Figure 4.52. Here we have essentially done the same, networking-wise, as you would when creating an MSCS cluster. The two NICs on the main subnet (192.168.7.x) have been joined to form the cluster address (192.168.7.155), with a second subnet added (10.0.0.x) for the heartbeat connection. The idea is that, just like in a server cluster, the inter-node traffic runs across the dedicated heartbeat NIC.

**Figure 4.52** Dual-NIC NLB Cluster

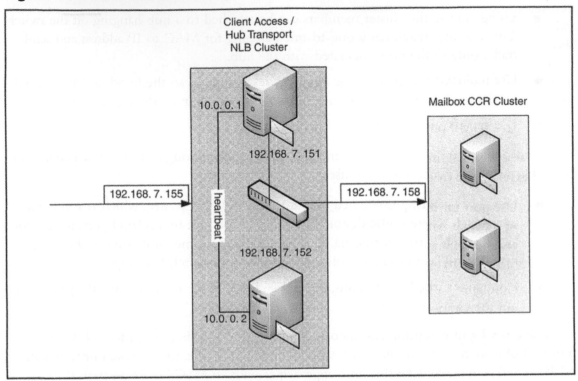

Now let's turn this idea on its head somewhat. When you configure an NLB cluster in Windows Server 2003, there is no place to specify traffic settings in the same way. In fact, the heartbeat communication within an NLB cluster is actually a broadcast from the NLB-enabled NIC. What does this mean? If you implement the system in Figure 4.52, you're wasting two network cards. The cluster won't use the "heartbeat" connection in this case. There is no way to control which traffic goes across which NIC, only the binding order of the NICs, which we will come to later. Try setting up this configuration—run it for a while using OWA sessions etc., and then check out the Status page for the heartbeat NIC. We doubt it will have seen much action.

**N**OTE

As a general rule, when writing this book we didn't want to write step-by-step instructions on how to set things up, because there is a wealth of information out there on sites such as isaserver.org and msexchange.org. However, this area seems to be woefully lacking in clear instruction, so in this case we'll go through the exact configuration of the cluster.

NLB clusters should always be configured using two network cards in each host. NICs are cheap, and it'll save you some hassle doing it this way. Servers want to talk to each other, and setting up a single-NIC cluster where the nodes can't communicate just causes pain. Now, let's look at what traffic travels across each NIC.

The first card we will call "frontend," the second "backend." Frontend is the card that hosts the NLB services, so the front-end network is the NLB-enabled network across which flows the incoming traffic toward the cluster IP address. The backend network hosts traffic between servers. This is to say, compared to an MSCS cluster network, the heartbeat and LAN traffic swap places!

Let's assume you are starting from the point of two individual, single-NIC servers with which you want to create the NLB cluster. These NICs have the addresses:

LW-CAS1      192.168.7.151/24

LW-CAS2      192.168.7.152/24

At present, these cards host all of the domain traffic between the servers and other hosts on the network. They are also registered in DNS, so another host looking for "LW-CAS1" finds 192.168.7.151. It's easier to have things remain this way, so these cards will handle the main LAN traffic.

Now we introduce the second cards, which will be on the "frontend" network and will host the cluster IP address, *not* the existing cards. The frontend network will host traffic coming in to the cluster and cluster heartbeat traffic. Figure 4.53 shows the optimal configuration for our NLB cluster.

**Figure 4.53** Our Optimized Network Load Balancing Cluster

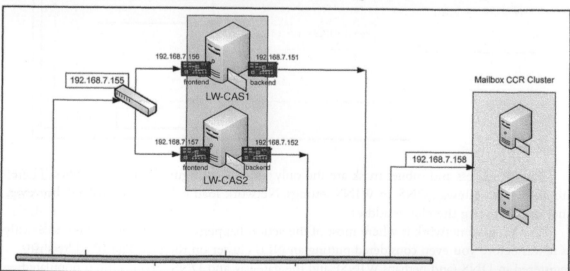

Let's take the frontend network first. The frontend network cards are assigned a dedicated IP address (DIP) and the cluster IP address. (The front-end NICs on both nodes each have the cluster IP address, but this apparent clash is taken care of by the NLB service.) The DIPs are only used for hosting the cluster address. The frontend network cards' configuration should look like Figure 4.54.

**Figure 4.54** The Frontend NIC has an Address Only

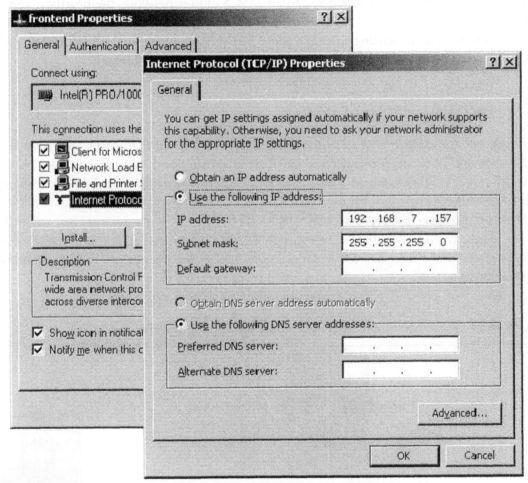

The IP address and subnet mask are the only settings configured on this network. There are no default gateway, DNS, or WINS settings. Network load balancing is enabled, however, and this is hosting the cluster address.

The backend network is where most of the action happens. This NIC is configured exactly as it was before you even considered putting an NLB cluster on the box. The IP address is registered in DNS (and perhaps WINS), and the gateway and DNS server settings populated.

In addition, this NIC is sitting at the top of the network bindings list, so outgoing traffic will go through this network.

To set up the two-node NLB cluster.

1.  **Configure two network cards in each node.**  These should be named "backend" and "NLB" and should be configured as follows:

|  | Node1 (LW-CAS1) | | Node2 (LW-CAS2) | |
| --- | --- | --- | --- | --- |
| NIC | Backend | NLB | Backend | NLB |
| IP Address | 192.168.7.151 | 192.168.7.157 | 192.168.7.152 | 192.168.7.157 |
| Mask | 255.255.255.0 | 255.255.255.0 | 255.255.255.0 | 255.255.255.0 |
| Gateway | 192.168.7.1 | | 192.168.7.1 | |
| DNS Servers | 192.168.7.150 | | 192.168.7.150 | |
| Register in DNS? | Yes | No | Yes | No |

2.  **Set network binding order.**  In Advanced Settings under the network properties, make sure "backend" is at the top of the Adapters and Bindings list (Figure 4.55).

**Figure 4.55** Backend Is the Primary NIC

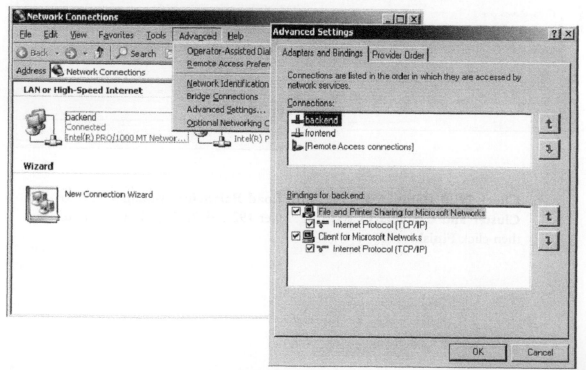

3. **Enable NLB.** On LW-CAS1, go to the properties of the NLB network card (frontend), enable NLB, and go to its Properties page. Remember, this is the second card we've added to the node. Enter an IP address for the cluster **of 192.168.7.155**, mask of **255.255.255.0**, and the cluster address of **nlbcluster.lochwallace.com**. The dedicated IP address should be 192.168.7.156 (the primary address of this NIC). Go to the Internet Protocol (TCP/IP) Properties page and add the cluster IP address (192.168.7.155) as a second IP address on that NIC. (Note: The cluster address *must* be the second address in the list.) (Figure 4.56.)

**Figure 4.56** Enable NLB

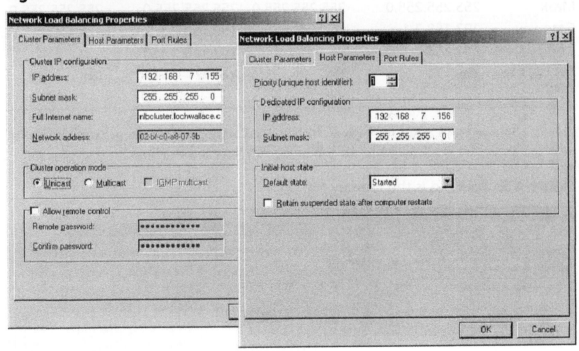

4. **Check NLB status.** Open **Network Load Balancing Manager**. Go to **Cluster and Connect to Existing**. Enter **192.168.7.156**, select the cluster, and then click **Finish**.

In the main NLB manager page, wait until LW-CAS1(frontend) shows the status "converged." Right-click the cluster name and select **Add host to cluster**. Enter **192.168.7.152**, and then select the NLB interface (192.168.7.157). It is important to attach to LW-CAS2 using the backend IP address, because if you use the frontend address you will experience connection problems and the cluster may not form properly. Make sure the IP address is 192.168.7.157, the correct mask, and that Default State is **Started**, and then click **Finish**. NLB Manager should look like Figure 4.57.

**Figure 4.57** Both Nodes Have Converged and Are Working Happily

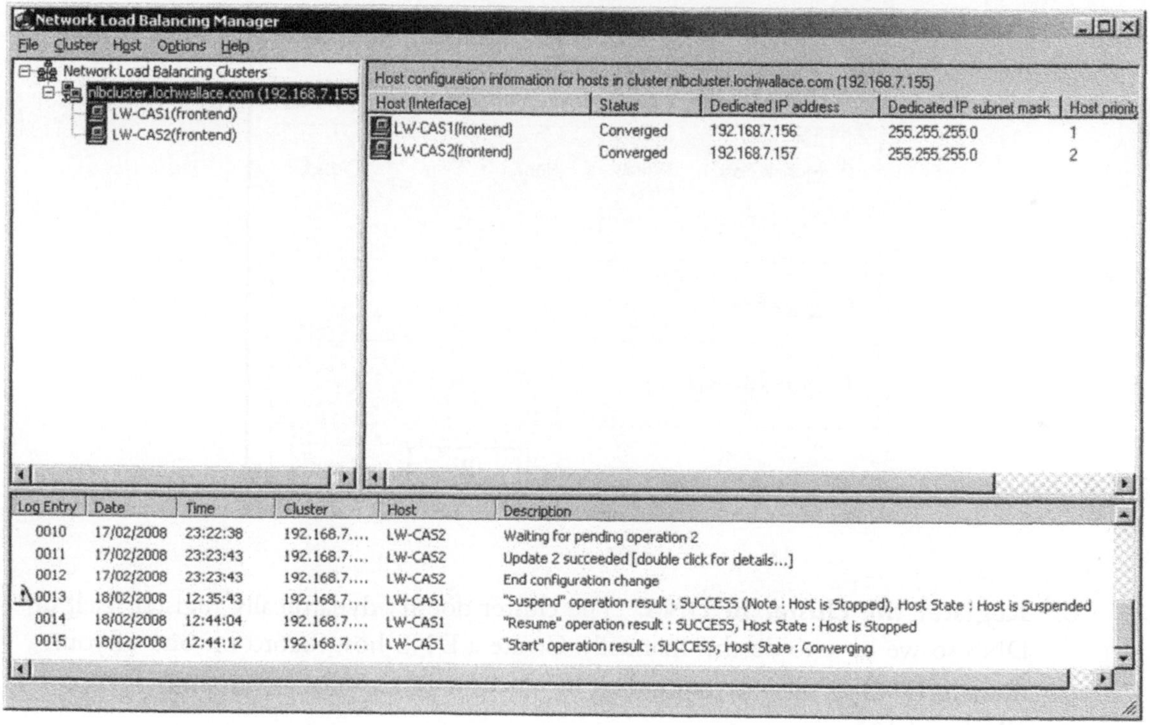

5.  **Configure port rules.**  In NLB Manager, right-click the cluster and select **Cluster Properties**. Go to the Port Rules tab and select the ports you want to cluster. In this case, add port 443 and set the affinity to Single, as in Figure 4.58.

**Figure 4.58** Configuring the Ports for NLB to Manage

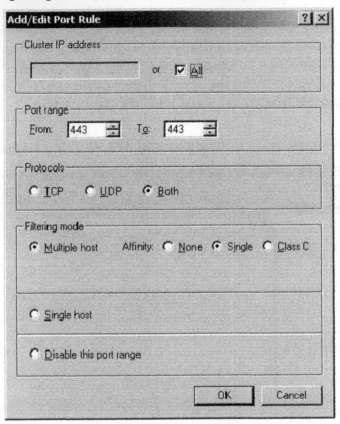

6. **Register the cluster in DNS.** The cluster doesn't dynamically register itself in DNS so we have to do this manually. Create a DNS host record on one of your domain DNS servers corresponding to nlbcluster.lochwallace.com and 192.168.7.155.

7. **Check that traffic is coming in the front and out the back.** There are many ways to check where traffic is coming from and to. A simple way is to use "netstat –an" on the backend cluster. Log on to any other server on the LAN and establish an OWA connection to the cluster address. On the active cluster node, run "netstat –an" and check with which servers it has TCP/IP connections. You'll notice that the traffic is coming from the backend addresses and not the cluster address.

We now have a working, optimal NLB cluster, making use of both NICs.

>   **Additional:** There is a welcome by-product of this configuration, where the
>   incoming traffic goes to the cluster IP and outgoing goes out the backend single
>   network cards—one way to avoid switch flooding on the NLB network is to plug
>   these NICs into a hub, and the hub into a switch. It's uncommon, however, to see
>   gigabit hubs, so this could pose a speed problem in some cases. However, because
>   typically the request traffic is much lower in volume than the response traffic,
>   you will find less load on that network than on the backend, so you're more likely
>   to get away with having a lower-speed hub.

In comparison to Network Load Balancing in Windows NT/2000 where you can create
only a single virtual server, Windows Server 2003 allows you to create multiple virtual
IP addresses/virtual servers and assign ports to any of those. For most publishing scenarios,
this isn't necessary, but if you want to provide more HTTPS services with different affinity
types, for example, this can be done using two virtual IP addresses.

There is quite a bit of technical information on NLB clusters in the Windows Product
Help. Unfortunately, it is all rather theoretical and doesn't go into how to configure an
NLB cluster. It does, however, allude to the kind of setup detailed previously. Go to the
Windows Help and Support Center, open the page titled "Multiple Network Adapters,"
and read "Multiple network adapters in unicast mode." If this kind of thing really floats your
boat, you can read some very technical information about it at the Windows Server 2003
Technical Reference site (http://tinyurl.com/24pywr).

## Designing & Implementing...

### Network Card Teaming and NLB

It is common to team network cards in servers to provide component fault tolerance
and traffic load sharing/balancing. Vendors such as HP provide utilities to manage
network teams for their cards, and they work by often over-writing the MAC address
of each network card. Since this is also what unicast network load balancing does, the
two need to be compatible—the network card driver should be NLB-aware, essentially.
If you normally team network cards for resilience, it is a good idea to do this for your
NLB clusters as well, but make sure it doesn't clash with the teaming software and
drivers.

Now that we've detailed the basic NLB cluster, let's look at how we might go about load balancing the various aspects of Exchange Server 2007 from a publishing perspective.

# SMTP Traffic—Incoming

SMTP traffic is the life-blood of your company's mail organization, so it's important to have SMTP traffic flowing constantly. In a large organization, there is usually more than one inbound route for mail, indicated in Figure 4.59 where mail comes into the organization via both firewalls/entry points. Mail Exchanger (MX) records in DNS tell sender SMTP servers that they can deliver the mail through either of the two entry points, thus providing backup routes in case one of the receiving servers is unavailable. Configuring MX records for your mail system is easy to do.

**Figure 4.59** Multiple Inbound Routes

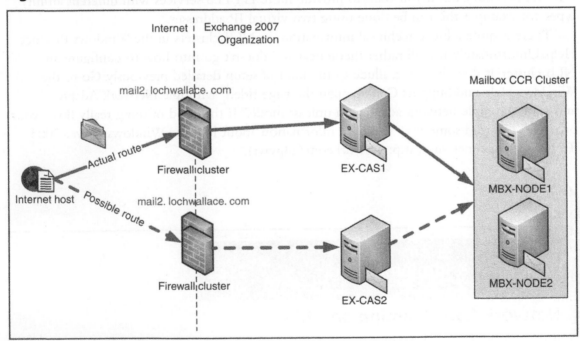

For this scenario, the MX records provide the failover capability, which means that the Hub Transport servers receiving the mail do not need to be load balanced; they can be set up as standalone servers, since the first firewall cluster will forward mail to the first Hub Transport server, and the second firewall to the second Hub Transport.

Note that although Figure 4.59 shows generic firewall devices, in the case of these being ISA servers the effect of the Hub Transport server being down is most likely going to be the same, since ISA—depending on the configuration—will likely fail the connection if it can't talk to the inside server, causing the mail delivery to fail over to the second firewall.

The MX records should be configured in a similar fashion to:

lochwallace.com MX preference = 1, mail exchanger = mail.lochwallace.com

lochwallace.com MX preference = 20, mail exchanger = mail2.lochwallace.com

Mail.lochwallace.com and mail2.lochwallace.com are addresses corresponding to your internal mail organization. Each receiving Hub Transport (or Edge Transport) server must have a Receive Connector configured to accept Internet mail.

You also could combine DNS round robin and MX records just as MS IT does. You basically set the same preference value for the MX records, so they are picked randomly (by the MTAs that supports this, which is most nowadays).

Counter-intuitively, mail will flow first to the address with the lower preference value, using the second as backup. If mail.lochwallace.com doesn't respond, mail will fall back to mail2.lochwallace.com.

Smaller organizations that do not have multiple routes in often use an SMTP store-forward service provided by their ISP. This provides a backup route for incoming mail in case your mail server doesn't respond and stores the messages sent to it for a number of days while your own server comes back online. Figure 4.60 shows such a setup.

**Figure 4.60** Load Balancing the Incoming SMTP Connections

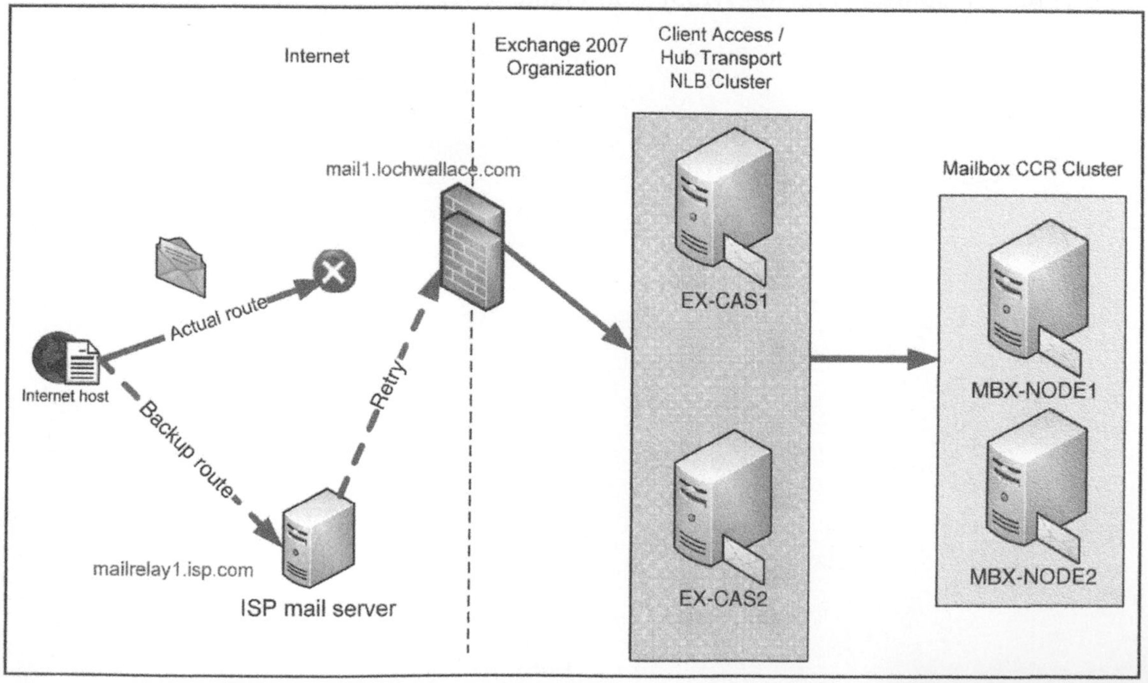

The problem with having one entry point for SMTP mail is that there is then only one route to the organization, and any breakage in the link will cause mail delivery to fail. Assuming you have failover firewalls configured, you must then figure out another way to introduce resilience into the next stage of mail delivery, the Hub Transport servers.

In this case, you must configure the Hub servers as an NLB pair to balance the load from outside. Unfortunately, although ISA Server 2006 can load-balance Web connections to internal standalone servers, it will not do the same for SMTP connections.

Load balancing SMTP connections in an NLB server is a supported configuration, but only if it is for Internet-facing connections. If you load balance the internal connections on port 25, Exchange will no longer be able to route mail between the NLB server and other Hub Transport servers since other Hub servers will try to address the node names rather than the NLB cluster (since the nodes are the Exchange servers, not the cluster). To address this issue, you can use a secondary NIC and create a Receive Connector for incoming mail, which can then be load balanced.

Luckily, our alternative NLB configuration makes it even easier since it's all ready for us. The backend NICs are the ones registered in DNS against the Exchange server names and so are the ones handling all the internal traffic (SMTP, Outlook client etc.), so the front-end NICs are there for us to play with—and already have NLB enabled.

## Configuring the Receive Connector

Receive connectors are created on a per-server basis, so we must create one per server. However, when it comes to the IP address on which the connector listens we select the NLB cluster IP address (192.168.7.155) as in Figure 4.61.

**Figure 4.61** Configuring the SMTP Receive Connector on the Cluster Address

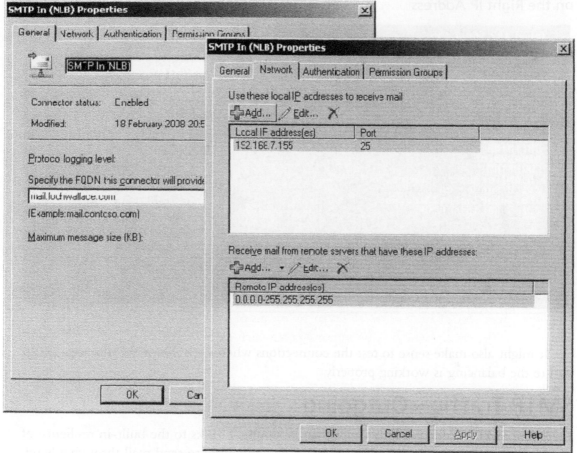

## Testing the Connector

To test the connector, simply stop or suspend each of the cluster nodes in turn and telnet to port 25 of the cluster IP address. If you can send a mail successfully, it's failing over okay.

Another way to verify which node is accepting the connection is to modify the FQDN in the first properties page in Figure 4.61 to something like mail1.lochwallace.com and mail2.lochwallace.com, as in Figure 4.62.

**Figure 4.62** Make Sure the Nodes Are Accepting the Connections on the Right IP Address

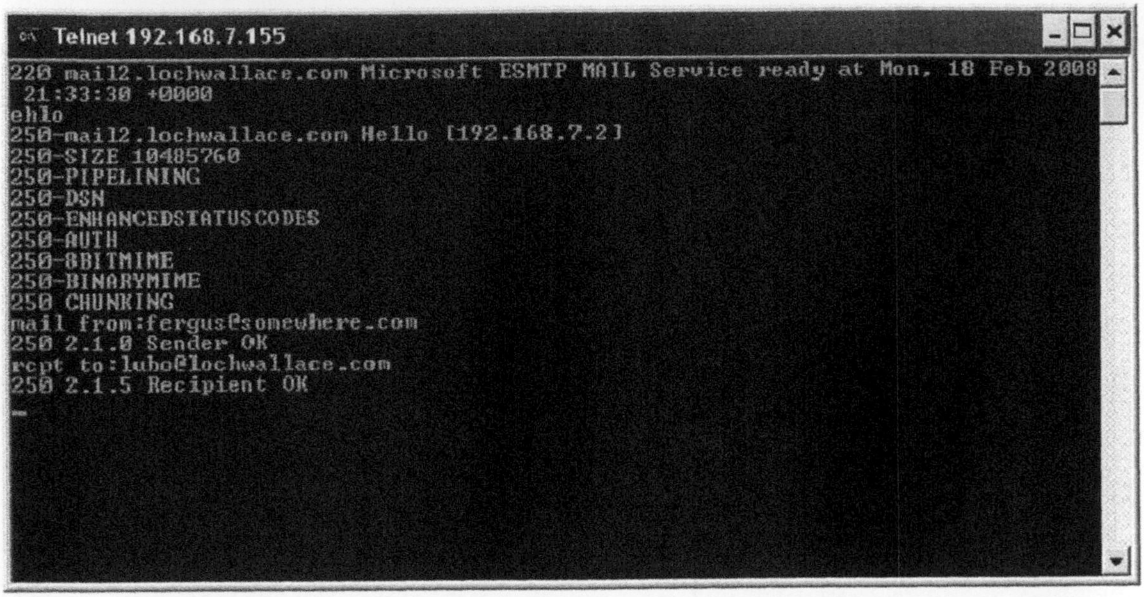

It might also make sense to test the connections when both nodes are running, just to ensure the balancing is working properly.

# SMTP Traffic—Outgoing

Outgoing SMTP traffic is a little easier than incoming. Thanks to the built-in resilience of SMTP flow in Exchange, multiple servers can be configured to send mail through a Send Connector. With the Internet connector, all we need to do is add the Hub servers we want to be allowed to send mail out to the *Source Servers* field of the connector. This ensures that if one of the Hub Transport servers goes down, mail will continue to flow out through the functioning servers (Figure 4.63).

**Figure 4.63** Providing Resilience through Multiple Routes

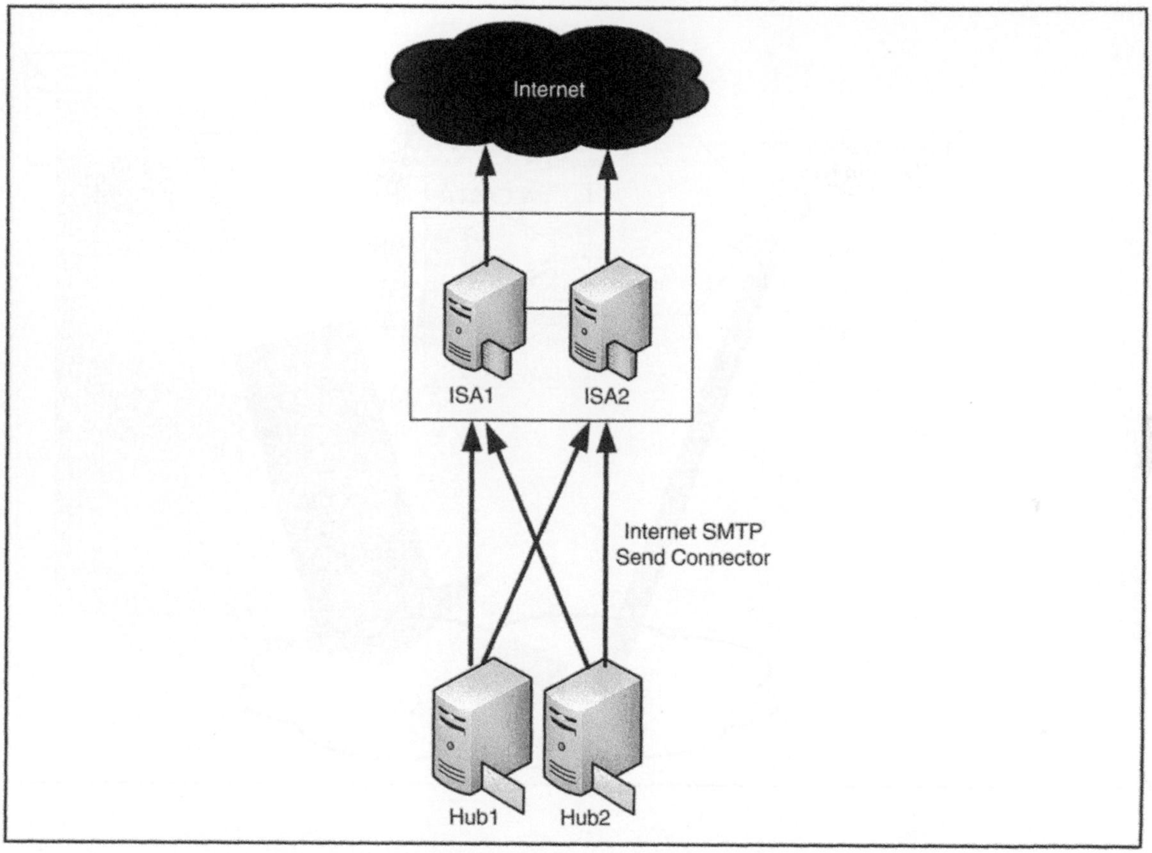

After configuring the Send and Receive Connectors for our NLB cluster, we end up with something like Figure 4.64. Incoming mail goes to a single IP address, but this is clustered by the NLB software so one of the servers will pick up the connection when the other is down.

Outgoing mail connections don't need resilience added since this is built in, within Active Directory sites. The Internet Send Connector incorporates both Hub Transport servers using Exchange's own resilience, so if one is down, the other sends the mail. Internal mail also flows through the backend NICs and behaves exactly as it does in a non-NLB environment.

**Figure 4.64** A Neat Resilient SMTP Solution

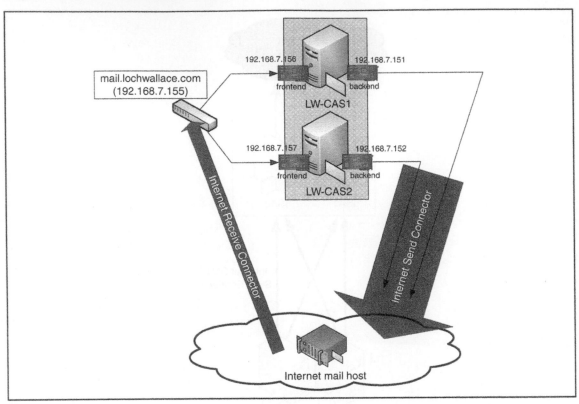

# Using an External Edge Transport Server

Edge Transport servers are designed specifically to sit on a perimeter network to sanitize SMTP mail in and out of the organization. Since ISA Server 2006 is typically used as a back-end firewall with another firewall at the front end of the perimeter, the ISA server will be sitting between the Edge server and the internal LAN.

If your ISA server is using the built-in SMTP filter, because an Edge Transport server needs to speak to internal Exchange servers to synchronize configuration content and transfer SMTP messages, a couple of things must be configured on the ISA server to let this happen.

SMTP Message Transfer Exchange servers talk the language of SMTP when talking to other mail servers. When transferring messages between themselves, however, they use an extended version of SMTP that includes additional verbs not understood by non-Exchange systems. The standard configuration of ISA Server 2006's SMTP filter does not take into account some of these verbs, as it's geared toward communication between Internet hosts. Typically, this setup will result in "500 5.1.1 – Unrecognized command" errors when delivering mail.

# EdgeSync

The EdgeSync process requires communication between the Hub Transport servers and the Edge Transport servers in the perimeter network. The EdgeSync service communicates over port 50636, so this port must be opened on the ISA server.

# Enabling SMTP

There are two possible methods to solve the SMTP issue:

- Disable the SMTP filter
- Add the Exchange verbs to the SMTP filter

Disabling the SMTP filter is relatively easy in ISA Server, but the question is, would you want to? If you're using it in the first place, this is possibly not the best method.

Adding verbs to the SMTP filter is done in the Add-ins section of ISA. Simply add the following verbs to the extensive list to allow the traffic between the Edge servers and the internal Exchange servers:

- PIPELINING
- DSN
- ENHANCEDSTATUSCODES
- STARTTLS
- X-ANONYMOUSTLS
- AUTH
- X-EXPS NTLM
- 8BITMIME
- BINARYMIME
- CHUNKING
- XEXCH50
- SIZE

Note that these verbs should not be advertised to Internet hosts through the front-end firewall.

## Enabling EdgeSync

To allow EdgeSync to work through the ISA server, create a rule with the following properties:

> **Action**: Allow
>
> **Protocol**: EdgeSync (create this rule with TCP50636)
>
> **From**: Internal Hub Transport servers
>
> **To**: Perimeter Edge Transport servers

EdgeSync is a one-way synchronization process so the traffic is required to be outbound only.

---

**NOTE**

EdgeSync also uses port 50389 to connect to ADAM, but this is done only locally. You will need to consider this if you are securing the Edge servers with the Security Configuration Wizard (SCW), but the ISA server does not need to allow this traffic through.

---

# Client Access

Client access methods in Exchange 2007 fall into two categories—Web-based and non-Web based. Much emphasis is put on the Web-based access methods—OWA, ActiveSync, and Outlook Anywhere—and almost none on the non-Web based protocols POP3 and IMAP. The functionality provided by POP3 and IMAP4 is more than accommodated by the Web services, so we are clearly being encouraged to use Exchange ActiveSync etc. as our means to get at Exchange data.

Of course, many people and companies do not use a Windows PC with Outlook or a Windows Mobile device, and as seems to be the way, these people are handicapped by not using conforming Microsoft products. Exchange 2007 offers full POP3 and IMAP4 support, of course, but a couple of things about the support for these protocols leave people at a disadvantage. The first was the woeful GUI support in RTM, forcing us to use the nice/nasty (whichever camp you fall into) PowerShell to configure it. That, thankfully, has been remedied in SP1, along with many "should-have-hads." The second is the lack of support for load balancing these protocols. OWA et al fall into the "Web protocol" camp and therefore can take advantage of ISA Server's capability to load-balance client requests to a Web farm of two or more independent Web servers. POP and IMAP are not able to take advantage of this, although they are able to take part in a Windows NLB cluster.

## Publishing Web Services Using a Web Farm

Publishing the Web services for Exchange 2007 is pretty much the same as publishing any other Web service. ISA Server 2006 provides particular functionality useful for Exchange publishing such as pre-authentication and application filters geared toward Exchange. The Exchange Publishing Rules work specifically with Exchange 2007's Web-based client access methods, making it easier for the administrator to configure publishing rules (Figure 4.65).

**Figure 4.65** Two-Node NLB Cluster

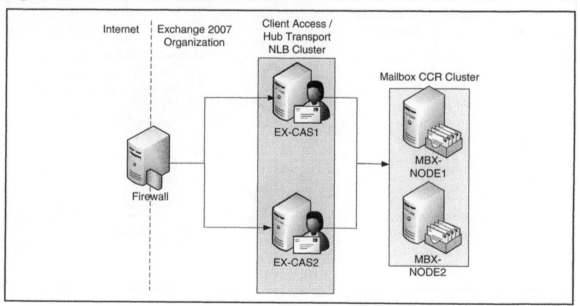

In an environment where you have two or more Client Access servers providing access to Exchange via Outlook Web Access, Outlook Anywhere, and Exchange ActiveSync, resilience can be achieved by creating an NLB cluster and configuring it to listen on HTTPS port 443 (and possibly HTTP/80 although seldom recommended). This involves extra effort in configuring additional network cards, creating the cluster, configuring the network to handle the NLB cluster properly, and administering and monitoring the cluster.

ISA Server 2006 provides an alternative mechanism for load-balancing Web servers (Figure 4.66). A single ISA server sitting in front of two or more Web servers can provide load balancing and resilience for client connections to those servers and will perform the following functions:

- Load-balancing to distribute traffic between Web servers

- Detection of offline servers and reliable failover to online farm members

- Draining, removing, and adding of servers to the farm without disrupting current connections

**Figure 4.66** ISA Decides Which Server to Forward Requests to and Keeps Session Information

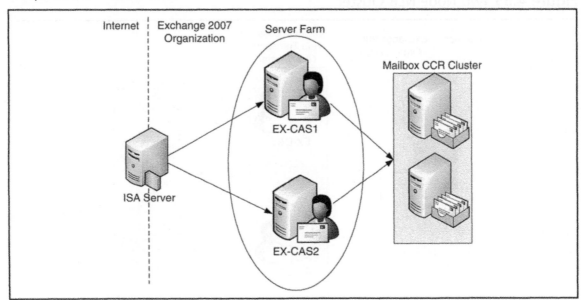

Web farm load balancing in ISA is appropriate for configurations where:

- All servers in the farm contain the same information; for example, mirrored servers.

- All servers in the farm perform the same function; for example, servers providing OWA, ActiveSync, and Outlook Anywhere.

Having the ISA server(s) perform the load balancing function has a number of advantages over hardware load balancers and/or NLB clusters:

- Load balancers that balance requests by source IP address are not effective if the clients are behind a NAT device and therefore the traffic appears to come from the ISA server. This could result in all the traffic going to one of the nodes or a random distribution of traffic, which would cause connections to fail. Because ISA is aware of the true source IP address in this case, it will balance the traffic effectively.

- ISA load balancing eliminates the need to purchase expensive load-balancing hardware.

- ISA load balancing is much easier to configure than NLB clusters, and the monitoring is built in.

- Adding or removing nodes in the Web farm is quicker and easier than doing it in an NLB cluster.

Web servers are grouped into a farm by creating a "server farm" object in ISA Server. The server farm object is used in the publishing rule instead of single server objects. When you create a server farm object, you must specify the servers to take part in the farm and a monitoring method for ISA to detect whether a failure has occurred with any of the nodes.

**Server farm members**  Specify the IP addresses (or computer names, which must be resolvable to the IP addresses) of the servers to take part in the farm.

**Monitoring method**  ISA must monitor each server in the farm to check that it is still running. This can be done by a URL request, a ping request, or a request to a specific port on the server (Figure 4.67). The default is the URL request, since this is more likely to detect a problem with the Web service itself as opposed to just the server. (If IIS fell over, for example, ISA will not detect the failure by pinging the server or connecting to port 25, for example.) An alert will be triggered if the servers do not respond within a certain time (five seconds by default).

**Figure 4.67** Specifying the Connectivity Verifier Information in the Server Farm Properties

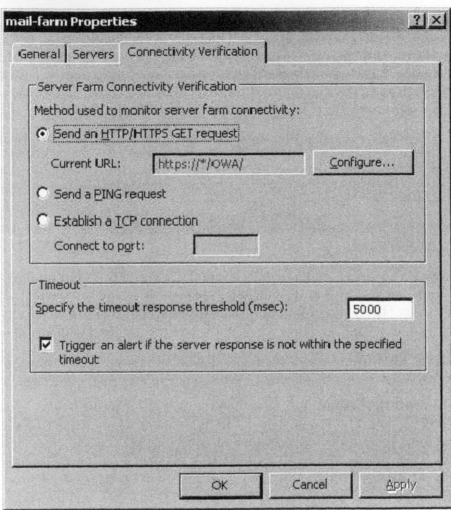

# Creating the Web Farm Publishing Rule

In the Lochwallace environment, we have two Client Access servers that are configured to provide Exchange Web services to internal and external clients using Outlook Web Access, Outlook Anywhere, and Exchange ActiveSync. We now need to create an ISA Server publishing rule that forwards incoming Web requests to the Web farm. The configuration of the publishing rule is very similar to when we publish a single server, the differences being the configuration of the Web farm and ISA's different behavior because of it, and the certificate considerations when spreading the same traffic between two servers.

Figure 4.68 shows the Web Farm tab of the publishing rule, which takes the place of the To tab.

**Figure 4.68** Specifying the Farm-Specific Rules for Publishing

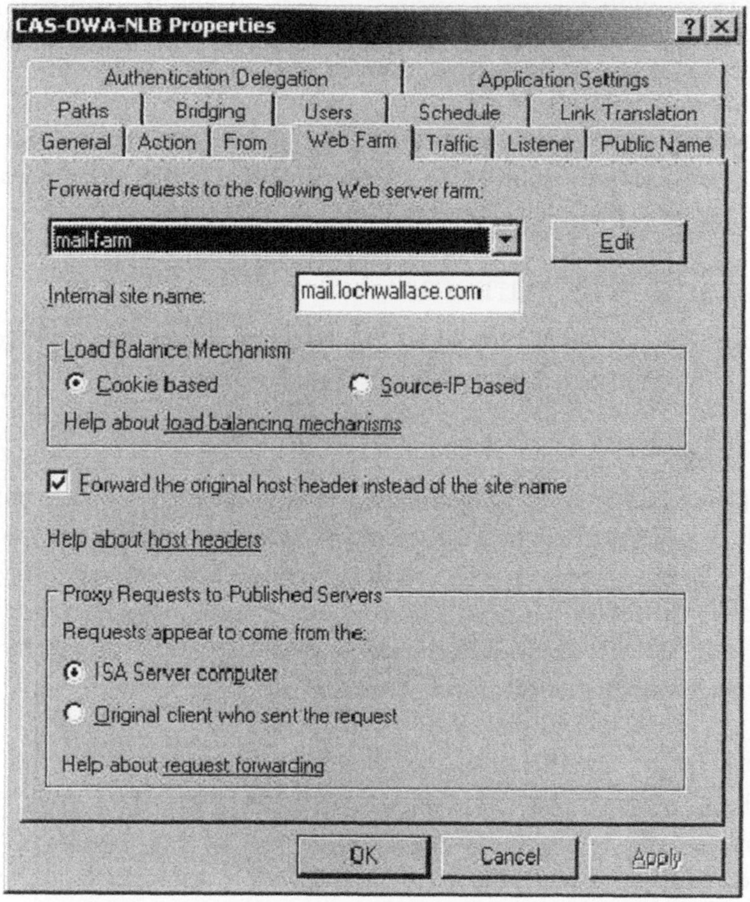

The Internal site name parameter is a bit strange. When publishing a single server, this is understood—it corresponds to the name of the server being published. However, when publishing a Web farm it also asks for an internal site name, and it's not clear what it actually means or what it does with this name. Let's look at how ISA Server uses this name:

**Publishing over HTTPS** If you're publishing the Web servers over HTTPS, you can use either a separate certificate on each server that corresponds to the server name, or a common certificate for each server. In the latter case, the Internal Site Name must correspond to the name on that certificate.

**Host header information** If the ISA server is configured to replace the host header of requests before passing them onto the published server, it uses the Internal site name for the host header. By default, however, ISA Server will forward the original host header, in which case it is not used.

**Link translation**  Link translation can be used on the ISA server to replace internal Web addresses with external accessible addresses. If link translation is used on the ISA server, the Internal Site Name should be the address of the server that is addressed internally.

Even if none of the preceding is applicable to your environment, the ISA Server rules engine may need to be able to resolve this address in DNS, so it is recommended that you use the name of one of the servers.

# Load Balancing Mechanisms

There are two methods by which ISA Server can spread the load between the Web servers—session- or cookie-based, and source-IP based.

## *Session-based Affinity*

Session affinity spreads traffic across servers based on Web browser sessions, which may contain a number of Web requests within the TCP connection. Session affinity ensures client stickiness by using cookies. Client stickiness is when a client reconnects to the same server within the Web farm even after the server has been rebooted. Session affinity is appropriate for Web browser sessions such as with Outlook Web Access or SharePoint. Outlook Anywhere and Exchange ActiveSync cannot use this kind of affinity.

## *IP-based Affinity*

IP affinity spreads the traffic load across servers based on the client IP address. Further connections from the same IP address are forwarded onto the same member of the Web farm. IP affinity is suited to applications such as Outlook and VPN software since they cannot handle cookies as in session affinity. Problems occur when you try to use IP affinity where clients are behind a NAT device or the ISA server is functioning as an upstream server. In this case, all traffic appears to come from a single IP address. In these cases, you must use session affinity.

## *Publishing All Web-based Exchange Services to the Web Farm*

You may be wondering how we publish OWA, Outlook Anywhere, and ActiveSync if the load-balancing mechanisms are not compatible. Luckily, the Load Balance Mechanism is particular to the rule, so just as we separated out to more than one rule previously because of authentication delegation differences, we can do the same here.

We used to be slightly frustrated with the Publish Exchange Web Access wizard for not letting us publish all of them at the same time, but we've come across a good reason for it to separate the OWA, Outlook Anywhere, and ActiveSync parts. Publishing all three to the same Web farm using the same load-balance mechanism just won't work, so we have to have a rule for each (almost).

If you have created the OWA publishing rule, you'll see that it has cookie-based balancing enabled by default. Go through the publishing wizard again for Outlook Anywhere, and specify exactly the same parameters for everything else in the wizard. When you open the rule in the firewall policy, you'll see that a number of options are different, but the main ones are the published paths (which of course we would expect) and the Load Balance Mechanism in the Web Farm tab. Source-IP based is automatically selected. (The other differences are that Outlook Anywhere uses Negotiate as the default authentication delegation method, and OWA uses a customized HTML form.)

So now we have two applications published to the same Web farm but using different load-balancing mechanisms. So what about ActiveSync? Since ActiveSync, like Outlook Anywhere, needs to use IP affinity, you might be able to simply add the /Microsoft-Server-ActiveSync/* folder to the Paths tab. The problem is that ActiveSync doesn't accept Kerberos or NTLM authentication on the server; you need to use Basic authentication. You could use Basic with Outlook Anywhere, but that would cause people to enter their credentials every time they log in, so it is better to create a third rule to accommodate ActiveSync. That's easy—we've done it twice already; we just need another one now. You should have the rules configured something like Figure 4.69.

**Figure 4.69** All the Rules Use the Same IP Address and Listener

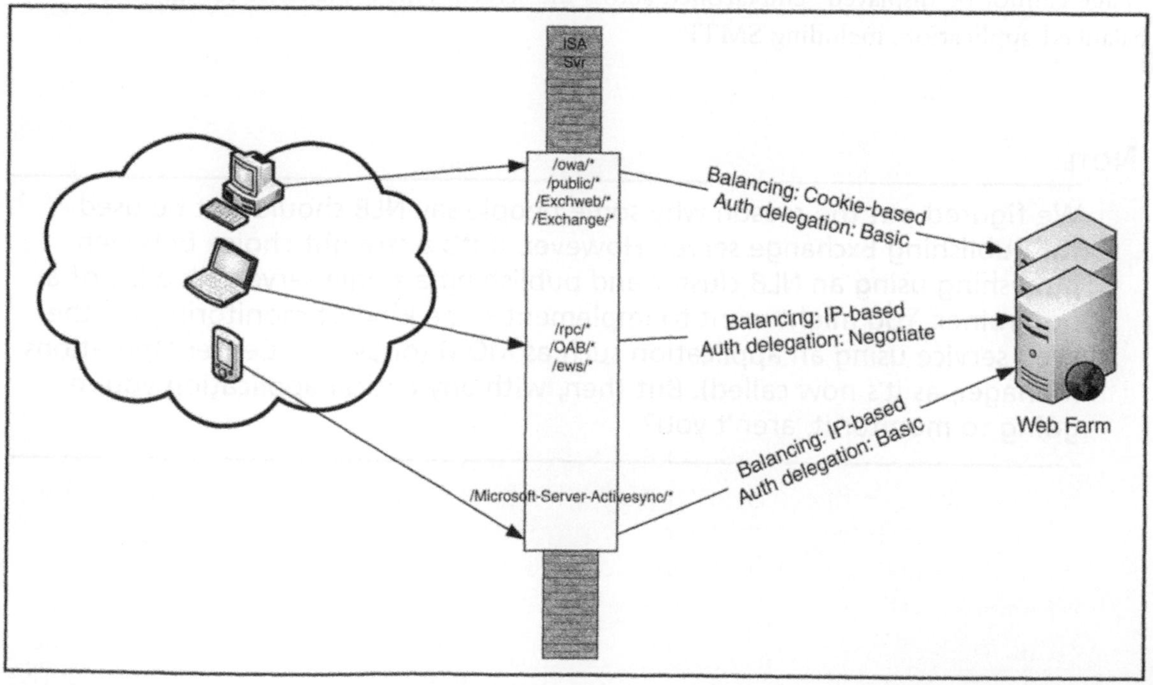

That was fairly easy, and has potentially saved a large amount of money that would have been spent on a hardware network load balancer, or a lot of pain setting up Windows NLB.

## Other Client Protocols

Perhaps in the last paragraph we spoke too soon, because the other protocols Exchange 2007 supports for client communication, IMAP and POP, are not supported using the Web farm arrangement. ISA Server only load balances Web connections, even when only IP affinity is required.

This leaves POP and IMAP users out in the cold slightly, and complicates things further if you need to integrate these protocols into your Exchange publishing configuration. Since it's not possible to use ISA's load-balancing feature, we have to fall back to using Windows Network Load Balancing. It also raises the question, "Should we just use NLB for all of the protocols and forgo the ISA load balancing?" To this we say no, for one very good reason—ISA Server's monitoring is much more effective.

When we looked at the connectivity verification methods available for the Web farm in ISA Server, it was suggested that the ping and TCP connection methods were rubbish because while the NLB mechanism would see when the server was down they wouldn't recognize when the actual Web service was not responding. The problem with Windows NLB is that it essentially uses the ping method of verification, so if, say, IIS crashes on one of the servers it will keep sending traffic to that server and the client will get something like "Page cannot be displayed" emblazoned across the screen. This is the same for any load-balanced application, including SMTP.

---

**NOTE**

We figured out the reason why some people say NLB should not be used for publishing Exchange server. However, if it's a straight choice between publishing using an NLB cluster and publishing a single server, it's a bit of a no-brainer. You might want to implement some kind of monitoring for the Web service using an application such as MOM (or System Center Operations Manager, as it's now called). But then, with any critical application you're going to monitor it, aren't you?

---

To configure NLB for the POP3 and IMAP4 services, we go back to the NLB cluster we configured earlier in the chapter. As well as adding the ports 25 and 443 to the NLB cluster, simply add the ports that correspond with the service that's being published, most likely 110/995 for POP3 and 143/993 for IMAP4.

# The Value of SAN Certificates

Throughout this chapter, as in most documentation for Exchange Server 2007, we talked in terms of issuing and working with Subject Alternative Name (SAN) certificates because it's something Exchange 2007 works with and each server issues to itself when it is installed. But when you consider the value of these certificates from the point of view of publishing with ISA Server 2006 (or any ISA Server version), it's not so clear that we should be considering them. Let's weigh up the sides.

SAN certificates obtained from commercial authorities are expensive. Even the cheapest ones can be many times the cost of a single-name certificate. You get an effect of increasing returns, however, as you pile more and more alternative names on the certificate you obtain for the same price. However, if you don't use these alternative names, what use is it?

## Internal SAN Certificates

Microsoft recommends you do not leave the self-certified SAN certificates in use in your Exchange environment. Best practice is to provide SAN certificates to each server from a trusted certificate authority. If this was a commercial one, it would become quite expensive, but you can of course create your own PKI infrastructure on your domain and issue certificates from there. This gives you an element of control in your environment as well, as it enables you to revoke and manage certificates.

Issuing a SAN certificate from your internal PKI infrastructure makes a lot of sense—for one thing, it doesn't cost you anything. In addition, Exchange servers play many different roles for different purposes, and clients/servers contact them through secure channels using different FQDNs, and separating out services to use multiple single-name certificates could be a difficult, if not impossible task.

However, when you consider access to Exchange from the Internet, it's a different story.

The problem with SAN certificates in a publishing scenario stems from one fact—*ISA Server does not recognize subject alternative names.* Sure, you can argue that it does because in certain circumstances, it looks at the top SAN, but in practice, this is of no benefit since that first SAN name must be the same as the subject name anyway. If ISA Server did work with

SAN certificates, this chapter would be much shorter because we would generally be able to publish everything through the one IP address and we'd all be happy. However, thanks to this restriction we have to find alternative ways to publish the likes of the Autodiscover service, using a separate certificate and hence second IP address, etc.

When you look at the examples in this chapter, all of them use a single FQDN to reach a particular server. This is a classic publishing scenario where single-name certificates would be used.

So what benefits do SAN certificates bring us in a publishing scenario? Well, none. Of course, the Exchange and ISA teams will get together and have a pow-wow about SAN certificates and ISA Server will support them, possibly in the next version. However, for the moment there is no advantage in buying an expensive commercial SAN certificate for publishing Exchange using ISA Server.

(If you simply open port 443 from the Internet to one of your CAS servers, it's a different story, but we would like to think you wouldn't do that or they might send round people in white coats.)

# A Typical Certificate Infrastructure

With the proliferation of public key infrastructures these days, led by the growing acceptance of certificate-based infrastructures as the basis of security and by applications such as Microsoft's Office Communication Server, which requires certificates for communication, it is unlikely that a large company does not have a certificate authority as a part of its domain. Creating and maintaining certificates from within this infrastructure is not the administrative nightmare as it was previously seen to be, mainly because it's likely to already be there in the first place. In addition, the cost of buying certificates seems disproportionate to what they actually do. Perhaps this is understating the value of commercial certification authorities, but paying $100 per year for something you can make on your own quite easily seems harsh.

The general way to go with certificates is to have commercial certificates on Internet-facing servers and internal ones for the internal Exchange infrastructure; servers that do not communicate directly with the Internet. Commercial certificates have the advantage that they are instantly recognizable and verifiable by clients and other servers since they come from a trusted source. This saves the distribution of internal root certificates to clients, for example. The advantages of internal certificates are that they are cheap, and give you all the flexibility you need for creating, maintaining, and controlling your secure environment.

With this in mind, one suitable design would be that in Figure 4.70. Here the ISA server has commercial certificates—*in orange*—corresponding to mail.lochwallace.com and autodiscover.lochwallace.com, whereas the internal servers have Subject Alternative Name certificates assigned to them from the internal CA—*in yellow*—for use within the Exchange organization. ISA Server forwards Web client requests onto the CAS Web farm with the name "mail.lochwallace.com" (as per Figure 4.70 ({the one referring to ISA 1 Rule vsd}). Because ISA doesn't need to use the same certificate when communicating with the published server as it gives to the client, it will recognize the FQDN from the SAN certificate and communicate as planned.

**Figure 4.70** External Certs for External Use, Internal Certs for Internal Use!

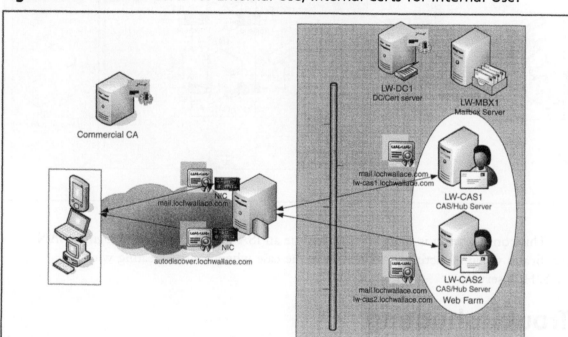

In this scenario, where the ISA server is doing the load balancing of traffic to the CAS servers, the CAS servers have a single IP address and an appropriate internal SAN certificate that they use for communication with all other servers.

In the Network Load Balancing publishing scenario (Figure 4.71), you can use the same internal certificates for both of the network cards on each node.

**Figure 4.71** No Need for Multiple Certificates per Server

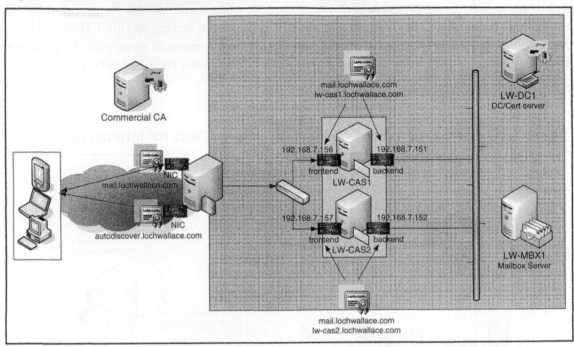

This configuration is quite acceptable since an ISA Server 2006 can recognize SAN certificates when it's acting as a client, as in the case when communicating with the CAS/Hub servers.

# Troubleshooting

Because of the complexity of the various processes involved in setting up a proxied publishing configuration, troubleshooting ISA is sometimes difficult. The logging capabilities of ISA are not the best, and usually interpreting the errors from the monitoring logs involves a trip to Google. Generally, though, it's important to keep some tips in mind and to understand the animal with which you're wrestling. Understanding ISA and its capabilities and intricacies is important. Because of its idiot-proof configuration tools, ISA is easy to configure but hard to get working.

## General Troubleshooting

There are so many links in the chain when publishing Exchange using ISA Server that it sometimes takes a lot of brain power when making a change to remember to make a modification elsewhere that corresponds. For example, it's quite common to get so tied up in making sure the server settings are correct that you forget the simple change on the client.

When troubleshooting problems and making changes to see what works and what doesn't, we suggest the following simple tips to start with:

**Always note down the changes.** Don't tell yourself, "It's just a small change, I'll remember it and put it back in a minute." It won't be just a small change; you'll end up making numerous modifications and soon it'll be a mess. Note each change you make, and underline each point where you think you've made progress—this can be the point to which you return when you've messed things up.

**Save the ISA configuration.** Back up the configuration as often as you can/feel fit. If that "progress point" you underlined is too far back in terms of number of changes, simply restore it from backup. Use the backup wizard at the server level, as this allows you to do a restore-import thus replacing all the rules currently in the configuration.

**Don't lose purpose.** It's easy to lose track of what you're trying to achieve and try something else that has a very slim chance of working. Keep in mind exactly what you're trying to achieve, and do it in bite-sized chunks.

**Separate rules and listeners.** This is more of a proactive measure. If you publish all of your services using a small number of rules, you're more likely to break something else while fixing the problem you're on. Understand the relationships between the rules (particularly the listeners involved) and be careful when making changes to components they have in common. It may look neat to have everything stuffed into a single rule (as you can do with ISA and Exchange), but you're asking for trouble.

**Start with a wide scope.** When creating rules, try to leave things as open as you can. Because ISA is so flexible—for example, with publishing multiple servers on a single listener—it allows you to narrow down rules to the nth degree. If you can get away with it, tell the rule to listen to all Web requests, not to require SSL, allow all users, etc. If you get it to work that way, it's easy to lock the rule down step by step and then work out where the rule breaks.

Other main points to consider are:

**Client authentication settings** This is easy to miss, but if you are testing using Basic auth prior to setting up NTLM auth for Outlook Anywhere, when you make the switch on the servers, remember to change the client too! Otherwise, you'll get endless logon screens in Outlook and end up throwing it out the window.

**Certificates** In the last section, we discussed certificates and the limitations you have to work with, particularly with respect to SAN certificates.

**ISA FQDN settings** Whether it's setting the SPN name for KCD or creating an SSL tunnel to the published server, make sure the server's FQDN is correct. Often, when this is not the case you receive a "Failed Connection Attempt" from the Web Proxy (Reverse) along with a 0x80090322 status code. This is a fairly generic code that can appear when the target name is incorrect or there is a mismatch between server names and certificates—unfortunately, even with the new logging features of the Supportability Update.

**Authentication methods** Client authentication using ISA server follows a chain: Client-ISA-Server. The client authentication method must match the one the ISA server expects. The delegation method, naturally, must also match the one the published server is expecting. It's easy to forget to follow the chain all the way.

# Outlook Anywhere Problems

Outlook Anywhere is particularly difficult to troubleshoot, as none of the logs will give you much of an idea of what's going wrong. While you can check on the connection from the client side using the Connection Status window (**Ctrl+Right-click** the Outlook icon on the taskbar's notification area and select **Connection Status**), it's difficult to know why it's not connecting as it doesn't tell you.

The most important thing to do when troubleshooting Outlook Anywhere is to know your enemy. Grab one of the extensive guides on the Internet and make sure you complete every step, and understand why each step is required and the consequences of it not being correct. This sounds vague, but it's important to know ISA Server and what each little check box does, as it's not often immediately obvious.

For specific ISA status codes relating to RPC over HTTP, check out the ISA Server Team Blog at http://blogs.technet.com/isablog.

# ActiveSync Troubleshooting

With later versions of the Windows Mobile operating system, the error codes in ActiveSync have become more specific and easier to pin down. Most errors in our experience involve certificate or server name issues. Ensure the root certificate is installed on the device and that the name of the Exchange server specified in ActiveSync refers to the FQDN of the external ISA interface (and that the appropriate listener is listening on that address).

ActiveSync device error codes in WM5 and later are typically in the format "850xxxxx" or "800xxxxx". There are some good guides that translate these codes into proper English out there on the Web. www.pocketpcfaq.com is one site with a list of errors and solutions.

**TIP**

You may not have a suitable mobile device to hand when you have to trouble-shoot or verify access to ActiveSync. If you open a Web browser and type in the URL https://mail.lochwallace.com/Microsoft-server-activesync, a working configuration will give you error code 501/505, Not Implemented or Not Supported. If you receive this, you can be pretty sure it's working successfully.

## ISA Best Practice Analyzer

The idea behind Microsoft's best practice analyzers is simple, but they have become extremely useful tools for ISA, Exchange, and other admins. The ISA BPA will point out any stupid configuration errors in the rule base and many hard to find errors, too. Particularly when you're troubleshooting issues and trying to get those publishing rules to work, run the BPA whenever you've made some changes so it can point to anything you've missed. It's much better to spend three minutes running the BPA than five hours finding that obvious problem in one of the rules.

Chapter 5 • High Availability with Exchange 2007

# High Availability with Exchange 2007

## Solutions in this chapter:

- **High Availability Strategies and Options**

- **Server Resilience**

- **Site Resilience**

- **Lab Configuration**

- **New and Improved in SP1**

- **Local Continuous Replication**

- **Cluster Continuous Replication**

- **Standby Continuous Replication**

- **SCR Deployment Scenarios**

- **Economics of Continuous Replication**

- **Troubleshooting High Availability Configurations**

# Introduction

Exchange availability has obviously become more and more important in the last few years since the importance of email and messaging has grown. You just need to look at the difference between the average customer who has an Exchange 5.5 environment and those who have shiny new Exchange Server 2007 environments. Over-zealous and target-driven salespeople notwithstanding, typically those customers with the highly available and scalable Exchange 2007 environments will have spent more money and effort than back in the days when they had three standalone Exchange 5.5 servers.

Not that those 5.5 environments weren't appropriate for the task—far from it—but in the mid-1990s it wasn't quite so important if some people were without mail for a few hours, or even days. And if you ever tried to set up a clustered Windows NT server, you'll realize why people didn't do that kind of thing often.

Exchange Server 2007 brought in some brilliant replication technology, similar to SQL's log shipping that allowed Exchange to replicate its data between servers or within the same server to a backup store. Service Pack 1 has upped the stakes somewhat by adding site resilience to this mix and adopting many new technologies that make setting up and maintaining highly available systems much easier, and dare we say cheaper, than before.

# High Availability Strategies and Options

*Availability* is a strange word, and means different things to different people. Typically, it is expressed in uptime values such as 99.99%, which means that the service will be running all year round save perhaps one hour of downtime. However, this is meaningless in some respects without a definition of *uptime*.

Consultants need to have a grasp of what availability is to the particular customer and to align the end product with their expectations. If a customer defines downtime as the whole company being unable to use Exchange, that's one thing, but if it's defined as "Jimmy in Marketing can't access his mailbox," then you're in trouble.

High availability can be tackled in a number of ways depending on the requirements and the specifics of the company. Usually, the requirements are defined in service level agreements (SLAs), which should be the starting point for a highly available Exchange design.

# Server Resilience

Server resilience refers to localized availability—within the same site and usually within the same cluster. If a server blows up, what are you going to do? Typically, server and server component failure is tackled using component resilience such as teamed network cards and RAID arrays and server clusters. The Microsoft Cluster Service (MSCS) is a solid platform for server resilience in Exchange 2007 and provides automatic failover of resources in case there is a problem with one of the servers. In Exchange 2007, Single Copy (SCC) and Cluster Continuous Replication clusters are based on the MSCS platform.

The main point of a cluster is to eliminate single points of failure, so that one breakage doesn't bring down the service. SCC clusters still have this single point of failure in the storage subsystem, and this is where Exchange's replication technology comes in. Cluster Continuous Replication (CCR) extends and modifies the classic cluster to use two copies of the data, therefore providing resilience for the storage as well.

The other local resilience feature for Exchange is Local Continuous Replication, which, being a storage-only resilience option, is more appropriate for companies investing in cheaper storage hardware such as direct attached disks but also want to take advantages of features such as offloading backup.

# Site Resilience

As the name suggests, site resilience is all about recovering service to another site if it becomes unavailable at the primary site. Site resilience used to conjure up thoughts of buildings blowing up and everybody running to a cold or warm production site down the road. Financial institutions, particularly banks involved in trading, are among those that have dedicated sites in case of terrorist attack or other major disasters at the "primary" site.

However, the ideas of primary and secondary sites are blurring as more and more companies, and particularly institutions such as universities, have multiple sites and high bandwidth connections between them. Some universities in England, for example, have sites close to each other with 10GB fiber links running between them.

For this reason, "site" resilience is a term that requires definition for each scenario. In most cases when talking about Exchange Server resilience, "site" refers to an Active Directory site, although this often correlates to a geographical location or campus.

The introduction of Standby Continuous Replication in Service Pack 1 brings site resilience to the masses without having to resort to third-party solutions. Provided the network infrastructure is up to the job, Exchange can provide resilience between sites, and between different subnets with CCR clusters on Windows Server 2008, so that service can potentially be resumed within minutes of a disaster at the first site.

Server and site resilience feature heavily in this chapter, as these are the big features of Service Pack 1 for Exchange.

# Lab Configuration

This chapter discusses and demonstrates a number of high availability scenarios using most of the methods available with Exchange 2007. The lab environment is detailed here to better describe the configurations and so the chapter can be followed using a similar test setup.

Again, the setup of the servers is not covered in any detail since, unless otherwise specified, they are all using standard configurations, and how to configure the servers is lower than the assumed knowledge of the reader. Figure 5.1 shows the full environment used for the chapter.

**Figure 5.1** High Availability and Backup Configuration

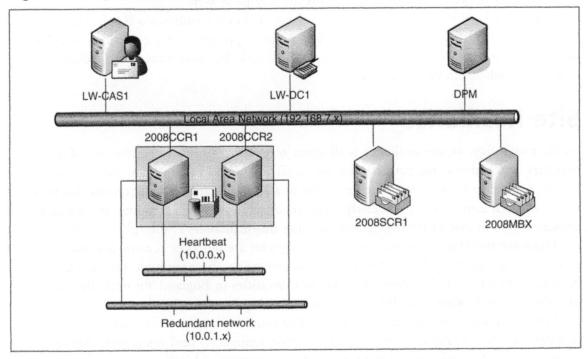

When setting up the environment, it's important to have some hefty hardware on which to run these virtual servers since particularly the Windows Server 2008 and the DPM servers take a lot of juice to run at any decent speed. If you have a production-spec VMWare ESX Server, good for you, but for the rest of us it's easy to reach a point where you might as well watch an episode of *Family Guy* while DPM is starting up. (See Table 5.1.)

**Table 5.1** Server Configuration

| Name | Software | Roles | NIC 1 (LAN) | NIC 2 (Heartbeat) | NIC 3 (Redundant) |
|---|---|---|---|---|---|
| LW-DC1 | Win2003 Std SP2 x64 | DC/GC | IP: 192.168. 7.150 <br> DNS: 192.168.7.150 | | |
| DPM | Win2003 Std SP2 x86 <br> Data Protection Manager 2007 | Backup server | IP: 192. 168.7.169 <br> DNS: 192.168.7.150 | | |
| LW-CAS1 | Win2003 Std SP2 x64 <br> Exch2007 Std SP1 x64 | Client Access <br> Hub Transport | IP: 192.168.7. 151 <br> DNS: 192.168.7.150 | | |
| 2008CCR1 | Win2008 Ent SP2 x64 <br> Exch2007 Ent SP1 x64 | 2008 CCR cluster node | IP: 192.168.7. 162 <br> DNS: 192.168.7.150 | IP: 10.0.0.5 <br> IP: 10.0.0.5 | |
| 2008CCR2 | Win2008 Ent SP2 x64 <br> Exch2007 Ent SP1 x64 | 2008 CCR cluster node | IP: 192.168.7. 163 <br> DNS: 192.168.7.150 | IP: 10.0.0.6 <br> IP: 10.0.0.6 | |
| CCR-CLUS2 | | Cluster | IP: 192.168.7. 164 | | |
| CCR-EXCH2 | | CMS | IP: 192.168.7. 165 | | |
| 2008MBX | Win2008 Std SP2 x64 <br> Exch2007 Std SP1 x64 | 2008 Mailbox server | IP: 192.168.7. 161 <br> DNS: 192.168.7.150 | | |
| 2008SCR1 | Win2008 Ent SP2 x64 <br> Exch2007 Ent SP1 x64 | SCR target (passive cluster node) | IP: 192.168.7. 166 <br> DNS: 192.168.7.150 | | |

# New and Improved in SP1

Service Pack 1 for Exchange Server 2007 introduces a number of new and improved features in the area of high availability. In particular, more options are now available for setting up site resilience and server resilience in high availability scenarios.

With previous versions of Exchange Server, depending on the requirements, site resilience had to be provided either by an offline/recovery solution or by using third-party tools to extend the functionality of Windows and Exchange. Third-party tools add complexity and cost to an environment, and are not always Exchange-aware in the sense that they organize with Exchange services what needs to be done or replicated for a consistent state. Typical SAN-to-SAN replication to another site takes place at the block level and replicates changes in the logs and in the databases themselves. In the event of a crash at Site1, there is no guarantee that the data at Site2 is consistent and ready to mount onto a recovery server.

Exchange Server 2007 introduced log shipping technology called Continuous Replication, which replicates only the log files (after initially copying, or "seeding," the databases), and the active Exchange server at the other end replays those log files in a manner that gives a consistent database. One of the big advantages of this log-shipping technology is its bandwidth efficiency. Most third-party Exchange replication solutions, such as HP's SAN-based Continuous Access product and Double-Take software, replicate Exchange data at the block level, and replicate the logs and the changes to the database files. This involves replicating the data twice: when the transaction is written to the log file, and when the transaction is written to (or modified in) the database. Continuous Replication replicates only the transaction log files (after database seeding takes place), and the Exchange services at the passive end commit the logs to the database.

This replication engine has found its way into one of the main features of SP1—Standby Continuous Replication—which provides options for site resilience without the need for third-party solutions or expensive SANs.

Other improvements in SP1 come courtesy of its support for Windows Server 2008, which provides cluster failover across multiple subnets, without the need to stretch LANs across geographical locations. It also enables replication over secondary cluster networks, giving CCR clusters added network resilience as well.

# Standby Continuous Replication

Standby Continuous Replication (SCR) extends the existing replication engine in Exchange Server 2007 to provide more deployment configurations by enabling the replication of databases to separate sites. SCR is meant to be deployed primarily by having a warm standby server (DR) environment in either a separate site or a separate server on the same site for added local resilience. In Exchange Server 2003, site resilience can be provided by maintaining a warm standby server in another location, ready to be built as a replacement when needed. There are two ways to implement the DR scenario in Exchange 2003, neither of them ideal. The server can be pre-built as an Exchange server, and after a disaster situation, the databases restored onto this server. In this scenario, client machines must be redirected to the new server, which necessarily has a different name from the original. The other scenario is a warm standby server with only Windows installed. In this case, when the original server goes down, the DR server is renamed to that of the original and Exchange installed using the /DisasterRecovery switch. No client Outlook profiles have to be redirected, but the procedure takes longer. In either scenario, there must be some way to get the databases to the DR server, either through replication or direct restore from tape or other media.

Exchange Server 2007 is more flexible in its disaster recovery techniques, as we'll discuss in the next chapter. Through the Autodiscover service and database portability, it is possible to restore a database to another Exchange server and have clients redirect themselves automatically in a DR situation. SCR provides the replication mechanism for this.

The SCR mechanism is also compatible with other types of replication, so they can be combined to provide more options for data and site resilience. LCR- or CCR-replicated databases can be replicated to a passive SCR node, providing server and site resilience in the same configuration. SCC clusters can also replicate their shared data to an SCR node.

# Windows 2008 Support

Exchange Server 2007 is the first version of Exchange that is able to run on Windows Server 2008. It can take advantage of a number of features particular to Windows Server 2008, such as geographically dispersed clusters, IPv6 and new cluster quorum configurations to provide more flexibility when designing and implementing Exchange.

## Multiple Site Failover

One of the features lacking in Windows Server 2003, which was exploited by third-party cluster add-ons, was cross-subnet cluster failover. Whereas Windows Server 2003 cluster nodes must all be in the same subnet (sometimes this required using a VLAN to spread across sites to accommodate it), "geographically dispersed clusters" are able to stretch across subnet boundaries—across routers—having one node in one subnet and another in a separate sub-net. Failover is almost as seamless as with a single-subnet cluster. The main difference is that the IP address cannot be transferred between cluster nodes in different subnets (Figure 5.2).

**Figure 5.2** A Two-Node CCR Cluster Straddling Subnets

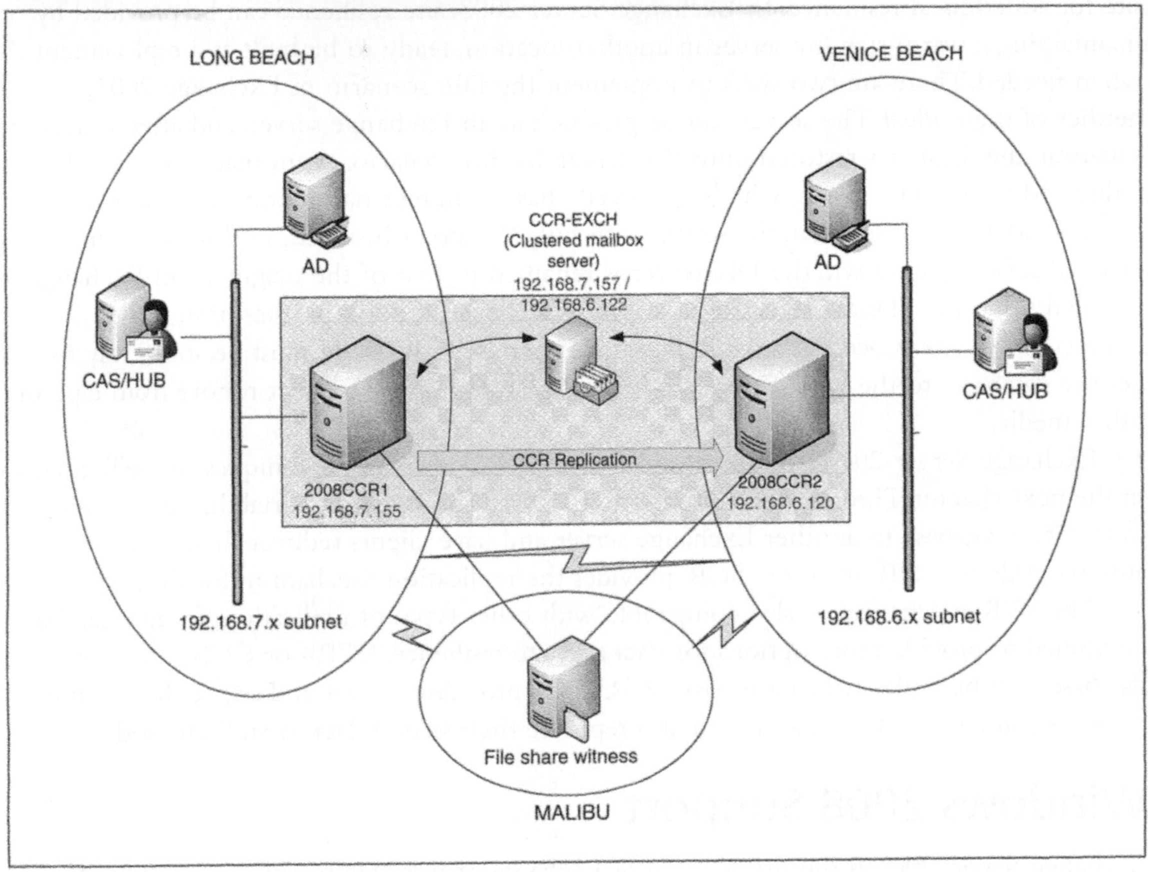

Because the cluster and Exchange server IP addresses switch between subnets, clients have the potential to become confused over which IP address actually holds the Exchange server they're looking for, so there is more reliance on dynamic DNS, which allows the active node to register itself in DNS as the clustered mailbox server (CMS) name. For this reason, the TTL of the DNS entries should be short. There may also be the requirement for clients to flush their DNS cache after failover.

# DHCP Support

Unlike previous versions of the Windows Server operating system, Windows Server 2008 supports using DHCP-assigned addresses for cluster nodes and for cluster IP Address resources. Previously, all IP addresses in a cluster configuration had to be assigned statically.

However, it is an all-or-nothing scenario—if the cluster nodes are assigned addresses by DHCP, the cluster will expect any cluster IP addresses to also be assigned via DHCP. If the cluster nodes are assigned statically, static addresses must be specified for each IP Address resource.

Microsoft's recommendation is to still use statically assigned IP addresses for Windows Server 2008 clusters in production environments, although many prefer using DHCP with reservations.

## IPv6

Windows Server 2008 and its cluster service now support IPv6, but only addresses that support dynamic DNS registration (AAAA host records and the IP6.ARPA reverse lookup zone). This applies to only global and site local addresses since link local addresses do not support dynamic registration.

IPv6 support does not mean you can run your entire network solely on IPv6, however. Exchange 2007 SP1 still requires that IPv4 is installed and that the network supports both IP versions.

## New Quorum Models

Windows clustering has changed a bit in Windows Server 2008. The new quorum models are similar to those in Windows Server 2003 but differently named enough to get a bit confusing. Previously (ignoring the single-node cluster model), there were three types of quorum available for MSCS clusters:

- **Single quorum cluster** This is the classic shared-storage cluster that's used in an SCC cluster, where there is a single copy of the quorum sitting on shared storage that all nodes potentially have access to.

- **Majority node set (MNS) cluster** Each node maintains its own copy of the quorum on a local disk. The nodes that are in a majority (for example, the group of three nodes out of the five that can talk to each other) have quorum and own the cluster.

- **MNS with file share witness** An extension to the MNS cluster model, this gives an additional "vote" to an external file share when deciding who has control of the cluster. This is useful for clusters with an even number of nodes, particularly for two-node clusters where otherwise a majority would be both nodes, and failure of one node means failure of the cluster.

Windows Server 2008 quorum configurations are mostly the same as in Windows Server 2003, but it's easier to approach them from the point of view of what you want to achieve, because there are a number of options.

For clusters with an odd number of nodes, you can use just the nodes themselves to provide the voting power for a majority within the cluster; for example, in a seven-node cluster you can have three fail and retain a majority. The Node Majority quorum configuration is appropriate for this situation, and is equivalent to the MNS cluster in Windows 2003. When you first create a cluster in Windows 2008, you are not asked what type of quorum you want;

rather, it creates a Node Majority configuration by default. Figure 5.3 shows a simple Node Majority cluster.

**Figure 5.3** A Three-Node Node Majority Cluster Spanning Sites

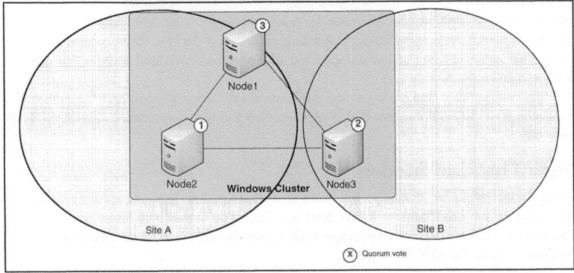

For simple two-node clusters, or any with an even number of nodes, an additional "vote" should be given to provide a majority in any situation. Otherwise, the loss of one node in a two-node cluster would mean loss of majority and the cluster would no longer be operational. In this situation, you have a choice between a Node and Disk Majority, and a Node and File Share Majority.

Node and Disk Majority is appropriate for clusters where the nodes are next to each other and is similar to the simple MSCS quorum configuration, except the loss of the shared disk alone means the cluster continues as long as the nodes can still communicate.

For geographically dispersed and special configuration clusters, such as CCR clusters, the Node and File Share Majority is appropriate. This is equivalent to the MNS with File Share configuration and uses a file share on a separate server as the third vote. Figure 5.4 is a comparison of the new Node and Disk Majority quorum and the classic Single Quorum configuration of Windows Server 2003.

**Figure 5.4** Win2008's New Method Is More Resilient than the Single Quorum

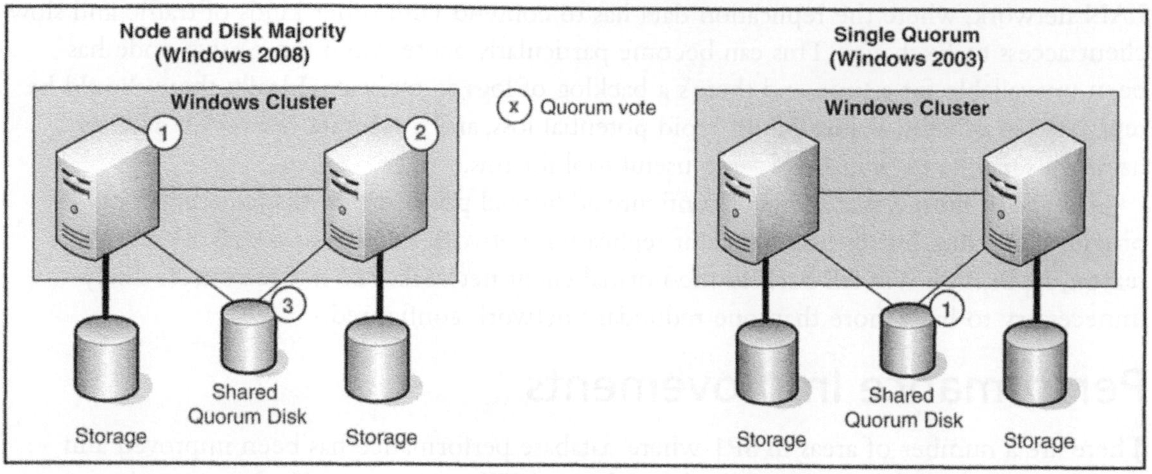

You can configure any of these additional quorum configurations after you create the cluster itself.

# Replication over Redundant Cluster Networks

Exchange 2007 SP1 enables you to configure CCR log shipping and database seeding across a mixed cluster network. Previously, all of the replication had to happen over the public network. This enables you to create additional mixed networks (networks configured to carry public and cluster traffic) for carrying replication traffic (Figure 5.5).

**Figure 5.5** Replication Happens Across a Separate LAN from the Production LAN

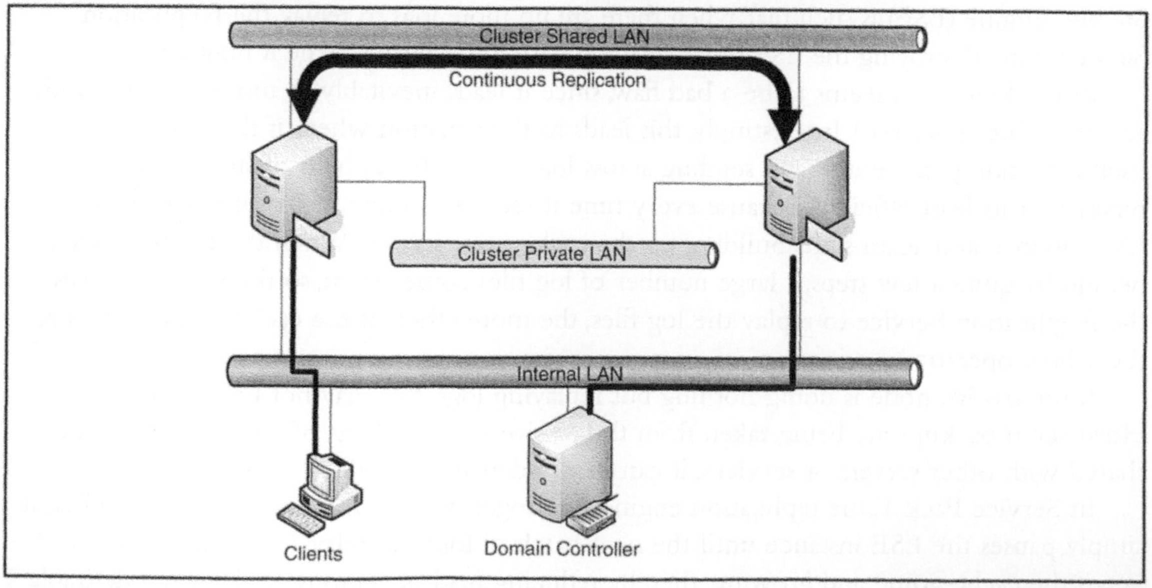

Why would you want to do this? The simplest reason is to avoid congestion on the main LAN network, where the replication data has to contend with other kinds of traffic and slow client access to Exchange. This can become particularly acute when the passive node has been unavailable for a time and there's a backlog of logs to replicate. Ideally, these should be replicated as quickly as possible to avoid potential loss, and a separate network—akin to having a separate backup LAN—is a useful tool for this.

It's worth noting that you can configure additional public networks for replication to provide resilience, but if the redundant replication network becomes unavailable for any reason, replication will fall back to the normal client network. For this reason, it's likely unnecessary to have more than one redundant network configured.

# Performance Improvements

There are a number of areas in SP1 where database performance has been improved and the idiosyncrasies of the ESE engine have changed. When designing Exchange environments, particularly storage, it may be important to know how the engine has changed to get a better feel of how much storage, memory, and CPU power is required, log file generation for backup window determination, and the like.

## Passive Node Log Replay

As mentioned in Chapter 1, there have been significant I/O reductions in the passive nodes of continuous replication scenarios. When log replay begins on a passive node, an ESE instance is created to manage the process. While it is replaying logs, ESE keeps in memory a cache of database pages it has read (the database cache) so it can read these pages quicker from memory and thus speed up the procedure. In RTM, the design of the replay function of the Extensible Storage Engine (ESE) is such that when there are no more logs to replay, the Replication Service stops, destroying the ESE instance along with the database cache it built up.

In hindsight, this seems to be a bad flaw, since it leads inevitably to more database reads and therefore more I/O. Interestingly, this leads to the situation where if the replication itself is working efficiently (and sending across log files in short bursts of small numbers), replay is at its least efficient, because every time it receives a burst of files it starts up that ESE instance and again starts building up the cache from scratch. When the passive node is behind by quite a few steps, a large number of log files come across, so the longer it takes the Replication Service to replay the log files, the more efficient the cache is and therefore the whole operation.

If the passive node is doing nothing but replaying logs, this may not be an issue. However, if backups are being taken from the passive node or parts of the disk system are shared with other servers or services, it can have a detrimental effect.

In Service Pack 1, the replication engine no longer discards the database cache; rather, it simply pauses the ESE instance until the next batch of logs to replay. This helps I/O as it keeps the cache going and growing, thereby reducing read operations. It also has a desirable side effect that it keeps the database cache in a "warm" state so failover to the passive node is quicker than before.

## Database Checksumming and Passive Node Backups

One of the benefits of the continuous replication mechanism is that, when using LCR and CCR, it's possible to take backups of the passive node rather than the active one. This reduces I/O on the active server, increases backup windows, and improves users' experience. In short, everybody's happy. However, because we're backing up the *copy* of the data rather than the data itself, how do we know that the active copy is in a consistent state? Backup operations, whether VSS-based or streaming-based, should check the state of the databases and logs backed up and flag when there's a consistency problem.

In RTM, the only way to check the state of the active copy—which is, after all, the one you should be worried about—is to back it up directly or manually performing an ESEUTIL check on the database. SP1 introduces a new online maintenance task that checks the consistency of the active database and finds any corruption. The Online Maintenance Checksum takes about half the online maintenance time window to scan database pages. Like the online defragmentation process, if t does not complete within the given time, it starts where it left off next time it runs.

This process is disabled by default as it requires significant amount of system resources, and it is only relevant if backups are performed on the passive node. Microsoft highly recommends taking backups from the passive node of a LCR/CCR system, so bear this in mind when designing such a system.

## Page Dependencies and Partial Merges

With almost every Exchange Server service pack comes an updated version of the Extensible Storage Engine. Beyond the implications of interoperability and backup/recovery, this can mean big differences in the performance profiles of Exchange; for instance, I/O performance, log file generation, and backup/restore performance. When ESE's method of performing operations changes, so does its performance profile.

SP1 for Exchange Server 2007 is no different. We already discussed passive node I/O improvements earlier, but other changes to ESE that have a slightly lesser effect are the removal of page dependencies and partial merges.

This is covered in great detail on the Exchange Team blog (http://msexchangeteam.com), but we'll summarize it here and its effect on storage and I/O.

Page dependencies were a method of reducing log files by linking two operations into one single operation. Page dependencies streamline operations such as move operations from being "Remove from here, write to here" to "Move from here to here." The dependency comes when moving a record from page A to page B, ESE is required to write the record to page B before it's deleted from page A. This has the effect of reducing log generation and avoiding data loss.

The disadvantages to this strategy include:

**Page recovery cannot be done in isolation.** Because one page operation may depend on another, recovering a single page from backup may require recovering another related page, and another and another. This would be incredibly time and resource consuming.

**Pages are written serially.** Because pages must be written in a certain order, according to the dependencies, it's more difficult for ESE to bunch together groups of write operations in the same area of the disk. This makes write operations relatively inefficient.

**More memory is required.** The online defragmentation operation reorganizes all the pages and therefore builds up huge dependency trees, requiring more memory to deal with it. According to Microsoft, this accounted for a need for an extra 512MB RAM per storage group in RTM.

Consequently, page dependencies were removed in SP1 at the expense of log file generation, which shot up by 33%. To counter this, the developers decided to remove partial merges within the database. Partial merges occur when a record is moved from one page to another without freeing up any pages in the hope that in the next online defragmentation pass, some space will be able to be freed up. This has the effect of compacting the database slightly tighter, thereby reducing disk space requirements. Since disk space is not at such a premium these days, this was not deemed so necessary. Removing partial merges had another effect on I/O, however. Because fewer move operations happen during online defragmentation, the I/O is much less—according to Microsoft's figures, this reduced "database churn" by around 80% and log file generation by 25%.

Overall, the ESE modifications in SP1 have a big effect on I/O, storage, and memory requirements. The Exchange Team provides a storage calculator (http://go.microsoft.com/fwlink/?linkid=84202) to help us calculate storage requirements, which they keep up to date when they make changes like this! In addition, the Mailbox Server Storage Design document (http://technet.microsoft.com/en-us/library/bb738147.aspx) is kept up to date for this purpose.

---

**NOTE**

Other documents and calculators of note are:

- **Planning Memory Configurations** http://technet.microsoft.com/en-us/library/bb738124.aspx
- **Planning Processor Configurations** http://technet.microsoft.com/en-us/library/aa998874.aspx
- **Planning Server Role Ratios** http://technet.microsoft.com/en-us/library/bb738159.aspx

---

# Transport Dumpster Improvements

The Transport Dumpster, the message delivery cache that is configurable on Hub Transport servers in a CCR cluster environment, now supports LCR deployments.

For situations where an LCR copy of a storage group is restored, the Restore-StorageGroupCopy commandlet has been modified to automatically submit a transport dumpster submission request to bring it up to date in a "lossy" failover situation.

So an administrator can find out some statistics about transport dumpster caches, the Get-StorageGroupCopyStatus commandlet has been updated. This can now report number of messages in the cache, oldest message, the availability of transport dumpster cache servers, and other information, which you can look up before initiating a restore. Knowing at least which HT servers are available before restoring can be useful so you can catch all the available lost messages during the process.

Other changes to the way the Get-StorageGroupCopyStatus task communicates with the servers in question improve the information available to the administrator. However, this change means that the commandlet talks to the server directly using synchronous RPC traffic, which should be taken into account if doing it over slow links.

# Reporting and Monitoring Improvements

There are a few known issues with storage group copy status reporting in RTM; for example, incorrect or inaccurate status reports on copies and problems with the underlying replay mechanism. The Get-StorageGroupCopyStatus has been updated to correct these issues, partly by changing the communication method it uses as mentioned previously.

A new cmdlet—Test-ReplicationHealth—checks various aspects of continuous replication environments (LCR, CCR, and SCR) to help proactive monitoring of the environment. It also integrates into the Microsoft Operations Management (or SCOM as it is now) management pack so your support people can react quickly to errors in the system.

Test-ReplicationHealth checks underlying cluster components first (node, quorum, and network status) and then examines the replication service and the status of storage group copies. It starts with the most important tests and moves down from there—quite refreshing.

# Management Console Additions

Although Microsoft is trying to make command-line junkies of us all, they once in a while throw us GUI-addicts a bone by adding new functionality to the Management Console. A few additions for managing clusters will make it easier for some of us to perform the operations and to remember that operations such as moving between nodes should be done in Exchange and not the Cluster Manager! The new Manage Clustered Mailbox Server wizard provides GUI access to operations such as stopping, starting, and moving the CMS.

# Local Continuous Replication

Local Continuous Replication (LCR) is a single-server solution that employs the asynchronous continuous replication mechanism of Exchange Server 2007 to replicate mailbox databases to a local copy on a separate disk array. This second copy can be activated in case of data failure or logical corruption on the active database. Figure 5.6 is a typical LCR configuration.

**Figure 5.6** Duplicated Storage Controllers and Disks Optimize the LCR Configuration

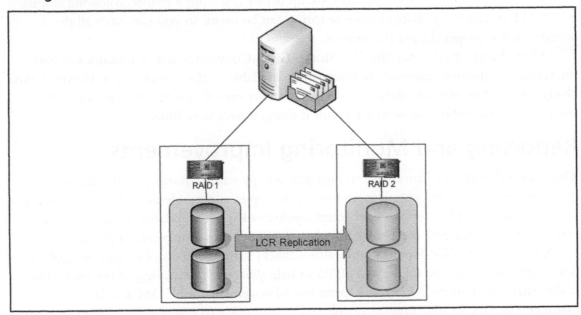

It is not necessary to have a separate storage controller, as it's possible to host both copies on different volumes on the same physical disk. However, a separate controller with separate arrays provides best resilience and efficiency, as discussed here.

LCR is designed to lower the total cost of ownership by providing the following features:

**Reduce recovery time for database disasters**  In case the active database copy becomes corrupt or the disk array breaks, the administrator can *activate* the passive copy in a matter of minutes and continue operation of the server.

**Offload VSS-based backups**  All types of VSS backup (full, copy, incremental, and differential) can be offloaded to the passive database copies. This means a reduction in the load on the primary storage subsystem, particularly if a separate disk controller is used. Consequently, this can lower the dependency on backup windows and raise the maximum database size limit on the server.

**Ease the backup burden** Although it doesn't eliminate the need for regular backups, having a second copy in sync can help reduce the number of full backups required on the server.

LCR provides a reasonable level of resilience against storage hardware failure at minimal cost, and is therefore ideal for companies where the mail system can handle a little downtime without major hardship.

Service Pack 1 now enables the Transport Dumpster to be used in LCR environments. Previously, the dumpster was available only for CCR environments (see the next section). Whereas a CCR failover is automatic, LCR failover (or passive copy activation) is manual. In both cases, the request for transport dumpster redelivery is made automatically by the Restore-StorageGroupCopy commandlet when failover occurs.

# Requirements

Hardware and software requirements for LCR are the same as for a standard standalone Exchange server. To hold the passive copy of the database requires a separate volume, which should at the very least be on separate disks and preferably on a secondary RAID controller. This will take full advantage of the performance benefits of LCR listed in the previous section.

LCR-enabled storage groups must conform to the "single database per storage group" rule common to all types of continuous replication. You cannot add a second mailbox store to an LCR-enabled storage group, nor is it possible to LCR-enable a storage group with more than one mailbox store present.

# Implementing LCR

Setting up Local Continuous Replication is easy. Where the effort and thought is required is in the planning of storage and utilizing the features of LCR in the best way possible. By this, we mean how to organize your LCR configuration to optimize I/O, backup, and recovery.

I/O optimization is handled by investing in a secondary RAID card and RAID array. Generally speaking, having the additional load of log shipping and database seeding on the same RAID controller and/or disks as the main database will slow the operational I/O of Exchange and make for a less optimal user experience in some cases, so separating out this extra storage task to a separate controller helps avoid any negative impact of LCR. It may be worth considering, however, the impact of the RAID controller cache on a situation like this. Given that the same write operation is happening on the production log disk and the LCR log disk, perhaps the cache would speed up write operations if both volumes were on the same controller.

Backup optimization is assisted by LCR by the fact that full backups are generally not required as frequently as when not using replication. Backing up the passive copy of the database frees up I/O on the active controller and adds very little overheard to the server itself in terms of CPU and memory usage. As with any Exchange server, however, you must take into account database sizes and therefore the strain on the system as a result of taking snapshot backups of the passive databases. Streaming Exchange backups cannot be taken from the passive node, but all types of VSS backup (full, copy, differential, and incremental) are possible and supported.

The main use for LCR is recovery optimization, but the efficiency of the recovery process is dependent on the planning and implementation of the LCR setup. Obviously in terms of resilience and fast recovery times, having the copies on a separate HBA and LUNs is the way to go, since this avoids a single point of failure in the disk system. (Having super-duper replication to another disk isn't going to help much if your single RAID controller blows up, for example.) Also consider that the disks housing the passive copy of the databases may be called upon to run the active databases and so should be specified accordingly, rather than sticking a couple of SATA disks onto your enterprise server because "it'll never be needed anyway." Famous last words.

Another advantage of the quick recovery method inherent in LCR restores (i.e., pointing Exchange to another existing set of databases) is that it increases the recommended maximum database size, since, unlike with streaming restores from tape for example, the recovery time is independent of the amount of data. There are other factors in play, of course, so it doesn't remove database size limits completely.

Enabling LCR can be done through the management shell, as can every operation in Exchange, but it's probably easier to enable it using the console. Simply right-click the storage group and select **Enable Local Continuous Replication**. After specifying the paths for the storage group copy and the database copy, LCR is enabled, the database is seeded to the second LUN, and log file replication commences. It couldn't be much easier (Figure 5.7).

**Figure 5.7** A Couple of Clicks and LCR Is Running

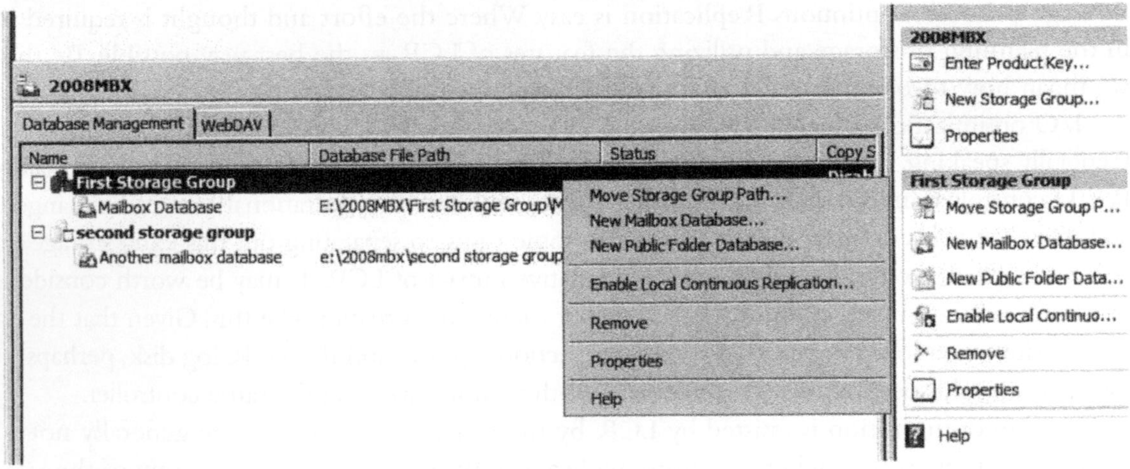

Using the management shell requires a two-stage process: enabling the database copy and then the storage group copy. It seems counter-intuitive to enable them in this order, especially as in the GUI, you simply enable replication on the storage group, and it enables the database automatically. However, Exchange complains if you try it the other way around. To enable LCR for the database in Figure 5.7, use the command:

```
Enable-DatabaseCopy -Identity "2008MBX\First Storage Group\Mailbox Database"
-CopyEdbFilePath "F:\LocalCopies\First Storage Group\Mailbox Database.edb"
```

To then enable the storage group copy:

```
Enable-StorageGroupCopy -Identity "2008MBX First Storage Group"
-CopyLogFolderPath:"F:\LocalCopies\First Storage Group" -CopySystem
FolderPath:"F:\LocalCopies\First Storage Group"
```

**NOTE**

In our test environment, we're being lazy and putting the logs and databases together on the same volume, but in a production environment, each should be on its own LUN.

You might agree that enabling LCR via the EMC is slightly easier than in EMS.

# Managing and Monitoring LCR

At a glance, you can check that LCR is behaving itself by looking at the management console. The properties of the storage group (Figure 5.8) tell you enough information to figure out how replication is, if there is any delay or problems, and, of course, where to find the passive copies.

**Figure 5.8** EMC Tells You Enough about the LCR Status for Most Occasions

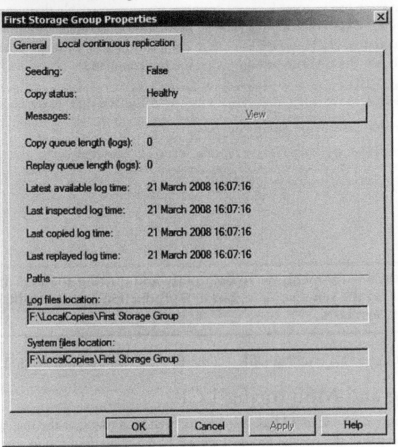

However, to obtain more information about the status of the LCR process and the active and passive database copies, use the Get-StorageGroupCopyStatus commandlet in the EMS. Issuing the command

```
Get-StorageGroupCopyStatus -Identity "2008MBX\First Storage Group" | fl
```

provides a host of additional information shown in Figure 5.9, including the last time the active or passive databases have been backed up and Transport Dumpster information.

**Figure 5.9** Sometimes the Shell Has Its Uses—Better Output

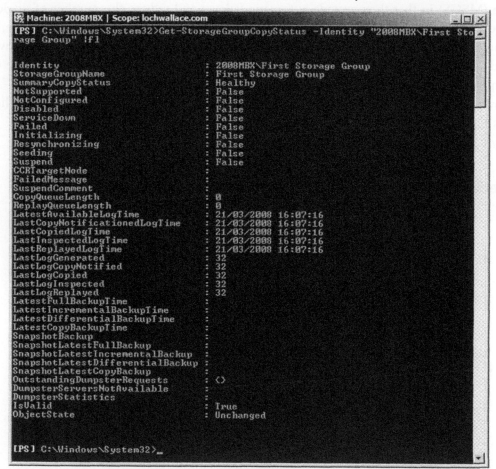

Despite the wealth of information provided by this commandlet, you're no closer to knowing if the actual database is in a consistent state. The new online maintenance task—Database Checksumming—checks the active database for inconsistencies, but there is no equivalent method of checking the passive copy other than activating the copy and letting online maintenance do its thing.

Another way to verify the integrity of a passive copy of the databases is by creating a VSS snapshot and checking its consistency using ESEUTIL. We cover this in the "Standby Continuous Replication" section later in the chapter.

# Cluster Continuous Replication

Cluster Continuous Replication (CCR) is an implementation of continuous replication that uses the failover capabilities of a Windows cluster while providing storage resilience through the log-shipping and replay functions of Exchange.

CCR clusters are similar to standard shared storage clusters based on Microsoft Cluster Service (MSCS) in that they provide automatic failover and reduce the number of single points of failure in the system. However, because CCR does not employ shared storage, and therefore avoids some complications this presents, it often makes for a more cost-effective method of achieving the same—actually more—resilience. CCR clusters also make use of a new type of quorum configuration called "Majority Node Set with File Share Witness" in Windows Server 2003, or "Node and File Share Majority" in Windows Server 2008. The witness file share is often situated on a hub-transport server, but can be located on any suitably located server. A standard CCR setup is shown in Figure 5.10.

**Figure 5.10** A CCR Cluster Using a File Share Witness

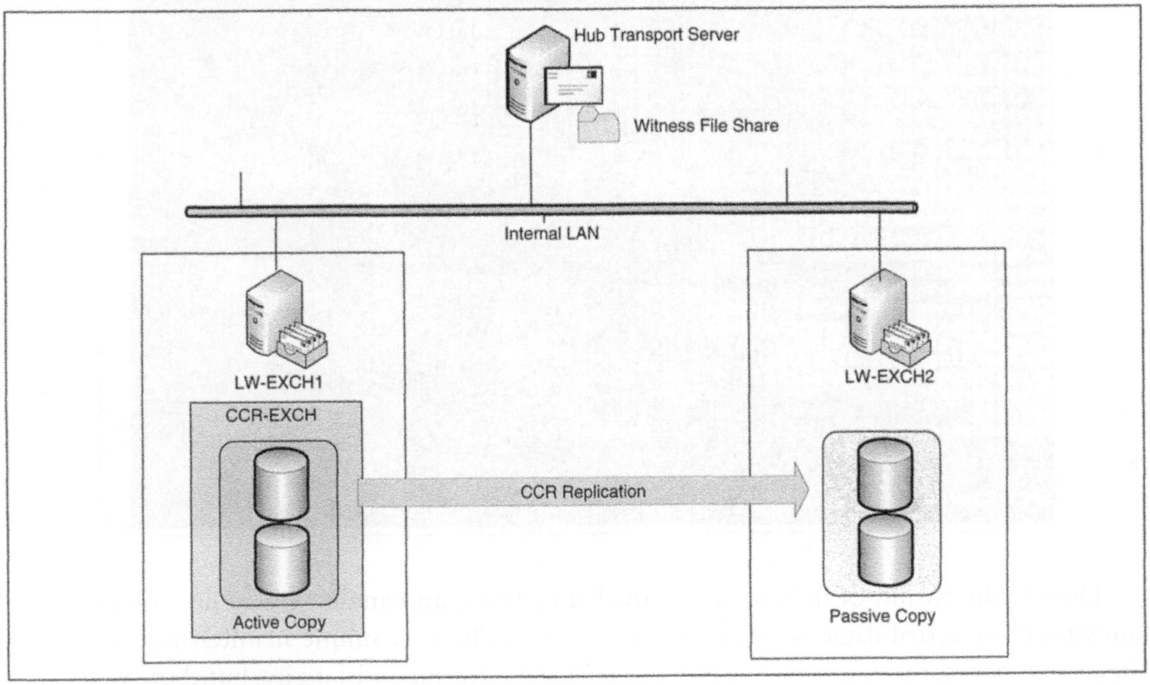

In terms of the Exchange replication, CCR differs from LCR only in that the databases and logs are stored on a separate server rather than on the local server. This separate server is a second node on the same MSCS cluster, and therefore provides cluster resilience and automatic failover on top of the data resilience of continuous replication. CCR also provides for scheduled outages in the same way as a Single Copy Cluster does, by enabling administrators to manually move the service (the clustered mailbox server) between nodes.

In contrast to SCC, or traditional clusters, CCR can be configured only with two nodes—an active and a passive.

CCR clusters provide the following advantages:

**Data resilience** Continuous replication provides some protection against database corruption. Corruption caused by a failed RAID controller on the active node, for example, will not be transferred to the passive database copy, and the cluster can fail over to the other node, and other copy of the mailbox databases, with minimum service outage.

**Cross-subnet configurations** CCR, when used in conjunction with Windows Server 2008, is able to span datacenters, providing automatic failover between geographical locations. The nodes must reside in the same Active Directory site, however.

**Backup from the passive node** The ability to offload backup responsibilities to the passive node frees up I/O and CPU cycles on the active node. Because it doesn't require resources on the server that serves clients, it also increases the available backup window and therefore the maximum possible database size. Only VSS-based backups are available on the passive node.

**Less reliance on backups** Although not a replacement for full backups, CCR makes a case for reducing the number and frequency of full database backups. It also provides an additional restore method prior to having to restore from backup tape.

**Flexibility** Being a clustered server, CCR clusters enable upgrades and patches to the OS and installed software with minimal downtime. A service pack update to the cluster, for example, involves only a single failing over of the mailbox databases, which can take a matter of seconds.

CCR clusters can be deployed in situations where otherwise a traditional (SCC) cluster may be used. CCR clusters have a number of advantages over SCC clusters that make them more appropriate in situations where cross-site failover is required, where shared storage is not present or not a possibility, and network bandwidth is of reasonably high quality (speed and latency). On the other hand, SCC clusters are more flexible on a local scale since they can expand to up to eight nodes on the enterprise versions of Windows, thereby making more efficient use of hardware.

# Requirements

Because it is a cluster configuration, CCR requires the enterprise versions of Windows Server and Exchange Server. The heartbeat and any redundant cluster replication networks require additional network cards and network infrastructure, and storage requirements are doubled due to the two copies of the same data.

For the cluster configuration, a file share witness is required on a separate server. Microsoft recommends that this be on a Client Access Server in the same site, but depending on the logical and geographical properties of the network, this may be in a separate location to both servers and on a standard file server.

# Implementing CCR on Windows Server 2008

Creating a Windows Server 2008 cluster for CCR is relatively simple because the minimum amount of information is required to create the cluster in the first instance (cluster name and IP address), and it has no particular hardware requirements above that required for Exchange 2007, in contrast to SCC clusters that required shared storage and components listed in the Windows Server Catalog.

While creating the cluster, allow Windows to validate the configuration. If you do not, the cluster may not be in a supported configuration.

## Networking

There are three network cards in the cluster created in this section. Typically, a cluster has two NICs—one for public traffic and one for the heartbeat communication. However, in SP1 it's possible to configure the CCR replication to take place over a "redundant" shared cluster network, so why not create a third network for this purpose? As with any Windows cluster, the binding order of the network cards is important (Figure 5.11). The main client network card must be at the top so the outbound traffic flows across that network unless destined specifically for one of the other local networks.

**Figure 5.11** The Top NIC Matters, the Others Can Be in Any Order

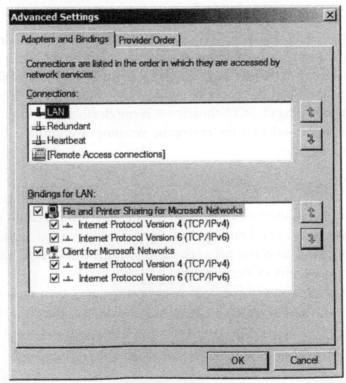

If installing nodes on different subnets, it's important to recognize the implications this has on networking. When the cluster fails over, both the cluster IP address and the Clustered Mailbox Server IP address change while the names obviously remain the same. For this reason, the configuration of DNS plays a major part in the speed of getting things up and running after failover. Clients must be able to access the new IP address, so the DNS entries for the shared resources should have a short Time To Live (TTL) value. It may be necessary to flush the DNS cache on some clients so they query the DNS server for the new address.

Configure the Heartbeat network to handle only the heartbeat traffic between hosts, but all other networks should be configured to host both client traffic and private (heartbeat) traffic. In Windows Server 2008, any network that hosts client traffic also can host the heartbeat, but in Windows Server 2003, you can select client only.

It is also best to rename the individual network cards on the hosts and the cluster network names, so it's easy to see which is which, as in Figure 5.12.

---

**NOTE**

Networks used for continuous replication traffic must be enabled for client and cluster traffic.

---

## Cluster Quorum

Windows Server 2008 clustering is markedly different from Windows Server 2003. The two cannot coexist in the same cluster, nor can they coexist within any of the Exchange continuous replication configurations. When you create a Windows Server 2008 cluster, by default a cluster is created with a Node Majority quorum, but a CCR cluster should use the File Share Witness style of quorum. In Windows Server 2003, to add a file share witness required a command line

```
Cluster res "Majority Node Set" /priv MNSFileShare=\\servername\sharename
```

In Windows Server 2008, the quorum can be set through the GUI. Through the Configure Cluster Quorum Settings option (Figure 5.12), you can configure any of the four available quorum configurations.

**Figure 5.12** The Quorum Type Can Be Modified after the Cluster Creation

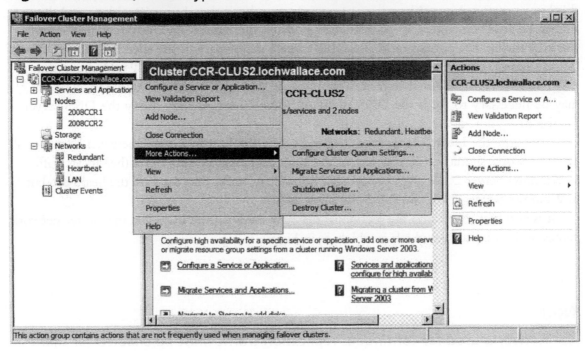

# Installing Exchange on the Cluster

When you install Exchange Server 2007 on a cluster node, you have the choice to create an active or a passive mailbox server. The difference between the two is simply that the active option creates a Clustered Mailbox Server (CMS)—the equivalent to an Exchange Virtual Server in Exchange 2003—and installs the Mailbox role on the node. Installing a passive cluster server installs the Mailbox role only. You can install the active and passive in any order, but typically installing a passive node is done on a cluster server that is the target for SCR replication.

> **NOTE**
>
> The mailbox role is the only role that can be installed on a clustered server.

When installing the active mailbox server, you can specify the location of the database files and the system files. It's easiest to do this when creating the clustered mailbox server, since moving the cluster databases later is more work. In a CCR cluster, Exchange won't carry out the entire move for you as it does in a standalone server (Figure 5.13). You must drop into the shell and use the Move-*StorageGroupPath −ConfigurationOnly* command to modify the configuration, and then manually move the databases on each node. This is obviously prone to errors that could prevent the server from failing over.

**Figure 5.13** It's a Little More Work to Move the Storage Group in a CCR Environment

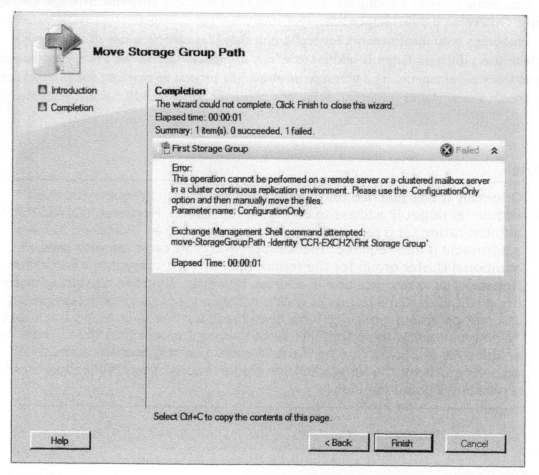

The passive node holds its copy of the databases on the same path as the active, as it must, so before installing the passive node make sure there is at least a volume with the same drive letter as the storage volume on the active node. It's not necessary to create any of the folders, by the way, as the replication engine will create these when it starts.

After installation of the passive node, the database seeding and log shipping starts automatically. Unlike in the other continuous replication scenarios, there is no other configuration required, but the cluster failover should be tested using the *Move-ClusteredMailboxServer* command to ensure the clustered server is performing correctly.

# Enable Replication over a Redundant Network

Enabling the database seeding and log replication over a redundant network is ideally something you want to do before Exchange starts replicating everything across the network of its choice. Unfortunately, you need to install Exchange to configure it, but then Exchange takes it upon itself to start replicating traffic at its leisure. If you have a lot of traffic to replicate on cluster creation, once the passive node has been installed, disable the replication for the time being by right-clicking the storage group and selecting **Suspend Storage Group Copy**. Otherwise, use the Suspend-StorageGroupCopy commandlet.

Enabling a redundant network for replication should ideally be a case of telling each node to use a different target IP address to which to replicate traffic, but because of the some dependency requirements, it's a bit more involved. The process of enabling the network actually creates a new cluster group consisting of a Network Name and IP Address resource.

> **NOTE**
>
> Originally it was planned that "redundant replication" require just the additional target IP address to configure replication. However, LOCALSYSTEM authentication (as is required) cannot be done using an IP address alone so a hostname is also required. The solution Microsoft came up with uses an additional cluster group for the redundant network, consisting of a cluster Network Name resource and IP address. However, Windows clustering doesn't bring Network Name resources online if they are not publicly accessible (an assumption would appear to have been made a while back along the lines of "who would want to do that?"), hence the requirement that the network be enabled for public traffic. The cluster creates a corresponding computer account in AD for the Network Name resource continuous replication uses for replicating DB and log files.

To enable the replication we must drop down into the shell again as there is no GUI interface for this:

```
Enable-ContinuousReplicationHostName -Identity <CMSName> -TargetMachine <NodeName>
-HostName <NetworkNameforReplication> -IPV4Address <IPAddress>
```

This command creates a new cluster group that contains an IP Address and a Network Name resource pertaining to the local node. The name and the IP address specified must be different from those already in use. The results of running this command on each node are in Figure 5.14.

It's not clear from the documentation what each parameter refers to, so here's a list of the appropriate parameters:

**Identity** The name of the clustered mailbox server (in this case, CCR-EXCH2).

**TargetMachine** The name of the cluster node that will own the hostname parameter; i.e., the local node.

**HostName** The Network Name for the cluster resource bring created.

**IPV4Address** The new IP address associated with the Network Name.

In our environment, on 2008CCR1 the command will be something like:

```
Enable-ContinuousReplicationHostName -Identity CCR-EXCH2 -TargetMachine 2008CCR1
-HostName 2008CCR1-Repl -IPV4Address 10.0.1.5
```

and on 2008CCR2:

```
Enable-ContinuousReplicationHostName -Identity CCR-EXCH2 -TargetMachine
2008CCR2 -HostName 2008CCR2-Repl -IPV4Address 10.0.1.6
```

This creates a cluster group for each node, as shown in Figure 5.14.

**Figure 5.14** A Name and IP Address Is Created for Each Node on the Redundant Network

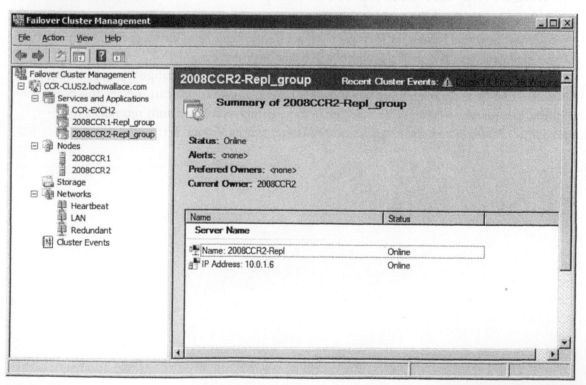

Name resolution is required for the new names and IP addresses, so you can either register each name in DNS or simply add the partner node addresses into the Hosts file on each node; for example, the following entry on 2008CCR1:

```
10.0.1.6 2008CCR2.lochwallace.com
```

The equivalent entry is added to the Hosts file on 2008CCR2.

## Testing Replication

When the cluster is set up and configured to replicate across the redundant network, you should test the behavior of the CR cluster during failure of the redundant network. The redundant network and the main client network provide resilience for replication since the replication service will send logs across the client network as a backup. You can test this by bringing down the redundant network manually.

Running the Test-ReplicationStatus commandlet brings up a warning on the ClusterNetwork test, but a quick glance at the Storage Group's Copy Status in the Management Console should show replication as "Healthy." This means the replication has failed over to the main client network, and of course, you can verify this by checking the contents of the log folder on the passive node.

## Configuring the Transport Dumpster

To provide the best protection for mailbox data when an emergency situation occurs, you should configure the Transport Dumpster to retain messages sent through the server so they can be replayed into the database when a lossy failover occurs.

The Transport Dumpster is configured through either the Exchange Management Console (EMC) or Management Shell (EMS). In the console, you can specify the two required parameters—Maximum size per storage group and Maximum retention time—under Hub Transport in the Organization Configuration (Figure 5.15).

**Figure 5.15** The Transport Dumpster Settings Are Global

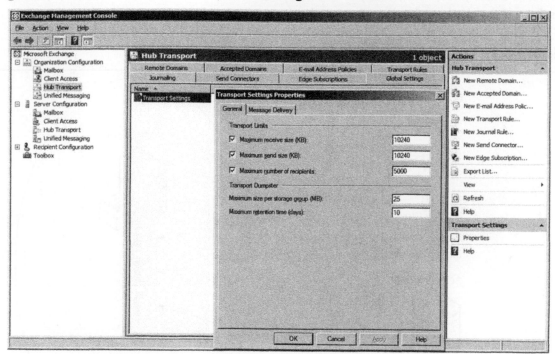

Alternatively, through the shell, the Set-TransportConfig commandlet can be used:

```
Set-TransportConfig -MaxDumpsterSizePerStorageGroup 25MB -MaxDumpsterTime
10.00:00:00
```

This command sets the maximum size per storage group to 25MB and a maximum age of 10 days.

# Standby Continuous Replication

Standby Continuous Replication (SCR) is the new replication method included in SP1 that gives administrators more options in terms of the distribution of data within and between sites for recovery situations. While it uses the same replication engine (Continuous Replication) as LCR and CCR, it is not designed for automatic resumption of service and so lacks the failover facilities of CCR.

Rather, SCR is a tool for implementing standby environments for recovery situations— either site recovery or server recovery. SCR provides a method of copying databases to a DR server, which can then host one or all of the databases in a disaster. A recovery scenario may involve the loss of one or more databases on the source server, or the whole source server itself. In either case, it is possible to either use the database portability feature of Exchange 2007 or use a server recovery method (using Setup /m:RecoverServer or Setup /RecoverCMS for clustered servers). Generally, it may be more appropriate to use database portability only when a subset of the databases has been lost on the source (Figure 5.16).

**Figure 5.16** SCR Can Replicate from or to Multiple Servers

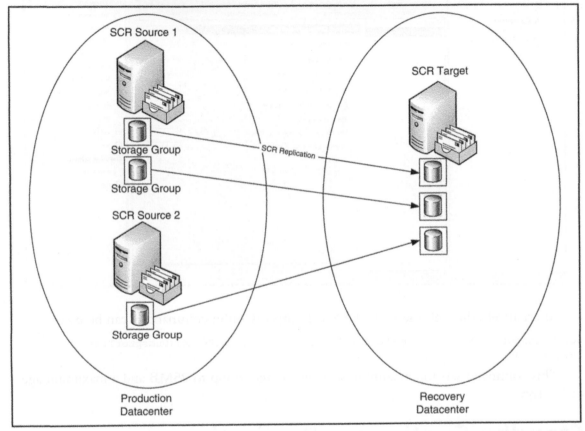

**NOTE**

Database portability refers to the fact that you can move a mailbox database to a different server in the same organization and mount it on that server without having to make any configuration changes on either server or database. In Exchange 2003, databases are portable, but a number of manual modifications must be made by the administrator when moving databases between servers. Exchange 2007 removed these requirements, which were imposed on the Exchange application level rather than the ESE level, to avoid the possibility of human error when orchestrating the database move. Public folder databases are not portable because of their structure and behavior, and must be replicated rather than moved.

Companies with a significant reliance on high availability and DR strategies, such as banks and financial institutions, have warm standby locations to use in the event of a major incident. For these companies, SCR provides much greater flexibility for implementing Exchange DR within their environment without complicating the configuration with third-party software or SAN replication. SCR, and continuous replication in general, is particularly useful where the WAN links are slow or there is much latency. In these cases, asynchronous synchronization must be used.

SCR can also be useful for server-resilience strategies within a single site. Standalone Exchange servers can replicate their databases to other individual or clustered servers, which can then be activated if the primary server goes offline. This is a similar situation to CCR, except SCR would be more appropriate in the following situations:

**Cross-subnet replication** If you're running Windows Server 2003, CCR is not applicable to nodes that are on different subnets. SCR, however, can replicate to a different subnet.

**Manual failover required** It's not always appropriate to have an automatic failover process for Exchange servers. Depending on the environment, failing over Exchange nodes may not be desirable if you can help it (especially if you are failing over to a remote site, when all of your users are local). You may therefore want to try to fix the primary node before activating databases on the recovery server.

**Hardware requirements** The hardware and the network infrastructure may not be appropriate or compatible for CCR and clustering.

**Cost** CCR replication requires Microsoft clustering, which is available only on the Enterprise versions of Exchange and Windows. SCR requires only Standard versions, so is potentially much cheaper for licensing.

**Active Directory site restrictions** CCR cluster nodes must be in the same AD site. SCR can replicate to a target in a different AD site.

**Multiple targets/sources** SCR supports replication from multiple source servers to a single target server and from a single source to multiple targets. CCR supports only one-to-one replication.

Another point worth noting is that in an SCR environment it's not possible to take backups of the target databases, unlike in a CCR environment where backups of the passive node are fully supported and recommended.

# Requirements and Features

SCR is an implementation of continuous replication that takes care of replicating data and replaying it into the target server and does not require a cluster configuration to implement.

The members of the SCR configuration can be cluster nodes but do not have to be. Hence, SCR is available in the Standard edition of Exchange Server 2007 SP1.

The other requirements for SCR are similar to the other types of replication (LCR and CCR):

- SCR-enabled storage groups can contain only one database.

- Replication can be one-to-many or many-to-one—you can configure a single source to replicate to many targets, or many sources to replicate to a single target.

- SCR includes a built-in, configurable delay for log replay to help avoid corruption on the source being replicated to the target in some situations.

Source and target server requirements:

- A source server can be:

  - A standalone Mailbox server

  - A clustered mailbox server in a Single Copy Cluster (SCC)

  - A clustered mailbox server in a CCR cluster

- A target server can be:

  - A standalone Mailbox server

  - A passive cluster node where the Mailbox role is installed but no Clustered Mailbox Server has been installed

**NOTE**

The operating system on the source and target servers must be the same version, so you cannot use SCR between Windows 2003 and Windows 2008 servers.

Target servers can have other roles installed as well as the Mailbox role, unless of course they are clustered.

## SCR and Public Folders

Public folder stores can be replicated within an SCR environment. However, because public folder replication uses a very different replication technique to continuous replication, public folder involvement in SCR should only be considered in particular cases.

The only valid sources for incorporating public folders into an SCR environment are a standalone Exchange server where replication is not enabled on the storage group containing the public folder database, or an SCC clustered mailbox server.

If public folder replication is disabled (in other words, there is only one public folder database in the organization), it is supported to replicate public folder databases using SCR. The storage group containing the public folder database must conform to the "one store per storage group" rule, however.

There are occasions when Microsoft does support SCR replication and public folder replication on the same database, and that is when public folders are being migrated either in to or out of an SCR-enabled storage group. You can replicate public folder data from a standalone server or SCC cluster into an SCR-enabled storage group as long as all other copies of the public folder database are removed when the data has finished replicating to the SCR group. Likewise, it is supported to replicate from an SCR-enabled group to another server in the organization. Clearly, the situation with using the two together is slightly precarious, and while it's possible to do it, Microsoft feels that the potential for problems is too great to support it officially.

# Implementing SCR on Windows Server 2008

If you like to have a graphical view of what's going on, which is useful when configuring an option and for viewing the configuration and any errors, you're out of luck here; SCR is strictly shell-based. Luckily, the management of SCR isn't too complex, but the lack of GUI interface does mean it's not immediately obvious what's going on when you open the Management Console. It is nice to have a full picture of the environment rather than having to look for something specifically.

## Activating SCR

Configuring SCR is simple:

```
Enable-StorageGroupCopy -Identity <NameofStorageGroup> -StandbyMachine
<NameofSCRTargetMachine> -ReplayLagTime 0.1:0:0
```

However, the simplicity of the configuration command implies a major assumption/requirement, which is that the target machine must have the same folder structure to contain the storage group files, database, and log files as does the source. For example, if the source databases sit on d:\Mailbox\SG1, the target server must have the same folder available for the SCR copy.

### *Storage Planning*

Replicating multiple sources into a single target has the potential for conflict and confusion, particularly if each source server is using the default location for its database files. Therefore, before implementing SCR there must be some planning in terms of database location and storage in general.

It's common for companies to configure their Exchange servers in a standard way, including of course standard hardware, software version, and so forth, and Exchange configuration in terms of database locations. The servers in our test environment all store the database files on the E: drive in a standard location (E:\Exchange Server\First Storage Group). This is going to cause problems when replicating storage groups from multiple servers (CCR-EXCH2 and 2008MBX) to one server (2008SCR1) since both storage groups will want to occupy that folder.

One option is to modify each mailbox server to store its databases on a different volume, so the stores from CCR-EXCH2 use drive E: and those from 2008MBX use drive F:. This does have the advantage of making storage planning on the SCR target easier since the volumes on the target match those in the sources.

However, a better strategy may be to use the same volume (drive letter) but create a folder on each source relating to the server itself, and create a subfolder for each storage group underneath it, as shown in Figure 5.17. For example, on CCR-EXCH2 you might store the files on E:\Exchange Server\CCR-EXCH2\First Storage Group and E:\Exchange Server\CCR-EXCH2\Second Storage Group.

**Figure 5.17** Keeping Multiple Storage Group Folders Apart

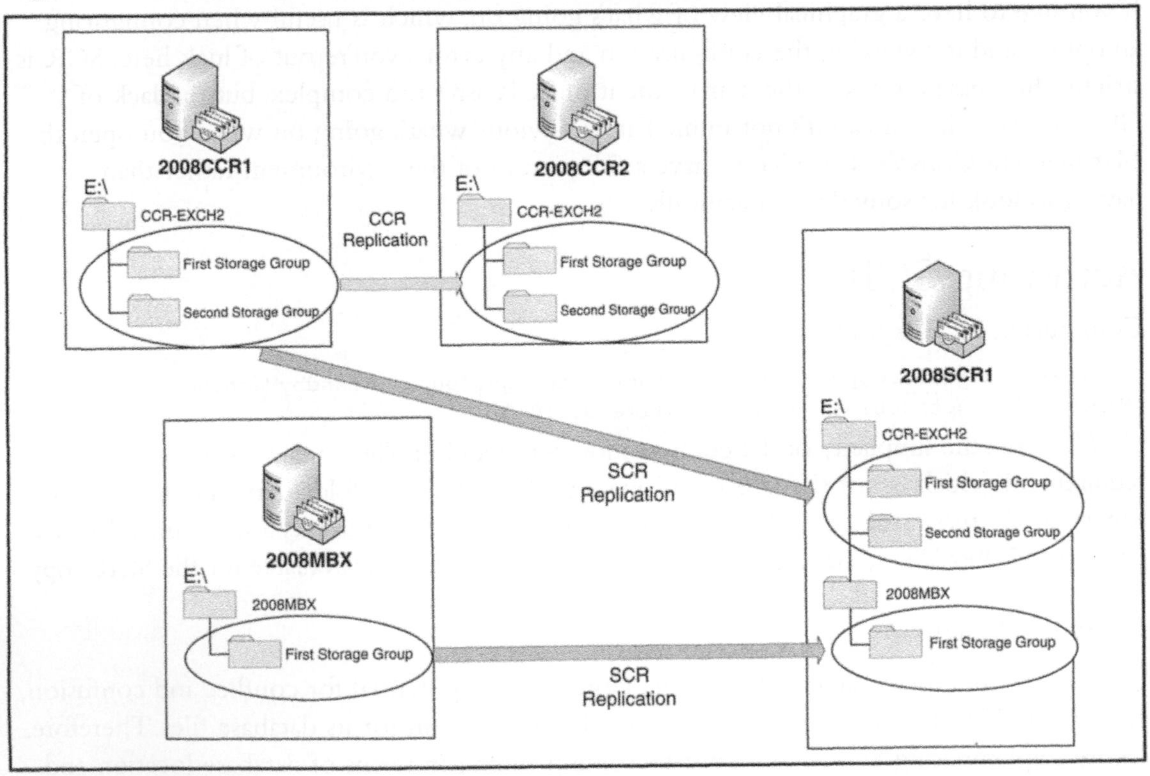

Replicating multiple databases to the same volume on the SCR target server may bring up issues with space and disk management. To counter this difficulty, you can configure mount points on the E: drive. For example, the 2008MBX\First Storage Group folder could be a

mount point that redirects to an F: drive on a separate storage array. Mount points are completely transparent to applications and fully supported in Exchange 2007 replication scenarios.

Obviously, in a production environment, each server will have separate RAID arrays for logs and databases, and providing a similar separation of databases/logs should be considered on the target server as well.

## Moving the Databases in a CCR Environment

Moving the storage group and database files in a standalone server can be done in the GUI under Database Management. Exchange will change the paths to the files in the server configuration and move the files. However, in a clustered environment, it's more involved—you need to modify the configuration and then manually move the files. Of course, it's necessary to move the files in *both* locations, since this data is being replicated.

If CCR server CCR-EXCH2 was installed with the default storage group\database location of "C:\Program Files\Microsoft\Exchange Server\Mailbox\First Storage Group," the operation to move them to the E: drive is:

1. **Suspend replication.** The CCR replication must be suspended for the duration of the move.

2. **Change the storage group path.** Use the Move-StorageGroupPath to change the location of the storage group files on the server. In this case:

```
Move-StorageGroupPath -Identity "CCR-EXCH2\First Storage Group"
-LogFileFolder "E:\CCR-EXCH2\First Storage Group" -SystemFolderPath
"E:\CCR-EXCH2\First Storage Group" -ConfigurationOnly
```

3. **Change the database path.** The database path also has to be modified in the shell using the following command:

```
Move-DatabasePath -Identity "CCR-EXCH2\First Storage Group\Mailbox
Database" -EdbFilePath "E:\CCR-EXCH2\First Storage Group\Mailbox Database.
edb" -ConfigurationOnly
```

4. **Move the database and storage group files.** Move the contents of the "First Storage Group" folder to "\CCR-EXCH2." This must be done on both nodes of the cluster! If the destination folder has not already been created, Exchange will create it.

5. **Mount the database.** This can be done in the GUI or by using the Mount-Database –Identity "CCR-EXCH2\First Storage Group\Mailbox Database" commandlet.

6. **Resume replication.** Resume the storage group copy replication in the GUI or by using the Resume-StorageGroupCopy –Identity "CCR-EXCH2\First Storage Group" commandlet.

Replicating from multiple source servers to a single target can present a number of challenges because of the prerequisites to SCR replication. Besides keeping the database paths separate and juggling disks and volumes for the databases, server recovery requires the installation paths to be identical on the source and target.

# Configuring Replication

To activate Standby Continuous Replication on a server, use the *Enable-StorageGroupCopy* command. This is the same command as used for Local Continuous Replication environments. Whereas LCR uses the –CopyLogFolderPath and –CopySystemFolderpath parameters to copy files onto a local volume, enabling SCR requires only two parameters—the storage group name and the target server name.

To replicate the storage group on 2008MBX to 2008SCR1, we issue the command:

```
Enable-StorageGroupCopy -Identity "2008MBX\First Storage Group"
-StandbyMachine 2008SCR1
```

There are no target folder parameters since these must be identical to the database folders on the source server.

---

**NOTE**

> To kick off SCR replication to a clustered target mailbox server, the Failover Cluster administration tools must be installed on the local machine. 2008MBX is a standalone server and so isn't able to configure the replication. However, rather than installing the cluster tools, you can configure the replication either from the target server or from any other clustered server. The command is the same.

---

On CCR-EXCH2 are multiple storage groups we want to replicate, so instead of enabling each individually we can enable replication for all of them by piping the results of the Get-StorageGroup commandlet into the Enable-StorageGroupCopy commandlet:

```
Get-StorageGroup -Server CCR-EXCH2 | Enable-StorageGroupCopy
-StandbyMachine 2008SCR1
```

This will enable replication for all the storage groups with the default parameters. Unfortunately, for a test environment, the default parameters include a 24-hour lag time. This is set so you can hopefully avoid the transfer of any corruption from source to target, but it's no good when you want to test it immediately. Therefore, adding the parameter "–ReplayLagTime 0" will cause the replication to happen immediately.

> **NOTE**
>
> When you enable SCR, the commandlet will warn you that database seeding needs to be manually run. Do this by first suspending SCR replication and then using the Update-StorageGroupCopy command. For the previous example, you could use the following command:
>
> ```
> Get-StorageGroup –Server CCR-EXCH2 | Update-StorageGroupCopy
> -StandbyMachine 2008SCR1
> ```

The destination folders are created automatically on 2008SCR1, as you can see in Figure 5.18.

**Figure 5.18** The SCR Target Storage Group Folders

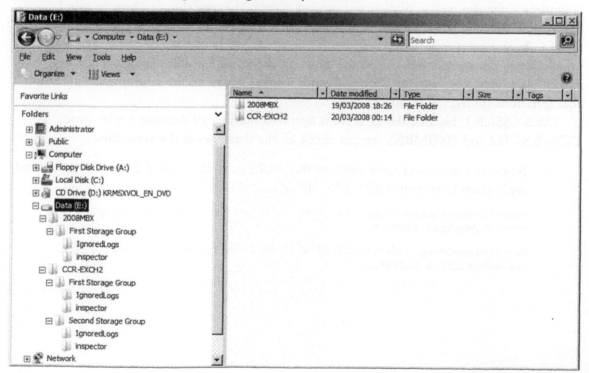

### *Creating a New SCR-Enabled Storage Group*

You can also enable standby continuous replication when you create a storage group using the New-StorageGroup commandlet. The following command creates a second storage group on 2008MBX and replicates it to the SCR target 2008SCR1:

```
New-StorageGroup -Name "Second Storage Group" -Server 2008MBX -LogFolderPath
"E:\2008MBX\Second Storage Group" -StandbyMachine 2008SCR1 -ReplayLagTime 0
```

Because this command specifies that SCR be enabled, again it must be done from a clustered machine since the target is a passive mailbox cluster node. However, the creation of a database within the storage group can be done on any machine using the New-MailboxDatabase or New-PublicFolderDatabase commandlet. No replication parameters are required since replication is set on the public folder level.

## Checking Passive Copy Integrity

Despite the extra online maintenance functionality in SP1 that checks database consistency (on the active node), it is recommended to verify the consistency of the database and log files on the passive node at regular intervals, especially if backups are being taken from the passive node.

Although the operation requires taking the databases offline, it doesn't involve any downtime since the passive node is not serving clients. The one thing to bear in mind, however, is that when the passive copy comes back online there will be a queue of log files ready to be copied across, which may impact network performance.

To verify the integrity of the passive node databases, take a VSS snapshot and run ESEUTIL against the snapshot. This technique works for any of the continuous replication configurations (LCR, CCR, and SCR).

On 2008SCR1, because the D: drive is host to a number of database copies (from CCR-EXCH2 and 2008MBX), we can check all the databases at the same time.

1. Suspend continuous replication on the database. In the case of 2008CCR1, suspend replication from both CCR-EXCH2 and 2008MBX:

   ```
   Suspend-StorageGroupCopy -Identity "2008MBX\First Storage Group"
   -StandbyMachine 2008SCR1

   Get-StorageGroup -Server CCR-EXCH2 | Suspend-StorageGroupCopy
   -StandbyMachine 2008SCR1
   ```

2.  Take a snapshot of the volume hosting the passive database copies; in this case, the E: drive:

```
Vssadmin create shadow /for=E:
```

Vssadmin creates the shadow and informs you of the path to the shadow copy, which we use to target ESEUTIL in the next step. The command window should look something like Figure 5.19.

**Figure 5.19** Creating a VSS Shadow Copy

3.  Resume replication activity for all of the databases. With the snapshot created, it's safe to resume the log shipping before checking the databases. To resume replication for all storage groups on both servers:

```
Get-StorageGroupCopy -Server 2008MBX | Resume-StorageGroupCopy
-StandbyMachine 2008SCR1

Get-StorageGroupCopy -Server CCR-EXCH2 | Resume-StorageGroupCopy
-StandbyMachine 2008SCR1
```

4.  Use ESEUTIL to verify the checksum of the databases. ESEUTIL.exe should be run with the /k switch against the VSS copy of the databases, so the normal "E:\" is replaced by the path to the volume shadow copy, as in Figure 5.20.

5.  You can also check the log files using the same utility:

**Figure 5.20** A Quick Check of the Database Suggests All Is Fine

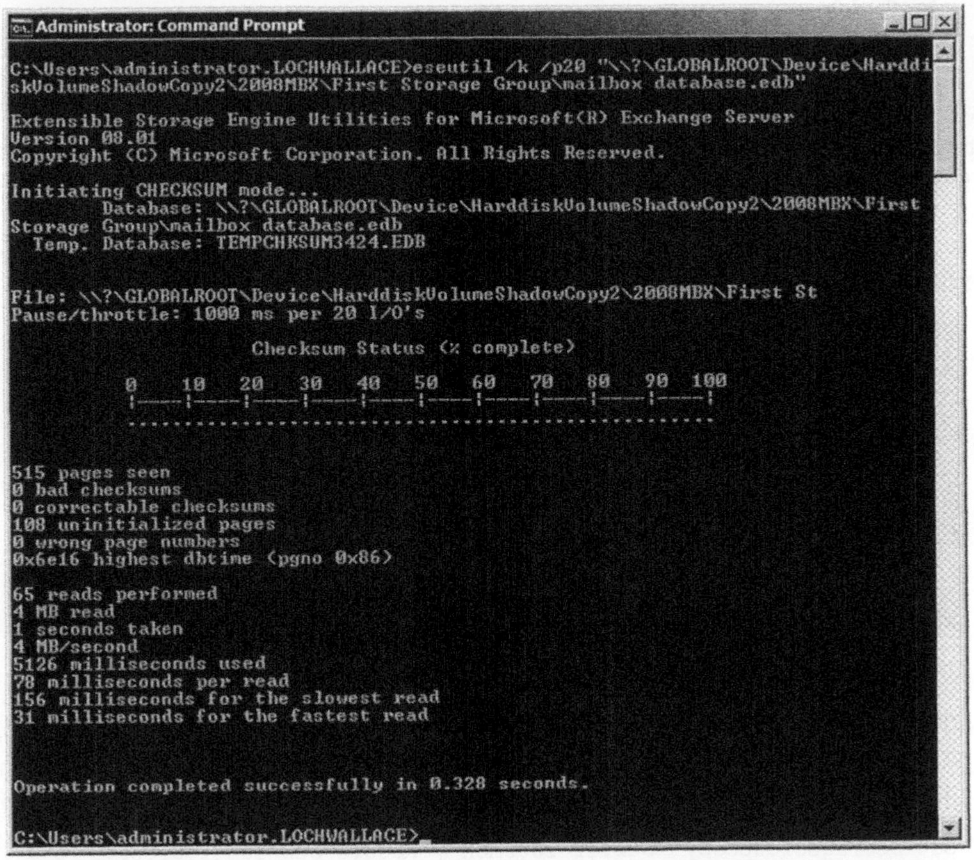

```
ESEUTIL /k "\\?\GLOBALROOT\Device\HarddiskVolumeShadowCopy2\2008MBX\First
Storage Group\E0000000001.log"
```

6. Assuming nothing is wrong with the database and logs, delete the volume shadow copy using the command:

```
Vssadmin delete shadows /for=E:
```

7. If corruption is found, suspend replication, delete the corrupt files, and re-enable replication. It may be necessary to reseed the database as well using the Update-StorageGroupCopy commandlet.

# Database Activation

Database activation refers to the manual process of mounting the replicated database on the target server. There are two ways to make this data available to clients, depending on the nature of the problem experienced. You can either mount the database on the target mailbox server directly (using "database portability"), or restore the entire mailbox server using the /m:RecoverServer or /RecoverCMS Exchange setup switches.

Which method to use depends on a number of factors: the nature of the problem (e.g., a single-database corruption or the whole server died), the replication topology (there may be multiple databases replicated to the same server, as in our example), and factors such as Recovery Time Objective.

Because the target database is an exact copy of the source, there are no operations necessary on the database; they only need to be mounted on the target server. Chapter 6 covers target database activation and other recovery scenarios.

# SCR Deployment Scenarios

As discussed, SCR's primary role is to provide site resilience without great capital expenditure in terms of hardware or software. Available in both versions of Exchange Server 2007 SP1, it enables high availability for smaller companies and those with huge IT expenditure.

# Nonclustered Mailbox Servers

Companies that don't have large budgets for implementing high availability strategies will typically host their data on single, standalone mailbox servers. Obviously, this is not a very resilient configuration since they have not invested in enterprise configurations (Enterprise software versions, for example) and therefore cannot take advantage of clustering technologies such as SCC and CCR. In these scenarios, SCR can add resilience by replicating data between the servers so that in the event of one server having a nasty accident, the data is present and recoverable on another mailbox server in the organization. This allows smaller organizations to maintain some resilience and reasonably fast recovery turnover without a huge investment in shared storage and expensive hardware.

One simple SCR scenario would be two mailbox servers sharing the user load for the organization but both storing the data from both servers (Figure 5.21). Because the active storage groups on each node are being replicated to the other node, the last server standing can take over the duties of the broken server without too much worry.

**Figure 5.21** Replicating Data between Two Standalone Mailbox Servers

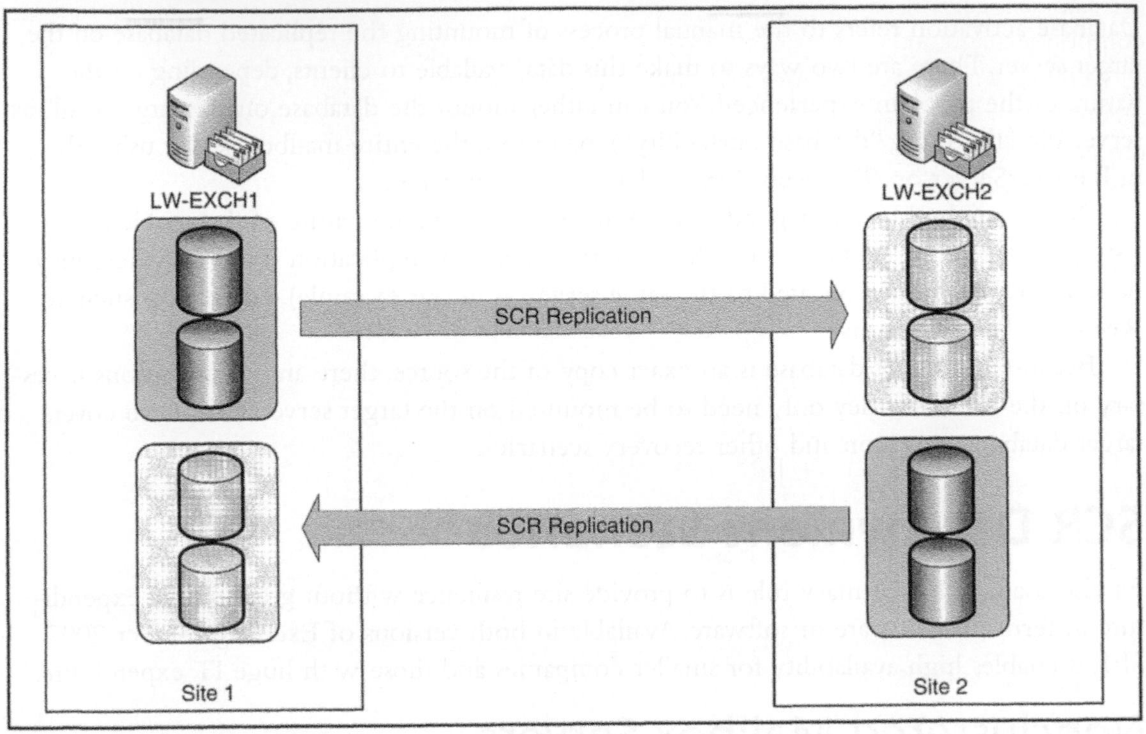

# Clustered SCR Target Mailbox Servers

If resilience is required in the SCR target environment and the production environment, it is possible to use a clustered server—either an SCC or a CCR cluster—as an SCR target. However, the cluster must not have a clustered mailbox server (CMS) present. As in Exchange 2003 clusters, where the binaries are installed first and then the Exchange Virtual Server created within Cluster Administrator, Exchange 2007 can be installed on both nodes of an MSCS cluster in passive mode. It seems slightly counter-intuitive, but the only difference between setting up an active Exchange node and a passive one in Exchange is that the active node setup creates a CMS.

By installing both nodes as a passive cluster node, the cluster is ready to create the CMS when required in a DR situation. In the meantime, while the logs are being replicated to one of the nodes, the Exchange Replication Service takes care of the mailbox store data.

If a disaster occurs, a CMS can be created using the RecoverCMS setup switch. This is covered in the next chapter.

# LCR/SCR Combination

A common scenario for using Exchange 2007's built-in resilience, particularly for smaller companies, is to marry the storage resilience of Local Continuous Replication with the site resilience of Standby Continuous Replication. Since both technologies are available in the standard edition of Exchange 2007 SP1, the only additional cost is additional storage components and an additional server.

The LCR component provides database and storage resilience, whereas SCR provides server and site resilience. In the case of database corruption or other failure, the swap to the passive copy of the database is very quick and can be as simple as modifying the mount point on which the databases are situated. SCR provides failover when the server or the site is no longer functioning, and database portability makes it easy even for an inexperienced administrator to mount the databases and get up and running again quickly.

# Economics of Continuous Replication

From a technical point of view, the new replication technologies are great for Exchange deployments because of the options they give those who design Exchange organizations. However, what also needs to be taken into account from Day 1 is the economics of the different scenarios possible for a particular company. Replicating data to an additional server somewhere else is all very well, but costs money in hardware and software, and convincing money men that sitting a server in a cold room out of town doing nothing until "doomsday" is always a difficult task.

Single copy clusters, based on the shared storage cluster model, are scalable up to eight nodes on Windows Server 2003 Enterprise. Starting with a two-node active-passive cluster (50% utilization), these can scale up to eight nodes with perhaps six nodes active at one time (75% utilization). Fifty-percent hardware utilization may be hard for some money men to swallow, but that is exactly the case with Cluster Continuous Replication (CCR) since only two nodes are possible in such a scenario. Would two CCR clusters replicating to an SCR target be preferable to a three-node SCC cluster (two active nodes) replicating to the same SCR target? It depends on many factors, but the latter would save a few thousand pounds/dollars for similar functionality.

The introduction of Standby Continuous Replication into the mix presents the possibility that you could be buying three servers and three copies of Windows and Exchange (two of them with the Enterprise version of Exchange), but having only one doing useful work. With SCR, this can be mitigated by replicating databases from multiple servers to a single server.

Often, designing a high availability environment ends up as an exercise in setting up the coolest new technology available (we've all been there!). However, weighing the best availability against the economic side will ultimately win the argument, be it with the finance director of your company or winning a bid to implement Exchange for a customer.

# Troubleshooting High Availability Configurations

High availability strategies are fine and dandy when all the complex data replication works without any input from the over-stressed IT staff, but sooner or later something will give you cause for concern, and as always, your success in dealing with issues depends largely on preparation and monitoring.

Before it even comes to troubleshooting problems in an HA environment, there must be some mechanism whereby somebody is notified of the problem. Larger environments may look to solutions such as Microsoft System Center Operations Manager (MOM) or Quest Spotlight on Exchange, whereas other smaller companies rely on manually checking server health as a part of their routine.

Using the Exchange tools to monitor its health is perfectly good for the job, if a little clunky at times. Particularly when it comes to Standby Continuous Replication, where everything is done through the command line, it's not always possible to get a nice view of everything that's going on, and some understanding of commandlets such as Get-StorageGroupCopyStatus is required to make sense of what's going on.

In high availability configurations, issues can arise from a number of directions, including cluster-related, network problems and Exchange itself. Usually, cluster and network issues can be ascertained from the Windows Event Log and general server behavior and are dealt with using traditional utilities such as Network Monitor, Netstat, ClusDiag, and the like. For Exchange issues we have the Toolbox and some commandlets to work with.

The following Exchange tools are useful for troubleshooting Exchange-related issues (and some cluster and network issues):

- **Exchange Troubleshooting Assistant** ExTRA provides a single interface to run tasks such as verifying database consistency using ESEUTIL, checking event logs for database-related events, and database management.

- **Exchange Best Practice Analyzer** ExBPA scans the configuration of the Exchange servers for misconfiguration and issues known to cause problems. The configuration is checked against a static list of known issues, which is updated regularly.

- **Get-StorageGroupCopyStatus** This commandlet provides a lot of information about the replication status for each kind of replication. Used with the –Standby Machine switch it reports on SCR copy status as in Figure 5.22. Without this switch it reports on the other replication method employed on the server, be that LCR or CCR.

Figure 5.22 suggests that replication isn't working as it should.

**Figure 5.22** The Commandlet Tells Us Something Is Amiss

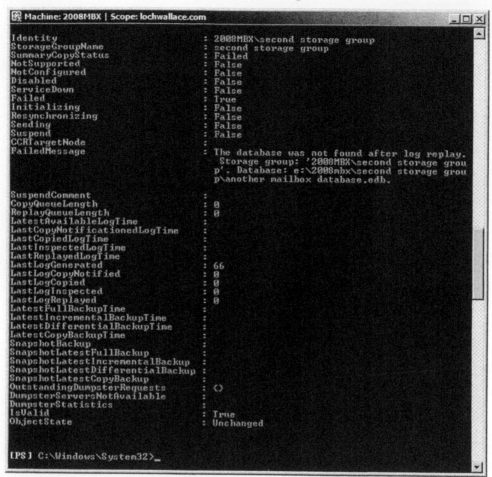

Here, the database has not been seeded to the SCR target, so the log files are being copied but not replayed. The database must be seeded manually after creating the SCR target.

Other issues can be discovered by checking relative values. For example, if the values of LastLogGenerated and LastLogCopied are out by a long way, this suggests there is something wrong with the replication service.

Some general troubleshooting tips and common errors can also be found on the Technet Web site athttp://technet.microsoft.com/en-us/library/aa996020(EXCHG.80).aspx.

Figure 5.22 The Commandlet Tells Us Something is Amiss

Here, the database has not been seeded to the SCR target, so the log files are being copied but not replayed. The database may be seeded manually after creating the SCR target.

Other issues can be detected by checking returns values. For example, if the values of LastCopyNotified and LastCopyInspected are out by a large way, this suggests there is something wrong with the replication service.

Some general troubleshooting tips and common errors can also be found on the Technet Web site at http://technet.microsoft.com/en-us/library/aa996029(EXCHG.80).aspx.

# Disaster Recovery Options

## Solutions in this chapter:

- Test Environment
- Backing up Exchange
- Restoring and Recovering Exchange

☑ Summary

# Introduction

When discussing this book with an old friend and colleague recently, we mentioned recovery and restore, to which he replied, "Oh you don't do restores any more, now you re-seed!" While this was meant to be taken with a slight pinch of salt, it does demonstrate some of the shift in how disaster recovery is viewed with Exchange 2007. It's been mentioned previously that the continuous replication technology of Exchange 2007 has lessened some of the backup requirements, raising the maximum recommended database size for mailbox stores and helping administrators sleep a little better at night.

With new technology such as this come new ways to preserve your data and network service, and new ways to recover from problems. Previously when confronted with a "disaster" in an Exchange environment, an administrator might have been confronted with a couple of options:

- Restore from backup tape
- Try to fix the database using ESEUTIL/ISINTEG

Nowadays, thanks to the high availability options there may be many more options:

- Fail over to passive database copy/node/server (LCR/CCR/SCR, respectively)
- Rewind to previous snapshot (using DPM or SAN-like snapshot technology)
- Restore from backup disk or tape
- Try to fix the database

The order of preference is probably not much different from the order laid out earlier.

Clearly, particular options are appropriate for particular situations, and some recovery options require some reconfiguration of the Exchange environment whereas others are simply a manipulation of the underlying storage.

Restoring a snapshot from a SAN arrangement, for example, is trivial. Exchange need not know what is happening; it just needs to be looking the other way while it's happening (in most cases only the databases are dismounted). On the other hand, restoring passive copies of the databases in continuous replication configurations is something entirely new for Exchange, particularly in an SCR configuration, and that will necessarily be the focus of this chapter.

# Test Environment

The test environment for this chapter is the one used in Chapter 5 with one addition: an additional SCR target machine has been added as a target for 2008MBX. This server (2008SCR2) receives the First Storage Group database files from 2008MBX so it can provide a full (standalone) server restore if 2008MBX dies (Figure 6.1).

2008SCR1 is a passive node in a cluster, whereas 2008SCR2 is a standalone Exchange server. 2008SCR2 will be used for a full server recovery operation.

**Figure 6.1** Multiple SCR Replication Streams for Multiple Recovery Options

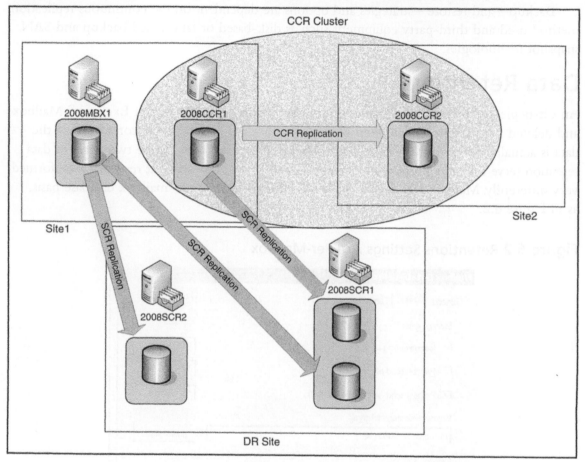

# Backing up Exchange

Backing up server applications in a corporate environment has always been a case of scheduling so they don't interfere with normal operations. Streaming Exchange backup windows may take a few hours every night, between online maintenance and other server backups, and has a major impact on the design of an environment, especially because of restrictions on database sizes.

The Volume Shadow Copy Service (VSS) introduced with Windows Server 2003 has helped in some environments to offload and speed up backup tasks, freeing up Exchange resources and decreasing the reliance on backup windows.

Continuous replication takes this a step further by enabling backups from a passive copy of the databases, thereby almost completely bypassing the active Exchange server when processing backups. (The active node still needs to process some information such as deletion of log files and ensuring logs have been replicated and committed.)

Backup—and restore—strategies and options are dependent on the continuous replication method used and third-party equipment such as disk-based or tape-based backup and SAN snapshot technologies.

# Data Retention

An oft-neglected method of data recovery is the retention facility within Exchange. Mailbox and deleted item retention can often obviate any thought of database restores because the data is actually still within the store but hidden from normal view. These two types of data retention serve the same purpose and are configured in the same way, but recovery is performed very differently. Mailbox and deleted item retention is set on a per-mailbox database basis, as in Figure 6.2.

**Figure 6.2** Retentions Settings Are Per-Mailbox

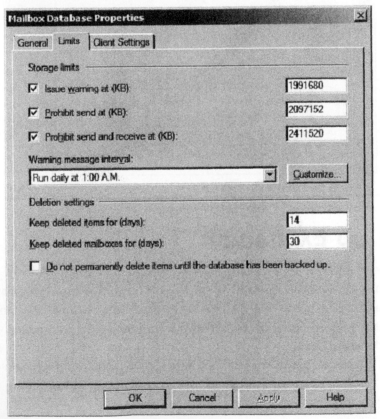

When mailbox retention is configured (by default, deleted mailboxes are retained for 30 days), a mailbox that has been deleted will not actually be removed from the database (purged) until the end of the retention period. It is merely tombstoned and deleted when its time is up. If a user account is deleted, for example, its mailbox is disconnected and is viewable in the Disconnected Mailbox area of the Exchange Management Console. Here it can be easily reconnected to another existing user account within the retention period. After the mailbox has been purged, it must be restored from backup.

Whereas deleted mailboxes are an administrative affair, deleted items retention is to do with the user. Many users never actually delete the items in the Deleted Items folder in Outlook, even if you set Group Policy to prompt them every time it closes. However, if you force deletion, or if the user kindly decides to delete these items, they too are retained for a period of time (14 days by default).

The recovery depends slightly on how the item was deleted. When you click **Delete** on an item, it goes first to the Deleted Items folder and then is purged from there. If you "hard-delete" an item (**Shift+Delete**) it is purged straightaway—it doesn't even see the Deleted Items folder. Exchange makes items from every folder recoverable via Outlook, but Outlook 2003 and Outlook 2007 behave differently. The registry key HKLM\SOFTWARE\ Microsoft\Exchange\Client\Options\DumpsterAlwaysOn(DWORD) tells Outlook whether it can recover items from every folder (value = 1) or only from the Deleted Items folder (value=0). Outlook 2007 has it on by default, Outlook 2003 off. Therefore, to bring Outlook 2003 up to the same functionality, simply modify or add this value.

To recover deleted items, users click on the folder from which the item was deleted and select **Tools\Recover Deleted Items**.

# Backup Methods

Traditionally, Exchange backups were taken through special streaming backup APIs in Exchange where the backup program would ask the Exchange services directly for a copy of the database and the store would provide a stream of consistent data for the application to store on its media. This kind of streaming backup uses resources and time on the Exchange box, hence many issues around backup windows when designing and managing Exchange environments. Windows Backup (NTBackup) is able to back up Exchange databases using these streaming backup APIs.

**NOTE**

The Microsoft IT group published some modifications they made to internal backup processes that realized significant benefits to backup speed. This is available at http://technet.microsoft.com/en-us/library/bb735157.aspx.

## Streaming and VSS-based Backups

With the advent of Windows Server 2003 and the Volume Shadow Copy Service (strangely abbreviated as VSS), Microsoft has been pushing toward using snapshot backups across the board. Exchange 2003 and 2007 both provide the requisite VSS writers for backing up this way, but NTBackup has never been able to use this writer, making the streaming option the only way to go. Third-party applications can make full use of the Exchange VSS writer, however.

The backup application bundled with Windows Server 2008 (Windows Server Backup) is not able to back up Exchange server. Again, it is not able to use the VSS writer of Exchange or the streaming backup APIs and consequently is no use for backing up Exchange. Although the Exchange Product Group is looking into providing a plug-in to enable this feature in the future, this leaves us searching for a third-party application that will support either VSS-based or streaming API-based backups. Given Microsoft's intention to do away with the streaming APIs probably in the next version of Exchange, a solution such as Microsoft DPM, which uses snapshot technology, would likely be the best choice.

> **NOTE**
>
> It is *possible* to back up Exchange using Windows Server Backup or any other non-Exchange aware snapshot utility, but it does not check the integrity of the database, and the chances of obtaining a consistent backup are lower than with an Exchange-aware program.

One of the changes made in Exchange Server 2007 SP1 is to disable remote streaming backups by default. It is common to have a network backup server that backs up other servers across the LAN. However, as part of Microsoft's recent super-secure initiatives, this kind of backup is now frowned upon because the backup data is not encrypted and is likely going across a public (client accessed) network. In Windows Server 2003, you can enable remote streaming backup using the following registry key:

```
HKLM\System\CurrentControlSet\Services\MSExchangeIS\ParametersSystem\
"Enable Remote Streaming Backup" (DWORD) = "1"
```

Windows Server 2008, however, disables all remote streaming backup and restore operations, regardless of this registry value.

Interestingly, using such a backup application that uses a local backup agent on the Exchange server is considered a local backup. This appears to be the way most network backup applications work, rather than talking directly to the Exchange services from the backup server.

## Other Snapshot Backups

Using Microsoft DPM server as a solution to backing up and restoring Exchange using snapshot technology does have its limitations in functionality and underlying method. Strangely, despite the availability of LCR copies for backup, DPM doesn't appear to use it, preferring to back up the active database instead.

There are a number of alternative and superior solutions out there. Many Storage Area Networks (SANs) provide much more advanced snapshot technology than VSS and can keep many copies of an Exchange database in much the same way as DPM. Of course, the cost is often prohibitive since to have an Exchange-aware replicated SAN infrastructure you have to have two of these SANs plus some (probably) costly Exchange-aware software that queries the database and checks the snapshot integrity. Many of these higher-end storage solutions obviate the need for continuous replication solutions, but then LCR, CCR, and SCR are aimed more at the lower end of the scale.

# Backing up in HA Configurations

In what we in this book refer to as "highly available" scenarios—those where Exchange 2007 continuous replication technology is employed—it is highly recommended to back up databases from the passive node. When the passive node of a CCR cluster is backed up, the replication service communicates this to the active node, indicating that the log files should be purged and the database header updated. These changes are then replicated back to the passive node, which does the same. Unfortunately, the new Standby Continuous Replication passive databases are not available for backing up—they are there only for disaster recovery purposes.

Solutions such as Veritas Backup Exec (and to some extent DPM) will back up the passive database, relieving the active storage system (disks and disk controller) of the effort involved in providing the snapshot and copying it to the backup server.

# Backing up with Data Protection Manager

Most companies will have backup solutions in place, either locally or using one of a proliferation of online (Internet-based) backup solutions on the market. It's a safe bet that any Exchange-aware backup application has now been updated to work with Exchange Server 2007, and therefore SP1.

Alternatively, the backup program that comes with Windows , NTBackup, is capable of taking streaming backups of Exchange 2007, which is still supported but will be dumped in future versions of Exchange in favor of VSS-based backups. Unfortunately, if you've taken the leap to Windows Server 2008, the Windows Server Backup program as it's now named, is not capable of backing up Exchange. Curiously, Microsoft, despite trying to point us all in the direction of VSS-based backups, has never thought it appropriate to make its own NTBackup capable of taking snapshot backups of Exchange. Now that they've taken the streaming API-based backup away in Windows Server 2008, we are left searching for another solution.

Of course, there is a plethora of third-party backup solutions out there, any of which will do the job with aplomb. However, for the purpose of demonstrating and discussing backups of high availability Exchange 2007 SP1 scenarios we are going to use Microsoft's own System Center Data Protection Manager, thankfully abbreviated to DPM to avoid RSI or early arthritis.

DPM is rather restrictive in the applications it can protect, being only capable of backing up certain Windows-based servers (file servers, Exchange, SQL, SharePoint and Virtual Server servers). However, this is more than enough to demonstrate Exchange backup and recovery, and it uses an interesting swift backup method similar to the log shipping in Exchange.

DPM uses a combination of VSS and log shipping to protect servers by keeping virtual (copy-on-write) snapshots from points in time almost as far back as you care to make them. By backing up Exchange every 15 minutes during the day, DPM can provide near-lossless recovery of Exchange and enable recovery to a particular point in the past. It does this by taking snapshots of the databases every so often (typically daily or weekly), and shipping/replicating log files from the servers at points throughout the day. Essentially, it takes a regular Full backup with incremental backups in between.

## Database Backups

When an Exchange server is first added to a DPM protection group, a snapshot of the database is taken and stored on the DPM server. This can be taken immediately or scheduled for a later time, probably when users have gone home. This snapshot forms the baseline for the backups (Figure 6.3). Every night/week/whenever specified, DPM takes an "Express Full" backup, which is the equivalent of a Full backup. An express full backup doesn't back up the entire database again; rather, it takes the difference between the baseline and the database as it is at the time of the backup, copies across the differences, and creates a snapshot on the DPM server to represent the entire database.

**Figure 6.3** The Initial Copy Is a Full Snapshot of the Database

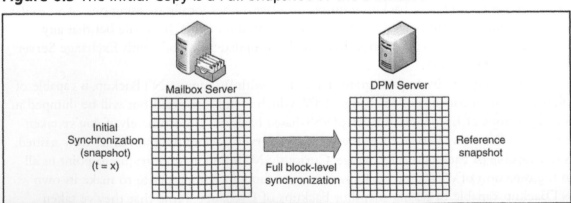

The express full backups are copied across to the DPM server where they can be used to create a snapshot of the databases at a point in time, using the reference (initial) snapshot and other express fulls (Figure 6.4).

**Figure 6.4** DPM Creates a Virtual Snapshot Using the Reference Snapshot and the Express Fulls

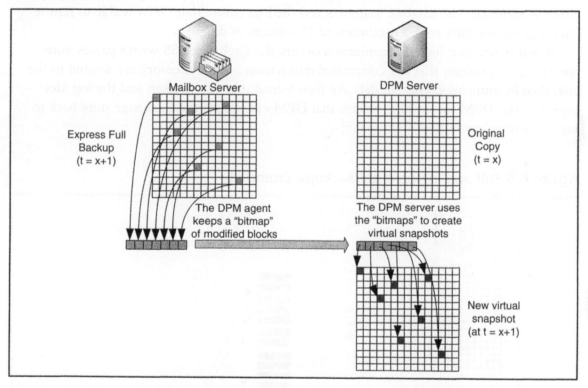

During the initial synchronization and the express full backups, the Exchange VSS writer ensures that all the data in memory is written to disk prior to the snapshot being taken. This ensures a consistent snapshot. Once the backup has been taken, and the data consistency verified on the DPM server, the transaction logs on the Exchange server are truncated.

**NOTE**

To have DPM verify the database consistency after the snapshot is taken, it must have a copy of the ESE.DLL and ESEUTIL.EXE files in the Microsoft DPM\DPM\bin folder. As DPM is a 32-bit system, it is necessary to use the 32-bit versions of these files.

Typically, an express full backup will be taken every day or every week. Further protection is obtained through log synchronization between these express full backups.

## Log Synchronization

Between the "full" backups, DPM employs a log shipping method whereby at certain intervals during the day (up to every 15 minutes) the committed log files are copied to the DPM server sequentially. The database snapshots and the logs ensure that DPM is able to restore Exchange to any time with a maximum of 15 minutes of data loss.

When transaction log synchronization occurs, the Exchange VSS writer pauses store operations and ensures that any committed transactions held in memory are written to the disk, thereby ensuring consistent data. An incremental snapshot is taken and the log files copied to the DPM server. This ensures that DPM can restore the Exchange store back to any of these points in time (Figure 6.5).

**Figure 6.5** Full and Incremental Backups, Essentially

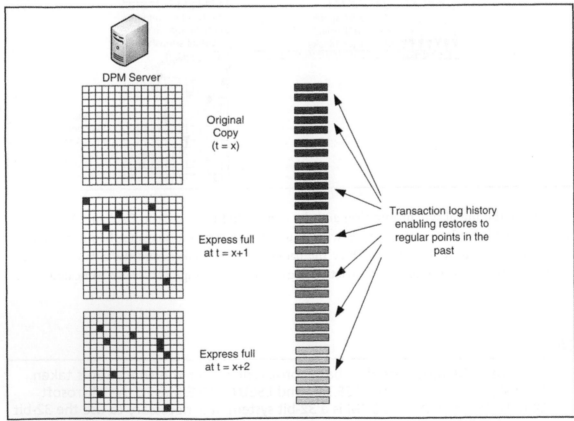

## Storage

DPM manages its own storage. Adding a raw disk to the DPM console allows DPM to format and manage it as needed so it can assign dynamic volumes to protection groups and individual components within those groups. Storage added to DPM must not already contain volumes, or DPM will see the disk but the space taken up by those volumes will be unavailable to it.

DPM carves up the available space by creating and removing dynamic volumes as shown in Figure 6.6.

**Figure 6.6** DPM Manages Its Own Storage, Which Is Visible in Computer Management But Not in Windows Explorer

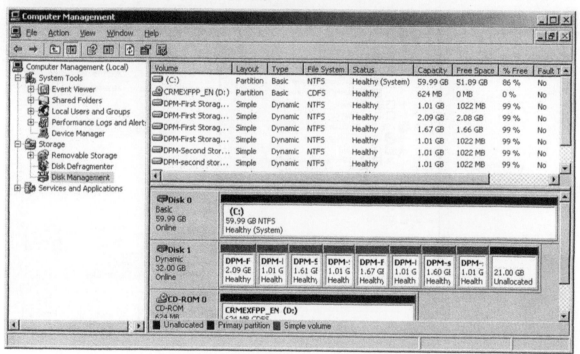

The volumes created by DPM are configured as numerous mount points within the \Microsoft DPM\DPM\Volumes folder.

## Server Protection

Protection policy is configured on a per-protection group basis. A protection group can contain any number of Exchange stores, file shares, and so forth, all protected according to the same policy specified on DPM. Figure 6.7 shows the selections on the Exchange servers in the test environment. The databases on 2008MBX are using LCR replication locally and are protected by the DPM server. CCR-CLUS2 (the cluster hosting the Clustered Mailbox Server CCR-EXCH2) is also being protected. 2008CC1 and 2008CCR2 are present because both nodes must have the DPM agent installed, but the databases are accessed via the CMS.

**Figure 6.7** Selecting Resources to Include in the Protection Group

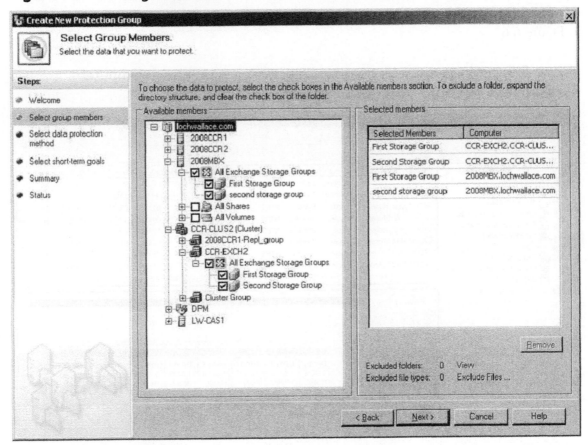

Microsoft recommends that the passive copy of a database be used for backing up, for reasons discussed earlier. However, there are a few complications with regard to continuous replication, which mean this is only possible for CCR clusters, not SCR or LCR.

Backing up a passive CCR database is possible because the replication engine communicates with its active equivalent to ensure the truncation of logs and update of the database header and so forth on the active node. SCR and LCR don't provide such a means to perform an Exchange-aware backup, so backups of LCR databases must be done on the active copy, and SCR-enabled databases on the source servers (which could be a passive copy of a CCR cluster, of course).

**NOTE**

**On DPM and LCR:** The documentation on DPM states that LCR-enabled databases can be backed up by DPM. However, when you try to select such databases when selecting protection group members, they don't appear. If you disable LCR, they suddenly appear again. This is because by default, when you enable LCR replication, the LCR VSS replica writer is enabled (presumably to enable VSS backups of the passive copy), but DPM can't use this writer. The solution is to disable it by creating a registry DWORD key named "EnableVssWriter" under HKLM\Software\Microsoft\Exchange\Replay\Parameters and setting it to "0."

When it comes to CCR clusters, however, DPM allows you to back up the passive node, and fail back to the active node if the passive is not available (Figure 6.8). The neat part of this is that, because DPM is cluster-aware, it will work out which node is running the passive copy and use its agent to perform the backup.

**Figure 6.8** DPM Sees the CCR Cluster and Presents Further Options

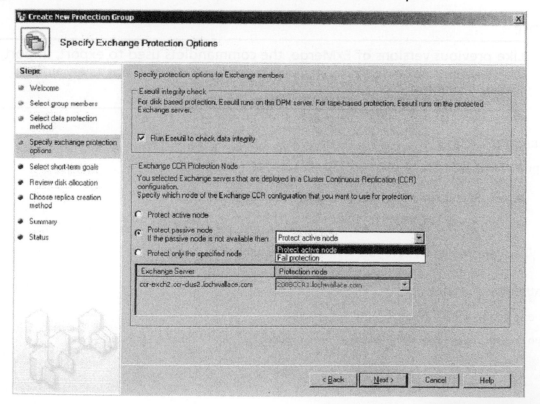

Because the passive node is essentially dynamic (it changes as the CMS fails over between nodes), the DPM agent must be installed on both nodes before you are able to select the CCR cluster for backup.

# Manually Backing up Using PowerShell

A method within Exchange 2007 enables you to back up mailboxes without the use of backup software, streaming or snapshot. Exporting mailboxes directly to PST files is not something we would ever advocate as a backup method, but it is worth mentioning as it provides a "backup backup" method (if you understand what we mean) for certain emergencies and allows you to take a copy of a single mailbox and store it on a file system somewhere. This is essentially your original brick-level backup, although backing up all mailboxes like this would be a killer in terms of storage because of the loss of single instance storage.

In fact, you're more likely to export a mailbox to a PST prior to purging it from the system, mainly for data retention and legal reasons.

Unfortunately, the EMC does not have the facility to export or import mailbox data, so you must use the Export-Mailbox command in the EMS. This can transfer mailbox contents from server to server or from server to PST file.

> **NOTE**
>
> Like previous versions of ExMerge, the commandlets used to export, import, and restore mailbox data in this way do not include mailbox rules, views, forms, and ACLs.

## *Prerequisites*

Export-Mailbox must be run on a 32-bit computer running:

- A 32-bit version of the Exchange management tools
- Outlook 2003 SP2 or later

The user must also have full access to the mailbox.

## *Exporting Mailboxes*

To export to a PST file:

```
Export-Mailbox -Identity {user} -PSTFolderPath {full pst file path}
```

Note that exporting multiple mailboxes in this way will do away with single instance storage, so what may have been a backup of 1 GB using a full Exchange backup may be many times that in PST files. PST files should be considered for temporary storage and archiving in some situations. Using PST files in Outlook, particularly across the network, is very inefficient when working with Outlook data.

For more information on network stored PST files, read, "Personal folder files are unsupported over a LAN or over a WAN link" (http://support.microsoft.com/kb/297019/en-us).

# Restoring and Recovering Exchange

Managing a messaging environment is perhaps something people don't look forward to, but Exchange Server 2007 SP1 makes recovery and restoration of Exchange databases easier with tools and methods that help minimize downtime and CTO anger. As a consultant, as with an administrator, it is important to have a grasp on these procedures and avoidance and mitigation strategies (such as those HA strategies described in Chapter 5) so a hardware disaster does not also become a career/reputation disaster.

# Recovery Tools in Exchange

Following on from the great success of the Exchange Best Practices Analyzer, Microsoft has brought in a similar tool to help diagnose and assist in righting any wrongs in an Exchange environment—the Troubleshooting Assistant (ExTRA). ExTRA encompasses a number of wizard-based troubleshooting tools that are designed to minimize the possibility of human error and make it easier for administrators. However, sometimes you just have to go back to the tried and tested command-line tools we've had since the dawn of Exchange-time.

## Toolbox Tools

The two main database troubleshooting tools within the Exchange Toolbox—Database Recovery Management and Database Troubleshooter—come under the umbrella of the Exchange Troubleshooting Assistant (ExTRA), as do the Mailflow Tools such as Message Tracking and the Mail Flow Troubleshooter.

### Database Recovery Management

The Database Recovery Management tool is a front end for performing actions on databases such as repairs and restores, cleaning up the log environment, and forth. These operations are not new to Exchange, but this tool, like the other Toolbox tools, provides a convenient front end for these actions (Figure 6.9) that should make it more idiot-proof than previously, when cracking open ESEUTIL was a more common occurrence.

**Figure 6.9** The Troubleshooting Assistant Brings Common Tasks into an Easy to Use Wizard Format

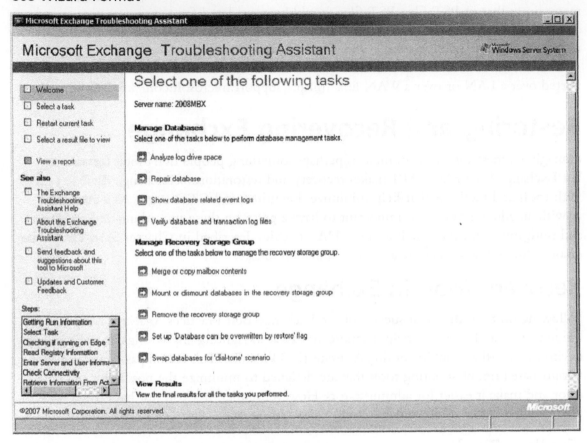

With the Database Recovery Management tool, you can:

**Analyze Log Drive Space** This shows information about the transaction log files and the disks that are hosting them. Besides compiling the number of logs and disk space used, it tells you the log file generation rate and how long it reckons you have until there isn't any space left. This isn't something that should happen, however, if the server is being backed up properly. If you do run into trouble, this tool also enables you to regain some space on the log drive by moving some log files to another location. This is akin to checking the Log Required value for the database (using ESEUTIL /mh) and removing the rest of the log files, but it can be done when the database is online.

**Repair a Database** This refers to a series of tasks involving ESEUTIL and ISINTEG to bring a corrupt database into a mountable and hopefully non-corrupt state. Run this if the database is not able to be mounted and it will go through a hard repair (ESEUTIL /p), database defragment (ESEUTIL /d), and up to two passes of ISINTEG –fix for all tests (to repair the logical structure of the database). This is last resort territory, and in any case, a copy of the database and log files should be taken before doing this.

**Show Database Related Event Logs** This task filters all database related events in the Application Event Log. It doesn't provide any additional information; rather, it makes the events easier to read.

**Verify Database and Transaction Log Files** This task verifies what state the database is in; for example, if it is in a "Clean Shutdown" or "Dirty Shutdown" state. This is some of the information available when running ESEUTIL /mh against the dismounted database file.

**Recovery Storage Group Operations** On the subject of making operations foolproof through the wizard interface, working with Recovery Storage Groups is much easier with the Exchange Troubleshooter. It takes you through creating the RSG, restoring databases, and the Dial-Tone Recovery operations described later in this chapter.

While the wizards do make things easier when performing standard operations, the fact that you can only use them to work on databases found through Active Directory configuration means sometimes you may need to use the command-line utilities when working with database files.

## Database Troubleshooter

The Database Troubleshooter tool is similar to the "Show Database Related Event Logs" task in that is scours the Event Log to find database-related issues, and then offers advice on how to resolve the issues such as referring you to Knowledge Base articles and useful tasks to perform within the Database Recovery Management tools.

# Command-Line Tools

Despite the "wizardification" of Exchange and many of the operations contained within the troubleshooter tools, if you're unhappy because you can't see what is actually going on behind the scenes, you can still run away from the wizards and delve into the low-level database tools.

**ESEUTIL** "Exchange Server Database Utilities" enables you to modify, verify, and fix Exchange databases from the command line. ESEUTIL can verify the health of databases, recover them by replaying log files, repair databases by discarding pages that cannot be fixed, and defragmenting databases. ESEUTIL is a low-level database tool that works against any database based on the Extensible Storage Engine and has no knowledge of the structure particular to Exchange.

**ISINTEG** The "Information Store Integrity Checker" is a higher-level tool that finds and fixes errors in databases at the application level. ISINTEG can understand and fix relationships between database tables, unlike ESEUTIL.

# Database Recovery

## *Restoring Databases to Another Server*

Exchange databases can be restored to any other server in the same Exchange organization, thanks to the database portability feature. It is much easier with Exchange 2007 than in previous versions of Exchange.

Databases generally must be ported between servers with the same Exchange 2007 revision and Windows operating system. It is possible, however, to move databases from Exchange 2007 RTM to SP1 servers, and from Windows Server 2003 to Windows Server 2008, but changes to the indexing of the database in the later version of Windows prevent you from moving back to a down-level Windows version. When the target system recognizes that the database is from a Windows Server 2003 server, Exchange will start re-indexing the database, which may cause I/O issues.

Database portability is covered in the section "Activating an SCR Database Copy" later in the chapter.

# Mailbox Recovery

In the old days of Exchange 5.5 and earlier, recovering individual mailboxes involved recovering an entire server and extracting the mailbox using Outlook or the ExMerge tool. With the advent of brick-level backup applications and the Recovery Storage Group in Exchange 2003, it became much easier.

The Recovery Storage Group is a special administrative storage group used for restoring databases and recovering mailboxes from backup. By restoring a mailbox database into an RSG (it won't handle public folder databases), you can merge mailbox data from a recovered mailbox into a production mailbox or export it into a PST file. Brick-level mailbox restores from third-party backup applications are generally easy to achieve, but the RSG method allows you to restore a subset of the mailbox data and to retrieve individual mails into a different mailbox for a legal enquiry or the like. As an example, the following commandlet restores mailbox data from Gordon's RSG mailbox into a subfolder of Lubo's mailbox:

```
Restore-Mailbox -RSGMailbox Gordon -RSGDatabase "RSG\Mailbox Database" -id "Lubo"
-TargetFolder "Gordon Email"
```

Once you have restored the database into the RSG, you can use the *Restore-Mailbox* command or the Exchange Disaster Recovery Analyzer (ExDRA) to export mail from a recovered mailbox to a mailbox in the production database.

## *Limitations*

Mailbox merge operations using an RSG, like the old favorite ExMerge tool, do not copy:

- Mailbox rules
- Search folders
- Views
- Forms
- ACLs

Most of these items will be retained if merging or copying data from a "dial-tone" recovery database into the original database, as may be the case with the Dial-tone Recovery situation in the next section.

# Dial-Tone Recovery for Immediate Service Continuation

Dial Tone recovery is a very useful method to get users back up and running when their mailbox database is unavailable. This may be because of database corruption or a server crash where you want to restore users to another server. In a situation where the mailbox database needs to be restored from backup (or if you want to repair the existing database so it will mount again), you can implement a dial-tone (empty) database to accommodate the inconvenienced users while you struggle with restoring the original. The dial tone's main purpose is to get users up and running with email (albeit with an empty mailbox) while their mailboxes are sorted out.

**NOTE**

Be aware that the primary purpose of the dial-tone database is to give you some breathing space while restoring or repairing the original database. When restoring from tape backup this is invaluable, but with the advent of disk-based snapshot backups and passive continuous replication database copies, it may be that restoring a database takes no more than a couple of minutes. In this case, it may be more hassle than it's worth to go through this procedure for the sake of a few minutes of peace and quiet.

The dial-tone recovery involves the following steps:

1. Create a new empty database for users.
2. Restore/repair original database and bring online.

3. Swap dial-tone and restored/repaired databases (optional but recommended).

4. Merge the two databases.

# Create Empty Database and Get Users Online

The first step in a dial-tone recovery is to get the users up and running again. To do this, move the old failed database and log files to a new location—clearing out the database folders—and mount the database in the management console. The Information Store service then creates a blank database in its place. When a user logs on to, or a mail is sent to his mailbox, the server creates a new mailbox in the empty, dial-tone database. At this time, the mailbox is devoid of the historical data and other settings such as forms, Inbox rules, and views, but these will be restored later from the original database.

One important aspect of this process is that the new mailbox retains the same unique ID (msExchMailboxGUID) as previously, which it obtains from the user object. This is important as merging process will use this to map the old and new databases to restore mail successfully.

## Exchange Recovery Mode

When Outlook is working in Offline mode (the default setting), it uses an encryption key to keep the data in the OST file secure. This key is unique to the mailbox database from which it came, so when Outlook starts up and sees a different (dial-tone) database instead, the keys don't match.

This is where the Exchange Recovery Mode comes in. Outlook recognizes that the database is different and gives the user a choice: work with the online database *or* the offline historical data (Figure 6.10). Obviously, it would be difficult to have Outlook integrate the two since they are from different sources, so this recovery mode is the ideal middle ground. It allows users to send and receive emails using the online database and refer back to old emails in the OST file.

**Figure 6.10** Outlook's Exchange Recovery Mode

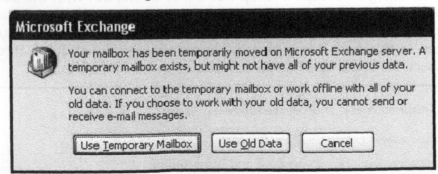

To switch between the two modes, you have to restart Outlook and choose the other option.

When the original database is restore on the server, Outlook automatically reverts to normal mode and works online with the database. Any new data created since the recovery operation began is not available but is migrated into the original mailbox as part of the final restore operation.

**NOTE**

When users log on to Outlook Web Access, they are presented with the new empty database until the restore operation is complete.

## Restore or Repair the Original Database

With the users happily working in their recovery environment, you have time to restore or repair the database. For this, we want to create a Recovery Storage Group.

**NOTE**

If the intention is only to repair the database using the ESEUTIL and ISINTEG tools, the RSG is not necessary at this time. It is necessary, however, when transferring mail between databases.

The aim is to restore the database into the RSG temporarily while users work off the dial-tone database as in Figure 6.11. RSGs are no longer created and manipulated within the management console; you must use either the shell or the Exchange Troubleshooting Assistant/Database Recovery Management tool.

**Figure 6.11** Users Work Against Their New, Empty Mailboxes for the Time Being

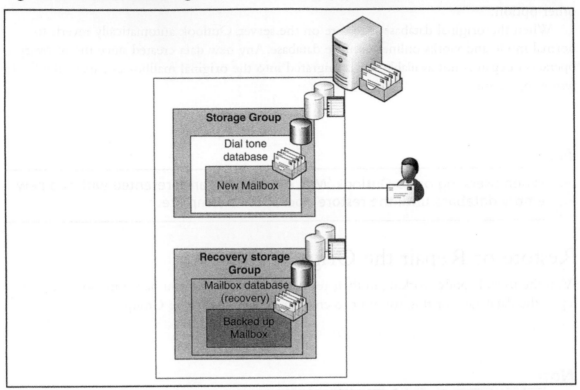

In the event of our "2008MBX\First Storage Group\Mailbox Database" needing to be recovered, we create a new RSG on 2008MBX corresponding to the First Storage Group. The location of the databases is important since ultimately you want this restored data to be placed in the same location as the original database. Restoring it to a different volume may be required because of lack of space on the LUN, but is not ideal since copying the data back to the original location may take a long time. By default, the ExTRA recommends a subfolder of the storage group location; for example, E:\2008MBX\First Storage Group\ RSG20080327143447). The ExTRA will also add the databases to the RSG automatically, which was a manual step in Exchange 2003.

In the Tasks page of the Troubleshooting Assistant are now a number of additional tasks available to manage the RSG. These are designed to make the whole dial-tone recovery process much easier and error-free (Figure 6.12).

**Figure 6.12** The Task-based Design of the Troubleshooting Assistant
Makes Recovery a Breeze

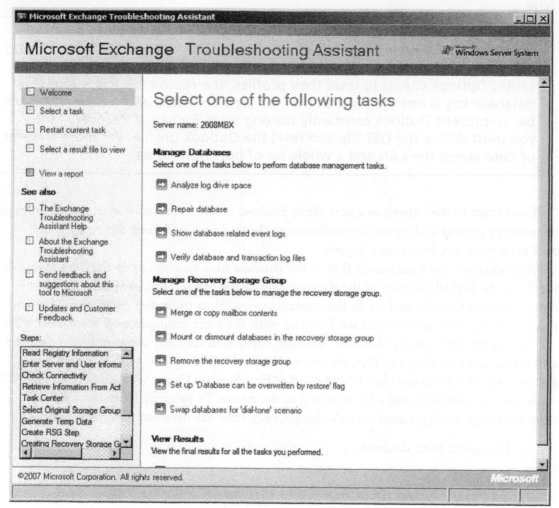

## Swapping the Databases

When the original database is recovered, fixed, and sitting in the RSG, you may want to
consider swapping the two databases so the restored DB is in the mailbox store and the
dial-tone is in the RSG. The reason for this is that it minimizes the amount of data that needs
to be transferred from store to store when merging the data. What would you rather copy,
the original 100 GB of data or the data that has been created in the last hour while you were
restoring the database? Another reason for swapping the databases so that you end up working
with the original is that the Restore-Mailbox commandlet cannot restore mailbox rules,
views, forms, or ACLs, so these will be retained only if you swap back to the original database.

**NOTE**

Of course, if you have doubts about the integrity of the original, restored database, you may wish to start afresh, but we don't recommend it—for two big reasons. The amount of data to transfer may be huge, as noted, and it causes Outlook clients to reset their profiles. The reason for this is that the database key is not the same as that for their OST files, and it now never will be. To prevent Outlook constantly starting up in Exchange Recovery Mode, you must delete the OST file and reset the Outlook profile. Yet more transfer of data across the LAN and a whole lot of hurt from users.

If you want to start afresh in a new clean database, create a new one after you've finished this recovery process and move the mailboxes gradually. Users will keep their sanity, and you'll keep your job. Everyone's happy.

Depending on the location on disk of the database files, you can swap the DBs by either modifying the logical location of the database files in Exchange Management Console, or simply swap the files themselves. In this scenario, we want to move the database files since they are on the same volume and we'll end up with the same configuration we started with.

The "Swap databases for 'dial-tone' scenario" option in ExTRA swaps only the database paths rather than moving the files. Be aware that this will leave you with a production database path of something like "E:\2008MBX\First Storage Group\RSG20080327143447," which may be confusing and a bit irritating in the future. To properly swap the databases so the Exchange configuration doesn't change, swap over the database files manually:

1. Dismount both databases.

2. Swap over the databases on disk.

3. Set "This database can be overwritten by a restore" flag on the main database (otherwise, you get the 0x80004005 error when attempting to mount it).

4. Mount the databases.

When users log on to Outlook again, the Exchange Recovery Mode message is gone and they are working with their old mailbox data again.

## Merging the Databases

The final operation is to merge the newly created data into the old mailbox. This can occur while users are working with their clients and is done by selecting **Merge or copy mailbox contents** in ExTRA. You should ensure that the merge traffic is going in the right direction (dial tone to original) because stopping it halfway through may get messy (Figure 6.13).

**T**IP

While Outlook is intelligent enough to recognize when the mailbox database has been reset, and leaves its local data intact, Windows Mobile and ActiveSync devices aren't so clever. These devices will synchronize all the content each time the database is changed, so it's best to try to keep mobile users from synchronizing during the recovery operation.

**Figure 6.13** Swap the Databases and Merge the Contents

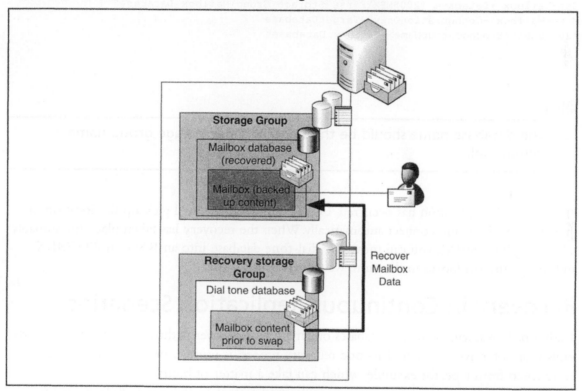

The wizard matches the mailboxes in the RSG and the original database automatically. By default, it uses the Mailbox GUID, but you may want to use another method such as Display Name, for example, if mailboxes have been deleted/recreated during the recovery operation.

During the merge operation, Outlook users will see items coming into Outlook as they work, until all the data is back in their mailboxes.

When the recovery operation is complete, use ExTRA to dismount the database in the RSG and then delete the RSG. You must manually delete the database files in the RSG folder.

# On Dial-Tone Portability

As with normal mailbox databases, dial-tone databases are portable. This means that it's possible to use an alternative server to create the dial-tone database. To do this, the name of the dial-tone mailbox database must be the same as the original on the other server. You also need to move the mailboxes between servers.

To move the mailboxes between servers without having access to the mailbox data (as the database is down), use the **Move-Mailbox** commandlet with the **–ConfigurationOnly** switch. If the database "2008MBX\First Storage Group\Mailbox Database" was down and we wanted to get all users up and running on server 2008SCR1, we'd use:

```
Get-Mailbox -Database "2008MBX\First Storage Group\Mailbox Database" |
Move-Mailbox -ConfigurationOnly -TargetDatabase
"2008SCR1\<StorageGroupName>\Mailbox Database"
```

> **NOTE**
>
> The database name should be the same, but the storage group name is immaterial.

When AD replication has occurred, Outlook 2007 clients will pick up the location of their new mailbox and connect automatically. When the recovery has taken place (presumably rebuilding 2008MBX), you can move the dial-tone database into an RSG on 2008MBX and merge the mailboxes in the same way as described earlier.

# Recovery in Continuous Replication Scenarios

Traditionally, restoring mailbox databases on an Exchange server without the use of third-party tools is an intensive task. The dial-tone recovery process is useful when the database has to be restored from tape, for example, which can take a matter of hours.

With the addition of the continuous replication feature in Exchange 2007, restoring a database is often not such a time- and resource-consuming process, as passive database activation may take only a few seconds. Activating passive database copies in replication scenarios differs slightly between implementations (LCR, CCR, and SCR), particularly in an SCR activation scenario where a server restore or database portability comes into play.

## Activating an LCR Database Copy

Local Continuous Replication is the simplest implementation of continuous replication in Exchange. The "Microsoft Exchange Replication Service" replicates log data from the production database onto another copy on the same server. For performance and resilience, the copy should be on a separate storage LUN and storage controller, although having the copy on the same disk array may provide some protection against database corruption.

When a problem occurs with the production—active—database, service recovery can be initiated relatively quickly by simply reconfiguring Exchange to point to the passive copy. This may be a case of modifying the location of the database and log files in Exchange Management Console or simply modifying the Windows mount points that redirect to the database location.

The server 2008MBX in the lab environment has its First Storage Group data stored in "E:\2008MBX\First Storage Group." LCR is replicating to a separate disk, "F:\Local Copies\First Storage Group." If the E: drive is no longer available, or database corruption occurs, we have to activate the copy on the F: drive.

## Modifying the Exchange Configuration

To activate the copy of the First Storage Group on 2008MBX, use the **Restore-Storage GroupCopy** command or the management console. Before this can be done, however, you may have to dismount the source database and suspend replication. It seems a bit strange when the database disk has been lost and Exchange still thinks it's mounted and trying to replicate.

To restore the copy and update the Exchange configuration to point to the location of the copy:

```
Restore-StorageGroupCopy -Identity "2008MBX\First Storage Group"
-ReplaceLocations
```

Alternatively, in the management console, right-click the storage group, select **Restore Storage Group Copy**, and select the **Replace production database path locations with this copy** option. This option (and the "–ReplaceLocations:$true switch) tells Exchange to update the configuration to use the location of the passive copy. No data needs to be moved; Exchange is just modified to point to the backup files.

If the passive copy of the database is in a dirty shutdown state, the recovery procedure will fail. To bring them into a clean shutdown state you must use the ESEUTIL tool. Sometimes, you can go into Database Recovery Management through the console, but you are only able to specify a database through the Active Directory configuration it obtains, rather than selecting an edb file on the file system. Use the following command to recover the database, importing the log transactions and bringing it into a clean shutdown state:

```
Eseutil /R E00 /L "F:\LocalCopies\First Storage Group" /S
"F:\LocalCopies\First Storage Group" /D "F:\LocalCopies\First Storage Group"
```

When the database is in a clean shutdown state (you can test this using ESEUTIL with the "mh" switch), the restore operation will work and the database location updated in Active Directory as in Figure 6.14. LCR is also disabled as part of the restore operation.

**Figure 6.14** The Database Path Updated and LCR Disabled

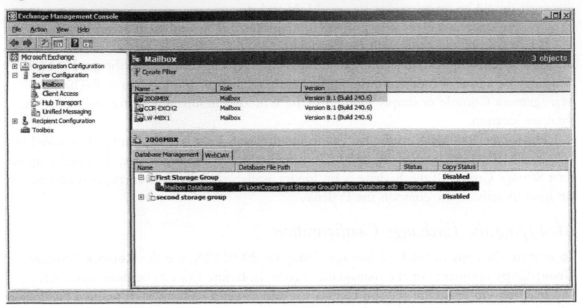

Depending on the nature of the problem with the original database, the Restore-StorageGroupCopy will copy the remaining logs from the original location to the passive location prior to mounting the database. Of course, if the whole source disk is gone this is not possible, and you receive a warning to that effect. Just accept this and click through to the next step.

## Modifying Operating System Parameters

Pointing Exchange to the location of the storage group copy may not be the best technique, because it involves modifying the Exchange configuration and potentially causes confusion if left like that for an extended period. However, it's possible to perform the recovery operation while keeping the Exchange configuration as it was.

Using this method, you have to end up with the passive copy of the storage group under the path "D:\2008MBX\First Storage Group." This can be done either by moving the passive copy files into that folder (probably not an option if located on a separate volume) or by using Windows volume mount points.

Volume mount points are relationships between folders and volumes in Windows. You can create a volume mount point on a folder called "Mount" that points to the E: drive. In Windows Explorer when you look in the Mount folder, you see the contents of the E: drive. Using mount points can speed up the recovery process.

We might want to configure 2008MBX so the database locations are on mount points (virtual locations, if you will) rather than physical folders. The First Storage Group is configured in the folder "C:\Mount\Databases\2008MBX\First Storage Group," and the passive copy is configured in the folder "C:\Mount\LCR\2008MBX\First Storage Group." As you can see in Figure 6.15, the Databases and LCR folders within C:\Mount point to the E: and F: drives, respectively.

**Figure 6.15** Configuring Volume Mount Points for the E: and F: Drives

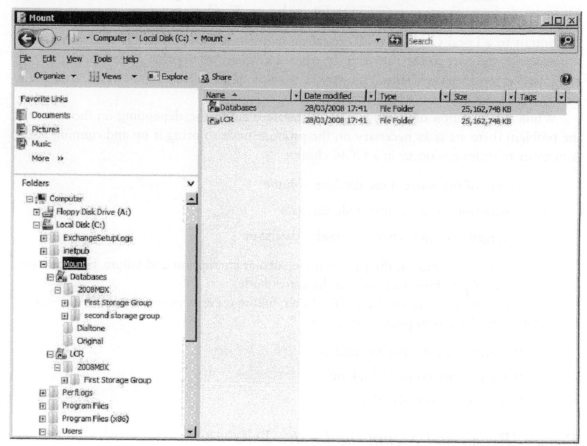

Imagine, then, the situation where the E: drive breaks and we need to recover to the F: drive. Rather than running the Restore-StorageGroupCopy commandlet with the –ReplaceLocations switch, we run it without the switch, so Exchange looks to the same location for the recovery files, and merely updates the mount point.

To do this, we must first remove the mount point using C:\Mount\Databases:

```
MountVol C:\Mount\Databases /D
```

Then, recreate the mount point to point to the E: drive:

```
MountVol C:\Mount\Databases \\?\Volume{72ff44cf-f5d9-11dc-a882-000c292cbf21}\
```

This points the Databases folder to the same volume as the LCR folder (E:). The ID of the volume is obtained by running the *MountVol* command with no parameters.

You should be able to use the drive letter when mounting volumes rather than the long volume ID, but this gives you a useful "The parameter is incorrect" error.

After recreating the volume mount point you can run the *Restore-StorageGroupCopy* commandlet to work with the passive copy without modifying the Exchange configuration.

# Recovering from a CCR Database Failure

In contrast to a Local Continuous Replication scenario, a CCR cluster is configured to automatically fail over to the passive node when a problem occurs that means the active node can no longer serve clients. This may be because of corruption in the active database or the loss of the LUN on which it resides.

While the activation of a passive CCR database is automatic, depending on the nature of the problem there are tasks necessary on the problem node to bring it up and running again. A number of issues can occur in a CCR cluster:

- Failure of the active node database volume

- Corruption on the active node database

- Divergence of the active and passive databases

Other issues can occur on the passive node, such as corruption and failure, but these are handled in a similar fashion to failure of the active node.

When a failure happens on the CCR cluster, follow these steps to recover service and bring the cluster back into proper operation:

1. Prepare/repair the passive database.

2. Bring the broken node back online.

3. Repair database replication.

## *Prepare/Repair and Mount the Passive Database*

The biggest priority after a failure is to get services back up and running, which means getting the database mounted.

Because each of the nodes in a CCR cluster has its own copy of the database, they are never going to be completely in sync while there is activity on the active node. When the active node goes down, the passive node makes a decision whether to mount its copy of the database based on the AutoDatabaseMountDial property (set using the Set-MaiboxDatabase commandlet or in the EMC). This determines how many un-replayed logs it can handle before it refuses to mount the database, as shown in Figure 6.16. If the number is above the threshold, the database will not mount automatically and you must manually recover the database using perhaps the recovery tools and the Transport Dumpster.

**Figure 6.16** The Passive Database Will Not Mount

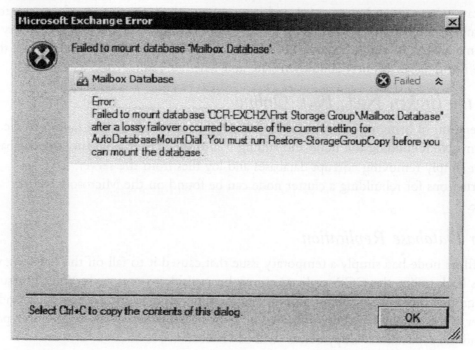

AutoDatabaseMountDial has three possible values:

- **Best Availability** The default setting, this allows a discrepancy of up to six log files between the active and passive nodes. If the value is less than six, automatic recovery will take place. If it is higher, the database will not mount and administrator intervention is required.

- **Good Availability** This allows a discrepancy of up to three log files for automatic recovery.

- **Lossless** This setting tells the passive node not to mount the database unless it has all the logs intact. It periodically attempts to copy the logs from the passive node, so if the active node returns with the logs intact, the logs will be copied and the database mounted again. If the logs are not intact, the database will not be mounted since it cannot mount it without data loss. Administrator intervention should be taken based on the amount of likely data loss and the likelihood of the logs being recovered against the downtime experienced by clients.

If the log files are not available to be copied over to the passive node, you can force a restore of the database using the Restore-StorageGroupCopy commandlet. This commandlet includes a request to the Transport Dumpster to resend all the mail in its cache, thereby hopefully bringing the transactions in the database up to date prior to mounting the database.

However, the Restore-StorageGroupCopy command doesn't always bring the database into a state where it can be mounted, and it is sometimes necessary to perform a restore and repair on the database, either using ESEUTIL or through the Database Recovery Management tool. Running a quick ESEUTIL /mh against the database tells you if the database is in a clean or dirty shutdown state and whether some repair is in order.

## Bring the Broken Node Back Online

The operation of bringing the failed node online again depends on the nature of the failure. It may involve rebuilding the node and adding it into the cluster, replacing the database LUN, or simply removing corrupt databases and log files from the server.

Instructions for rebuilding a cluster node can be found on the Microsoft Technet Web site.

## Repair Database Replication

If the offline node had simply a temporary issue that caused it to fall off the network, when it comes back online the CCR replication may be available to start again. You can resume the storage group copy in this case by running the Resume-StorageGroupCopy commandlet. However, if the storage failed there may be no copy of the database left on the now-passive node, and the replication "Copy Status" will be "Failed."

Bringing back the CCR replication in this case requires a re-seeding of the database file to the passive node using the Update-StorageGroupCopy commandlet as in Figure 6.17. When the passive node is brought back online with a new empty database LUN, log replication is restarted automatically but the database must be seeded manually.

**Figure 6.17** Reseeding the Database to the Passive Node

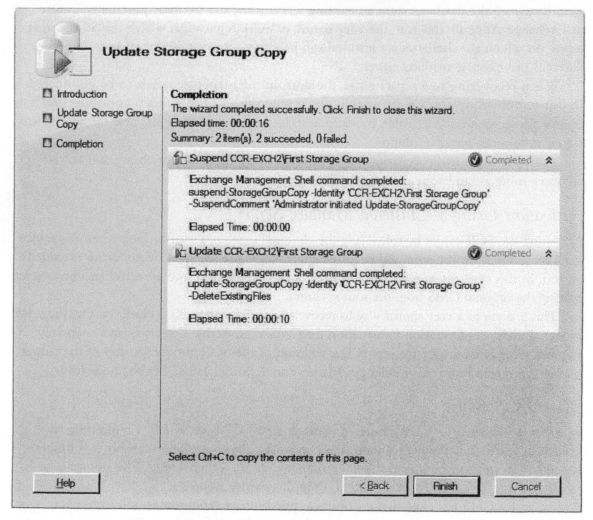

## Activating an SCR Database Copy

Different failures call for different measures, and recovery strategies are, after all, what we write about. SCR–based recovery tends to be used for server failure scenarios because SCR is geared toward site resilience rather than server resilience (although it can be used for server resilience in many scenarios).

When an entire Exchange mailbox server is out of action, you will likely want to recover the server to the state it was prior to the problem that killed it. We say *likely* because these days the dependencies, or rather the relationship between database and server, are less stringent. There is less need to restore original servers than there was in previous versions of Exchange Server because it's easier to move a database onto another Exchange mailbox server.

For example, if an entire server breaks, rather than recovering that server you may simply wish to restore the databases onto an existing server using the database portability feature of Exchange. After all, this is in the very nature of SCR replication where the SCR target server on which the databases are restored can be either a recovered server or an entirely different pre-existing mailbox server.

When recovering to a separate site, the domain infrastructure needs to be considered. In our test environment, we are working on a single site, so the domain controller and Hub/CAS server are still available. In addition to having both of these available in the DR site, we must consider name resolution.

There are three main scenarios for an SCR recovery, database portability, and server recovery using a standalone or a clustered server.

## Activation Using a Clustered Mailbox Server

Activating the SCR target by recovering the clustered mailbox server is done when the source mailbox server is no longer available; for example, when the site goes down for an extended period. In this case, the target passive cluster node is converted into an active mailbox server hosting the original CMS from the source cluster.

This is done in a very similar way to recovering an Exchange 2003 cluster in that the setup process gathers configuration information for CMS from Active Directory and essentially assumes the role of the source server. The addition of the SCR process on top of the cluster recovery presents additional challenges, mainly concerning database health and recovery.

## The DR Scenario

In our test scenario, the CCR clustered mailbox server CCR-EXCH2 is replicating to 2008SCR1, which is the passive (and only) node of a cluster server, ostensibly in a different site although in this case it is in the same subnet as all the other servers. The storage group "First Storage Group" is replicated by SCR to this passive node.

CCR-EXCH2 has exploded, or been dropped into a swimming pool. Either way, it's no longer working and there is not much hope of getting it back. We want to resurrect CCR-EXCH2 on the SCR target server (2008SCR1) and recover the databases. It is accepted that data loss may occur since some log files may not have been replicated to the SCR target location.

## Preparing the Database(s) for Recovery

To prepare the SCR database copy to be mounted, the Restore-StorageGroupCopy command needs to be run against it. Although the same commandlet is used for all three of the continuous replication scenarios, the –StandbyMachine parameter specifies that we are working with an SCR copy.

The Restore-StorageGroupCopy cmdlet does the following:

- Marks the DB as mountable
- Disables the replication process (at least it's supposed to)
- Reports on the amount of data loss resulting from the recovery
- Attempts to copy missing logs from the source

In reality, however, the disabling of SCR doesn't seem to work so this has to be done manually.

The following command restores the SCR copy of the First Storage Group from the cluster:

```
Restore-StorageGroupCopy -Identity "CCR-EXCH2\First Storage Group"
-StandbyMachine 2008SCR1 -Force
```

For SCR, the –Force parameter must be used when the source is not available. Without this switch, the commandlet will try to copy the remaining log files from the source and fail.

Figure 6.18 shows the result of the *restore* command. It informs you that it expects some data to be lost in the process.

**Figure 6.18** Forcing a Restore of the SCR Copy

**NOTE**

With the pipelining possible in PowerShell, you can restore all replicated databases at once. In the case of our test environment, since all SCR replicas have 2008SCR1 as the target and we want to restore them all, we can use the command *Get-StorageGroup | Restore-StorageGroupCopy –StandbyMachine 2008SCR1 –Force*. This restores all applicable SCR targets in the organization.

## *Configuring the Clustered Mailbox Server*

To configure the clustered mailbox server:

1. **DNS resolution**  It is likely that the server recovery process will involve a change of IP address for the clustered mailbox server, since more often than not the SCR recovery will be in a different subnet. The first thing to take care of, therefore, is DNS resolution.

   ■ When using a Windows Server 2008 cluster (such as CCR-DR), the DNS record for the CMS (CCR-EXCH2) must be deleted from domain DNS. When the CMS is recovered using the /RecoverCMS switch, its name will be reregistered by the setup program.

2. **Recover the Clustered Mailbox Server**  At this point you can recover the CMS on the DR cluster by running:

   ```
   Setup.com /RecoverCMS /CMSName:CCR-EXCH2 /CMSIPAddress:192.168.7.165
   ```

   ■ (On this occasion, the IP address is the same as the CMS being recovered, but it needn't be.)

   ■ As Figure 6.19 shows, the setup fails, as there are SCR target databases on the server for which replication has not been disabled.

**Figure 6.19** Setup Fails Unless All SCR Is Disabled

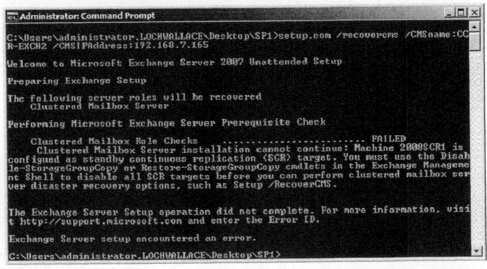

3. **Disable SCR replication**  The quickest way to disable all the SCR replication in which the target server is involved is to use our friend the pipe symbol:

   ```
   Get-StorageGroup Ð Disable-StorageGroupCopy –StandbyMachine –2008SCR1
   ```

■ This enumerates all storage groups in the organization and disables SCR replication to the target 2008SCR1. As you can see from Figure 6.20, this is not the cleanest way to achieve what we need, but it works. Any storage group that doesn't replicate to 2008SCR1 throws up an error but no action is done on them.

**Figure 6.20** Disabling SCR Replication, Even When It's Not Enabled!

4. **Attempt CMS recovery again** With the replication disabled, attempt the CMS recover again using Setup.com:

```
Run Setup /RecoverCMS /CMSName:CCR-EXCH2 /CMSIPAddress:192.168.7.165
```

■ This time, it completes successfully and is shown within the Failover Cluster Manager on 2008SCR1, as shown in Figure 6.21. The first attempt to recover the CMS may fail, with the CMS Network Name resource remaining offline. In this case, it is probably possible to bring the resource online manually and retry the Setup.com /RecoverCMS operation.

**Figure 6.21** The Recovered CMS

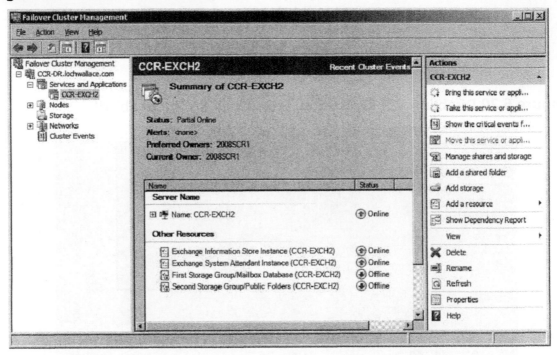

## Recovering the Databases

After the CMS has been successfully recovered to the recovery cluster, all that is left to do is mount the databases. If the database recovery process was successful, the database is in a Clean Shutdown state and is ready to be mounted. Check that the databases are in a Clean Shutdown state using ESEUTIL /mh. If they are in Dirty Shutdown mode, use ESEUTIL /r to perform a soft recovery and make them clean.

When the databases are mounted, clients should be able to connect to the new server without manual intervention. The cause of problems at this point is only likely to be name resolution since nothing has changed in terms of the Exchange configuration. Only the IP address of the server (which to the clients is the same server as before) has changed.

## Disadvantage of Using a Clustered Target Server

One thing that should be clear in this scenario is the importance of designing the SCR replication topology, particularly with regard to the types of target servers to choose.

The main disadvantage of using a clustered mailbox server as the target is that once you have recovered the CMS, you can no longer use the *Restore-StorageGroupCopy* command. On a single mailbox server there is no problem with this.

If you have to restore all the source databases at the same time in a disaster, you must run this commandlet against all databases before you recover the CMS. However, if you need to recover further databases after this, you may incur more data loss (and perhaps stress) by having to resort to the ESEUTIL utility (Figure 6.22).

**Figure 6.22** Restore-StorageGroupCopy Isn't Possible when a CMS Is Present

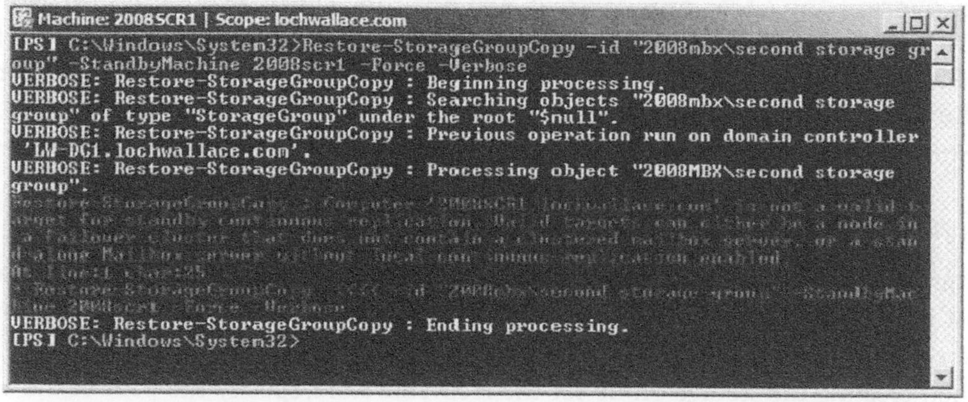

The only option in the situation in Figure 6.22 is to get down and dirty with our old friend ESEUTIL.

## Activation Using Database Portability

To activate an SCR target database on a different server from its original host, we need to use the database portability feature of Exchange. Unlike the server recovery method, this method requires some reconfiguration within Active Directory—moving the location of the mailbox database and reconfiguring mailbox settings to point to the new mailbox store—and depending on the clients may require client reconfiguration as well.

What it boils down to, operationally, is little more than a restore of an offline database backup onto a separate server because we are attaching a copy of some database files onto a new storage group and mailbox database.

## Restore the Database

As with the cluster recovery, the database files need to be restored using the Restore-Storage GroupCopy commandlet. This tries to copy any remaining log files from the source server and bring the database into a mountable state. It also lets you know if it expects that any data is missing and therefore it will be a "lossy" restore.

If the database is in a Dirty Shutdown state, use ESEUTIL /r to perform a soft recovery and bring it into a Clean Shutdown state so it can be mounted.

> **NOTE**
>
> In the case of the test environment for these last two chapters, the SCR target server is a Clustered Mailbox Server. When recovering a database from a single server, the *Restore-StorageGroupCopy* command must be used prior to recovering the CMS; otherwise, it will not run. Therefore, when recovering a CMS it's useful to know exactly which databases you are recovering and do so before creating the CMS. Otherwise, you will be stuck with ESEUTIL to bring the database into a mountable state, which may result in higher data loss.

## *Configure the Destination Storage Group and Database*

The target storage group and mailbox store may already be configured on the SCR target server, if it is a standalone Exchange server. In the case of our test environment, the target is a clustered server so this needs to be done after the CMS has been recovered.

When creating the storage group for the recovered store, specify the path of the SCR destination. In the case of 2008MBX, this is C:\mount\Databases\2008MBX\First Storage Group. Use the command:

```
New-StorageGroup -Server CCR-EXCH2 -Name 2008MBX-SG1 -LogFolderPath
"c:\mount\databases\2008MBX\First Storage Group" -SystemFolderPath
"c:\mount\databases\2008MBX\First Storage Group"
```

When creating the database, we need to specify a filename, which cannot be already present, so we can use the same path but a slightly different name (Figure 6.23):

```
New-MailboxDatabase -StorageGroup "CCR-EXCH2\2008MBX-SG1" -Name
"2008MBX-DB1" -EdbFilePath "C:\mount\databases\2008MBX\First Storage Group
\mailbox database-DR.edb"
```

**Figure 6.23** Creating the Database Using the Console Is Easier

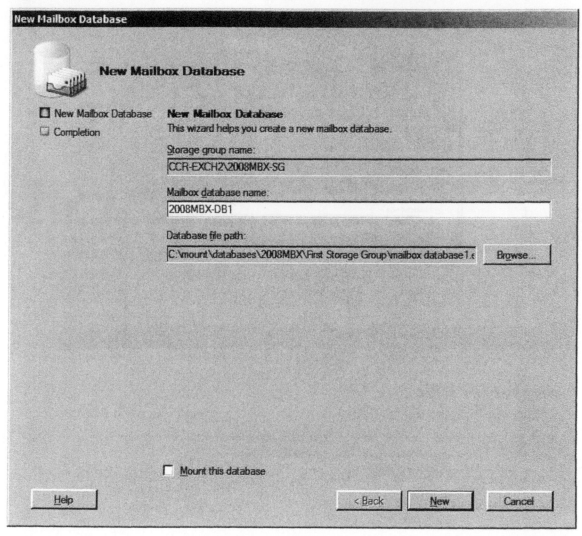

Now we don't have to fool around with reconfiguring Storage Group and database locations using the "–ConfigurationSonly switch; we only have to rename the database file to reflect the one we just specified (mailbox database-DR.edb) and we are ready to go. Figure 6.24 shows the new DR storage group and database we created and configured to point to the SCR target database file.

**Figure 6.24** The New DB Points Toward the SCR Target Files

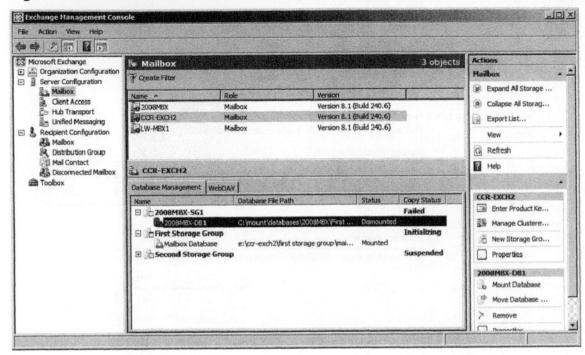

## *Mount the Database*

Now, with any luck, the database will just mount. Just one thing though, oft forgotten, is to mark the database as "can be overwritten by a restore" since we're mounting a "foreign" database. The *Set-MailboxDatabase* command can be used for this:

```
Set-Mailboxdatabase "CCR-EXCH2\2008MBX-SG1\2008MBX-DB1" -AllowFileRestore:$true
```

Mount the database using the command:

```
Mount-Database "CCR-EXCH2\2008MBX-SG1\2008MBX-DB1"
```

(In certain situations, PowerShell assumes the "–Identity" switch so we needn't include it.)

The mailboxes are not quite ready to be used, however, since AD had them marked down as sitting on a server named "2008MBX."

## *Modify Active Directory Settings*

By now, your users are probably itching to get back onto Outlook to email their loved ones that the earthquake miraculously killed all the servers but none of the staff. However, before they connect to their recovered mailboxes we need to tell AD that they have moved. AD still thinks Lubo's mailbox is on 2008MBX\First Storage Group\Mailbox Database, and so Outlook is trying and trying with no joy.

To change the location of all the mailboxes on the recovered database, use the Move-Mailbox commandlet with the –ConfigurationOnly switch. For our 2008MBX server:

```
Get-Mailbox -Database "2008MBX\First Storage Group\Mailbox Database" |where
{$_.ObjectClass -NotMatch '(SystemAttendantMailboxÐExOleDbSystemMailbox)'}|
Move-Mailbox -ConfigurationOnly -TargetDatabase "CCR-EXCH2\2008MBX-SG1\2008MBX-DB1"
```

This command filters out the non-user mailboxes (SystemAttendantMailbox and ExOleDbSystemMailbox) and changes the configuration of the user mailboxes on the original database to reflect the new, recovered database. Figure 6.25 shows Jackie and Lubo's mailboxes that have been moved from 2008MBX.

**Figure 6.25** Once the Configuration Has Been Changed in AD, Users Can Access Their Mailboxes Again

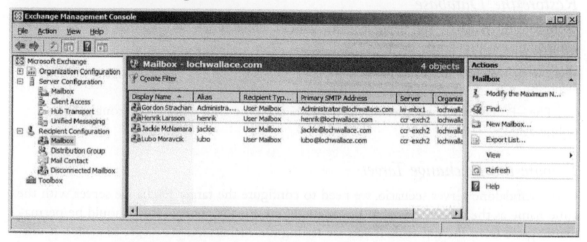

Depending on how the network, particularly Active Directory, is configured, users may face a wait to get back online with Outlook while AD replicates the mailbox location changes to the relevant global catalog servers.

Outlook 2007 or Outlook Web Access users will find that they will be able to reconnect without manual intervention. However, if the source server (2008MBX) is offline, which in our case it is, users using Outlook 2003 and earlier will have to reconfigure their Outlook profiles manually to point to the new Exchange server. If 2008MBX were still online—for example, if we were recovering from corruption in that database—it would redirect the down-level Outlook clients automatically, saving your administrator much hassle.

## Activation Using a Standalone Server Recovery

Activating an SCR copy on a standalone server is somewhat stranger than the clustered method. To recover the whole server we must use Setup with the /m:RecoverServer switch. This installs Exchange Server with the same configuration as the previous server (the SCR source). Note that the configuration details come from the Active Directory object, and any local customizations on the source server are lost unless you have them backed up.

The slight strangeness is that in order to be an SCR target, Exchange must be installed on a server, but you can't use the RecoverServer switch on an existing Exchange server. The answer, in a recovery situation, is to uninstall Exchange and then reinstall/recover it. If your whole site blows up, you're probably not under too much time pressure to get this Exchange server back up and running, but still it's not ideal.

So, in the test environment we have 2008MBX replicating its First Storage Group via SCR to 2008SCR2, configured using the command:

```
Enable-StorageGroupCopy -Identity "2008MBX\First Storage Group" -StandbyMachine
2008SCR2 -ReplayLagTime 0.0:1:0
```

## Restore the Database

To restore the database and bring it into a state in which it can be mounted, use the same commandlet as previously used:

```
Restore-StorageGroupCopy -Identity "2008MBX\First Storage Group" -StandbyMachine
2008SCR2 -Force
```

The −Force switch assumes that 2008MBX is offline and will not be brought back online again.

## Prepare the Exchange Target

In the standalone server scenario, we need to configure the target Exchange server with the same name as the source server. At this point, of course, the source server should be permanently gone from the network. If you are testing this scenario, don't forget to switch it off, and don't switch it back on again.

Some third-party applications allow you to have a standby Exchange server and switch its NetBIOS name on the fly, enabling you to avoid the process of uninstalling Exchange, changing the server name, and reinstalling. Using just the Microsoft tools, we have to go through these steps:

1. **Uninstall Exchange on 2008SCR2.** Leaving the database files intact, remove Exchange 2007 from the target, or DR server. This needs to be done because it's not possible to rename the server when Exchange is installed, and we need to reinstall using the RecoverServer switch so it picks up the configuration from AD.

**NOTE**

To save a little time, rather than uninstalling all of Exchange 2007, you can remove all the Exchange roles, leaving the Administrative Tools intact so it's not necessary to reinstall these after the server rename.

2. **Reset computer AD account.** The computer account of the source server must be reset in Active Directory so we can put the target server in its place.

3. **Rename server.** Remove the target server (2008SCR2) from the domain, rename it to "2008MBX," and re-add it to the domain. It's not possible to give the server the name of an existing server in Active Directory.

4. **Reinstall Exchange 2007.** Log on to the new 2008MBX server and install Exchange 2007 SP1 once more using "Setup /m:RecoverServer." Because there is already an Exchange server object in AD with the name of your server, the setup program will adopt the configuration of the source server from the settings in AD.

When Exchange is reinstalled on the target server, it has taken the place of the source server and is ready to mount the databases that were synchronized previously using SCR.

## Check the Database

It is likely that the recovery process was not able to bring the database(s) into a Clean Shutdown state. Check what state the database is in by using ESEUTIL /mh.

If the database shows "Dirty Shutdown," use ESEUTIL with the /R switch to perform a database recovery. It will probably be necessary to add the /a switch to allow it to recover the database with data loss. The /a switch will be necessary if additional log files are required to perform the recovery operation but these files have not been replicated from the broken source server.

## Bring Database Online

Assuming the database files are in the same location as they were, simply mount the database and the mailboxes will be ready to use. Because they are on the same server name as before, users can log straight on to Exchange and work without reconfiguring mailbox settings as is necessary when using database portability.

# Restoring SCR after a Recovery

Whether to restore SCR functionality after a disaster recovery depends on the situation. A third company site may be configured for Exchange replication, or the company might move to another location to re-start operations.

Whichever situation you find yourself in, the mailbox data needs to be transferred from one site to the other. There are a number of methods to achieve this:

**Mailbox Moves and Replication** With a high-speed, low-latency WAN link between the sites, you may opt to simply move mailboxes and replicate public folder databases and other data across to new servers you set up in the target site. This is a relatively easy method that depends particularly on factors such as time-scales, staff movement, and network speed. If users were to move gradually to the new site, for example, mailbox moves could be synchronized with this people movement.

**Server Forklift** Another method is to simply move all the hardware to the new site. This involves slightly more than simply moving everything and switching it on, and may require a lot of network reconfiguration, but is a viable method for an all-at-once office move.

**SCR Replication** SCR will provide site resilience for the period of the upheaval, so if high availability is required for this period of time it may make sense to set up replication again either back to the broken site or to a different site where the company has its operations. This may be appropriate for university campuses where SCR is used between sites and one suffers a power-failure for a few days, for example.

## Reconfiguring SCR Replication

In the SCR replication scenario, the process of reconfiguring the SCR replication to the new site is the same as for the original setup of SCR between the production and DR sites. SCR replication is enabled between source and target, the databases seeded, and replication resumed.

However, in the case of a site failure that has not affected the source mailbox servers as such, the primary site, when it is brought back online, will still contain the original mailbox databases, and it is possible to use these as the basis for the replication rather than having to reseed the whole database again.

To avoid conflict between the source and target servers, it is important to reconfigure the source environment prior to reconnecting the sites. For example, if server or CMS recovery has been used, these servers must be removed from the original environment since they have been recovered in the DR site.

### Removing a Clustered Mailbox Server

Where the clustered mailbox server CCR-EXCH2 has been recovered in the DR site, it must be removed from the original production site. This can be done by removing the CMS only while keeping the Windows cluster intact, using the command:

```
Setup.com /ClearLocalCMS /CMSName:CCR-EXCH2
```

This command clears the CMS from the cluster, leaving a passive-passive Exchange cluster that can then be used as an SCR target ready for either a controlled switchback to that site or as a DR server.

### Managing the Controlled Switchover

Performing a controlled switchover for an SCR pair is similar to performing the database activation in a disaster recovery scenario. However, when using the Restore-StorageGroupCopy commandlet in a controlled manner, do not use the –Force switch since the source databases are present and available from which the commandlet can copy the remaining log files.

# Transport Queue Database Recovery

Mailbox and public folder databases are not the only things that can go awry when problems occur. Exchange 2007 Hub Transport and Edge Transport servers store their SMTP mail queues in ESE-based databases as well, and these are susceptible to the same kind of problems and corruption when storage failure or other problems occur.

The queue database on a transport server is stored by default in the C:\Program Files\ Microsoft\Exchange Server\TransportRoles\data\Queue folder and consists of the following files:

---

**Database Files:**

| | |
|---|---|
| Mail.que | The queue ESE database file |
| Trn.chk | The database checkpoint file |

**Transaction Log Files:**

| | |
|---|---|
| Trn.log | The current transaction log file |
| Trntmp.log | The next transaction log file created in advance |

---

**Continued**

| Trnxxx.log | Further transaction log files created when necessary |
| Trnres00001.jrs and Trnres00002.jrs | Placeholder log files (these simply take up space so the database has some leeway if the disk fills up) |
| Temp.edb | The queue database schema verifier file—not a log file but located in the log file folder |

## Recovering a Queue Database

Because of the transient nature of the transport queues, backing them up doesn't make much sense. The best you can hope for, if the queue database becomes corrupt, for example, is to fix the database. If it's necessary to recover a queue from an ailing server, you can move the queue to another production server and recover it there.

To recover a queue database on another transport server:

1. **Move the queue database and log files.** Move all the files in the Queue folder to a temporary location on another transport server. If it is not already stopped, you may have to stop the Exchange Transport service (MSExchangeTransport) before moving them. If the affected server is to be brought back into service, simply restart the transport service and a new queue database will be created.

2. **Perform a recovery of the database.** The ESEUTIL tool will attempt to replay logs transactions into the database and make it possible to mount it. Use the command:

   ```
   Eseutil /r Trn (Trn is the log base file name)
   ```

3. **Defragment the database.** It is a good idea to defragment a database after recovery using ESEUTIL with the /d switch.

4. **Clear the existing queue database.** The server on which you are working also has a queue database that will be replaced as part of the recovery. Before doing that, this queue must be emptied and all mail delivered:

   a. Pause the Transport service so no more mail comes into the queue:

   ```
   Net stop MSExchangeTransport
   ```

   b. Monitor the queue and ensure all mail is delivered. Retry queues if some mail is not deliverable.

c.  If some mails is not deliverable, you can export them to files using the console commandlet:

```
Get-Message -Queue "Unreachable" | Export-Message -Path
"<LocalDirectory>"
```

These messages can be recovered later by moving them into the Pickup folder on a transport server.

d.  Stop the Transport service on the server.

5.  **Replace the queue.**  Replace the existing queue files with those from the stricken server and restart the MSExchangeTransport service.

6.  **Check the queues to make sure the messages are delivered from the new server.**  There may be a number of messages stuck in various queues on the new server. If the new server is in a different AD forest or has different Exchange roles from the original, some messages may be stuck in the Undeliverable queue. You can try to manually resubmit these messages and those stuck in the Retry state.

---

**NOTE**

---

If a queue recovery operation takes longer than the message delivery timeout value—two days by default—you should extend this timeout value so the system doesn't give up and send nondelivery reports to the senders. You can do this by configuring the TransportServer object:

```
Set-TransportServer -MessageExpirationTimeout <dd.hh:mm:ss>
```

---

# Summary

Exchange Server is quite a resilient system based on tried and tested transactional database technology. Although the underlying database technology is going to change in a future version, the "database formerly known as Jet" continues to do the job for Exchange.

Even in a monumental crash in an Exchange environment, with the right backups and disaster recovery procedures and infrastructure in place, there is no reason why this should spell disaster for the company. Native Exchange technologies provide assistance at every level—high availability options such as clustering protect against downtime, and disaster recovery options such as Standby Continuous Replication and dial-tone database recovery enable relatively speedy return to production in many cases. There is also a plethora of third-party applications and hardware not covered in these chapters that make HA and DR operations easier.

This chapter, and indeed the book, covers merely a subset of what is possible in Exchange Server 2007 SP1. We tried to cover the interesting bits and make it accessible to most, but further reading is always a browser away on Microsoft's excellent Technet site—http://technet.microsoft.com/en-gb/library/bb124558(EXCHG.80).aspx.

# Index

Printed and bound by CPI Group (UK) Ltd, Croydon, CR0 4YY

03/10/2024

01040342-0002